Ordinary Heroes:
Six Stars in the Window

Dan Oja

To our neighbors, Joe and Arlene Hardiner, thank you for all you've done over these many years.

MediaTechnics Corporation
22 W. Bryan St. #240, Savannah, GA 31401
www.mediatechnicscorp.com

Ordinary Heroes: Six Stars in the Window is published by MediaTechnics Corporation.

Copyright © 2008 by Dan Oja.
All rights reserved. No part of this publication may be reproduced, stored in any retrieval system, or transmitted in any form or by any means electronic or mechanical including photocopying, recording, or otherwise, without the prior written permission of the the publisher.

Published by
MediaTechnics Corporation
22 W. Bryan St. #240, Savannah, GA 31401
www.mediatechnicscorp.com

Developmental Editor	June Parsons
Copy Editing	Green Pen Quality Assurance
Design and Composition	MediaTechnics Corporation
Cover design	MediaTechnics Corporation
Video and Web Content	MediaTechnics Corporation

Ordinary Heroes: Six Stars in the Window is published in several formats using the innovative BookOn™ technology from MediaTechnics Corporation. For more information on the digital versions of this product, visit our Web site at www.sixstarsinthewindow.com.

In the digital version of the book, each chapter title is linked to a Web page with resources related to that chapter. Also in the digital versions of this book, figures linked to media elements and Web resources include the following markers:

★ Click here for Web Info

★ Click here to watch video

If you are using the paper version of the book, you can view the media elements and Web resources by using your Web browser to go to www.sixstarsinthewindow.com/media.

Trademarks
BookOnCD and BookOn are trademarks of MediaTechnics Corporation. All other trade names and trademarks are the property of their respective owners.

Disclaimer
As much as possible, this story is an accurate portrayal of the experiences of the Koski brothers in World War II. The dates, places, names, and major events in this book are based on books, unit histories, military records, unpublished manuscripts, letters, interviews with family members, interviews with the surviving Koski brothers, and interviews with veterans who served with the Koski brothers. However, some events have been simplified and some minor events, thoughts, conversations, and letters have been reconstructed to fill gaps in the story. If you discover errors or have additional information related to the events and people in this book, please contact the author at the publisher's address.

ISBN:
978-0-9817823-0-0 hard cover
978-0-9817823-1-7 digital BookOnCD and BookOnDownload
978-0-9817823-2-4 digital BookOnPrint

Library of Congress Control Number: 2008931606

Printed in the United States of America
1 2 3 4 5 6 7 8 9 10

★★★ Ordinary Heroes: Six Stars in the Window ★★★
Table of Contents

Table of Contents iii

Dedication vi

Foreword vii

Introduction viii

1. The telegram 1

2. God's plan 5

3. Mama is calling me! 8

4. The promise 10

5. A nice, quiet sleep 13

6. War is a fearful thing 18

7. Their finest hour 26

8. Sleeping bears 30

9. A lot like hunting deer 36

10. The fog of war 41

11. For all the good I did 45

12. Where are you going buddy? 48

13. Why we fight 54

14. Pretending to be soldiers 56

15. Silver wings 59

16. Our landings have failed 64

17. You know it's no picnic 69

18. Red dust and pasties 73

19. On borrowed time 77

20. Someone's son 79

21. Six blue stars in the window 86

22. Bridges and buzz bombs 92

23. Who fears? 100

24. Ready for duty 109

25. Two down 112

26. I'm going to come back 116

27. We could'a been killed 119

28. Who will sleep here next? 121

29. You'd better finish up! 125

30. Don't they know they're the bad guys? 129

31. Why go for 40? 133

32. Last-ditch defense 136

33. We thought you were dead! 139

34. I can't think of any other way 141

35. A little bit of good 144

36. My mother loved me 148

37. Don't be in a rush to leave here 150

38. Some uncertainty exists 157

39. Maybe they were going to be all right 159

40. The ones who weren't so lucky 163

41. What was it like? 166

42. Not your burden 172

43. Just scared kids in uniform 175

44. God is with us 180

45. Don't blame us 186

46. This might be hell 188

47. Rendezvous 195

48. I'm almost there	199
49. Mountain of hope	203
50. Until the day I die	207
51. Such happiness doesn't last forever	210
52. Wrong place, wrong time	212
53. Has anyone heard from George?	216
54. Lie in the dark	218
55. Where I'm going	219
56. Give 'em heck boys	224
57. Valley of the shadow	225
58. One bridge too far	230
59. For him, the war was over	232
60. The last hill	234
61. I'm not gonna lose my whole damn squad!	238
62. SUD to KIA	241
63. Forget it, all of it	244
64. We have to let it go	247
65. To our graves	253
66. Aftermath	255
67. Don't you recognize me?	261
68. Not forgotten	263
Afterword	266
Credits	267
Bibliography	268
Index	270

★★★ Ordinary Heroes: Six Stars in the Window ★★★
Dedication

This book is dedicated to all the men and women who were asked to give so much in World War II.

It is particularly dedicated to the six Koski brothers:

> Frank Alfred "Al" Koski
> Carl Arthur "Art" Koski
> George Harold "Jiggs" Koski
> Oscar Henry Koski
> Reuben Arnold Koski
> John Leslie Koski

These are my uncles. They are also some of the finest men I have ever known.

This book is also dedicated to the men who served with the Koski brothers, particularly those ordinary and extraordinary heroes from the 332nd Engineers Regiment, the 352nd Squadron of the 301st Bomb Group Heavy, and the 85th Regiment of the 10th Mountain Infantry Division. It is not possible to list all of the veterans who assisted with this project, but special mention must be made of Tom Jones, Warren Babcock, James Winterbottom, James Orwig, Tustin Ellison, Al Wiedorn, Carl Cossin, and Bill Kehres for the countless hours they spent helping me with this project. These men are my mentors, my friends, and my heroes.

It is further dedicated to the extended Koski family for their support and encouragement throughout this project. This story is part of your heritage, something to be cherished and shared with future generations. Again, I cannot list everyone who helped, but I feel that special mention should be made of Edna Mae Koski Oja, Oscar Koski, Mary Morissette, Carl Arthur Koski, Christine Gupta, Julie Wolf, Susan Oja, John W. Koski, Karen Adair, and Brett Stephens for their continued support and assistance during this extended project.

Finally, it is dedicated to my parents, Edward Oja and Edna Mae Koski Oja. You raised your children to value the contributions of others and this book is one result. I only wish that Dad could be with us to see the final version.

Last, but not least, it is dedicated to my wife, June Jamrich Parsons, and her parents June and Dr. John X. Jamrich. This book would not exist without your continued encouragement and support. It would definitely not be what it is without your advice and extensive edits over countless revisions. You helped make it what it is.

Dan Oja

★★★ Ordinary Heroes: Six Stars in the Window ★★★
Foreword

Far from the center of international politics or world conflict, in the center of Michigan's Upper Peninsula, there is a small, quiet town called Ishpeming. While it may be a loose translation at best, Ishpeming is said to mean "heaven" in the local Native American language. As a family of faith, Alfred and Elizabeth Koski and their children probably would not have referred to their home as heaven, but it was about as close to it as most of them could imagine.

The peaceful northern woods of Michigan surrounding Ishpeming are a world away from the streets of Berlin, the World War II battlefields of Belgium, or the mountains of Italy, but all would play a role in the family's story.

This is their story. It is a story of heroes: my heroes. As I write, my heroes are dying. Soon they will all be gone, but their story will not go with them. Theirs is a story that deserves to be told and remembered. It is a story of a family that persevered through our nation's darkest financial times, through loss, and separation to leave a legacy of respect and admiration that is difficult for those of us who have known them to put into words.

Over the last 230 years, the American engine of freedom has produced a world that is so affluent, in historical terms, that we seem to have lost the idea of what a real struggle is. The twelve Koski children came from a different time. The struggle of their generation was about more than rising gas prices or a lack of cell phone service. Their generation stood together against a man whose name has become synonymous with evil and against the movement he spawned. They stood together in the war that erupted around the world following his rise.

Ordinary Heroes is not only a story about the Koskis. It is an American story. The details varied, but the gist of the story was repeated in households from coast to coast. Ambitions were put on hold and our soldiers marched off to war, leaving their loved ones to wonder how many would return and what kind of world would be left even if they did.

Ordinary Heroes is also a story of the world. The United States did not stand alone in World War II, nor did its enemies. This is a story of courage and persistence to be emulated and of mistakes that should not be repeated. It is a story of the triumph of freedom, and of lessons that seem to have been forgotten. It is a story of the cost that evil will extract from the good and the free if it is allowed to grow beyond its youth.

The Koskis would not have called themselves heroes. They were not apt to draw attention to themselves. Prior to 1940, the brothers probably would not have called themselves soldiers, either. They were soldiers, though, because that is what their circumstances required them to be. They met the challenge of their day, and they, and so many of their contemporaries, are heroes. Like so many of those heroes, they did not talk much about the war and we are all worse off for not knowing the depth of their experience and their wisdom. Much of what we do know is preserved here in this tale of heroes...real, ordinary heroes.

Carl Arthur Koski

★★★ Ordinary Heroes: Six Stars in the Window ★★★
Introduction

Ordinary Heroes: Six Stars in the Window is the true story of one family, six brothers, and a world at war. It is also the story of a very special generation—the story of America's fathers and uncles and grandfathers, the story of ordinary Americans who rose to meet the extraordinary challenges of their time.

Ordinary Heroes starts with a look at the life of the Koski family against the backdrop of events of the 1930s. The focus of the story gradually narrows to the three brothers who served significant time in combat. In large part, this is the story of those three brothers and the men they served with.

As much as possible, this story is an accurate portrayal of the experiences of the Koski brothers in World War II. The dates, places, names, and major events in this book are based on books, unit histories, military records, unpublished manuscripts, letters, interviews with family members, interviews with the surviving Koski brothers, and interviews with veterans who served with the Koski brothers. In the interest of telling a complete and accurate story, I have—when necessary—recreated missing details based on the actual events and the actual people who were present at the time. The events are real, the people are real, the places are real, and the dates are as accurate as possible, but some letters, conversations, and thoughts expressed in the book have been reconstructed. My purpose in the reconstruction was not to change or re-write history—my purpose was to fill in the gaps to bring the story of these ordinary soldiers to life in a compelling, yet accurate and complete fashion.

Through the use of technology, *Ordinary Heroes: Six Stars in the Window* makes it possible for you, the reader, to review much of the documentation and source materials upon which the book is based.

If you are reading the digital version of this book, you can click the chapter headings for more information pertaining to that chapter, including links to source materials.

You can also click the links under many photos to watch video clips or display additional information on the Web.

The video links include actual World War II footage of major events and interviews with family members and veterans talking about the events in their own words. Many of the Web links include scans of original letters and documents, providing further insight into the extensive research on which this book is based.

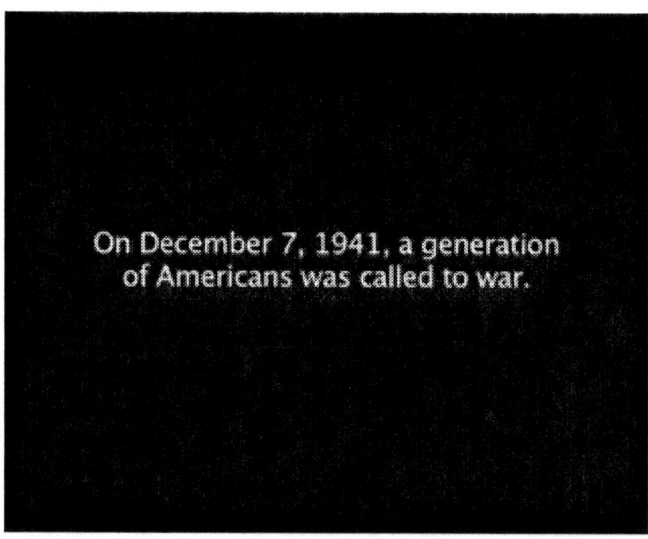

★ Click here to watch video

Figure 0-1: If you are reading a digital version of this book, click the link above to watch the introductory video and start your journey into the world of Ordinary Heroes.

If you are reading the paper version of the book, use your Web browser to go to www.sixstarsinthewindow.com/media to view the same information and videos.

Dan Oja

★★★ Ordinary Heroes: Six Stars in the Window ★★★
1. The telegram

May 4th, 1945: Lilly Koski closed the door and carefully locked it behind her. It felt strange to lock the door. In years past, the house had been so full of people. Somebody was always home and there was never any need to lock the door.

Since her mother died fourteen years earlier, Lilly had stayed home to take care of her father, six brothers, and five sisters. But now all six of her brothers were off to war. Her sisters had moved out of the house, were working, or were going to school. Her father was still working at the iron mine and was gone for most of the day. With no one to take care of during the day, Lilly now worked a part-time job in the lunch room of the Gossard factory. She enjoyed working. After years of taking care of her brothers and sisters with no pay and little thanks, it felt good to get out of the house and be paid for her work.

As Lilly walked along the road, she couldn't help but smile as the morning sunshine warmed her face. It was a bright spring morning in the tiny mining community of West Ishpeming, nestled in the iron-rich hills of Michigan's Upper Peninsula. Only dirty patches of snow remained in the ditches alongside the road and here and there a few brave wildflowers reached for the sun.

Everyone was optimistic that the war was nearly over. After three and a half years of fierce fighting, setbacks, and heavy losses, Nazi Germany was on the verge of defeat. Just two days ago, Lilly had read about the German surrender in Italy. Yesterday, the newspapers reported that Hitler had killed himself and Berlin had fallen. The rest of the Germans were supposed to surrender any day now.

Lilly sang quietly to herself as she walked, dreaming of the day when all six of her brothers would return from the war. The boys would resume their lives and—in her mind at least—everything would be as it had been in the years before the war.

Wrapped in her own pleasant thoughts, she didn't notice the dark green car that passed her, heading back towards West Ishpeming. She didn't see it turn and go up the hill to the Koski house. She just kept walking, blissfully unaware of the events that were about to unfold.

The green car pulled to a stop in front of a neat white house with ruffled curtains in the windows. The corner lot was encircled with a wire fence fastened to rough log posts.

A man in uniform stepped out of the car. He opened the gate and climbed the sagging wooden steps. He knocked on the door. As he waited, he nervously fingered a yellow piece of paper and his eyes fell on a small red and white banner bearing six blue stars. "This family has six sons in the service," he thought sadly. "They've already sacrificed so much."

He knocked again and called out, "Hello! Hello! Is anybody home?"

No one answered.

A neighbor was hanging clothes in her yard across the street. Pinning a sheet to the clothes line, she yelled to him, "They're all gone for the day. You might try Ann's."

The man turned toward the woman. "Ann?" he questioned.

★ Click for Web Info

Figure 1-1: A flag with six stars, similar to the one that hung on the door of the Koski house during WWII.

"Ann is one of the Koski girls," said the neighbor. Pointing up the street, she added, "She lives in the green house just over the hill."

The man climbed into his car and disappeared over the hill. He stopped at the green house, walked onto the porch, and rapped on the door.

He heard a singsong voice calling, "Be right there!" In a few seconds the door opened. Ann Koski stood in the doorway. Her blonde hair glistened in the sunlight. She flashed a dazzling smile, which disappeared when the man handed her the yellow piece of paper.

Ann unfolded the telegram and glanced at its contents. The man in uniform awkwardly reached out a comforting hand. Ann shook her head violently and pushed him away, then retreated into the house. She stood in the middle of the living room, unsure what to do. "Oh my God," she whispered. "Oh my God."

She slowly turned toward the door. Making a decision, she stumbled down the steps clutching the telegram in one hand, dragging her bewildered young daughter behind her with the other. Picking up speed, she half-walked, half-ran four blocks to her sister Martha's house.

Her young niece Jackie was sitting in the front yard, playing with a toy. Ann stopped and asked, "Where's your mother?"

"She's in the house," replied Jackie. "My Dad's there too and Auntie Eleanor. Can we have a tea party?" she asked playfully.

"Not now sweetie," replied Ann. "Stay here. I have to talk to your mother."

Ann hurried inside. Martha was sipping coffee with her older sister Eleanor when Ann burst through the door, the crumpled yellow sheet clutched in her hand. Martha turned her head, startled. It wasn't like Ann to burst in without knocking.

Ann leaned against the washer, panting from her run. She held the yellow paper towards Martha. Her lips trembled as she forced out one hoarse word: "Telegram!"

Martha placed her coffee cup on the washer and reached for the telegram. She adjusted her glasses and quickly scanned its contents. As the words seared her consciousness, she screamed, then sagged to the floor.

Jackie heard the scream from outside and ran into the house crying, "What's wrong Mama? What's wrong?"

Jackie saw her mother crumpled on the floor by the washing machine, sobbing. Her aunt Eleanor stood next to Martha, reading a telegram. Eleanor lowered the telegram, her eyes filled with tears. In a grave voice she said, "Something very sad has happened."

Eleanor turned toward Martha's husband. Her voice trembled as she tried to rein in her emotions. "Jack, I think you should get Edna Mae from school."

Jack nodded and left the house, walking across the street to the West Ishpeming School.

Inside the school, Mrs. Lindholm had just scrawled the poem In "Flanders Fields" on the board. Her eighth-grade students were industriously copying the poem into their workbooks.

> *We are the Dead. Short days ago*
> *We lived, felt dawn, saw sunset glow,*
> *Loved, and were loved, and now we lie*
> *In Flanders fields.*

The youngest Koski girl, Edna Mae, was sharpening her pencil near the window when she glanced out and saw Jack coming up the sidewalk. She tugged at one of her pigtails and wondered why he was walking so quickly.

Moments later, Jack entered the classroom. He talked quietly with the teacher. Mrs. Lindholm gestured to Edna Mae, "Get your things Edna Mae. You won't be coming back today."

Jack took Edna Mae by the hand and they walked out of the school together. She saw her sisters Ann, Martha, and Eleanor climbing into the car. As she slipped into the back seat, they handed her the telegram. She quickly read it. "It can't be true!" she thought. Then she looked at her sister's faces and she knew that it was true.

They drove into town, pulling to a stop in front of Ishpeming High School. Jack hurried into the school, returning a few minutes later with Evelyn. Textbooks cradled in her arms, Evelyn squeezed into the car with her five sisters. She glanced at the telegram and said flatly, "I knew it."

They drove around the block and stopped in front of the Gossard. Eleanor got out and spoke to someone at the door.

A few minutes later, Lilly Koski emerged, still wearing her cafeteria apron. She saw the car parked at the curb. The front door was open and her sister Eleanor stood waiting, a piece of yellow paper clutched in her hand.

Lilly saw her sisters sobbing inside the car. She stopped in the doorway, a puzzled look on her face. She couldn't understand why her sisters would come to get her in the middle of the day.

Lilly watched as Eleanor slowly stretched out her hand, holding a crumpled piece of paper.

Time stopped.

That wasn't just a yellow piece of paper. It was a telegram. With the world at war, Lilly knew the kind of terrible news that telegram could bring.

"What's this?" Lilly murmured softly to herself. "Dear God, this can't be happening."

Martha took a step forward and offered the telegram to Lilly. "It's from the War Department." she said in a halting voice.

Lilly didn't move. She didn't want to touch the telegram. She didn't want to read it.

She reminded herself that this didn't have to mean the worst. Maybe one of the boys was just injured or missing. She hated to think of one of her brothers in a hospital or prisoner of war camp, but it was better than...

Then came the awful thought—who could it be?

Probably not Al. He should be safe with the Coast Artillery in Washington state.

Probably not Art. Yes, he was in Europe, but he was building railroad bridges with the Engineers. He shouldn't be anywhere near the front lines.

It couldn't be Reuben. He was in Chicago with the Navy and had just been home on leave a few weeks ago.

It shouldn't be George. He'd been in some sort of accident, but according to his last letter he was recovering in a hospital in France.

Her thoughts turned to Johnny, her youngest brother, the last to go to war.

Foreboding images of Johnny as a young boy flashed through Lilly's mind, images of Johnny and Edna Mae rolling batteries across the kitchen table to knock down tin soldiers, images of Johnny enthusiastically marching around the house with a broomstick on his shoulder chanting "Hup, two, three four! Hup, two, three four!"

With a chill, she remembered Johnny's most recent letters. After weeks of waiting in a replacement depot, he had finally been assigned to an infantry outfit in northern Italy. "But no," Lilly tried to reassure herself, "It couldn't be Johnny. The war in Italy is already over."

Then she thought, "Oh, dear God! It can't be Oscar!"

A fleeting smile touched Lilly's face as she remembered Oscar as a brave, but perhaps overly-adventurous young boy, leaping from the second story window with a table cloth tied to his belt as a make-shift parachute.

Then another image came to Lilly's mind, an image of Oscar leaping out of a flaming B-17, parachuting down towards the earth as German soldiers waited below, guns at the ready.

Lilly shook her head to dispel that horrible vision.

"This isn't right," thought Lilly, "The war is almost over. The boys should be coming home soon."

Eleanor took another step toward Lilly, bringing that terrible telegram closer. Lilly stood rooted to the spot, unable to move back, unwilling to reach out for it.

Eleanor held the telegram out, waiting for Lilly to take it. Lilly's breath came in shallow gasps as she slowly reached out. She knew that in the next few seconds her world would change forever.

★ Click here to watch video

Figure 1-2: Edna Mae, the youngest of the Koski sisters, was fourteen years old when the family received the telegram.

★★★ Ordinary Heroes: Six Stars in the Window ★★★
2. God's plan

Life had never been easy for Finnish immigrant Alfred Koski or his family. Alfred was born near Perho, Finland on August 14, 1882. In 1900, his parents purchased one-way tickets for Alfred and his siblings, put the children on a ship, and sent them to America. The Koski parents did not travel to America with their children—perhaps because of lack of funds—and they never saw their children again.

None of the Koski children spoke English, but after getting off the ship in New York City, they did their best to make their way in this strange new land. Somehow, seventeen-year old Alfred ended up in the Upper Peninsula of Michigan where he found work in the underground iron mines. Underground mining was grueling and often dangerous work, but Alfred stuck with it and he made a place for himself in the growing Finnish-American community in the central Upper Peninsula.

Alfred felt at home in Upper Michigan as one of tens of thousands of immigrants from Finland, Sweden, and Norway who migrated to the snow belts of Upper Michigan, Wisconsin, and Minnesota. They loved the lakes, the forests, and even the long winters, which reminded them of their homelands.

Alfred became active in the local Apostolic Lutheran Church, a fundamentalist church with strong ties to Finland and the Finnish community. The members of the church were a rather severe lot. They did not believe in drinking or dancing or non-Christian music. They placed their faith in God, hard work, and a strong personal moral code.

It was through the church that Alfred met his future wife, Elizabeth Honkala, a Finnish girl who came to America as a baby. They were married on July 29, 1905. Their first son, Frank Alfred, was born two years later and another son or daughter was born every two or three years after that.

Alfred purchased a small, partially built house in West Ishpeming, a few miles walk from the underground iron mines where he worked. The first floor of the Koski house included a pantry, kitchen, parlor, and dining room. The second floor had three bedrooms: one shared by the five girls, one shared by the six boys, and one for Alfred Koski and his wife.

Like most of the houses of that time, the Koski house did not have an inside bathroom. It only had an outhouse attached to the back of the barn. The outhouse stank in the heat of summer and was dismally cold in the winter when the outdoor temperatures often dropped to twenty degrees below zero. Winter or summer, old Sears Roebuck and Montgomery Ward catalogs served as toilet paper.

★ Click here for Web Info

Figure 2-1: Ishpeming is located near the center of Michigan's Upper Peninsula, or U.P.

The stock market crash of 1929 had little immediate effect on the Koski family, but they definitely felt the effects of the Great Depression which followed. The economy slowed to a near standstill. Businesses failed and millions lost their jobs. Alfred Koski continued to work in the mine, but his hours and his income were drastically cut. He bought forty acres of forest near Cooper Lake, a few miles from his house, and chopped down trees to carve out a small family farm. As the Depression lingered, that little farm became an increasingly important source of food for the family. Hunting, fishing, and berry picking assumed new significance as ways to augment their meager diet.

★ Click here for Web Info

Figure 2-2: During the depression, a friend of the Koski brothers (left) shows off his refurbished bicycle. George has his hands on his head. Oscar has a bandage on his head from an accident with a double-bladed axe. Art is standing with his arms crossed.

Everybody, including the children, had chores—real chores, not just little tasks like taking out the garbage or setting the table. In the spring and summer, they worked on the family farm at Cooper Lake, planting, watering, weeding, and making hay for the milk cows. In the fall they cut, split, and stacked tremendous quantities of firewood to heat the house through the long northern winters. In the winter, they brought in armloads of firewood and shoveled the snow that blanketed the area for as much as eight months of the year.

Figure 2-3: Ishpeming merchants dig out after a snowstorm in the late 1930s.

But life wasn't all work. When they finished their chores for the day, the children often sat in the hayloft singing or playing music on a harmonica or Jew's harp. Their father didn't approve of music other than church hymns, but when he wasn't around, the Koski children sometimes played popular tunes. Johnny often recited famous speeches or heroic poetry with such passion that even the older boys couldn't help but smile as they listened to his spirited performances.

The entire family, girls as well as boys, loved being outdoors. When they had an afternoon free, they'd go fishing in the Carp River. If they had more time, they'd hike out to Dead River or Flat Rock to swim, fish, hike, or pick wild blueberries. Even a hard day of work at the family farm was not without its rewards. As soon as they finished their chores, they'd run to the lake, strip off their clothes, and go skinny dipping in the cool waters of Cooper Lake.

As was typical at that time, there was a clear distinction between the roles of men and women. As the father, Alfred's main task was to support the family. He worked in the iron mine, kept milk cows, and worked the farm near Cooper Lake.

★ Click here to watch video

Figure 2-4: Johnny Koski pointing to a turtle in Cooper Lake, near the family farm.

His interaction with the children consisted mainly of providing discipline when needed, working with them to maintain the farm during the summers, and supervising their work at the wood pile during the fall and winter.

As the woman of the house, Elizabeth took care of the children and the chores involved in running the house. As her family grew, it became increasingly difficult for Elizabeth to manage by herself, so Lilly, the oldest daughter, dropped out of school in the sixth grade to help her mother with the chores and the younger children.

On Easter Sunday, 1931, as the family walked home from church, Lilly and her Mother lagged behind, thinking about the minister's rather graphic description of Christ's suffering on the cross. A little further up the road, they found Johnny, then only five years old, sitting on the side of the road, crying to himself.

Her mother leaned down and gently asked, "What's wrong Johnny?"

Johnny answered, "I'm crying because of the bad things those people did to Jesus. Momma, why does God let bad things happen?"

Lilly watched as her mother reached down, picked up Johnny, hugged him to her chest, and answered, "Sometimes God lets bad things happen. We may not understand why, but we must remember God has a plan. There is always a purpose, even for bad things."

Her mother then looked at Lilly over Johnny's shoulder and continued, "You must always remember this. Everything, everything that happens is part of God's plan."

As she had so many times before, her mother once again reminded Lilly, "If anything ever happens, you must promise that you will take care of the children."

Lilly was just twenty-one years old at the time. She had no idea what the coming years might bring, but she replied as she had always replied, "Don't worry mother, I will take care of them."

Figure 2-5: Elizabeth Koski with baby Carl "Art" and daughter Eleanor. The oldest daughter Lilly is standing in the doorway wearing an apron. Lilly would have been only about nine years old in this photo, but she already was her mother's helper.

★★★ Ordinary Heroes: Six Stars in the Window ★★★
3. Mama is calling me!

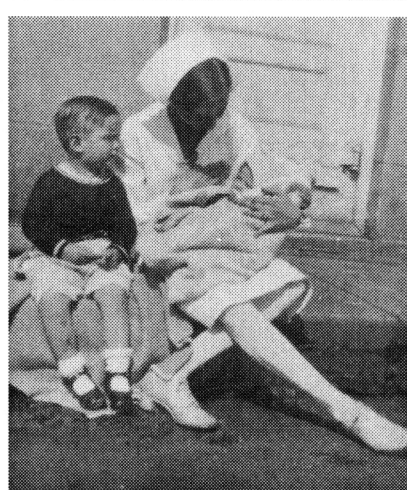

★ Click for Web Info

Figure 3-1: Johnny Koski watching the nurse care for the baby, Edna Mae, after their mother died.

In the spring of 1931, the Koski family suffered a grievous blow. On April 22, Elizabeth gave birth to her twelfth child, Edna Mae. Six days after Edna Mae was born, Elizabeth died from a blood clot related to the pregnancy.

At age forty-seven, Alfred Koski was left a widower with twelve children, the youngest just a baby, whom he had to to somehow support on the meager income from his job at the iron mine.

Dr. Erickson, who had cared for Elizabeth during her pregnancy, took pity on the family. He kept the baby in the hospital for almost six months and arranged for nurses to visit the Koski house after Edna Mae was sent home. Dr. Erickson knew the family did not have money to pay the bill, but he also knew that Alfred Koski would be too proud to leave the bill unpaid. The good doctor solved the dilemma by never sending the Koski family a bill for his services.

Alfred Koski rarely smiled after his wife died. He didn't have time or energy to play with his kids. He didn't read to them, take them fishing, or tell them bedtime stories. He worked to keep food on the table, he kept order in the house, and he made sure all the children went to church. That was all he could do, it had to be enough.

Alfred Koski was a somewhat stubborn man. He refused to accept charity, even during the darkest of times. In his mind, it was essential that the Koski family pay its own way in the world.

To outsiders, it sometimes looked like the family needed help. A few weeks after their mother died, their cousin Nina Clark came to check on them. The children were called in for lunch, but one boy remained sitting on the edge of the hayloft above the barn. That boy's name was Carl Arthur, but everyone called him Art—everyone except cousin Nina, who insisted on calling him Arthur.

Cousin Nina called to him, "Arthur, it's time to eat! Arthur come down from that roof!"

★ Click here to watch video

Figure 3-2: Alfred Koski on the steps of the Koski house.

Art pretended he couldn't hear her. He didn't come down, he just continued to swing his legs over the edge of the loft. When Nina stood under the hayloft and called to him again, he tried to make her go away, yelling, "It's not my turn to eat today. I ate yesterday."

The family was so obviously poor that Nina believed Art when he told her that he only ate every other day. She jumped in her car and drove off, a determined expression on her face.

Later that afternoon Nina returned with cans of food from the Salvation Army. She proudly presented the canned food to the family so the "boys could eat every day."

Alfred clenched his jaw, but said nothing as Lilly accepted the food. As Lilly scurried to put the cans in the pantry, Alfred gravely thanked Nina for the food, then sternly told her, "Never bring more food to this house again. The Koski family does not accept charity."

Although Lilly always managed to put some food on the table, she couldn't fill the psychological void left by the death of their mother. The youngest children were particularly affected by the death of their mother.

When the youngest, Edna Mae, mistakenly called Lilly "mother," the older children rather cruelly reminded told her, "She's not your mother. You don't have a mother. Your mother is dead!"

Evelyn, the next-to-youngest daughter, held elaborate funerals to bury dolls she had declared dead. One day, some years after her mother died, Evelyn marched out of the house carrying Edna Mae's favorite doll, the one with a china head.

"This doll is dead!" proclaimed Evelyn as she buried the doll in the back yard during yet another funeral service. Edna Mae was heartbroken to see her favorite doll being buried, but she didn't argue as her older sister seemed to knew more about such things than she did.

Johnny, the youngest boy, told Lilly he often dreamed that his mother was standing over him in a white gown while he slept. Sometimes she would lean down towards him, but just as she was about to pick him up in her arms, he would wake up, and she would be gone.

Edna Mae didn't remember her mother, but she dreamed about her anyway. Several times she had a particularly vivid dream in which she and Johnny were playing in the yard of the West Ishpeming School. Johnny would suddenly stop playing, cock his head to one side, and run up the stairs into the school yelling, "Momma is calling me! Momma is calling me!"

In her dream, Edna Mae ran into the school after Johnny, anxious to finally see her mother. She would see Johnny fling himself into the arms of his mother, who stood at the top of the stairs, dressed all in white. Edna Mae always ran up the stairs as fast as she could, desperate to hug her mother, but the dream always ended before she reached her mother.

Edna Mae often lay awake at night, reviewing that dream, trying to get a clear look at her mother's face. As Edna Mae replayed the dream in her mind, she thought it rather odd that her mother was barefoot and had mud between her toes.

★ Click here to watch video

Figure 3-3: Students on the steps of West Ishpeming School. The steps that Johnny ran up in Edna Mae's dream were just inside the doors.

★★★ Ordinary Heroes: Six Stars in the Window ★★★
4. The promise

Lilly, the oldest daughter, had been her mother's helper since childhood, so it seemed natural for her to become the surrogate mother for the Koski family, cleaning, cooking, and raising the younger children. She was only twenty years old, but she shouldered responsibility for the family, mothering the youngest children and baby Edna Mae.

Lilly struggled constantly to feed the family in the lean times of the Great Depression. Alfred Koski's modest income just wasn't enough to feed thirteen hungry people. The older brothers and sisters sometimes found work and contributed money when they could, but Lilly still found it difficult to provide food for the family. Sometimes she served oatmeal for breakfast and again for supper, but somehow she always managed to put something on the table.

Precious cash had to be used to buy some things such as flour, but as much as possible Lilly based her meals on products from the Koski farm, their dairy cows, and whatever the boys could bring home from the woods.

★ Click here for Web Info

Figure 4-1: The Koski boys a few months after their mother died. From left to right: Johnny, Oscar, Reuben, George, and Carl "Art." The oldest brother Al is not in the photo.

Root vegetables were stored in the cool, dark basement and wild blueberries and strawberries were made into preserves and stored on shelves that lined the rough stone walls of the basement. The preserves in those clear jars proved very tempting to the youngest Koski children. One winter day, Lilly heard voices in the basement and decided she had better check it out. As her eyes adjusted to the gloom, she saw Oscar sitting on the floor surrounded by opened jars of fruit preserves. He had a big blue bowl in his lap and was eating preserves with a spoon.

Lilly gasped, "Oscar, what have you done?"

Oscar tried to reassure her with all the innocence of an eight-year old boy. "It's alright. I just took one spoon from each jar. Nobody will even notice!"

Of course, once the seal on the jars was broken, the preserves had to be eaten, so the family did not eat fruit for the remainder of that winter.

Although they had very little money, the Koski family did try to celebrate special occasions. Once, during the worst years of the Depression, Alfred Koski told Lilly to prepare the house for special visitors from Finland.

Lilly bustled about the house, setting the table with her mother's best table cloth, glass candlesticks, and the best china cups, the ones without the chips in the brim. Lilly even sent Edna Mae to Kallatsa's store to buy a bag of bismarcks.

Those store-bought pastries were a rare extravagance. Lilly baked bread and an occasional pie, but she didn't bake anything as fancy as those bismarcks so she knew the children would be fascinated with them. When Edna Mae returned, Lilly took the bag of bismarcks and put them in the pantry, admonishing her siblings, "Don't eat these bismarcks! They are for company."

When the guests arrived, the children stood in the door to the parlor and watched quietly while Lilly served Alfred Koski and his guests. The guests drank their coffee and ate their bismarcks, calously ignoring the Koski children who closely watched every bite.

By the time the guests left, the bismarcks were all gone. The waiting children didn't get any, they had just watched as the visitors ate them all. This may seem harsh by today's standards, but this was the 1930s. Children didn't rule the family as they do today. Just because a child wanted something didn't mean he or she was going to get it. Adults and children alike were used to going without, and to not getting everything they wanted. This was the Great Depression and hardship was a part of life.

★ Click here to watch video

Figure 4-2: Koski relatives visiting Alfred Koski during the bismarck incident. Alfred Koski, wearing glasses, is seated on the left.

Duty was also a part of life in those difficult days. Unlike later generations that obsess endlessly about what they want to do, generations that lived through more difficult times understand that there are things that have to be done, challenges that have to be met. If something needs to be done and if you're the only person willing or able to do it, then that becomes your duty. You do what you have to do. What you want isn't really very relevant.

Lilly understood her duty to the Koski family.

She was an attractive young lady and had caught the eye of various young men, including George Sarberg, a quiet fellow who lived just a few blocks away.

In the summer of 1938, twenty-eight year old Lilly Koski walked with George through the hayfield across the street from the Koski house. Her cotton dress fluttered around her knees, its faded flowers a pale echo of the bright buttercups that bloomed in the field. George was in love with Lilly and he was trying, once again, to persuade her to marry him.

"Lilly," he said. "You've done your share and more. You've taken care of your brothers and sisters long enough. You know I love you. And I think you love me. Please say you'll marry me."

Lilly shyly glanced at him, then continued walking across the hayfield. The offer was tempting. She loved George and his quiet, gentle ways. She knew she wasn't getting any younger and she did want to have a family and children of her own.

Ever since her mother died she had devoted herself to the family. But that was seven years ago. Wasn't that enough? Would it be so selfish to get finally get married, to finally say "someone else must take over now"?

Lilly took a breath, about to tell George that she would marry him.

Then she remembered the promise she made just before her mother died. She remembered her promise to take care of the children if anything ever happened. She had kept that promise for seven years. She could keep it for a while longer.

As Lilly walked beside George, she knew she couldn't let her mother down, she couldn't let her brothers and sisters down. Her answer to George had to be the same as it had been the last time, and the time before that.

Lilly stopped walking, turned to George and said very softly, "George, you know that I love you. I'll always love you. But I cannot marry you."

Trying to hide his disappointment, George asked, "But when Lil? When will you be free to marry me?"

Lilly thought of Edna Mae, just eight years old, then replied, "George, I can't marry anyone until the family doesn't need me anymore. I can't marry until Edna Mae is grown."

George wanted to reach out to Lilly, he wanted to try to convince her to change her mind. But he sensed her resolve, so he just shoved his hands deeper into his pockets and softly replied, "That's a long time Lil."

Tears glistened in Lilly's eyes as she looked back towards the Koski house and said the most difficult words she would ever say in her life.

"That's going to be years from now. I'll be a middle-aged woman. I can't expect you to wait for me. I can't see you anymore George. You should find someone else."

Lilly turned away from George. She turned away from her own future with him and resolutely strode back to her duties at the Koski house, leaving George Sarberg standing alone in the field.

★ Click here to watch video

Figure 4-3: Sisters Evelyn (left) and Edna Mae (front) are wearing white dresses. Family friend Jeanette "Jenny" Traise (back) is standing behind Edna Mae. Lilly Koski is on the right, wearing the dark print dress.

★★★ Ordinary Heroes: Six Stars in the Window ★★★
5. A nice, quiet sleep

Autumn 1938: During the early 1930s, Al, the oldest Koski brother, worked in the iron mines and saved enough money to purchase forty acres south of Ishpeming, in an area known as Flat Rock. It wasn't prime land—mostly sand, ferns, jack pines and wild blueberry bushes. Near a small lake—actually more of a pond—Al and his brothers built a crude cabin from logs and scraps of lumber. The camp wasn't much—just a shack with a couple of second-hand windows and a tar paper roof. But the Koski boys loved that rustic old camp and they spent many happy weekends there hiking, fishing, and hunting. In the winter, the boys hunted for rabbits. During the summer they fished and in the early fall, they hunted ruffed grouse locally known as "partridge."

Figure 5-1: George Koski with a pistol outside the Flat Rock hunting camp.

The biggest event of the year was the opening day of deer season, which has always been an unofficial holiday in the Upper Peninsula of Michigan. Many businesses and schools closed for the day as almost all able-bodied men and boys headed to crude shacks fondly referred to as "deer camps."

By the fall of 1938, Johnny, the youngest of the Koski brothers, was thirteen years old and desperate to go deer hunting. Johnny mounted a campaign to convince his brother Al that he was ready to hunt deer with the rest of the brothers. As the oldest brother, Al was the mentor for the younger boys, taking them to camp and teaching them how to fish, hunt, and "get along in the woods." Al owned the hunting camp and ran it with a firm hand, so Johnny knew he had to convince Al that he was ready to start hunting deer.

As Lilly dished up an early breakfast of oatmeal in the Koski kitchen, Johnny continued his campaign. "Come on Al!" pleaded Johnny. "Let me go to deer camp this year! I've been hunting rabbits and partridge for years now. I can move pretty good in the woods and you know I can handle a gun. Other fellas my age are going hunting this year."

Al finally relented. "Okay, you can come to deer camp with the gang this year, but you'll hunt with me and you'll do exactly as I say. You won't go hunting on your own unless I say you can."

Johnny leapt into the air with his arms raised. "Hooray! You won't be sorry—you'll see!"

Going to camp wasn't anything new for Johnny, but this year was going to be different. This year he would join them at deer camp, finally crossing the all-important boundary that separated the men from the boys.

In many ways, Johnny had grown up at that camp, in the company of his brothers. When he was only five years old, on his first overnight stay at the hunting camp, Johnny heard a rustling sound inside the walls of the primitive cabin as he lay in his bunk.

"What's dat noise?" Johnny asked, with more than a touch of the local Finnish-American accent.

Al replied, "That's just mice running around inside the walls. Don't worry about them!"

Johnny couldn't sleep and lay nervously in his bunk, listening to the mice as they moved around inside the walls. Finally he asked, "Why are the mice in the walls?"

The older brothers chuckled in their bunks at the question, a question which had no logical answer, a question that adults wouldn't think to ask.

Al replied in his usual serious way: "Well Johnny, I think it's because they find it satisfactory to make their nests inside the warm walls."

Johnny always seriously considered everything his big brother Al told him. He eventually made some connection between the mice and his sister's jobs at a clothing factory in Ishpeming. After a few minutes, his young voice piped up again in the dark, "So, the mice work in the satis-factory!"

The other brothers laughed heartily for several minutes. As they started to fall asleep, one of the brothers chuckled in the dark, setting the others off again. They didn't get to sleep for some time as the cabin would grow quiet, then one or another of the brothers would chuckle in the dark as he thought about Johnny's comments.

The older brothers sometimes took advantage of Johnny's youthful gullibility. Later that summer, Johnny was walking back to the camp after dark with Art and Al. A bird whistled in the bushes and Johnny asked, "What's that?"

With a straight face, Al told him, "That's a bear. They can whistle, you know. They do that to lure you into the bushes."

Johnny listened solemnly, his eyes wide in the dark woods. Just then another bird whistled in the bushes close behind them. "Bear!" Johnny shouted in panic. He took off like a rabbit, racing down the darkened road to the camp.

Art and Al followed along at a more sedate pace. Back at the cabin, they told the story to the other brothers. From then on, the older boys teased Johnny mercilessly about whistling bears. Johnny's response was always the same. He would stand up straight, put his fists on his hips, and state, "That's not funny! Alfred told me that bears can whistle."

But Johnny was much older now—all of thirteen years old—and he was trying very hard to fit in as his older brothers got on with the serious business of checking and rechecking their guns and other equipment. Afterwards, they sat in the rustic hunting camp, drinking strong, black coffee and talking about where they were going to hunt the next morning.

George looked at his little brother and teased, "You're not gonna get buck fever, are you Johnny?"

Johnny looked down at his cup of coffee for a long time thinking. He'd heard stories about first-time hunters who bumbled a clean shot. Some hunters got too excited, failed to take careful aim, and missed. Others could not pull the trigger. Faced with the reality of a deer in their rifle sights, they were unable or unwilling to end the life of the beautiful animal standing before them.

Johnny understood why those men could not pull the trigger. Most men have a natural reluctance to killing, particularly when it comes to killing something as beautiful as a deer. But Johnny also understood that meat didn't come from a store, it came from animals. If a person was going to eat meat—any kind of meat—then some animal had to be killed to provide that meat. Buying meat from a store didn't eliminate the killing, it just moved the burden of the killing to someone else.

To Johnny and the other Koski brothers, a man didn't try to shirk his responsibilities by pretending that unpleasant things didn't exist. Being a man meant doing what was necessary, even if it was unpleasant or even if you were afraid. Being a man meant looking life—or death—in the eye and doing what needed to be done.

Like every lad, Johnny desperately wanted to join the men at deer camp. But there was more to it than male bonding. Poor families like the Koskis, struggling to make ends meet during the Depression, barely had enough money for essential store-bought items like flour and sugar. If they didn't hunt, they weren't going to eat very much meat. Johnny wanted to do his part in providing food for the family.

But that didn't mean killing a deer would come easy for a sensitive boy like Johnny. Just the previous spring, Johnny and his brothers found a bear cub caught in a beaver trap. Some of the older brothers wanted to shoot the cub to put it out of its misery, but Johnny pleaded for them to give the little fellow a chance. "I'll take care of it!" he said. "I can make it better!"

The older brothers relented and helped Johnny free the cub from the trap. It tried to bite and scratch, but they managed to stuff the cub into an old pillow case, which Johnny carried home. Lilly was hanging clothes on the line in the yard when the boys returned home with the squirming sack. The older boys egged Johnny on, saying "Show Lilly what you have in the bag!"

Johnny carefully reached into the squirming sack and pulled out the struggling bear cub. Seeing the bear, Lilly squealed and ran into the house, leaving a sheet flapping on the line while the boys doubled over with laughter.

Johnny cleaned and bandaged the cub's foot. Mindful of the sharp claws and teeth, he then held it while one of the brothers took pictures. Johnny put the cub in the rag box in the basement and cared for it while it recovered. A few weeks later, Lilly was home alone when she heard a crash in the basement. She lifted the trapdoor, peered into the dimly lit basement, and saw the bear eating jam from a broken jar. The cub turned and saw her, then galloped towards the steps.

Lilly dropped the trapdoor and dragged a heavy wooden dresser over it while the bear pawed at the trapdoor from below. When Johnny came home from school he found Lilly sitting on the dresser on top of the trap door. She had been there for hours, afraid to move. Lilly made it clear that the bear had to go. The bear's foot was mostly healed, so Johnny brought it back to the woods at Flat Rock and set it free.

★ Click here to watch video

Figure 5-2: Johnny Koski holding the bear cub with the bandaged foot.

Johnny felt good about having helped that bear cub. If he hadn't been there to save the cub, it probably would not have lived. But he had been there, and that cub did survive and grew into a full-sized bear. For the rest of that year, and for several years after, that bear periodically ambled past the hunting camp. It didn't seem afraid of the boys and never made any threatening moves. It seemed almost like that bear remembered Johnny and came back to check on him from time to time. While Johnny thought about the bear cub, George waited impatiently for an answer. Getting no response, George banged his coffee cup on the table and repeated his question: "Well? Are you gonna get buck fever Johnny?"

Johnny looked George in the eye. Killing a deer wouldn't come easy for him, but refusing to do so would mean stepping back from manhood. That wasn't acceptable. Johnny was determined to prove that he was a man.

"No," Johnny replied, "I'm not gonna get buck fever. I told you I was ready and you'll see that I am."

The next morning, several hours before dawn, Al and Johnny set out from the camp. Johnny was carrying the old Krag rifle—the same one that all Koski brothers used until they purchased their own rifles. On this, his first outing, he wasn't expected to use that rifle. As they followed a path into the dark forest, Al told Johnny, "Just follow me and watch carefully. If you do all right today, tomorrow you can lead and I'll follow along to see how you do."

They hiked to one of Al's favorite hunting spots on a small hill overlooking a deer trail, sat down next to a tree, and waited. They waited, and waited, sitting in the cold for hours. Johnny's coarse red-and-black-checked woolen hunting clothes made him itchy and the minutes dragged past as he tried not to think about scratching. When the itching became unbearable, Johnny would shift position or scratch and Al would sternly whisper, "Shhh! Don't be making noise like that!"

The minutes dragged on as the woods around them slowly brightened with the coming dawn. Finally, just after sunrise, they saw a large buck stepping carefully along the trail. The buck was suspicious, stopping frequently to sniff the air, but it didn't catch their scent and didn't see them waiting motionless near the base of the tree. Al slowly raised his rifle, waited until he had a clear shot, then squeezed the trigger.

The loud retort of the rifle echoed from the neighboring hills. The deer fell, kicked a time or two, then lay still. Al checked to make sure the deer was dead, then told Johnny to stay with the deer while he got help to drag the deer back to camp.

Johnny sat on a log with his rifle and waited. This had been a good day, maybe the best day of his life.

Johnny was watching a hawk circle in the distance when he heard movement in the brush. He figured it was Al, trying to sneak up on him, so he called out, "Alfred, is that you?"

Nobody answered and the noise came even closer. Suddenly, a large black bear burst out of the bushes. It saw Johnny, reared up on its hind legs and charged, mouth open and large white fangs glistening with saliva. This wasn't his cute little bear cub. This was a full-grown adult black bear and it was very, very mad!

Johnny, the thirteen year old first-time hunter, didn't hesitate. He coolly raised his rifle, aimed, and fired. Johnny's bullet hit the bear in the mouth, breaking off a large front tooth, then passing through its neck. The bear tottered for a moment, then fell backwards, dead, less than thirty feet away.

Al returned sometime later with Art, ready to drag the deer back to camp. Johnny was sitting on the log with the Krag rifle across his lap. From the expression on Johnny's face, Al knew something had happened. As Al walked closer, he asked Johnny if everything was all right.

Figure 5-3: Johnny Koski with hunting rifle and hat, about the time of his first deer hunt.

Johnny replied, "Yeah, everything's okay." Then he added, "While you were gone, a bear charged me and I had to shoot him."

Al frowned, "Johnny, you shouldn't make things up like that. You know lying is wrong."

Johnny replied, "I ain't making this up." He smiled proudly and pointed to the bushes on the other side of the log, "Maybe you should take a look in those bushes over there."

Al stepped around the log and was astonished to see a large black bear sprawled on the ground. The bear had been killed with a single shot. From the angle of the shot, he could tell the bear was standing up on its hind legs, with its mouth open, when Johnny shot it.

Al was impressed. He looked back at his baby brother and smiled with pride. Faced with an upright, charging bear, many men would have run. Many more would have shot in haste—and missed. It took a lot of nerve to stand still and take careful aim at the looming figure of an attacking bear.

That evening, Johnny told the story of the charging bear over and over again. He could tell that his brothers looked at him a little differently. He wasn't just little Johnny anymore. He was only thirteen years old, but he had faced a tough situation, a situation that none of his brothers had faced. He hadn't run and he hadn't panicked. He had proven that he wasn't a child anymore.

As the brothers sipped their coffee and talked about the bear, Art crumpled up some old newspapers and pushed them down into the old cast-iron cook stove. He lit the match and flames lapped over a quotation from a recent speech by Neville Chamberlain, Prime Minister of Great Britain:

> My good friends, for the second time in our history, a British Prime Minister has returned from Germany bringing peace with honour. I believe it is peace for our time. Go home and get a nice quiet sleep.

Like most Americans, the Koski brothers hadn't paid much attention to events in Europe. They didn't know what was happening in Germany. They didn't know that halfway across the globe frightened politicians had thrown away the last good chance to stop the Nazi menace.

In a misguided attempt to avoid another war with Germany, the leaders of France and England had given in to Hitler's demands and allowed him to take over a large section of Czechoslovakia. Those politicians did not understand that appeasing a man like Hitler would not prevent war. Appeasing Hitler only strengthened his position with the German people and made war even more likely.

If the leaders of France and England had stood firm and had been willing to fight, they could have put an end to Hitler and the Nazi menace while his armies were still weak. But they didn't stand firm, and millions of people would die in the resulting war.

But even if the Koski brothers had known what was happening in Czechoslovakia, they probably would have felt it was not relevant to their lives. As Neville Chamberlain was to later say, it was "a quarrel in a faraway country between people of whom we know nothing."

On this night in the fall of 1938, as the newspaper burned in the stove, the Koski brothers prepared their simple supper of coffee, bread, and beans. They then climbed into their bunks for a nice quiet sleep without a thought about the events unfolding in Europe—events which would soon engulf them all.

Figure 5-4: Having signed the Munich Pact, Neville Chamberlain believed he had secured "peace for our time." That was a serious miscalculation. Giving Hitler the Sudetenland did not satisfy him, it only encouraged further aggression.

★ Click here to watch video

★★★ Ordinary Heroes: Six Stars in the Window ★★★
6. War is a fearful thing

October 1939: Johnny was looking forward to his second season at deer camp, hoping that this year he'd finally get his own deer. He'd spent hours cleaning and polishing the old Krag rifle. If ammunition hadn't been so expensive he would have spent every afternoon after school shooting at old tin cans to improve his aim. But he didn't have money for ammunition and he did have school, so he sat at the kitchen table, doing his homework and watching his older sisters come and go.

Outside, Art and Al were cutting firewood with a saw blade attached by a rubber belt to the rear wheel of an old Model T truck. It was a crisp autumn day, but they worked up a sweat as they maneuvered the heavy logs through the spinning blade. Reuben and George were supposed to be helping stack the logs, but they'd wandered off somewhere as younger boys tend to do.

Art was a big lad, five foot ten and over 150 pounds, and he easily hefted his end of the logs. Al was smaller—just five foot seven and 125 pounds—but he was tough as nails and handled his end of the logs with apparent ease.

A man parked his Model A in front of the house and made some snide remark to Art and Al as he walked into the house to visit their father. When the man went in the house, the brothers looked at each other, grinned, then walked to the back of the man's car. Art grabbed the bumper and lifted the back of the car off the ground, while Al put a block of wood under the axle, leaving the back wheels slightly off the ground. They went back to cutting wood.

The man came out of the house, started his car, and put it in gear. Nothing happened, so he stepped on the gas. The engine raced and the rear wheels spun, but the car still didn't move. The man gave Art and Al a dirty look, turned off the car, then stalked back into the house to complain to their father. As soon as the door closed, Art lifted the car while Al removed the block of wood. Both boys went back to cutting wood.

Moments later, the man came out with their father. He was saying, "Dose poys did sumpin and now my car, she no go! Here, I show you!"

He jumped in the car, started it up, dropped it in gear and stomped on the gas. The rear wheels spun gravel and the car fish-tailed down the hill while the man wrestled with the steering wheel in an attempt to keep the car on the road.

Their father watched as the car skittered down the gravel road. He then put his hands on his hips, turned, and looked sternly at the brothers. Art and Al just glanced at him as they continued to feed logs into the saw blade. Their father yelled something, but Al just put his hand up to his ear and wiggled it to indicate that he couldn't hear over the din of the saw. Their father gave up and went back into the house. As he disappeared, both boys burst into laughter.

To the Koskis, that Ford truck was an exceedingly useful general-purpose machine. They used it to haul everything from firewood to manure to people. They coaxed it along two-track roads deep into the woods and pushed it across streams and through mudholes. It even served as a portable power plant for devices such as the sawmill.

Like everyone else in the Upper Peninsula, they knew that much of the iron ore used to manufacture Ford cars and trucks had been mined in Ishpeming or Negaunee. They also knew that much of the wood used in the manufacture of Ford automobiles came from the Ford lumber camp in the little town of Alberta, just south of L'anse, Michigan. They even knew people who claimed they'd seen Henry Ford with his good friend Thomas Edison on one of his many trips to the Upper Peninsula. But they didn't know there was a darker side to Henry Ford.

Henry Ford had been a strident anti-Semite since the early 1920s. For years, he owned and published a small newspaper called the *Dearborn Independent* which prominently featured articles on the "Jewish problem." The *Dearborn Independent* published an English version of *The Protocols of the Learned Elders of Zion*, a fictional document which spelled out the alleged secret plans for Jewish domination of the world.

Henry Ford was not the only anti-Semite in America. Many influential figures in the government of the United States, the War Department, and the U.S. intelligence services believed that the Jews were responsible for many of the problems of the world. Even members of the clergy jumped on the anti-Semite bandwagon. Father Charles Coughlin of Detroit portrayed the "Communist Jews" as the source of America's problems in strident radio addresses, sermons, and newsletters .

Henry Ford was one of the most influential anti-Semites in America, using his significant prestige and wealth to further his views. His influence extended to the anti-Jewish policies adopted by the Nazi party. During the Nuremberg trials after the war, Baldur von Schirach, one of the key figures in the elimination of Jews from Vienna, made the following statement: "The decisive anti-Semitic book which I read at that time, and the book which influenced my comrades, was Henry Ford's book, *The International Jew*. I read it, and became anti-Semitic."

★ Click here for Web Info

Figure 6-1: Left to right: President Herbert Hoover, Henry Ford, Thomas Edison, and Harvey Firestone at Edison's 82nd birthday in Ft. Meyers, Florida on February 11, 1929.

Adolf Hitler himself was a fan of Henry Ford, both for his anti-Semitism and for his exceedingly efficient production line manufacturing methods. For a time, a large portrait of Henry Ford hung prominently in Adolf Hitler's office. During an interview with the *Chicago Tribune*, Hitler stated, "We look on Henry Ford as the leader of the growing Fascisti movement in America. We admire particularly his anti-Jewish policy which is the Bavarian Fascisti platform. We have just had his anti-Jewish articles translated and published. The book is being circulated to millions throughout Germany." During a 1931 interview, when a *Detroit News* reporter asked Hitler why Henry Ford's portrait hung on his wall, Hitler candidly replied, "I regard Henry Ford as my inspiration."

Looking back, it can be difficult to understand the strength of the anti-Semitic movement of that time. All over the world, people faced brutal poverty. There was no work, there was very little food. Massive inflation wiped out life savings and crippled economies. The German mark plummeted in value from four marks to a dollar, to 7,000 marks to a dollar, finally becoming almost worthless as the exchange rate hit one million marks to the dollar. In their suffering, the people of the world looked for someone to blame. Individuals and political parties gained popularity by presenting the Jew as the scapegoat, the cause of the world's problems.

People lost faith in the ability of their governments to overcome the problems facing them. Many people felt that democracy had failed. They believed the future belonged either to fascism or to communism. As Anne Morrow Lindbergh, wife of the famous aviator Charles Lindbergh, put it, "The wave of the future is coming and there is no fighting it," suggesting the war in Europe was not a "fight between good and evil" but a struggle between "forces of the past" and "forces of the future."

In Germany, Italy, Yugoslavia, and the Soviet Union, strong, charismatic leaders gained power with tantalizing promises for those with no other hope for the future. Adolf Hitler combined elements of racism, anti-Semitism, totalitarianism, and intense patriotism, to craft a message that resonated with the German people. He blamed the problems of Germany on racial impurity, the Jews, and the German leaders who had betrayed Germany by signing the Treaty of Versailles, which ended World War I. In return for total power, Hitler promised to restore the German nation to its place of greatness and to bring the Aryan race to power over all other peoples.

Hitler combined his extreme political views with modern industrial methods to produce a war machine of unprecedented power, a war machine that he intended to use with extreme brutality. In August of 1939, Hitler made his intentions clear in his Obersalzberg Speech, saying,

★ Click here to watch video

Figure 6-2: Adolf Hitler and the Nazi party offered the German people hope in a time of despair and were rewarded with the enthusiastic support of the people.

> Stalin and I are the only ones who visualize the future. So in a few weeks hence I shall stretch out my hand to Stalin at the common German–Russian frontier and with him undertake to redistribute the world.
>
> Our strength lies in our quickness and in our brutality, Genghis Khan has sent millions of women and children into death knowingly and with a light heart. History sees in him only the great founder of States. As to what the weak Western European civilization asserts about me, that is of no account. I have given the command and I shall shoot everyone who utters one word of criticism, for the goal to be obtained in the war is not that of reaching certain lines but of physically demolishing the opponent. And so for the present only in the East I have put my death-head formations in place with the command relentlessly and without compassion to send into death many women and children of Polish origin and language. Only thus we can gain the living space that we need. Who after all is today speaking about the destruction of the Armenians?
>
> Colonel-General von Brauchitsch has promised me to bring the war against Poland to a close within a few weeks. Had he reported to me that he needs two years or even only one year, I should not have given the command to march and should have allied myself temporarily with England instead of Russia for we cannot conduct a long war. To be sure a new situation has arisen. I experienced those poor worms Daladier and Chamberlain in Munich. They will be too cowardly to attack. They won't go beyond a blockade. Against that we have our autarchy and the Russian raw materials.
>
> Poland will be depopulated and settled with Germans. My pact with the Poles was merely conceived of as a gaining of time. As for the rest, gentlemen, the fate of Russia will be exactly the same as I am now going through with in the case of Poland. After Stalin's death—he is a very sick man—we will break the Soviet Union. Then there will begin the dawn of the German rule of the earth.

> The little States cannot scare me. After Kemal's death Turkey is governed by cretins and half idiots. Carol of Romania is through and through the corrupt slave of his sexual instincts. The King of Belgium and the Nordic kings are soft jumping jacks who are dependent upon the good digestions of their overeating and tired peoples.
>
> We shall have to take into the bargain the defection of Japan. I give Japan a full year's time. The Emperor is a counterpart to the last Czar—weak, cowardly, undecided. May he become a victim of the revolution. My going together with Japan never was popular. We shall continue to create disturbances in the Far East and in Arabia. Let us think as 'gentlemen' and let us see these peoples at best as lacquered half maniacs who are anxious to experience the whip.
>
> The opportunity is as favorable as never before. I have but one worry, namely that Chamberlain or some other such pig of a fellow will come at the last moment with proposals or with ratting. He will fly down the stairs, even if I shall personally have to trample on his belly in the eyes of the photographers.
>
> No, it is too late for this. The attack upon and the destruction of Poland begins Saturday early. I shall let a few companies in Polish uniform attack in Upper Silesia or in the Protectorate. Whether the world believes it is quite indifferent. The world believes only in success.
>
> For you, gentlemen, fame and honour are beginning as they have not since centuries. Be hard, be without mercy, act more quickly and brutally than the others. The citizens of Western Europe must tremble with horror. That is the most human way of conducting a war. For it scares the others off.
>
> The new method of conducting war corresponds to the new drawing of the frontiers. A war extending from Reval, Lublin, Kaschau, to the mouth of the Danube. The rest will be given to the Russians. Ribbentrop has orders to make every offer and to accept every demand. In the West I reserve to myself the right to determine the strategically best line. Here one will be able to work with Protectorate regions, such as Holland, Belgium and French Lorraine.
>
> And now, on to the enemy, in Warsaw we will celebrate our reunion.

The speech was received with enthusiasm. Hermann Göring, one of Hitler's top generals, is reported to have danced like a wild man. Any Germans who might have had misgivings about the speech remained quiet.

With benefit of hindsight—knowing what Hitler said, what he did, and what he meant to do—it is difficult to reach any conclusion but that he was a most evil person. But any individual, no matter how evil, can cause only limited harm. With the overwhelming support of the German people, Adolf Hitler gained control of the German nation, one of the most technologically advanced nations in the world. With near-total control of that industrialized nation, he was in a position to cause incalculable harm to the rest of the world. And he proceeded to do just that.

To the Western world, Hitler presented quite a different face. In speech after speech, he declared that Nazi Germany sought only peace. "Nationalist Socialist Germany wants peace because of its fundamental convictions," he cried. "Germany needs peace and desires peace!" and Germany neither intends nor wishes to interfere in the internal affairs of Austria, to annex Austria, or to conclude an Anschluss [merging of Germany and Austria]." But at the same time that he was making those peaceful-sounding speeches, Hitler was orchestrating a massive military buildup that went far beyond the limits imposed by the treaty that ended World War I.

People see what they want to see. Painful memories of World War I were still fresh and the people of the Western world desperately wanted to believe that peace with Hitler was possible. The Times of London, like many western newspapers, bought into Hitler's story, remarking about one of his speeches, "The speech turns out to be reasonable, straightforward, and comprehensive. No one who reads it with an impartial mind can doubt that the points of policy laid down by Herr Hitler may fairly constitute the basis of a complete settlement with Germany."

The political leaders of France and England also tried to convince themselves that Hitler was a reasonable fellow, someone with whom they could negotiate. British Prime Minister Neville Chamberlain continued to seek some common ground with Hitler, some way to avoid war. As he was to say in a speech later that year, "war is a fearful thing, and we must be very clear, before we embark on it, that it is really the great issues that are at stake."

Unfortunately, by the time it became clear that the great issues were at stake, it would be too late—too late to stop the war that would claim millions of lives.

★ Click here to watch video

Figure 6-3: Neville Chamberlain wanted to avoid war, but Hitler's ambitions made peace impossible.

On August 22, 1939, Germany and Russia reached agreement on a non-aggression pact. A portion of the agreement provided for the division of Polish territory "in the event of a territorial and political rearrangement." This agreement cleared the way for Germany to invade Poland without fear of a Russian attack.

On September 1, Germany invaded Poland. Great Britain demanded that Hitler withdraw from Poland. Instead, the Germans pressed the attack, destroying the rest of the Polish Air Force. On September 2, Edouard Daladier, the French Prime Minister, and Chamberlain offered to attend a peace conference to reconsider the Polish issue if Germany would withdraw its troops. The Germans did not respond.

On September 3, Chamberlain sent an ultimatum to Hitler, requiring a response within two hours. Once again, Hitler did not reply. At 11:00 a.m., Chamberlain declared that a state of war existed between England and Germany. At 5:00 p.m., France also declared war on Germany.

Poland needed immediate military assistance, but neither France nor England moved to provide meaningful assistance to the beleaguered Poles. Within a week, 170,000 Polish troops were encircled. On September 17, the Soviet Union invaded Poland from the east. Ten days later, overrun by German and Russian troops, abandoned by the rest of the world, Poland surrendered.

World War II had begun. The forces were in motion. The future of the world hung in the balance.

The Koski brothers were not paying particular attention to events in Poland.

★ Click here to watch video

Figure 6-4: Nazi Germany invaded Poland on September 1, 1939, drawing Great Britain and France into the war.

Instead they were watching the escalating conflict between Finland and the Soviet Union. The Soviet Union pressured Finland to give up territory north of Leningrad and lease the Soviets a sea port for a naval base. Finland refused. On November 26, 1939, the Soviet Union attacked Finland.

The Finns were outnumbered fifty to one, but they inflicted heavy losses on the Russian troops through guerrilla tactics. The Soviet troops were well equipped with tanks, artillery, and automatic weapons. The Finns fought back with surprise attacks, booby traps, snipers, and flaming liquor bottles filled with a mixture of kerosene, tar, and gasoline. Although such bottles had been used in previous wars, it was during the Finnish Winter War that they were named Molotov cocktails, after Vyacheslav Molotov, one of the primary Russian negotiators with whom the Finns had been unable to reach a compromise short of war.

Most Finns fought as light infantry, traveling on homemade skis and wearing bed sheets as camouflage. Finland also had a small air force that courageously took to the skies to oppose the much larger Russian air force. Some of the Finnish pilots compiled astounding records, such as Lieutenant Sarvanto, whose record shows thirteen confirmed and four unconfirmed kills. On one occasion, Lieutenant Sarvanto flew into a formation of seven Russian planes. In four minutes, he shot down six Russian fighters, while another Finnish pilot took out the seventh. All together, Finnish pilots shot down 240 Russian planes, while losing only 62 planes of their own.

Finnish snipers took a horrible toll on the Russian troops. One sniper, a Corporal Hayhä, killed more than 500 Russians. A captured Russian officer, interrogated by the Finns, explained what the war was like from the Russian side.

> The first Finns that I personally saw were the two that took me as prisoner after my regiment was destroyed. We couldn't see them anywhere, yet they were all over the place. If anybody left the campsite, he met with certain death. When we sent our sentries to take their positions around the camp, we knew that within minutes they would be dead with a bullet hole in the forehead or the throat slashed with a dagger. This invisible death was lurking from every direction. It was sheer madness. Hundreds, even thousands of my men were slaughtered.

The United States and France expressed stern disapproval of the Soviet attack on Finland, but did not offer any military support for Finland. The League of Nations impotently demanded that the Soviets stop the attack.

Although their governments would not help Finland, volunteers showed up from Sweden, Norway, Denmark, France, and England. There was even one volunteer from Jamaica and two Japanese men, who for some reason, felt compelled to risk their lives to help the beleaguered Finns fight the Russian juggernaut.

Only one country was willing to provide significant assistance to help Finland repel the Russian invaders. That country was Nazi Germany. So, as little Finland struggled for survival against the Russian war machine, Finnish soldiers fought alongside German soldiers in a classic case of "the enemy of my enemy is my friend."

Of course, the Nazis were helping Finland for their own reasons. They could not afford to let the Russians control the Norwegian ports or the Swedish iron mines which the Germans so desperately needed to build their war machines.

Most Americans didn't know much about Finland. If they thought of Finland at all, they thought of the music of Jean Sibelius or Finnish athletes such as Paavo Nurmi. Few remembered that stubborn Finland had been the only country that insisted on repaying its World War I debt to the United States. Few thought tiny Finland had any chance against the mighty Soviet army.

But as recent immigrants, the Koski family knew firsthand the ingrained stubbornness of the Finnish people. They knew how much the Finns hated the Russians and believed that somehow the Finns would find a way to defeat the Russian invaders. But, they also knew the war would cost the Finns dearly, both in money and in lives.

The human cost of the Finnish-Russian war was brought home to them when they received a letter from Finland with a photo of a Finnish cousin who had been killed while fighting against the Russians. They didn't know where he had been fighting or how he had been killed. They just knew the stark outlines of the story: a young man went to war and would not return.

★ Click here for Web Info

Figure 6-5: A Koski cousin named George Koski was just one of some 22,830 Finns and 126,875 Russians killed in the Winter War.

One day, the Koski brothers were listening to a local Finnish-language radio station as it described the brave Finnish soldiers fighting the Russian invaders. Suddenly, the door opened and their father walked in. The boys knew their father did not approve of radio and they expected to be scolded. But surprisingly their father sat down in his rocking chair and listened to the rest of the newscast. From then on, their father would join them as they listened to the news of the Finnish soldiers fighting on skis to defend their homeland.

During those broadcasts, the boys learned how much their father hated the Russians with their "yellow teeth like corn." They learned how their grandparents sent their children to America to get them away from the Finnish Socialists and Russians. Alfred Koski told the boys hard stories of Finnish refugees forced out of their homes by the Russians, and of others who had been forced to work for the Russians in the forests or the mines.

The Koski boys were surprised to hear the depth of their father's feelings on the Finnish–Russian war. They could not help but notice his pride in the Finnish soldiers who were out-fighting the Russians through surprise, cunning, and courageous action.

Some weeks later Johnny and his young friend Bobby Emmanuelson skidded to a stop on their homemade skis alongside the ramshackle Koski barn. As they knocked the ice off their skis, Bobby said, "My Dad says the Finns ambushed the Russians again last week. They hid in the woods, attacked, then skied away before the Russians could come after them. How'd you like to be one of those ski soldiers Johnny?"

Johnny Koski just grinned at his enthusiastic young friend. They both knew he couldn't think of anything better than being a ski soldier.

One of their favorite winter games was ski troopers. They would swoop through the forest on their homemade wooden skis, envisioning themselves as Finnish ski troopers, gliding unseen and unheard behind the Russian invaders. They would attack an unsuspecting stump or rock, then quickly glide away before the imaginary Russians could bring their armor and artillery into play.

Inspired at the thought of the brave Finnish soldiers defending their homeland, Johnny stepped up on a log and began to enthusiastically recite the words to one of his favorite poems, *I Have a Rendezvous with Death,* by Alan Seeger, a young soldier who died in World War I:

> *I have a rendezvous with Death*
>
> *At some disputed barricade,*
>
> *When Spring comes back with rustling shade*
>
> *And apple-blossoms fill the air—*
>
> *I have a rendezvous with Death*
>
> *When Spring brings back blue days and fair.*

"Aww Johnny, why do you always have to do that one?" asked Bobby. "Do Hiawatha instead!"

"Okay, okay," said Johnny. He took a deep breath, then launched into one of Bobby's favorite poems, *The Song of Hiawatha* by Henry Wadsworth Longfellow.

As Johnny recited the poem with his usual gusto, his young friend Bobby sat on a log and listened intently. Both Johnny and Bobby loved poetry, particularly poems of far-away places, brave men, and heroic deeds. As poor kids in rural northern Michigan, they didn't think they'd ever travel far, or participate in any great deeds. But the world had other plans.

★ Click here to watch video

Figure 6-6: By the 4th grade, Johnny Koski could recite numerous heroic poems from memory.

★★★ Ordinary Heroes: Six Stars in the Window ★★★
7. Their finest hour

Through the winter of 1939–1940, England and France were technically at war with Germany, but very little happened. Hitler consolidated his hold over Czechoslovakia and Poland, while the Belgians, French, and English strengthened their defenses. The English called this time the "Phony War," the Germans called it Sitzkreig or "Sitting War." English pilots dropped propaganda leaflets over Germany. The English and French expanded production of military supplies, but no actions were taken to attack German troops or expel them from Poland.

On January 18, 1940, the Koski brothers listened to the radio as Edward R. Murrow reported on English expectations: "The question most people are asking in England these days is: will the Germans attack in the spring?" Drawing on his experiences in Berlin, reporter William Schirer replied, "Ed, I don't know a single German who isn't sure that there will be plenty of action in the spring. But what kind it will be and where, no one knows…"

Alfred Koski had relented and let the boys listen to the radio, but that was one of the few instances in which he changed his mind about anything. Like most Finns, once he formed an opinion, he stuck with it. Once he decided to do something, he did it.

The Finns have a word for that sort of determination: *sisu* (see-soo). Sisu is one of those terms that doesn't have an exact English translation. It's a combination of stubbornness and determination. It is determination past the point of reason. Sisu gives men the stubbornness to fight just a little longer, even though they know they cannot win. Sisu is what sustained the Finns through forty-two wars with the Russians, even though they lost every one.

Sisu might be a Finnish word, but it is not a uniquely Finnish trait. It can be found in all nations and in all people. Sometimes, when the need is very great, a leader will emerge—a leader with the stubbornness, the sisu, the determination to succeed despite all odds. Such a leader can change the fate of a nation or the world. In the early years of World War II, when the need was very great, such a leader emerged in England.

In April of 1940, Germany invaded Denmark and Norway. In May, the advance continued as Germany invaded Belgium, Luxembourg, the Netherlands, and France. In a stunningly successful maneuver, the Germans feinted with an attack on Belgium, then poured tanks through the heavily wooded Ardennes, trapping most of the French, British, and Belgian forces.

Neville Chamberlain, the Prime Minister of Great Britain, was forced to resign when it became clear that his policy of appeasement had failed miserably. Winston Churchill, a bulldog of a politician, who had repeatedly warned of the dangers of Nazism, was selected as the new Prime Minister and assumed the

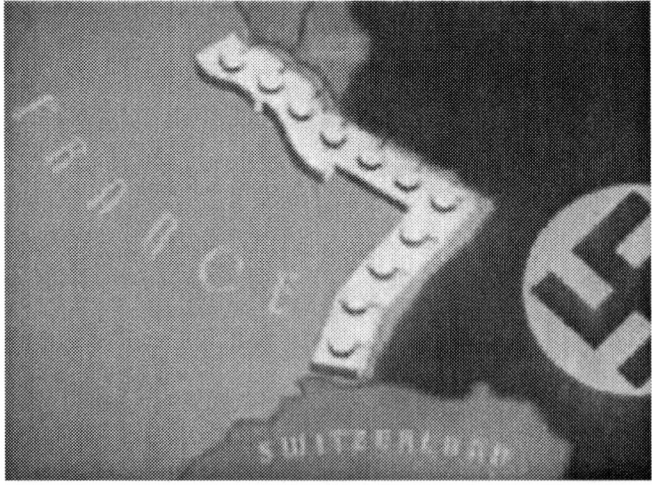

★ Click here to watch video

Figure 7-1: The French believed the Maginot Line would stop the Germans. Holland and Belgium believed Hitler would respect their neutrality. Military strategists believed the Germans could not attack through the Ardennes. Hitler proved them all wrong with a stunningly successful attack through the Ardennes forest.

task of rescuing the remnants of the English Army and preparing for the defense of England.

At the end of May, England struggled to rescue 400,000 troops trapped on the beach at Dunkirk. By June 4, the evacuation at Dunkirk was complete. France and Belgium capitulated. Rumania and Bulgaria joined the Germans. Germany faced no significant resistance in all of western Europe. England stood alone against the might of the Nazis in Europe.

As the rising tide of Nazism threatened to engulf all of Europe, the United States of America boldly declared itself neutral. The fate of Western Civilization hung in the balance, but the United States did not want to get involved.

★ Click here to watch video

Figure 7-2: Thousands of ships and boats of all sizes converged on Dunkirk in a heroic effort to rescue the remnants of the British Army trapped on the French coast.

On May 13, 1940, Winston Churchill outlined his grim vision for the future in a speech to the House of Commons:

> I would say to the House as I have said to ministers who have joined this government, I have nothing to offer but blood, toil, tears, and sweat.
>
> We have before us an ordeal of the most grievous kind. We have before us many, many long months of struggle and suffering.
>
> You ask, what is our policy? I will say it is to wage war by sea, land, and air. War with all our might and with all the strength God has given us, and to wage war against a monstrous tyranny never surpassed in the dark and lamentable catalogue of human crime. That is our policy.
>
> You ask, what is our aim? I can answer in one word. Victory. Victory at all costs—Victory in spite of all terrors—Victory, however long and hard the road may be, for without victory there is no survival.
>
> Let that be realized. No survival for the British Empire, no survival for all that the British Empire has stood for, no survival for the urge, the impulse of the ages, that mankind shall move forward toward his goal.
>
> But I take up my task with buoyancy and hope. I feel sure that our cause will not be suffered to fail among men. At this time I feel entitled at this juncture, at this time, to claim the aid of all and to say, "Come then, let us go forward together with our united strength."

★ Click here to watch video

Figure 7-3: Winston Churchill steadfastly refused to accept the possibility of defeat.

On June 18 1940, as it became clear that France would fall, Winston Churchill gave one of his most famous speeches in the House of Commons:

> What General Weygand called the Battle of France is over. I expect that the Battle of Britain is about to begin. Upon this battle depends the survival of Christian civilization. Upon it depends our own British life, and the long continuity of our institutions and our Empire. The whole fury and might of the enemy must very soon be turned on us. Hitler knows that he will have to break us in this island or lose the war. If we can stand up to him, all Europe may be free and the life of the world may move forward into broad, sunlit uplands. But if we fail, then the whole world, including the United States, including all that we have known and cared for, will sink into the abyss of a new Dark Age made more sinister, and perhaps more protracted, by the lights of perverted science. Let us therefore brace ourselves to our duties and so bear ourselves that, if the British Empire and its Commonwealth last for a thousand years, men will still say, "This was their finest hour."

On June 23, the French signed an armistice with the Germans. The northern two–thirds of France was to be occupied by the Germans. The southern one–third was to be governed by the French, but pledged to cooperate with the Germans. The French-controlled portion of the country was run by Philippe Petain from the southern French city of Vichy and became known as Vichy France. Most of the French colonies in Africa allied themselves with the Nazis. On June 23 1940, Adolf Hitler triumphantly toured Paris. Most of Europe was under control of the Nazi party. Only a small number of Frenchmen, many of whom were in England, pledged to continue fighting the Nazis.

★ Click here to watch video

Figure 7-4: Nazi troops advanced into France with a speed that bewildered the French and surprised even the German commanders.

Many people throughout Europe, as well as in England and Germany, believed the Germans had won the war. All that remained was the formality of a German–English peace agreement. The English could not win and the Americans would not fight. Logic dictated that the English people must accept German rule of the European continent and come to terms with the Nazis.

Against logic, against hope, Churchill refused to negotiate for peace with Germany. Churchill understood that a negotiated peace would leave most of Europe under Nazi rule for the foreseeable future. Given time to consolidate the occupied territories, the Germans would inevitably attack and conquer Great Britain.

Churchill had no good options. He could continue to fight, hoping that some miracle—perhaps American intervention—would allow him to prevail. Or, he could make peace with the Germans, wait for them to build their forces, then face attack by an overwhelming force. Churchill decided to continue the fight.

Anticipating a negotiated peace, Hitler was initially reluctant to commit to an attack on England. When Churchill refused to negotiate with him, Hitler approved plans for an all-out air attack on England. This was to be followed by an amphibious landing code-named Operation Sea Lion.

By mid-August, 1940, England was under almost constant attack by the German Air Force, or Luftwaffe. The Battle of Britain had begun. Armed with great courage, skill, and a relatively sophisticated radar network, the Royal Air Force, or RAF, fought valiantly to stop the Germans. But RAF losses were extremely heavy, forcing Prime Minister Churchill to the realization that "A few more weeks of this and Britain would have no organized defense of the skies."

Churchill recognized that the fate of Great Britain depended on the gallantry and skill of the RAF fighter pilots. In a speech to the House of Commons on April 20, 1940, he remarked, "Never in the field of human conflict was so much owed by so many to so few."

If the Germans gained air superiority over England, Operation Sea Lion would be launched and England would almost certainly be overwhelmed. As German bombers thundered overhead, a German invasion of England seemed imminent. The government of Great Britain was forced to make plans for a German invasion of England—plans that included guerrilla warfare against the German invaders and possible relocation of the British government to Canada.

Many Germans believed the British people would rise up to form a new government, a government that would seek peace with the Germans to stop the bombing of English cities. However, English determination grew as the bombing continued.

★ Click here to watch video

Figure 7-5: Winston Churchill understood that if England lost the Battle of Britain, "the world would sink into the abyss of a new dark age."

Churchill battled periods of depression, which he called "the black dog," but he remained determined to defend England. In a speech to the House of Commons on June 4, 1940 he said "We shall fight on the beaches, we shall fight on the landing grounds, we shall fight on the fields and in the streets, we shall fight in the hills, we shall never surrender."

This wasn't hyperbole. Churchill knew that within a matter of weeks, British citizens might well be fighting the Nazis in the streets and hills of England. At dinner one night, he put down his knife and fork and advised his wife and pregnant daughter-in-law, "If the Hun comes, I am counting on each of you to take one with you before you go."

But on August 23, the course of the war changed when a navigational error caused German bombers to mistakenly drop their bombs on London instead of the aircraft factories and oil tanks that had been their assigned target. In retaliation for the bombing of London, British bombers attacked Berlin, killing ten people and wounding twenty-nine. This was the first time Berlin had been ever been bombed.

An outraged Hitler ordered the Luftwaffe to switch to bombing raids of London and other population centers. As the German bombers attacked the English cities, the RAF was able to regroup. By mid-September, the tide turned in favor of the RAF and the British planes slowly beat back the attacking Luftwaffe. Although the bombing of England continued, the Luftwaffe was unable to gain air superiority over England. Operation Sea Lion was postponed, then finally called off.

For the time being, England was safe from invasion, but the war was far from won. Hitler still controlled most of Europe. The British people realized they could not win the war without American involvement.

That fall, the Koski brothers listened as CBS News correspondent Edward R. Murrow reported from London, "Many Britons believe that this world, or what's left of it, will be largely run from either Berlin or from Washington." Which would prevail had not yet been decided.

★★★ Ordinary Heroes: Six Stars in the Window ★★★
8. Sleeping bears

November, 1941: It was dusk and most of the Koski brothers had returned to the cabin from a day of deer hunting. Only Johnny and Reuben were still out. Suddenly Johnny burst into the cabin, breathing heavily and repeating the strange phrase, "My stomach is hot! My stomach is hot!"

Somebody handed him a drink of water and he finally calmed down enough to tell them what had happened. "I was working my way through that valley on the south side and I climbed over a fallen pine tree. I put my foot down on the other side of that log and I thought I felt something move. I didn't know what it was, so I stamped down really hard."

"The thing under my feet moved and growled! I looked down and saw black fur under my foot. It was a bear! So I pointed my rifle down and shot, then shot again."

He pointed to his Krag rifle, "I shot until my gun was empty, then ran back here as fast as I could. I can't believe it! I stepped right on that bear and woke him up!"

The Koski brothers grabbed their rifles and streamed out the door with Johnny. They walked briskly through the woods, Johnny leading the way and chattering excitedly the whole while. As they approached the fallen log, Johnny warned them, "That's the tree. Be careful! I think that bear is still under there."

Art poked around in the bushes with the tip of his rifle. Nothing moved, so he pulled the branches aside. Sure enough, there was a big black bear lying dead under the fallen tree.

Johnny endured a lot of teasing after stepping on that bear. That night, Al pulled his pipe out of his mouth and said in his gravelly voice, "You know, Johnny, I don't recommend stepping on a sleeping bear. You'll wake him up for sure and then you'll have your hands full." He puffed on his pipe, then continued, "Yup, I'd leave those sleeping bears alone if I was you."

That advice might have been a little late for Johnny, but it would have been good advice for Hitler. While Germany overran much of Europe, two of the greatest powers in the world, the Soviet Union and the United States of America, slumbered like hibernating bears. It would be better for Hitler if they were not awakened.

Joseph Stalin, the dictator of the Soviet Union, did not believe that Germany was a threat to the Soviet Union. Stalin had apparently either not read or did not believe Hitler's statements in Mein Kampf, "When we speak of new territory in Europe today we must think principally of Russia and her border vassal states. Destiny itself seems to want to point out the way for us here... This colossal empire in the East is ripe for dissolution and the end of the Jewish domination in Russia will also be the end of Russia as a state."

On June 22, 1941, Germany attacked Russia. Over three million German soldiers and 3,300 tanks crossed the Russian border. Some historians believe this attack on Russia may have been Hitler's fatal mistake. The Nazis and the Russians were uneasy allies at best and war between them was probably inevitable, but many historians believe Hitler could have postponed that war for several years. If Hitler had focused his efforts on England, he might have been able to invade England or inflict enough damage to persuade Churchill to settle on his terms. The Americans would not have been able to use England as a base from which to bomb Germany. Without England, it would have been almost impossible for the Americans to launch a successful invasion of Europe. Hitler could have later turned his focus to the Russians, either reaching some sort of compromise with them or focusing all his military might to crush them. The Thousand Year Reich could have been reality. Instead Hitler left England unconquered and attacked Russia, creating exactly the type of two-front war that German military minds had always warned against. The Russian bear had been awakened, but America still slumbered.

In the fall of 1941, Americans were bitterly divided on the issue of neutrality. Many Americans felt that if the U.S. supplied the Allies with war materials, the Allies might be able to win the war without involving U.S. troops. Others felt that any assistance to the Allies risked U.S. neutrality and would lead to U.S. involvement in the war. Both sides wanted to avoid sending U.S. troops to war. Neither side was willing to accept that the war could not be won without U.S. troops.

Some Americans argued the war had already been lost, that America must learn to live with a Europe dominated by the Nazis. The famous American aviator Charles Lindbergh gave a speech to the America First Committee in New York City. In the speech he reiterated the noninterventionist position that the war in Europe was as good as lost:

★ Click here to watch video

Figure 8-1: Isolationists and interventionists argued passionately about American involvement in the war.

> It is not only our right, but it is our obligation as American citizens to look at this war objectively, and to weigh our chances for success if we should enter it. I have attempted to do this, especially from the standpoint of aviation, and I have been forced to the conclusion that we cannot win this war for England, regardless of how much assistance we extend.
>
> I ask you to look at the map of Europe today and see if you can suggest any way in which we could win this war if we entered it. Suppose we had a large army in America, trained and equipped. Where would we send it to fight? The campaigns of the war show only too clearly how difficult it is to force a landing, or to maintain an army, on a hostile coast. Suppose we took our navy from the Pacific, and used it to convoy British shipping. That would not win the war for England. It would, at best, permit her to exist under the constant bombing of the German air fleet. Suppose we had an air force that we could send to Europe. Where could it operate? Some of our squadrons might be based in the British Isles, but it is physically impossible to base enough aircraft in the British Isles alone to equal in strength the aircraft that can be based on the continent of Europe.

★ Click here to watch video

Figure 8-2: Famed aviator Charles Lindbergh argued strongly that America should not get involved in the "war that cannot be won." His message resonated with many Americans who did not want another war.

Many Americans agreed with Lindbergh. If the war in Europe was hopeless, why should America become involved?

Wouldn't it be better to focus on defense and get used to the idea of dealing with a Europe ruled from Berlin? Even if the Allies could win the war in Europe, what gave America the right to intervene in European politics? Many wondered why America should play policeman to the rest of the world.

In May of 1941, the looming war finally touched the Koski family when the oldest brother, Al, received his draft notice. On June 3, 1941, in a scene that was to be repeated millions of times in the coming years, the Koski family drove Al to the train station and tearfully waved goodbye as he boarded the train for boot camp.

★ Click here to watch video

Figure 8-3: Alfred Koski posing with a 155 mm cannon, one of many guns installed on the west coast of America to fend off a possible Japanese invasion.

Al trained as a gunner with Battery C of the 57th Coast Artillery at Camp Callan, San Diego. He was one of ten thousand young men at Camp Callan being trained to defend the shores of America against enemy invasion. From 6:00 a.m. to 5:00 p.m., the soldiers drilled in their blue denim fatigues, marching in the soft sand of the parade ground under the hot California sun.

There were a number of recruits from Ishpeming at Camp Callan, including Guido Bonetti, Albert Hillman, Leonard Leinonen, Strom Russo, and Nataline Belpedio. Nataline Belpedio wrote a letter, parts of which were published in the *Mining Journal* for the folks back home: "Every Saturday we have inspection. You should see the boys polishing their rifles and making up there bunks. Everything has to be just so, our shoes have to be shined, hair cut, teeth brushed, we have to be clean shaven and our clothes neat, every-thing in our foot lockers arranged according to orders." He continued, "The pace here is terrific. They turn out soldiers like Henry Ford turns out cars. No time is wasted. They don't let you forget you're in the Army. We drill and drill and then we drill some more."

In the autumn of 1941, his basic training complete, Al applied for early release from the Army as an essential worker in the iron mines. His early release was approved and on September 28, 1941 he was discharged. As he was discharged, Al received a letter signed by Brigadier General F.P. Hardaway, which read in part, "You have done your part in actively participating in the program of the Army of the United States, and now you are about to again participate, actively, in the national defense movement in civilian life."

Believing his military obligations fulfilled, Al married his fiancee and started building a house in West Ishpeming, just a few blocks from his father's house.

By November of 1941, all six of the Koski brothers were back in the Upper Peninsula. Al was married, George was taking classes at the Michigan College of Mines (later Michigan Technological University), and the other four brothers were home.

Like most Americans, the Koski brothers read the newspaper accounts, listened to the radio reports, and tried to pretend there was some alternative to war. The war was like a whirlpool and America just went around and around, drawing ever closer to the brink.

On the first weekend in December, 1941, the Koski brothers and a few friends were out at hunting camp. As they dug into a stack of pancakes and pot of hot coffee, they talked about the war in Europe and what role, if any, America should play in it.

One of their friends said, "I still don't see why this war is our problem. We know the English and the French could have avoided the whole thing if they had fought Hitler right off the bat. They knew he was bad, but they let him build up his armies anyway."

One of the other fellows pitched in "They gave him Czechoslovakia without a fight. Now, after they waited too long and have been whupped good, they want us to help them. I don't know, I think it might be a little late for that. It seems to me they're on their own now."

The first fellow joined in, "Yeah, they haven't attacked us. Hitler is Europe's problem, not ours. Who made us boss of the world?"

Al poured himself another cup of coffee. "You're right when you say it would have been better if the English and the French had taken a stand early on. They could have whipped Hitler in the early days and saved the world a lot of misery. But they didn't. They didn't understand what they were dealing with, so they gave him what he wanted and hoped he'd go away."

He paused and took a drink of coffee, then continued, "They made mistakes, but I don't see that those mistakes change anything. Hitler controls most of Europe. Do you really think he'll be satisfied with Europe? He's a rabid wolf and we're going to have to fight him sooner or later. I don't like the idea of Americans fighting Hitler in Europe, but I'd rather fight him in Europe than America. Do you really think we have any other choice?"

One of the other boys said, "Okay, maybe Hitler has to be stopped, but why is it up to us? Why do we have to be the ones to do it?"

Art replied, "When you get right down to it, we're gonna have to do it because we're the only ones who can do it. The Brits, the Canadians, the Australians, and all the rest are doing their best, but they can't win this war without us. Anybody who thinks so is dreaming."

The other boys grumbled, but didn't really have any response. Deep in their hearts, they knew Al was right. Sooner or later America was going to have to fight Hitler. They also knew that they, as young men in their late teens and early twenties, would be on the front lines of any war. So, they kept hoping that the Hitler problem would somehow go away.

George had brought along his latest crystal radio set, hoping to prove that his new antenna design would allow him to receive a useable signal at the camp. The homemade radio didn't need batteries or electricity, but required a very long wire antenna stretched between the cabin and a tree. George hovered over the little set, moving a big paper clip back and forth on the coil, listening intently to his little headset. Suddenly he yelled, "Quiet! I got something!" The brothers stopped talking as George listened intently. Moments later he turned to the brothers and said, "I only got part of that, but I think the Japanese attacked us at someplace called Pearl Harbor."

The boys scrambled into the old pickup truck and sped back to West Ishpeming. When they reached the Koski house, Al's wife rushed out to meet them, sobbing as she relayed the news, "The Japanese attacked Pearl Harbor! They've killed a lot of sailors and everybody says we're going to war!"

The Koski brothers ran into the house to listen to the news for themselves. Eric Sevareid reported on the mood of the crowd that had gathered in front of the White House "You can't perhaps judge the temper of a whole nation just from these crowds, but here at any rate there is not

★ Click here to watch video

Figure 8-4: Upon hearing the news of Pearl Harbor, all young Americans knew America was going to war.

the slightest sign of any dismay, or misgivings, or regret...I saw the French people go to war and they did it with reluctant misgiving and the deepest regret, which was written plain on every face. Of that, I see nothing at all here."

When the broadcast ended, George turned off the radio. The family sat quietly, thinking what this might mean to the world, to the family, and to themselves.

Al spoke first. "No question about it, this means war, war against the Japanese and probably against the Germans as well."

He looked somberly at his young wife, then continued, "I'll be recalled for sure. Jeanette, I guess the house will have to wait. I'm afraid you'll have to move back with your parents until this thing is over."

Al continued, "Art, George, Reuben—you'll probably have to decide between joining up and getting drafted. If you volunteer, you might get some choice about what you do. If you get drafted, you'll go where the Army wants you to go. You'll each have to make that decision for yourself."

"Oscar, you're still in high school. With any luck, you might not have to get into this."

He turned to his youngest brother. "Johnny, this will surely be over before you get out of school. If the rest of us end up in the service, it will be up to you to help father."

Al soon left with his young wife. They'd been married for less than two months and knew they would soon be separated, perhaps for a very long time.

Art left a short time later to visit his red-haired girlfriend, Jeanette "Jenny" Traise. He and Jenny had been dating for a while, but Art didn't want his brothers to tease him about having a girlfriend, so he hadn't told the rest of the family about her.

The next day, the front page of the local newspaper, the *Mining Journal*, carried an expected but ominous article titled "Expansion of Armed Forces Expected." As Al had anticipated, all enlisted reserves were being called back to active duty. The article explained that the selective service system would soon draft large numbers of men for military service.

On December 8, Congress declared war on Japan. On December 11, Germany and Italy declared war on the U.S. In return, Congress declared war on Germany and Italy. The die was cast.

★ Click here to watch video

Figure 8-5: On December 7, 1941, forces of Imperial Japan attacked Pearl Harbor.

On Dec 9, President Roosevelt gave a radio speech to the country:

Fellow Citizens:

Powerful and resourceful gangsters have banded together to make war upon the whole human race. Their challenge has now been flung at the United States of America. The Japanese have treacherously violated the long-standing peace between us. Many American soldiers and sailors have been killed by enemy action. American ships have been sunk, American airplanes have been destroyed...

Together with other free peoples, we are now fighting to maintain our right to live among our world neighbors in freedom and in common decency, without fear of assault...

We are now in the midst of a war, not for conquest, not for vengeance, but for a world in which this Nation, and all that this Nation represents, will be safe for our children. We expect to eliminate the danger from Japan, but it would serve us ill if we accomplished that and found that the rest of the world was dominated by Hitler and Mussolini.

We are going to win the war, and we are going to win the peace that follows. And in the dark hours of this day, and through dark days that may yet to come, we will know that the vast majority of the members of the human race are on our side. Many of them are fighting with us. All of them are praying for us. For, in representing our cause, we represent theirs as well —our hope and their hope for liberty under God.

As the Koski brothers listened to the President's stirring speech, they understood that at least some of them would soon be called to join the war effort. They believed that America would win in the end, but they didn't know that victory would take so long or come at such a terrible price.

★ Click here for Web Info

Figure 8-6: Franklin Roosevelt in his wheelchair, with his dog Fala and Ruthie Bie, the poster girl for the March of Dimes. Roosevelt was rarely photographed in his wheelchair and many Americans did not know that their leader was disabled.

★★★ Ordinary Heroes: Six Stars in the Window ★★★
9. A lot like hunting deer

January, 1942: In early January, Al Koski received a letter informing him that he was being recalled to active duty as of February 16, 1942. But Al was not destined to be the first Koski brother to enter the wartime Army.

A few days later, George received his induction notice, followed by orders to report for duty. George didn't want the rest of the family to worry, so he didn't tell them when he had to leave. They knew he had been drafted, but assumed he would leave later in the spring.

On Friday, January 15, Edna Mae saw George's duffel bag at the foot of the steps. She asked him, "George, are you going to the Army now?"

George shook his head and answered, "No, Edna Mae. Don't worry, I'm not leaving yet."

After breakfast, George picked up his duffel bag and walked out the front door. Edna Mae ran to the barn to get her Dad, who was milking the cows. But by the time they got out to the yard, George was heading down the hill in a car driven by Lilly's suitor, George Sarberg. They turned a corner and then both Georges were gone.

★ Click here to watch video

Figure 9-1: George Koski was the first of the Koski brothers to leave after Pearl Harbor.

Edna Mae started to cry, but her father told her, "God will watch out for George. He will be all right." As Edna Mae and her father gazed at the tire tracks on the snowy road they had no way of knowing that all twelve Koski children would never again be together.

A month later, Al boarded a train to return to the Army. Two of the six Koski brothers were now in uniform. Art knew he would be drafted soon and Oscar expected his draft notice before he graduated in the spring.

Reuben was granted the first of several six-month deferments as an essential worker in the iron mines. For a time at least, Reuben's contribution to the war would consist of mining iron ore used to make the ships, tanks, and guns needed for the war. Johnny, the youngest son, was still a junior in high school, safe from the draft and too young to enlist.

On February 23, President Roosevelt gave one of his fireside radio chats. He asked Americans to look at their maps as he explained the grave situation facing the world. During the President's speech, a Japanese submarine fired sixteen shells off Ellwood Beach, just west of Santa Barbara. No one was injured, and the shelling caused only $500 of damage to a shed and a catwalk. The Coast Artillery and civil defense forces stepped up their preparations for Japanese attacks and possible invasion.

Figure 9-2: The oldest son, Al Koski, was called back to active service in February, 1942. Al is on the left, his father Alfred is in the center, and Lilly is on the right.

In February of 1942, Art received his draft notice. He passed the initial physical exam in Marquette and in early May he reported to the induction center in Milwaukee, Wisconsin.

At the induction center, when asked which unit he wanted to serve with, Art replied, "The Mountaineers, of course!" Like so many young men from the mountain and northern states, he had read magazine articles about the elite mountaineers and ski troopers and wanted to serve with them.

As a Finnish lad, with plenty of outdoor experience, he figured he'd be a natural for the ski troops. But the Army had other ideas.

★ Click here to watch video

Figure 9-3: Like all of the Koski brothers, Art reported to the induction station in Milwaukee, WI.

Art had earned very good scores on the math tests and had worked as a surveyor in the mines, so the Army assigned him to the newly formed 332nd Engineers which were assembling at Camp Claiborne, Louisiana.

Figure 9-4: Carl "Art" Koski.

Art hoped he'd get home after induction, to say goodbye to his family and to Jenny. But the Army wanted the 332nd brought to full strength as quickly as possible, so Art was shipped directly from Milwaukee to Camp Claiborne, arriving there on May 15.

Art was assigned to the survey team of Headquarters and Service Company, or H&S Company, the outfit responsible for planning and coordinating construction projects. The actual construction was done by other units or "letter companies" of the 332nd: Company A, Company B, Company C, Company D, Company E, and Company F.

Art missed the cool north woods and he missed his Jenny. He wrote to her almost every day. On May 30, he wrote:

```
Dear Jenny,

Here it is, another weekend comes and I'm not any-
where close to home. Just think, I'm over 1300 miles
from you. Today when we were on a hike I was thinking
about you, wondering what you were doing at that time
(about 2:00 p.m. Saturday afternoon). I could picture
you at Dead River enjoying the weekend while I was
marching on a hot dusty road. When I say hot, I mean
hot. Lots of guys passed out, one even died from
heat, but it didn't phase me one bit, old Art just
kept hoofing it along.

Sometimes I think hell must be right underneath
Claiborne. The sun is so hot, the buttons on my over-
alls are burning circles in my undershirt. We take a
bath and wash our clothes every day, it's so hot and
clammy here.
```

```
            You asked about the time here. The clocks are exactly
            the same time as at home. Every night, particularly
            on Wednesdays and Saturdays at 7 o'clock, I feel
            lonesome.

            The food here is a little better than I had at home
            and it'd be a lot better if someone shot the cook. He
            doesn't know how to boil water and he's in charge of
            our food.

            Hope I'll see you soon,

            Art
```

★ Click here for Web Info

Figure 9-5: Letter from Art to Jenny.

Most of the men at Camp Claiborne weren't used to eating fancy food, but they still had a difficult time adjusting to Army food. Clyde Fritz was the H&S Company mess sergeant, but his only previous cooking experience came from making stew on hunting trips. Even the least fussy of the men agreed there was some room for improvement in the food.

The wives of some of the officers and enlisted men visited the camp during June and July of 1942. After tasting the food for themselves, they volunteered to work with the mess officers to teach them how to make the most of the ingredients provided by the Army. Their advice covered such things as adding more eggs and flour to cornbread so it wouldn't fall apart, not over-boiling the coffee, and beating the powdered eggs to make them fluffier. The wives even convinced the cooks to keep a perpetual pot of stew simmering on the back of the stove, an improvement greatly appreciated by the night guard and any other men who got back to base too late for dinner.

That perpetual pot of stew became the source of numerous stories, each with a variation of the same punch line. Apparently one of the cooks put his dirty socks in a pot of soapy water and set them on the back of the stove to soak overnight. One of the H&S men came in from guard duty and dipped a bowl in what he thought was the stew pot. The next morning, he complained to the cook that it was the worst stew he had ever eaten, saying, "There weren't any meat or vegetables in it. All I found was the skin from that chicken we had last Sunday."

★ Click here for Web Info

Figure 9-6: Carl "Art" Koski at Camp Claiborne, Louisiana.

In early June, Art received word that his sister Ann was marrying John Solka, who everybody called "Buster." Art wrote to Jenny, "If you go to Ann and Buster's wedding, kiss the bride for me. I'll send a thousand and one kisses in this letter. Give Ann one and keep the other thousand for yourself." Art also wrote that he had volunteered to be a scout for his unit. He figured after years of hunting he could "move around in the woods pretty good."

The men of the 332nd soon learned how they would contribute to the overall war effort. Combat troops require constant supplies of equipment, spare parts, fuel, food, ammunition, and replacement troops. Eventually the Allies would land in Europe. As they pushed the Germans back into Germany, supplies would become a growing problem as the Allied supply lines grew longer, while the German supply lines grew shorter. The Engineers would be responsible for repairing the transportation infrastructure to support the Allied advance.

The transportation infrastructure of Europe had been heavily damaged during the German invasion of Western Europe and the Allied bombing. It would sustain even more damage from the Allied advance and sabotage from the retreating Germans. Engineer units, such as the 332nd, would need to quickly repair the transportation infrastructure so supplies and reinforcements could get to the Allied troops at the front. The Engineers could not win the war alone, but without the Engineers, the Allied invasion would be doomed to failure.

The motto on the 332nd Engineers logo, "To build, to conquer," reflected the crucial role of Engineer units in war. Some time later, as the Engineers started to understand the scope of their assignments and the incredibly short schedules, they gave themselves another unofficial motto: "The difficult we do immediately, but the impossible may take a little longer."

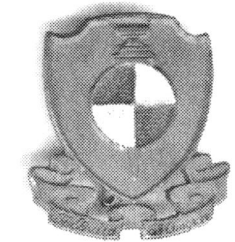

★ Click for Web Info

The officers of the 332nd were given just nine weeks to transform the civilian engineers, surveyors, and construction workers into an efficient Army Engineer Regiment. It was a challenge. At an average age of 29, the men of the 332nd were older than the men in most other units and they didn't always take to Army discipline as readily as younger men.

Figure 9-7: 332nd Engineer Regiment pin: "To build, to conquer."

Most of the men in the 332nd had extensive engineering, surveying, or construction experience, but there were many things they needed to learn if they were to function as an effective Engineer unit. They trained intensively, learning how to operate the Army's heavy equipment and how to build bridges and roads "the Army way." At the same time, they went though the equivalent of basic training with calisthenics, infantry drills, and weapons training. To Art's way of thinking, they spent way too much time exercising and marching in the heat and humidity of the Louisiana summer.

Few of the officers in the 332nd had any significant military training. Their inexperience led to confusion on the drill field when they bellowed orders such as "Round, face, march!" and "As scrimmages at five yards, come ahead!" The enlisted men did their best to interpret the muddled orders and, after six weeks of intensive training, the men and the officers finally began to function like an Army unit.

As in all Army camps, living conditions were primitive. Art lived in a pyramidal tent, with seven other enlisted men, sleeping on an army cot with a thin mattress, two sheets, and two wool army blankets.

Thundershowers were a constant nuisance, soaking the tents and loosening the lines. Gusts of wind blew the tents over, exposing everyone and everything inside to the wind and the rain. Art learned that anything that got wet, stayed wet for days in the humid Louisiana climate.

★ Click here to watch video

Figure 9-8: A soldier of the 332nd Engineers, possibly Art Koski, rushes past tents on his way somewhere, perhaps to the mess hall to eat another "scientifically" prepared meal.

Art hated the heat and humidity of Louisiana in the summertime. He was a northern boy. For him, anything over 75 degrees was hot. Exercising in 95-degree temperatures and high humidity, while wearing a heavy army uniform was sheer torture. As he sat in his sweat-soaked clothes and guzzled water at the end of a day, he often thought to himself, "I'll take 10-below over this any day. Once this war is over, I'm never going south of Escanaba again."

The Engineers were not expected to get into combat situations. They were supposed to build bridges, not shoot Germans. The U.S. Army didn't have enough rifles, because most of the reserve weapons had been sent to England to replace the weapons lost in the mass evacuation at Dunkirk, so the men of the 332nd got the "short course" on marksmanship—three days on the firing ranges, shooting old Springfield bolt-action 1907 rifles and a few old British Enfield rifles.

The men also practiced blocking roads by tying sticks of TNT to a series of trees, then blowing them up to create a maze of fallen tree trunks known as an abatis. The officer in charge of the drill told them, "Properly planned, a roadblock of this type can even stop tanks."

Art wasn't the only man who thought to himself, "Things will have gone awfully wrong if we find ourselves trying to stop German tanks."

By early July, the men of the 332nd knew they would be leaving Camp Claiborne soon, but they didn't know where they were headed. Rumors abounded—Alaska, Africa, England, the Pacific—but no one knew for sure. Near the end of June, Art wrote to Jenny that the 332nd Engineers expected to be sent to Alaska to work on the Alcan Highway. Art looked forward to leaving the hot south and seeing some of the Alaskan wilderness. He didn't know if Alaska would be as nice as his beloved Upper Peninsula, but he felt anything had to be better than "Lousyana" in the summertime!

Art continued to miss Jenny. On July 6, he wrote that he had just spent a long day guarding German prisoners of war who had been captured in Africa. He also wrote that he "dreamed we were getting married. Boy were you ever pretty all dressed up for the occasion. I spoiled it by waking up. I hope that actually will happen soon." Art ended the letter with a sketch of two hearts joined by an arrow.

In other letters to Jenny, Art expressed confidence in his ability to handle any assignment. In one letter he told Jenny that the captain and the sergeant had given him "special hell today for not giving them the proper salute while carrying a gun."

Art admitted he had slipped up with the salute, but said "if it comes to fighting, they won't have anything to say cuzz I think there's more hell in me than a dozen other soldiers put together. I hope."

On July 9, the Engineers held a practice battle using guns loaded with blanks. Apparently the officers thought the exercise was successful, but in his letter to Jenny, Art wondered how well the Engineers would do if they had to fight trained soldiers.

During the practice battle, Art served as scout for H&S Company. As he explained to Jenny, "in case of trouble, I'll go ahead of everyone else and locate the enemy." With the boundless confidence of youth, he told Jenny not to worry, "hunting men is a lot like hunting deer" and "the enemy will be dead before they know I'm anywhere around."

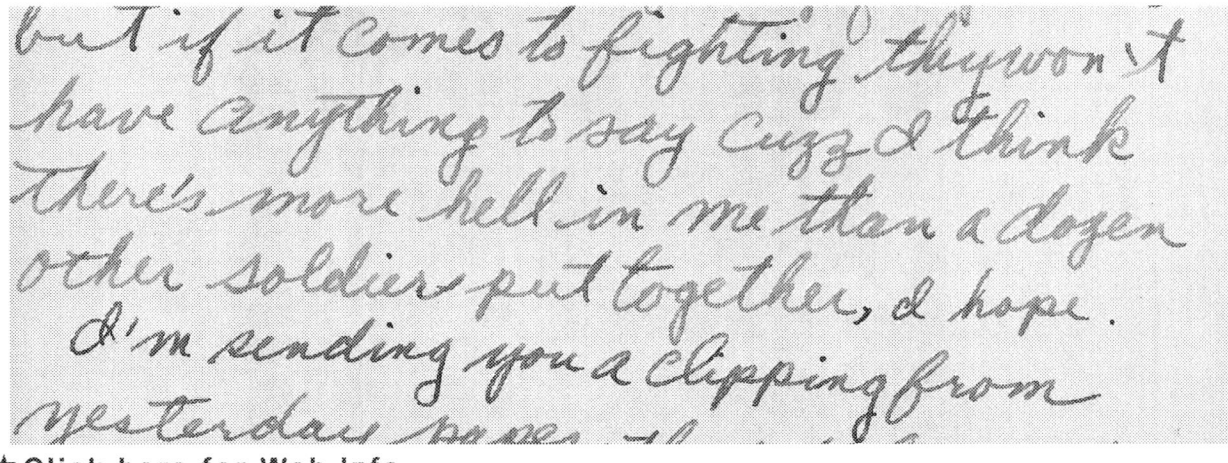

★ Click here for Web Info

Figure 9-9: A portion of one of the many letters that Art wrote to Jenny.

★★★ Ordinary Heroes: Six Stars in the Window ★★★
10. The fog of war

February, 1942: Al Koski reported for duty with the 63rd Coast Artillery in Seattle, Washington. Like his brother Art, Al had worked as a surveyor in the iron mines. He received additional training as a surveyor while serving with the Coast Artillery in 1941. So it came as no surprise when Al was assigned to a crew surveying potential antiaircraft emplacement sites.

Antiaircraft defense of the west coast of the U.S. was a significant priority at that time. No Japanese plane could fly all the way from Japan to the U.S., but as the Pearl Harbor attack demonstrated, Japanese aircraft carriers could launch air significant attacks against American targets near the coast.

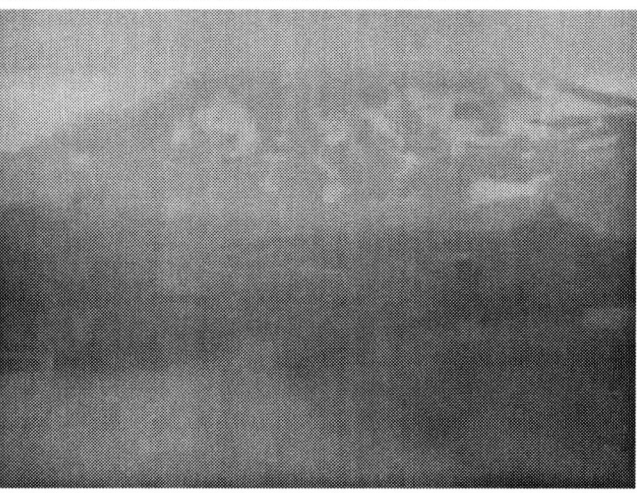

★ Click here to watch video

Figure 10-1: The Army, Navy, and Air Force built bases and stationed men and equipment throughout Alaska and the fog-shrouded Aleutian Islands.

After the attack on Pearl Harbor, Japanese forces advanced on targets all over the Pacific: Kuala Lumpur, Hong Kong, Singapore, Thailand, Malaya, Borneo, New Guinea, Java, Guadalcanal, the Philippines, and Burma. Country after country and island after island were overrun by the seemingly unstoppable Japanese.

By the spring of 1942, U.S. Army strategists became concerned about a possible Japanese invasion of Alaska and the Aleutian Islands. The Americans viewed the Aleutian Islands as eventual stepping stones for attacks against the Japanese mainland. Likewise, the Japanese viewed the Aleutians as stepping stones for an invasion of Alaska and North America. The U.S. Army decided to fortify the islands such as Attu, Kiska, and Unalaska against Japanese attacks.

In the spring of 1942, Al Koski was sent to Unalaska, a tiny island about halfway down the Aleutian Island chain, to survey potential sites for antiaircraft emplacements.

★ Click here for Web Info

Figure 10-2: The Aleutian islands, stretching from the coast of Alaska into the Bering Sea, were viewed as crucial stepping stones by both Japanese and American commanders.

Early on the morning of June 3, Al walked down to the dock to get a better look at the surrounding terrain. On the way, he passed a squad of soldiers painting camouflage patterns on top of a Quonset hut. It was just 4:00 a.m., but that far north, it was already light. Al stood on the dock, looking for potential antiaircraft sites in the snow-covered mountains overlooking Dutch Harbor. A low-morning fog drifted over the low peninsula obscuring the rows of barracks under construction.

A sailor pointed out a group of planes approaching from the far side of the harbor. The sailor muttered uneasily, "Our planes don't approach like that." The planes swooped low over the harbor. As they neared the dock, they opened fire. Machine gun bullets sprayed the docks and bombs exploded in geysers of water. Someone yelled "Japs!" and everyone dove for cover.

The next thing Al knew, he was in the cold water, paddling to stay afloat. His left ear was ringing, but he otherwise seemed uninjured. On the shore, he saw soldiers running for cover. Thick smoke rose from oil storage tanks that had been hit by the Japanese bombs. As quickly as they came, the Japanese planes disappeared into the fog. As Alfred scrambled out of the freezing water he saw painters belatedly sliding down the rounded sides of the Quonset hut and scrambling for cover. Wounded men were calling for help and plumes of smoke rose on all sides.

Al joined in the search for wounded men. A sailor running alongside him muttered, "Damn Japanese!" Another sailor chimed in, "What do they think they're doing? They can't attack Alaska and get away with it!"

The air attack on Dutch Harbor was a prelude to a Japanese invasion of the Aleutian Islands. On June 6, the Japanese landed 500 marines on the island of Kiska. They captured the American Naval weather detachment, consisting of ten men and one dog. One man escaped, but was recaptured after 50 days of near-starvation in the bitter cold.

On the same day, the Japanese 301st Independent Infantry Battalion landed on Attu. Attu's population consisted of 45 native Aleuts and two Americans. Charles Jones was a ham radio operator and weather observer and his wife, Etta, was a teacher. Charles was captured by the Japanese, interrogated, and killed. The Aleuts were taken prisoner by the Japanese. Etta Jones was sent to Yokohama Japan as a prisoner of war.

The U.S. government believed civilian morale would be hurt by news of the Japanese invasion, so it tried to limit news coverage of the situation in the Aleutians. Although the news blackout successfully curtailed reports by the U.S. news media, it could not silence the Japanese propaganda machine that proudly proclaimed the successful invasion of the Aleutian Islands.

For the rest of 1942 and the first months of 1943, the U.S. Army Air Forces repeatedly bombed Japanese-held Kiska and Attu. Despite these attacks, the Japanese dug in deep and refused to leave. The situation could not be allowed to continue so the American Army prepared to invade the islands of Attu and Kiska.

On May 11, 1943, thirty-four ships landed 16,000 American soldiers on the north and south sides of Attu. After eight days of bitter fighting, the American northern and southern forces linked up,

★ Click here to watch video

Figure 10-3: Alfred Koski was sent to Dutch Harbor in the Aleutian Islands to survey antiaircraft sites intended to protect against Japanese air attacks.

splitting the Japanese forces. Realizing the battle was lost, the Japanese killed their own wounded, injecting them with morphine, then throwing grenades into the medical tent. On May 29, the remaining Japanese soldiers launched a desperate banzai attack. In bitter fighting, the Americans beat back the frenzied attack. Rather than face defeat, 500 of the remaining Japanese committed suicide. Of the approximately 2,600 Japanese soldiers on Attu, only 28 were taken prisoner. The rest were killed or committed suicide.

★ Click here to watch video

Figure 10-4: The Battle for Attu was a desperate struggle fought under exceedingly harsh climatic conditions.

In the battle to retake Attu, 549 Americans were killed, 1,148 injured, 1,200 suffered severe injuries from the bitter cold, 614 were stricken with disease, and 381 were lost due to miscellaneous causes. All together, the Americans suffered 3,829 casualties, or 25 percent of the invading force—losses reflective of the bitter combat that would characterize battles with the Japanese throughout the war.

With Attu back in American hands, the focus turned to Kiska. Anticipating fierce fighting in the battle to retake Kiska, the Allies assembled a force of 34,426 soldiers, including 5,300 Canadians. The 87th Mountain Combat Team of the U.S. Army, a specialized infantry unit trained in winter and mountain warfare, was assigned a leading role in the invasion of Kiska.

Before dawn on August 15, 1943, Operation Cottage was launched as Allied soldiers landed on the rocky fogbound beaches of Kiska. At first the landing was unopposed. Soldiers stealthily moved ashore and fanned out over the island in search of the Japanese. Visibility was extremely limited in the foggy darkness and freezing rain mixed with snow.

Suddenly the GIs came under fire. They couldn't see the enemy through the heavy fog and snow, but they fired back as best they could, aiming at the sound of rifle shots. The battle dragged on the rest of that day and into the night, both sides groping blindly in the limited visibility.

On the second day it became apparent that a terrible mistake had been made.

In the dark and the fog, the Allied soldiers had been shooting at each other. No Japanese soldiers remained on the island. All Japanese forces had secretly evacuated before the invasion.

Seventeen Americans and four Canadians were killed by friendly fire or booby traps. Fifty Allied soldiers were wounded and 130 soldiers were diagnosed with a condition known as trench foot.

★ Click here to watch video

Figure 10-5: The Allied invasion of Kiska took place under terrible conditions, with rain, fog, and snow hampering operations.

Trench foot is a fungal infection that typically occurs when soldiers stand in water-filled trenches or wear wet boots and socks in near-freezing conditions. The feet go numb. The skin turns red or blue and often peels off. Severe cases can turn gangrenous and require amputation. Trench foot was a major problem in the cold, wet trenches of World War I, and it reemerged in World War II, first in Alaska, but later in Europe during the winter of 1944–1945.

When the troops returned from Alaska, they were surprised to be greeted as returning heroes. America needed heroes. It needed some good news after a string of repeated defeats by the Japanese.

The soldiers of the Kiska invasion had not fought the Japanese, but they had landed on an island believed to be held by the enemy, fully expecting bitter opposition by a determined foe. They had suffered casualties and had learned first-hand about the chaos and confusion, the "fog of war," that cloaks every battlefield.

After returning from Kiska, the 87th Mountain Combat Team became part of the 10th Mountain Infantry Division, an elite outfit trained for mountain and winter warfare. They would face the enemy again in the mountains of Italy in the final months of the war.

Al Koski recovered his hearing and continued to serve with the 63rd Coast Artillery. In December of 1943 he was transferred to the 213th Anti-Aircraft Artillery Battalion where he continued work on the coastal defenses of Alaska and the state of Washington.

★ Click for Web Info

Figure 10-6: 213th Coast Artillery pin: "The First Defenders."

★★★ Ordinary Heroes: Six Stars in the Window ★★★
11. For all the good I did

July 18, 1942: In his southern drawl, Master Sergeant Tom Jones informed the soldiers of H&S Company they were about to leave Camp Claiborne: "Listen up! We're leaving Camp Claiborne soon and your mail is going to have to go to an APO address. Fill out these forms and send them home so your folks know where to send your mail."

The men were somber as they filled out the forms as they knew the APO address meant the 332nd was being shipped out of the country.

★ Click here to watch video

Figure 11-1: During WWII, troops rode, slept, and ate on trains, but they usually didn't know where they were going.

Two days later the Engineers of the 332nd Regiment climbed onto trains. None of them knew where they were headed. Rumors about their eventual destination abounded—Alaska, England, Africa—but nobody knew for sure. Art was very hopeful they were being sent to Alaska to work on the Alcan Highway. As he boarded the train he heard one of the other men say, "This is it! Alaska here we come!" That sounded good to Art. The cool wilderness of Alaska seemed like his kind of place.

The trains headed north, all the way to Chicago. As they lurched through the rail yard, Art looked at the other trains sitting on the tracks and thought, "Chicago! After all that time down south, this feels so close to Jenny and the good old U.P. One of those trains out there is probably going to be in Ishpeming tomorrow. Wouldn't it be grand to be on it? I wonder how long it will be before I get this close to her again?"

Art and the other men peered anxiously out the windows of the train, trying to determine if they were turning west, towards Alaska and the Pacific, or east, towards Europe or Africa.

Art's hopes of seeing Alaska were dashed when the train turned east, eventually stopping at Camp Kilmer, New Jersey, a major port of debarkation for troops being sent to Europe. The men heard later that a different Engineer unit had been sent to Alaska. The 332nd was going to England to participate in the coming invasion of Europe.

At Camp Kilmer, the men of the 332nd were issued new M1 Garand rifles. They didn't have time to fire them, but became somewhat familiar with them as they removed the Cosmoline that had protected them during shipment. During the next few days trains carrying the remaining units of the 332nd arrived at Camp Kilmer. Soon the entire Regiment, consisting of 52 officers and 1,239 enlisted men, was assembled at Camp Kilmer.

Every man was issued a photo ID card. Most of the men were given 24 or 48-hour passes and many took advantage of the opportunity to visit New York City, which was just twenty-two miles to the north.

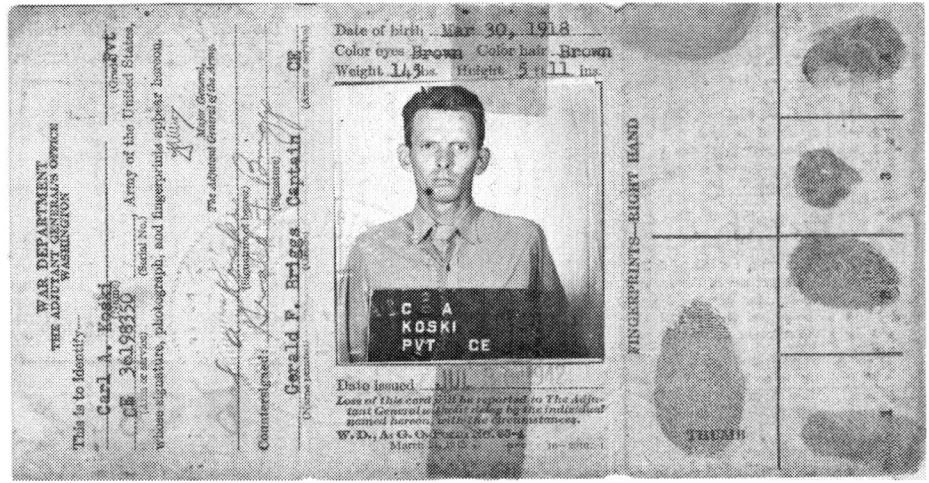

Figure 11-2: Carl "Art" Koski's ID issued at Camp Kilmer.

On July 31, Art wrote to Jenny to tell her she might not hear from him for a while, maybe for a week or more. He promised to tell her more when he could.

At 1:30 a.m., on August 5, after less than two weeks at Camp Kilmer, the men of the 332nd took a train to Manhattan where they boarded the *USS Argentina*, a luxury liner that had been converted into a troop ship. The *USS Argentina* left port at daybreak on August 6, passing the Statue of Liberty just as the sun rose. The ships moved in single file through the submarine nets at the mouth of the harbor, then took positions in the convoy that would cross the ocean.

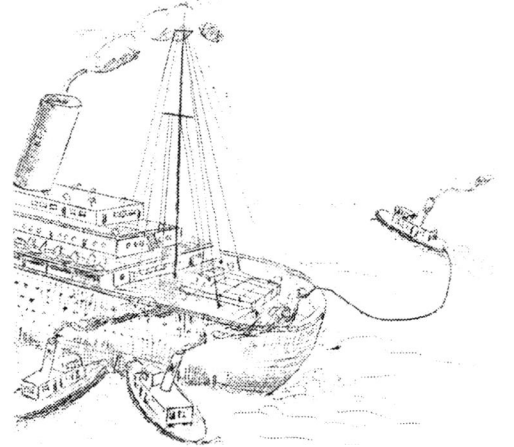

Figure 11-3: Sketch of 332nd Engineers boarding the USS Argentina.

The convoy included eleven troopships: the *West Point*, the *Argentina*, the *Barry*, the *Brazil*, the *Monterrey*, the *Uruguay*, the *Manhattan*, the *Batory*, the *Orcades*, the *Andes*, and the *HMS Queen of Bermuda*. The troop ships were protected by airplanes, the battleship *USS Arkansas*, the light cruiser *USS Brooklyn*, and fourteen destroyers.

Copies of a letter from President Roosevelt circulated among the men. In the letter, Roosevelt explained they were part of the largest expeditionary force to ever leave the United States, over 85,000 men. But what made an even bigger impression on the men was the part of the letter that explained they were "in for the duration" and would not come home until the war had been won.

Most of the men had never seen the ocean before, let alone a warship. As they looked around at the vast convoy, one of the men said, "Sure makes you feel safe to see those cruisers and destroyers out there, doesn't it?"

One of the other men snorted, "Safe! Hell, with this many ships we're just one big, slow-moving target. Those German subs just have to sit still and we're sure to run right over them. I'd feel safer crossing in a rowboat!"

The ships sailed north to Nova Scotia. After two days at sea, they anchored for more than a day, while Canadian troops boarded two British ships. The convoy then headed east across the Atlantic. To make it harder for German submarines to track them, the ships followed a zigzag course across the ocean. At irregular intervals, all of the ships in the convoy would turn sharply in one direction or the other in an attempt to confuse any Germans who might be trying to predict their course.

All went well until Friday, August 14, when the convoy received word that the destroyer *Spencer* had spotted a German submarine. The convoy quickly changed course to avoid the area where the submarine had been spotted.

The entire convoy went on alert. Sailors manned the guns and lookouts with binoculars anxiously scanned the horizon searching for a periscope or the track of a torpedo heading towards them. The GIs were ordered to don their life jackets and carry a canteen full of water at all times.

Crammed below decks, the Engineers could only sit and wait—wait for the all-clear signal, or the dreaded sound of a torpedo exploding against the ship's hull. Minutes dragged by, slowly turning into hours. Some of the men tried to sleep, their heads cradled by bulky life jackets. Some played cards, others talked or just sat quietly, lost in thought.

★ Click here to watch video

Figure 11-4: The trip from the United States to England was particularly dangerous during the height of the Battle of the Atlantic when German submarines prowled the waters of the North Atlantic hunting convoys of ships bound for England.

Art spent many hours thinking about Jenny, the good times they'd had, and the future he hoped they'd have together after the war. He fished her photo out of his shirt pocket and gazed at it, thinking it would be a shame to die here, in the middle of the Atlantic Ocean.

He thought to himself, "If it ends here, I might just as well have stayed home with Jenny, for all the good I did."

Figure 11-5: Photo of Art's sweetheart, Jeanette "Jenny" Traise wearing ice skates.

★★★ Ordinary Heroes: Six Stars in the Window ★★★
12. Where are you going buddy?

August 14th, 1942: Art and the other Engineers sat below decks for hours, wearing their uncomfortable life jackets and waiting for something to happen. Long after midnight, they heard an announcement: "Remove your life jackets and return to your quarters."

No one told them what happened to the German submarine. Perhaps it lost track of the convoy when they changed direction, perhaps it was low on torpedoes, or perhaps the captain saw the formidable escort and decided to look for easier prey. In any event, the Engineers were more than ready to get off the ship. On dry land, they could do something useful for the war effort. On the ship they were just torpedo targets.

Early the next morning, two British planes flew out to meet the convoy and guide the ship to port. After eleven days at sea, the *USS Argentina* dropped anchor in the Firth of Clyde on the Scottish coast. Art and the men of the 332nd Engineers had arrived in Europe.

Later that afternoon, the men were ferried to shore near the Greenock train station. They immediately boarded trains for the 400-mile trip from Scotland south to Newport, Wales. The men did their best to sleep in their seats as the train click-clacked through the night. They got off the train late the next morning and marched four miles uphill to a large hilly field, where they ate their first meal in England: bread fried in mutton gravy with hot tea to drink. The Americans did not like the taste of mutton, but they were so hungry they ate every bite anyway.

★ Click here to watch video

Figure 12-1: Landing in England, the GIs found themselves part of a gigantic buildup of troops from all over the world.

The 332nd Engineers moved into British Army tents set up on the lawns of a large country estate near Malpus Court, South Wales. The next day they started work on their first construction project in England, a camp with Nissen huts for 1,500 men. The Nissen hut had been developed by the British during World War I. It was a simple pre-fabricated building with a wooden floor and a curved corrugated metal roof. The Engineers were familiar with the Quonset hut, which was the American version of the Nissen hut, but they had ever seen a Nissen hut. They had no idea how the things went together, but they eventually figured it out and assembled a total of 118 Nissen huts. Two were used as kitchens, two as mess halls, one as a recreation facility, and the rest as barracks.

Art soon learned something of the English language as spoken in England. He learned that a "spanner" was a monkey wrench, a "lorry" was a truck, and the "bonnet" meant the hood. After a confusing encounter with an English engineer, one of the exasperated mechanics complained, "I wish they'd speak plain English! This is almost like being in foreign country or something."

Like every soldier in his unit, Art was busy from dusk to dawn. Jenny hadn't heard from him since the last letter he sent from Camp Kilmer, New Jersey and he knew she would be worried about him. Five days after arriving in England, he got his first break and he walked three miles to the nearest town to send her a telegram. He didn't have much money and he had to pay by the word, so the message was brief: "Greetings. All well and safe. Love."

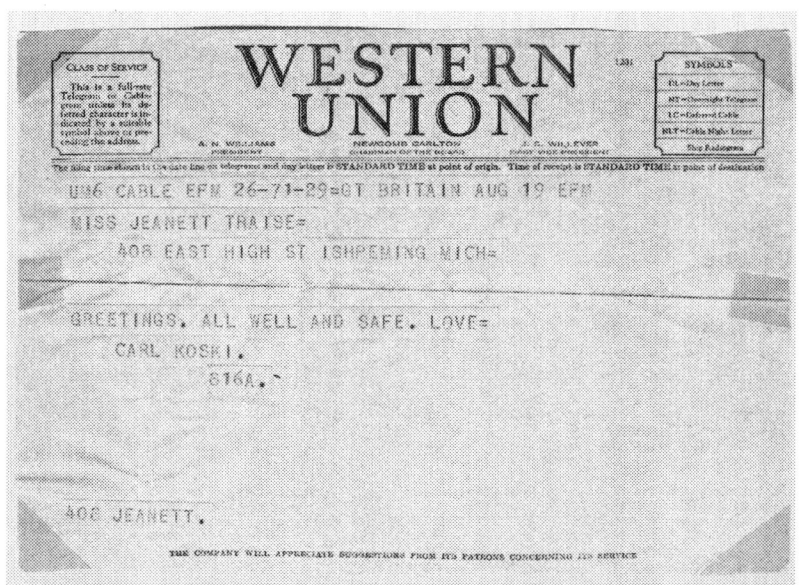

Figure 12-2: The telegram Carl "Art" Koski sent to Jenny on his arrival in England.

Art thought the countryside was beautiful, with it green rolling hills and sturdy stone and brick houses. He laughed when somebody told him that King "Art" and the Knights of the Round Table were supposed to have held their meetings in the nearby town of Caerleon.

In mid-September, Art and the other men of H&S Company moved to Benham Valence Castle, about two miles west of Newbury, Berkshire, England, where they stayed for the next nine months. It was a beautiful country manor, surrounded by expansive lawns and a formal garden with clipped hedges and fanciful topiaries. The building faced south, overlooking a lake. A hunting and fishing lodge stood on the shore of the lake. The family that owned the manor stayed in the main living quarters, while the H&S men stayed in the servant's quarters and out-building. Art had never seen anything quite so grand as Benham Valence Castle and he felt he had come a long, long way from the little village of West Ishpeming.

★ Click here for Web Info

Figure 12-3: The manor house at Benham Valence Castle as it looked in 1942 when H&S Company bunked in the servant's quarters.

A few days later, H&S Company hosted a party at Benham Valence Castle. Art didn't want to go to the party. He didn't drink, he didn't dance, and he wasn't interested in any girl besides his little red-haired Jenny. "I don't want anything to do with that party," he told Sergeant Gatewood. "Other guys want to go, so I'll stand guard tonight."

Sixty-three English girls from the British Army attended the party and most of the men enjoyed it immensely. Sergeant Warren Babcock, the man responsible for maintenance of H&S Company vehicles, later told Art that most of the girls were from the British Auxiliary Territorial Service or ATS. Many were volunteers from various European nations and wore the name of their country on their uniform. Warren had been particularly impressed with a pretty blond girl from Finland. He teased Art that he missed out by not going to the party, but Art just shook his head and said guard duty had been fine with him and he didn't need any other girls.

Shortly after arriving at Benham Valence Castle, the 332nd Engineers attended training sessions covering the Bailey bridge and the British Railway bridge. Art thought the Bailey bridge was particularly interesting. A bridge that could be transported on trucks and assembled by hand in a matter of hours could prove very useful when they started rolling across Europe. There were many variations of the Bailey bridge, including the double-double and the more difficult triple-triple version. The crews trained hard under the direction of British engineers and officers who had attended the famous Bailey Bridge School at Ripon, Yorkshire.

To polish their skills, they held bridge-building competitions where the letter companies raced to complete Bailey bridges. As their skills increased, the times got very competitive. In one competition, A Company completed its bridge just one minute faster than D Company.

Art sent Jenny numerous V-mails. A V-mail was a regular letter that was processed on a Recordak machine and shipped as one frame on a roll of 16-millimeter film. Seventeen hundred letters fit on each 100-foot roll of film, greatly reducing the volume and weight of the letters sent between soldiers and their families, freeing up space on the ships for more essential items such as food and ammunition. Once the letters arrived in the U.S., they were printed from the film and mailed.

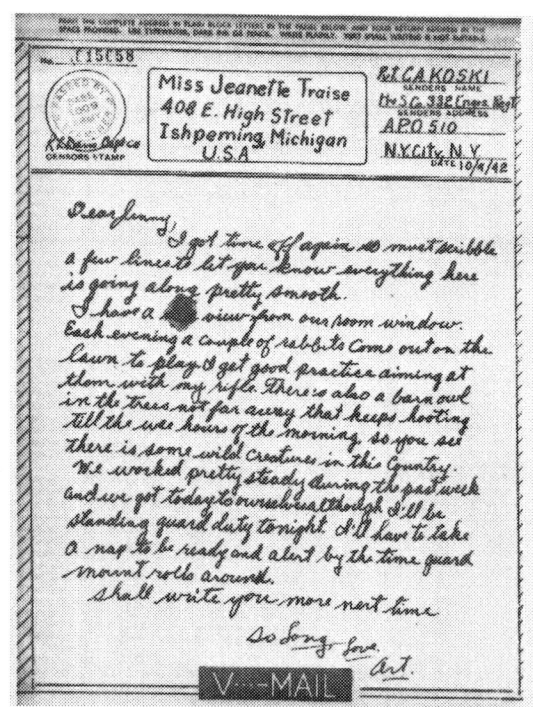

Art's V-mails expressed his disappointment about missing another hunting season, but he told Jenny, "next year at this time I hope to be there and then maybe we can make up for lost time."

October arrived, bringing with it the first hints of fall and the human costs of the conflict to come. Two men of the 332nd died, one of a heart attack and another when his courier motorcycle slid out of control on wet pavement. Those first deaths in Europe had a negative effect on morale. Those two soldiers weren't ever going to see their homes or loved ones again. In somber moments, the men of the 332nd wondered how many more men would be lost before the war was over.

★ Click here to watch video

★ Click here for Web Info

Figure 12-4: One of many V–mails from Art to Jenny.

In November, Art received a "snag of letters from home yesterday from Eleanor, Edna Mae, Rube, and yourself and I can't figure out how to answer them all. We can't write about anything we do or where we are, etc. so it finally boils down to the point where a letter hasn't got anything to it more than saying I'm all right." He asked Jenny to write as often as she could. "That's a great morale builder for us guys over here. It's like a shot in the arm when we get a letter. No kidding, it makes us feel happy for days afterwards."

Figure 12-5: Sketch of English cottage by Sgt. Tom Jones. This could well be the cottage where Art stayed when he wrote the letter to Jenny.

By December, the air had a definite chill. Art sat in the gardener's cottage "warming his shins" by the fire as he wrote to Jenny. He continued to miss her writing, "I dreamed that we were putting up our own home. I hope I don't have to wait too many years in this dog-gone army before I get out and get started on it."

As the holidays approached, Art and the other men spent more time thinking and talking about home and their loved ones. The Army tried to help, serving a traditional Christmas turkey dinner with all the trimmings. Art wrote that most of the men behaved themselves during Christmas and no one drank too much. Christmas 1942 was Art's first Christmas away from home. It was quiet and peaceful, but it wasn't Christmas at home.

The Engineers used their skills to make their own lives a bit easier. In celebration of Memorial Day 1943, Warren Babcock and some of the men from H&S Company decided to try making ice cream. They jacked up the rear of a Jeep and placed it on blocks to hold it off the ground. They bolted a broken drive shaft to each of the rear wheels and welded paddles to the end of each drive shaft. Underneath each paddle they positioned a half-barrel. Inside each half-barrel they placed a container made from two five-gallon cans. They filled the cans with powdered milk, water, and sugar and packed the barrel with salt and ice scavenged from a nearby brewery. With the Jeep running slowly in first gear, the paddles churned the milk while the ice and salt in the barrel cooled the mixture. For a while, nothing seemed to happen, but eventually the mixture started to thicken and soon they had enough ice cream for the entire Regiment.

Figure 12-6: Men of H&S Company wait for a taste of ice cream from Warren Babcock's homemade ice cream maker.

The machinists and mechanics of the 332nd built other devices as well. Some devices, like the ice cream, maker worked quite well. Others, like their over-powered washing machine, were less successful. When they turned that device on, it spewed suds, water, and wet clothes all over the ground and everyone standing nearby.

The Engineers were kept busy working on one project after another. Sometimes, it seemed that all of England was gong to be converted into an Army camp or an airfield. On June 24, H&S Company was moved to the site for Northway Camp, about a mile east of Tewkesbury. The Engineers discovered that the proposed site was a swamp and had to devise a series of drainage ditches to dry the land before construction could begin. Once the land dried, they constructed a series of long buildings. Since these buildings had vertical walls, they were able to put windows in the side walls, letting in more light than would have been possible with the rounded Nissen huts.

Near the end of July, H&S Company moved again, this time to Stockbridge Hospital south of Winchester, Hantshire. The men of H&S Company were quartered at Dunbridge House, which was a fishing lodge on the Test River.

That evening, Art looked longingly at the river and said, "I betcha there are fish in that river."

Several other men murmured agreement and looked wistfully at the gently flowing water.

Finally someone said, "How about we mosey down and take a closer look?"

One thing led to another. Master Sergeant Tom Jones was working on construction drawings when he noticed a group of men standing down by the river. Walking down to investigate, he found Art and a group of soldiers, standing by the edge of the river watching another man who stood motionless, knee-deep in the river, holding a homemade spear held over his head.

Master Sergeant Jones was about to order the soldier out of the river, when an elderly Englishman walked up behind the soldier standing in the river and tapped him vigorously on the back.

Without looking to see who it was, the soldier said, "Go'way! Can't you see I'm trying to catch a fish?"

The Englishman rapped him soundly on the shoulder again. Exasperated, the soldier lowered his spear and turned around.

The Englishman, who was the owner of the fishing lodge, sternly informed the men they must not fish in the river. That order was later confirmed by their captain who explained that the Brits had the odd notion that the fish in the rivers belonged to the Lords who owned the estates. That didn't sit too well with the Americans, who were used to catching fish anywhere and anyway they could. But orders were orders and from then on the GIs were careful not to get caught fishing in that river.

Figure 12-7: Tom Jones was working in this house when he spotted the men spearfishing in the river.

The Army tried to keep the soldiers out of trouble by providing occasional recreational activities such as USO shows featuring well-known entertainers. When the USO brought Bob Hope over to perform for the 332nd, most of the men from H&S Company headed over to watch the show.

On the way to the show, the men walked past a fenced area where German and Italian prisoners of war from Africa were being held. One of the German prisoners yelled in surprisingly good English, "Hey GIs! We're going to New York! Where are you going?"

One of the engineers stopped, looked the German prisoner in the eye and replied with great conviction, "We're going all the way to Berlin, buddy, all the way to Berlin."

Of course, the engineer meant that figuratively. He meant the Allies were going to go all the way to Berlin. He never thought the 332nd Engineers would go all the way to Berlin and had no intention of going there personally.

★ Click here to watch video

Figure 12-8: As the buildup in England continued, the Allied commanders analyzed the German defenses, trying to identify the best possible location for the coming invasion.

★★★ Ordinary Heroes: Six Stars in the Window ★★★
13. Why we fight

February, 1943: As the spring of 1943 approached, three of the six Koski brothers were in the Army. George was with the 103rd Anti-Aircraft Group in Orlando, Florida. Al had been promoted to Master Sergeant and was serving with the 63rd Coast Artillery in Seattle, Washington. Art was with the 332nd Engineers in England. Oscar, Reuben, and Johnny were at home, as were the six Koski sisters and their father.

It had taken time for the United States to mobilize for war, but by the end of 1942, the United States began making significant contributions to the Allied war effort in Europe and Africa. In November, the U.S. invaded North Africa, joining the British troops who had been battling German and Italians in Africa since 1940. In January of 1943, the U.S. Army Air Forces started bombing runs over Germany. In the east, the Soviet Union regained the initiative, defeating the Germans at Stalingrad, Kursk, and Kharkov.

The Allies were making headway, but the war was far from over. Oscar realized it was only a matter of time before he was drafted. He had two choices: wait to be drafted or volunteer. After careful thinking, he decided to volunteer for the Army Air Forces. Like many young men, he thought the Air Force had more handsome uniforms and preferred the thought of flying high over the enemy instead of crawling around in the mud while people shot at him.

Oscar visited the local recruiter and was told he couldn't join the Army Air Forces because too many men had already volunteered for the Army Air Forces. The recruiter recommended that Oscar join the Army Signal Corps and apply for a transfer to the Army Air Forces. So, on March 12, 1943, Oscar joined the Signal Corps.

A few days after joining up, Oscar boarded the train to Fort Sheridan, near Chicago, Illinois, to take an initial battery of physical and intellectual tests. Oscar scored well on the tests and was slated for transfer to the Army Specialized Training Program or ASTP, a program in which intelligent recruits were sent to college campuses across the country for an accelerated series of college courses.

Oscar felt uneasy about the ASTP. He figured he was going to have to fight sometime, so he'd just as soon get it over with. Oscar requested an interview with an officer and said he would prefer to join the Army Air Forces rather than participate in ASTP. The officer said he'd see what he could do. The officer apparently arranged something, because Oscar soon found himself on a train, headed for Army Air Forces Basic Training in Atlantic City, New Jersey.

When Oscar and the other recruits got off the train in Atlantic City, they were herded onto buses, presumably heading to a training base. They were surprised when the bus stopped downtown on Atlantic City Boulevard in front of the Hotel Chalfonte. A sign over the door indicated that Hotel Chalfonte was an Army Air Forces training facility, so the men stepped off the bus and sauntered into the hotel.

As he walked into the lobby of the hotel, Oscar noticed the ornate window trim and fancy carpeting. Clearly this had once been a luxury hotel, although the luxurious furnishings had been replaced with sturdy Army-issue chairs and tables.

The names of the new recruits were checked against a list. They were given uniforms and assigned rooms in the converted hotel. When Oscar got to his room, he stretched out on his bunk and thought, "This isn't anything like the Army barracks Art and Al described in their letters. Maybe life in the Air Force isn't going to be so bad after all." He fell asleep thinking pleasant thoughts of life in a luxury hotel in Atlantic City.

Very early the next morning, Oscar and the rest of the recruits were rudely awakened by a very large sergeant with an extremely loud voice. They jumped out of bed, dressed, and rushed downstairs to line up in front of the hotel.

The large sergeant, whom the recruits immediately nicknamed "Tiny," proceeded to introduce the recruits to the joys of basic training: "You might be sleeping in a hotel, but you are NOT here on vacation! You're in the Army Air Force now. My job is to turn you into soldiers and by God I'm going to do it if it kills you."

After roll call, the men marched to the outskirts of Atlantic City for calisthenics and close order drills. As he sweated in the predawn air, Oscar wryly whispered to the recruit next to him, "This is more like the Army training I expected, but I would have been fine with the luxury hotel thing."

Day after day, for four weeks, the intensive training continued. The days started early, with reveille at 5:30 a.m. Breakfast was at 6:10 a.m., supper at 6:20 p.m. Every hour between was packed with physical training, marching, and rifle practice. In the evenings, the recruits watched educational movies on topics such as "Why We Fight" and memorable Army films on the effects of venereal disease.

On one of their infrequent days off, Oscar and his buddies walked down to the harbor. Oscar could see the wreckage of several ships outside the harbor and he asked the other men if they knew what had happened. One of the guys said, "They were hit by German subs. They sank a lot of ships around here last year."

Oscar sat on a rock and stared at the wreckage. This was close, too close. This war was supposed to be fought in Europe and the Pacific, not in America, yet the Germans had attacked ships right here, just outside the Atlantic City harbor.

Oscar had never agreed with the people who argued America should stay out of this war. He had never agreed with the isolationists who argued, "It's not our war! Let the Europeans sort it out! Why do we have to die to clean up the mess in Europe?"

But now, looking at the wreckage of those ships, Oscar understood more clearly than ever before, that America's choice had not been between fighting the Axis powers or staying out of the war. The choice had been between taking the fight to the Axis powers on the battlefields of Europe and the Pacific, or waiting for them to grow stronger, then fighting them on American soil. Viewed that way, it was a pretty easy choice.

★ Click here to watch video

Figure 13-1: In WWII, the U.S. military made extensive use of movies to educate new recruits.

★★★ Ordinary Heroes: Six Stars in the Window ★★★
14. Pretending to be soldiers

May 1943: Just before he graduated from Ishpeming High School, Johnny finally received his induction notice. He knew it was coming, as almost every young man was drafted as soon as they graduated from High School.

He went for a preliminary physical in Marquette, after which the doctor shook his head and gave him the bad news: "You only weigh 112 pounds. Son, I'm afraid you're going to have to sit this war out. I'm marking you 4F, unfit for service."

Johnny pulled on his clothes, then asked, "If I gained weight could you reclassify me?"

The Doctor looked puzzled, then said, "Maybe you didn't understand me. If you're classified as ineligible, you won't have to fight in this war. You can stay home."

Johnny indignantly replied, "Oh, I understand all right. Most of our neighbors and four of my brothers are already in the service. If I don't get into this war, I'm always going be 'Johnny who stayed home while everybody else went to war.' No siree, I'm sorry, but that's not good enough! I have to get in so I can do my part in this war."

The Doctor shrugged and said, "Look kid, there's nothing I can do. The Army makes the rules and I just follow them. Even if you gained weight and got reclassified, the war would be over before you got overseas. You've got four brothers in the service. Your family is doing enough for this war. Be happy that you don't have to go, and get on with the rest of your life."

Johnny buttoned his shirt and stalked out of the doctor's office, determined to find some way to change his classification. By the time he got home, Johnny decided he would do his best to gain weight in the hope that he'd get another opportunity to join the military. He exercised and started to eat as much as he could. When he could find the money, he bought bananas and drank milkshakes to put on extra weight. He made a pull-up bar out of a piece of old pipe and mounted it on the side of the barn. After a while, regular pull-ups got too easy, so he copied his brother Reuben and started hooking his toes through the holes in cement blocks to increase the weight as he did his pull-ups.

A few weeks later, Johnny's friend Bobby ran up to him, waving a newspaper in the air. "Look at this Johnny! You can join the ski troops!"

Johnny grabbed the paper and immediately focused on an article titled "U.S. Army Wants More Ski Troops." The Army was looking for volunteers to join the mountain troops. Over 100 men from the Upper Peninsula had already been selected for service with this elite group, including ten men from Marquette County. Those interested were directed to contact Arthur Heibel with the National Ski Patrol for an application form. Johnny finished the article, then slowly handed the paper back to Bobby.

"Bobby," he said, "they're not going to take me. I didn't pass the physical for the regular Army. What makes you think I could get into the ski troops?" Johnny's shoulders sagged as he turned and headed back towards home.

Johnny graduated from Ishpeming High School on June 17, 1943. The shadow of war loomed over the ceremony. The salutatorian's speech was entitled "To Win This War" and the valedictorian spoke about "When This War Is Over." As the new graduates left the auditorium, and the band played "Auld Lang Syne," Johnny wondered how many of his classmates would go to war and not return.

After so many years of Depression and war, most people's clothes were getting a bit ragged. As his sister Eleanor wrote about Johnny's graduation:

```
His buddy wanted to go to the graduation so badly. He
didn't have a pair of pants to wear other than the
one with a hole in the buttocks. As Johnny's pants
didn't fit him, I was in a quandary. We decided to go
anyway, and I would walk close behind him so no one
could see the hole in his pants.

It was a tearful evening. Many of the audience sobbed
out loud. We all knew these young graduates would be
in military service very soon and that this little
graduation could well be their last hurrah.
```

The Koskis didn't have enough money for commercial graduation photos, so Johnny stood outside the Koski house in West Ishpeming wearing his graduation gown while his sister Lilly took his photo. Johnny was somber as he stood for the photo in his cap and gown. Graduation was supposed to be a time to look ahead to the future, but until the war was won, the world faced a very uncertain future.

His father gave Johnny a watch for graduation. It was the nicest present Johnny had ever received and became his most valued possession.

One of Johnny's classmates, Ben Hassinger, volunteered for the Marines during his senior year. Ben was scheduled to leave for basic training soon after graduation. Johnny and Ben had been in the same classes through 8th Grade and went to Ishpeming High School together. Johnny was disappointed that Ben was entering the service while he was staying home. Johnny told Ben, "This isn't right. My brothers are in the war, our neighbors are in the war, and now you're going to war, while I sit here at home. I gotta get into this fight and do my part somehow." But with his 4F classification, it appeared that Johnny was not going to play a part in this war.

★ Click here to watch video

Figure 14-1: Johnny Koski poses for a photo after graduating from Ishpeming High School.

Just a few months after Johnny graduated, tragedy struck, not in the service, but at home. Johnny's sister Ann had been married for just thirteen months and thirteen days when her husband, John "Buster" Solka, was killed in an explosion in the Negaunee Iron Mine. Ann and her baby daughter Christine moved back to the Koski house. Ann was devastated by the loss of her husband, but Johnny became enthralled with baby Christine who he thought was "cute as the dickens."

But not even baby Christine could keep Johnny's mind off of the war. If anything, his 4F classification only strengthened his interest in the military and his desire to serve his country.

Johnny found an old policeman's cap that he painted white and stashed under the seat of the family's old Model T. Throughout that summer and fall, Johnny and his young friend Bobby made frequent trips to Cooper Lake for loads of firewood. Each time they drove away from the Koski house, Johnny reached under the seat and pulled out that old policeman's hat. He'd plop that hat on his head and both boys would sing with enthusiasm as they bounced along the bumpy road to Cooper Lake:

> *From the Halls of Montezuma*
>
> *To the shores of Tripoli*
>
> *We fight our country's battles*
>
> *In the air, on land and sea*
>
> *First to fight for right and freedom*
>
> *And to keep our honor clean,*
>
> *We are proud to claim the title*
>
> *Of United States Marines.*

In the fall of 1943, while Johnny and his cousin Roy Honkala were hunting out at Flat Rock, they posed with their rifles, pretending to be soldiers. Johnny put on his white painted police cap and they both held their hunting rifles at their sides as they gravely shook hands, like generals meeting after a great battle.

Neither Roy nor Johnny knew that in less than a year, both would be soldiering for real.

★ Click here to watch video

Figure 14-2: Johnny Koski (left) and his cousin Roy Honkala (right), pretending to be soldiers. Johnny is wearing the policeman's cap he had painted white.

★★★ Ordinary Heroes: Six Stars in the Window ★★★
15. Silver wings

May, 1943: After four weeks of basic training at the Hotel Chalfonte, Oscar and the other Army Air Forces recruits were ordered to line up outside the hotel with their duffel bags. As their names were called they climbed onto buses for the trip to the train station. Because of strict security, they weren't told where the trains were headed.

Oscar didn't mind not knowing where he was going. He was just happy to be done with basic training, and even happier to see the train heading north. After Art's descriptions of training in the brutal heat of Louisiana, Oscar wasn't looked forward to a summer in the hot and humid south.

The train finally stopped and the men were transferred to buses for another ride to an unknown destination. When they got off the buses, they found themselves on the campus of Allegheny College in Meadville, Pennsylvania. At Allegheny College, the cadets were enrolled in college-style courses to prepare for the specialized air crew training that lay ahead.

Figure 15-1: Oscar Koski in flight suit at Allegheny College in 1943.

Oscar enjoyed his six weeks of training at Allegheny College. He thrived on the challenging course work. It also didn't hurt that, aside from the recruits, most of the students at Allegheny College were young women who enjoyed the company of the air cadets in their dashing uniforms.

Like many young men, Oscar had thought of fighter planes as offensive weapons. But he soon learned bombers were the offensive arm of the Army Air Forces. It was bombers that carried the fight to the enemy, hitting military installations and destroying infrastructure. Fighters were defensive, primarily tasked with destroying enemy bombers and protecting Allied bombers from enemy fighters that were trying to shoot them down.

★ Click here to watch video

Figure 15-2: Colleges and universities around the country played a major role in military training for World War II.

Before the Japanese attacked Pearl Harbor, the U.S. military focused primarily on defense. Since no hostile country had planes capable of attacking across the Atlantic or Pacific oceans, defense meant preventing enemy ships from reaching the U.S. coast.

The United States relied on a multilayered defense against enemy ships. The navy's job was to intercept and destroy enemy ships in the open ocean. Any ships that made it past the navy were to be stopped by the gigantic guns of the Coast Artillery and planes of the Army Air Forces. If the ships got through and enemy troops landed on U.S. soil, the army would attack them with ground forces. That wasn't a bad plan—if the U.S. could afford to focus on defense and ignore the rest of the world.

Each branch of the service jealously guarded its place in the overall defensive plan. In 1938, the Army Air Corps (as the Army Air Forces was known until July 21, 1941) demonstrated it could navigate precisely over water for long distances by intercepting a cruise ship some 700 miles from shore in the Atlantic Ocean. The Navy, threatened by what it saw as an attempt to infringe on its traditional role, convinced the War Department to limit all Army Air Corps flights to within 100 miles of the coast. The Navy would retain responsibility for threats outside the 100-mile boundary. The Coast Artillery and the Army Air Corps would be limited to action against enemy ships that managed to get within 100 miles of the coast.

Under those constraints, the Army Air Corps couldn't justify long-range bombers. Many members of the Army Air Corps believed the country needed long-range bombers, but they also knew they wouldn't be able to get permission to design or build such planes in the face of strong antiwar sentiment. Instead, they designed the B-17 Flying Fortress, literally a mobile fortress that would patrol the shores of the country against enemy ships. The B-17 featured long-range capabilities, ostensibly to allow long patrols along the U.S. coastline. But, fortunately for the country—and the rest of the world—this long-range capability meant B-17s could also be used as long range bombers, if and when the need arose.

★ Click here to watch video

Figure 15-3: The B-17 Flying Fortress was to play a major role in World War II.

Finding and hitting a small ship in a large ocean was not going to be easy. Navigation at that time primarily consisted of following roads or railroad tracks across country. Bombardiers considered themselves lucky if they managed to drop their bombs on the correct city. But the U.S. Army Air Corps committed itself to precision bombing and set about developing the necessary techniques and equipment, such as the top secret Norden bombsight. The Norden bombsight was a mechanical analog computer which dramatically increased accuracy. It accounted for the altitude and movement of the plane to release the bombs at the exact moment so they would hit the designated target. For maximum accuracy, later versions of the bombsight controlled the airplane as it approached the target.

When the Japanese attacked Pearl Harbor, the U.S. was forced into the war. The U.S. declared war against Germany, Italy, and Japan, but had no realistic way to bring the war to any of those countries. U.S. leaders were faced with a choice: either stay home and wait for the Japanese or the Germans to attack the continental U.S., or find some way to bring the war to the enemy.

★ Click here to watch video

Figure 15-4: Allied bombers relentlessly pounded German targets; American bombers attacking by day and English bombers attacking by night.

Allied leaders understood it would take years for the Allies to assemble the men and equipment needed to launch a successful invasion of German-occupied territories. The U.S. Army Air Forces turned to the B-17 bomber as the only available weapon that could reach German targets. Orders were pushed through and soon new B-17 bombers arrived in England for use by the RAF and the fledgling 8th Army Air Force. By the summer of 1942, B-17s started to attack German targets, first in occupied France, then throughout Europe and into Germany.

The Allies did not have a fighter plane with sufficient range to accompany the bombers on long flights, so the bombers had to provide their own defense against enemy fighters. The bombers were equipped with multiple .50 caliber machine guns and flew in massive formations, precisely arranged so machine guns from many planes could fire on fighters attacking from any angle.

In the early years of the war, British pilots had suffered heavy losses during initial daylight bomb runs, so they switched to night bombing. Flying at night made it harder for the Germans to find and attack the bombers, but it also made it much more difficult for the bombers to locate and hit their targets. The British resorted to dropping massive loads of bombs in the general area, hoping at least some of the bombs hit the target. But the effectiveness of night bombing was limited at best. The RAF's own studies of bomb damage in 1941 indicated that for every ten bombers that claimed to have hit the target, fewer than three had gotten within five miles of the target. The unfortunate truth was that the majority of bombs were being dropped in the wrong place.

While the RAF focused on night bombing, the U.S. Army Air Forces focused on precision bombing. Strategists believed that with the right equipment and proper training, a group of bombers could accurately hit specific targets such as factories and marshaling yards. Such accuracy would pay huge dividends by destroying the enemy's ability to produce and distribute war materials, while limiting unnecessary civilian casualties.

There was one major problem with this strategy: precision bombing required daylight flights, so the crews could locate the targets. That meant the U.S. planes had to fly over enemy targets during the day, making it much easier for German antiaircraft gunners and fighter pilots to locate and attack the bombers.

Even with daylight precision bombing, many bombs missed the target. To help ensure destruction of the target, the Army Air Forces adopted a policy of sending large numbers of bombers flying in tight formation. When the lead plane dropped its bombs, the rest would follow suit. If all went well, the bombs from all of the planes would drop in the same area, obliterating the target.

As they studied the air-war strategy, Oscar and the other cadets started to understand what that strategy would mean to them as combat air crews. It was an ominous future. They would fly over enemy territory in broad daylight in large formations of heavily armed bombers. Their planes would be attacked by ground-based enemy antiaircraft gunners and enemy fighters from the time they crossed enemy lines until they crossed back into Allied territory. Because the missions would take place over enemy territory, any crew members who bailed out or survived a crash landing would find themselves behind enemy lines.

After completing the Army Air Forces courses at Allegheny College, Oscar was sent to a Classification Center in Nashville, Tennessee where he and other recruits completed an exhaustive series of tests to determine which men would be trained as pilots, navigators, or bombardiers. He and the other cadets received copies of *Together We Fly,* an Army Air Forces publication that described the classification process and the important jobs performed by the bombardier, navigator, and pilot of each crew.

Most of the young men who entered the Army Air Forces dreamed of being pilots. Specifically, they wanted to be fighter pilots, dashing knights of the sky engaging in heroic one-on-one combat with enemy fighters. Few young men wanted to be bomber pilots. Even fewer aspired to become navigators, bombardiers, radio operators, or gunners. The Army Air Forces needed fighter pilots, but it also needed bomber pilots and other crewmen. The classification tests were designed to evaluate aptitude and assign each cadet to the most appropriate job.

Oscar was selected for training as a navigator, but before starting his navigator's training he was sent to Harlingen Field in Laguna Madre, Texas for gunnery training. Navigators and bombardiers doubled as gunners, using the nose and cheek guns to fire at enemy fighters attacking from the front of the plane. During gunnery training Oscar learned how to operate and maintain a .50 caliber machine gun, and how to track and hit a moving target.

Oscar's next stop was Selman Field in Monroe, Louisiana for preflight school. During this fifteen-week course, he received initial training in meteorology, mathematics, physics, aircraft identification, military science, and the organization of the Army Air Forces. Even the calisthenics were specially selected to develop the physical attributes deemed necessary for a future navigator.

After completing gunnery and preflight training, Oscar arrived at Ellington Field in Houston, Texas for navigation training. There he finally began a detailed study of various methods of navigation.

He started with piloting or visual navigation, which consisted of watching for distinct landmarks on the ground below and comparing them with features on a map to determine his current location. This method worked well when the navigator had a clear view of the ground and could spot readily identifiable features such as lakes, rivers, roads, railroads, or towns.

Oscar then tackled dead reckoning, learning how to estimate his position using all available information, including the starting location or point of departure, heading, air speed, and estimated ground speed.

Oscar learned that airplanes are constantly affected by the wind. If there was no wind, and the airspeed indicator showed 200 mph, the plane would be traveling over the ground at 200 mph. But, if a 50 mph wind was blowing from the front, the airspeed indicator might show an airspeed of 200 mph, but the plane would only be traveling 150 mph over the ground. Or, if the 50 mph wind was blowing from the rear, the airspeed indicator might show 200 mph, but the plane would actually be moving over the ground at 250 mph.

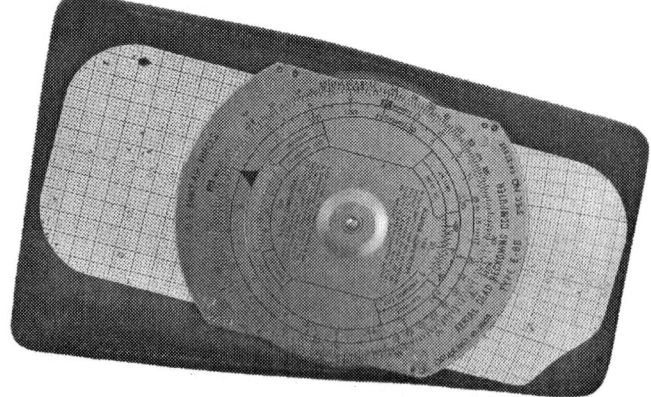

★ Click here for Web Info

Figure 15-5: WWII E-6B Aerial Dead Reckoning Computer.

Drift was also a problem. If an airplane was traveling north and if there was no wind, the plane would be heading directly north. If there was a wind blowing from the west, the plane would drift off course. The compass would still indicate that the plane was pointed north, but the actual course over the ground would be in a northeasterly direction.

In actual practice, adjusting for drift was even more difficult than it sounds. The wind never blows at a constant speed and direction. Navigators had to try to calculate the average wind speed and average wind direction and apply a correction factor to their calculations.

This was before the invention of the electronic calculator, so the navigator performed these calculations in his head, with a small E6B manual "computer," or with pencil and paper. He did this while squatting on a little bench in front of a small table in an airplane that was constantly bouncing around due to prop wash from the other planes in the formation.

At typical flight altitudes, the temperature inside the plane was from −30 to −50 degrees Fahrenheit. The air was too thin to breathe at those altitudes, so navigators wore heavy mittens and breathed through an oxygen mask. The oxygen system provided much lower oxygen pressure than usual, so everyone, including the navigator, felt light-headed and drowsy for most of the trip. It was under these less than ideal conditions that navigators performed the calculations to guide the plane to the target and back home again.

Oscar also learned how to determine his plane's position from radio signals. A radio-direction finder showed the bearing to a known radio station. By plotting the bearings for two or more radio stations, Oscar learned to estimate his current location with reasonable accuracy.

Finally, Oscar tackled celestial navigation, determining location based on the angle of the sun or stars. Celestial navigation was used for centuries on ships and could be very accurate. It was of limited use on combat air missions because of the time required to take the sights and make the calculations, and because most U.S. combat missions were flown during the day, which prevented use of the stars for navigational purposes. But the Army Air Forces wanted to make every effort to enable its navigators to get the planes to the target and back again. So, Oscar learned a whole new set of terms essential for celestial navigation, including sidereal time, right ascension, declination, and azimuth. He memorized key constellations and stars, then practiced until he could determine his location with a sextant and a set of astronomical tables.

During the last weeks of training, Oscar flew many navigation training missions. Each flight carried an instructor, a pilot, and a group of students. The students practiced plotting routes to locations specified by the instructor. They also planned special routes for rendezvous and search missions.

★ Click for Web Info

Figure 15-6: WWII Navigator's wings.

Finally, graduation day arrived. Each cadet was fitted with an officer's uniform for the graduation ceremony. Oscar checked his uniform in a mirror and practiced adjusting his officer's cap to just the right jaunty angle. After the graduation speech, the newly commissioned flight officers raised their right hands and repeated the oath of office, solemnly swearing to support and defend the Constitution of the United States against all enemies, foreign or domestic.

As Oscar proudly walked back toward the barracks, he saw two enlisted men walking toward him. They stopped and saluted the newly minted officer. A bit self-consciously, Oscar returned the salute.

Oscar was now an officer in the U.S. Army Air Forces. He hoped he'd measure up to the job that lay ahead.

★★★ Ordinary Heroes: Six Stars in the Window ★★★
16. Our landings have failed

November, 1943: Just before Thanksgiving of 1943, Art and the 332nd Engineers moved to Grims Ditch, Dorset. Despite it's bleak name, Grims Ditch was set in a pretty valley crisscrossed with paths used by meandering sheep. The "ditch" was an ancient earthworks built by Celts, Druids, or some other early people. On Thanksgiving Day, the Engineers enjoyed another traditional Thanksgiving dinner made from a few of the 1,600,000 turkeys that had been shipped from the U.S. to England for the troops.

★ Click here to watch video

Figure 16-1: While the Allies prepared for the coming invasion, the Nazis prepared to drive them back into the sea.

The Allies had made some progress in the war. They had pushed the Germans and Italians out of North Africa. They had landed in Italy and fought their way to Naples. The Germans still controlled France and most of Europe and they were busily fortifying the coast of Europe against an Allied invasion.

Art thought about Jenny constantly and wrote to her at every opportunity. He also thought about deer hunting, conjuring up vivid memories of every deer season he had enjoyed with his brothers. In early December, Art received a letter from Johnny, with a photo showing the deer he and Reuben shot that year. Art saved the photo to remind himself of the hunting he was going to do when the war was over. On the back of the photo, he wrote, "Johnny and Rube got their bucks this year. Looks like it don't it?"

Before Christmas, Art sent a letter to his sister Ann. He said he was glad to hear that she and Christine were doing well and that "This lousy war better get over with soon or I won't know my closest relatives." He hadn't heard from his brother George for some time, writing, "He was changing from place to place so often I lost track of his correct address." Art ended the letter optimistically, saying he "may be there much sooner than one may expect."

On Christmas Eve, Art and the men of H&S Company attended a Christmas party. The Salisbury Congregational Church sang traditional Christmas carols. Art and the men enjoyed the show, singing along with great enthusiasm.

As he sang Christmas carols, Art fondly remembered past Christmases in the Koski house and daydreamed of the future when he and Jenny could spend Christmas together in their own house.

On January 2, H&S Company moved to Cowesfield House, about a mile from the village of White Parish, Wiltshire. Officers stayed in the manor house while enlisted men stayed in pyramid-shaped tents on the expansive lawns.

Figure 16-2: Johnny Koski with deer, November, 1943.

★ Click here for Web Info

Figure 16-3: Sergeant Tom Jones painting while in England.

In his spare time, Master Sergeant Tom Jones continued working on his sketches and water color paintings. At Cowesfield House, he held an exhibit of his art depicting historical scenes, buildings, and projects completed by the men of the 332nd.

While H&S Company was based at Cowesfield House, one of the mechanics noticed a large grandfather clock stored in the garage of the manor. In his spare time, he examined the clock and finally repaired it. He then proudly told the caretaker he had fixed the old clock in the garage.

The caretaker exploded, "You fixed that clock! Why did you do that? That clock stopped working when the old man died. It has not run since. Whatever made you think we wanted it fixed? I say, you're just going to have to put it back the way it was."

The man grumbled, but the caretaker would not relent so the mechanic opened the clock and removed one of the pieces so the clock would not work.

During their stint in England, the 332nd Engineers worked on a wide variety of projects including railroad depots, railroad tracks, bridges, radar installations, runways, and camps with housing for over 40,000 men.

The letter companies (A, B, C, D, E, and F) of the 332nd worked on several mysterious projects, including two dams built to exacting, but clearly inappropriate specifications. The engineers kept telling their supervisors that the dams weren't right for that location, but were told to "shut up and build them according to the specs."

Much later the men learned that the mysterious dams were replicas of strategic dams located on the Ruhr River in Germany. The replicas were used to train British Royal Air Force pilots who, in May of 1943, flew a daring and successful low level bomb raid in which they "skipped" specially designed bombs across the surface of the water to destroy the dams.

Some projects were clearly related to the invasion, an invasion that even the Germans knew was coming. In March of 1944, men in Company A of the 332nd Engineers began work on a large facility that later served as the headquarters for Operation Overlord, the Allied invasion of "Fortress Europe." The entire facility was camouflaged with nets to hide it from German planes. Twenty-two air raid shelters were constructed, along with buildings for headquarters and living quarters. Miles of cinder paths were laid and camouflaged. Finally, the entire area was surrounded with barbed wire.

★ Click here to watch video

Figure 16-4: General Eisenhower and his staff worked diligently to plan all aspects of the invasion. Of course they did not have computers—just maps and pens and paper. French railroad bridges were primary targets, destroyed to hinder movement of German supplies and reinforcements.

That spring, Art's regiment became part of Engineer Group 2, which consisted of three General Service Regiments, one Engineer Dump Truck Company, one Engineer Welding Detachment, one Engineer Maintenance Company, and three Combat Engineer Battalions. This formidable engineering group could tackle just about any type of heavy construction project, from roads to railroads to bridges to harbors. The inclusion of the Combat Engineer Battalions was somewhat worrisome to the construction engineers as Combat Engineers had a reputation for being in the thick of the fighting, usually working with front-line troops, blowing up fortifications, removing mines, and repairing bridges under direct enemy fire. It seemed obvious to Art that Engineer Group 2 was going to operate very close to the front lines.

Captain Robert Towne arranged for the men of H&S Company to receive additional training in construction of fixed and floating Bailey bridges, erection of steel trestles for railroad bridges, railroad reconnaissance, demolition, removal of mines and booby traps, marksmanship with rifles and machine guns, and map reading. By mid-April, training intensified further in preparation for the invasion of Europe. The men performed thirty minutes of calisthenics every morning before breakfast and practiced combat skills such as using bayonets, identifying aircraft, first aid, constructing tank traps, demolition, and identifying poison gases.

On May 11, Art's regiment hiked with full packs into Langley Woods. He slept in a pup tent for two nights as the entire regiment prepared for field operations. On the bivouac, Art noticed the medical unit practicing recovery and treatment of soldiers with simulated wounds. He nudged the guy next to him and said, "I sure hope those guys don't have too much to do when we get across the Channel."

Figure 16-5: Warren Babcock maintained the vehicles used by H&S Company of the 332nd Engineers.

England was bursting with Allied troops and equipment. The invasion was coming soon. Art could feel it in the air. His sense of foreboding was heightened when the Engineers were told to mark their clothes with their last initial and the last four numbers of their serial number. Somebody said that was so they'd get their clothes back from the Army laundry. Somebody else said it was to help identify their bodies if their dog tags got blown off.

★ Click here to watch video

Figure 16-6: Commandos in one-man submarines risked their lives to get samples of beach sand from Normandy beaches.

Sergeant Warren Babcock and the men of the Service company worked around the clock, waterproofing the vehicles and heavy construction equipment the 332nd would take across the Channel. They installed air intake and exhaust snorkels that extended to the top of the vehicle, loosened the fan belts so the fan wouldn't push against the water, and waterproofed the spark plugs. They tested the waterproofed vehicles by driving them through deep water-filled trenches.

Every detail was meticulously planned, including the optimal tire pressure for driving on the beaches. Army Rangers made secret trips to German-occupied

France to collect sand samples from the beach where the 332nd would land. The Engineers compressed the sand and tested it to determine the best tire pressure for their trucks and other wheeled vehicles.

As the reality of the coming invasion sank in, some of the men started to have second thoughts about participating. One soldier from H&S Company had lied about his age to get into the service. He was a husky kid, but he'd been only fifteen years old when he signed up. He confessed to the captain that he had lied about his age when he enlisted and argued that he should not take part in the invasion. The captain told him, "Tough luck son. You should have thought about that before you lied about your age," and refused to transfer him. The soldier started to act crazy, hoping to get a transfer. One day he was driven off in a Jeep by two MPs. No one knew what happened to him after that.

★ Click here to watch video

Figure 16-8: In early June of 1944, a mighty flow of men and material began moving to the English coast in preparation for the invasion.

Everyone in the 332nd knew the invasion was imminent—almost everyone in England knew it—but very few knew exactly where or when it would take place. Even those officers attending top-secret briefings knew only that the attacks would be launched on D-day at H-hour, "the exact time and place to be announced."

On the night of June 5, 1944, the Engineers of the 332nd heard the unmistakable rumble of aircraft. Art and the other men ran outside to see a huge armada of planes passing overhead. Every plane in England seemed to be in the air that night, including fighters, bombers, and Lancasters pulling gliders. There had been no official announcement, but as he watched the planes swarm overhead, Art knew this had to be the start of the invasion. It was too big an effort to be anything else.

Seeing the size of that air armada, Art felt confident the Allied invasion would quickly drive the Germans back from the beaches. General Eisenhower, the man in charge of the attack, was not so confident. During the long night of June 5, as General Eisenhower waited for progress reports, he penned the following announcement to be released to the press if the invasion failed.

```
Our landings in the Cherbourg-Havre area have failed
to gain a satisfactory foothold and I have withdrawn
the troops. My decision to attack at this time and
place was based on the best information available.
The troops, the air and the Navy did all that Bravery
and devotion to duty could do. If any blame or fault
attaches to the attempt it is mine alone.
```

★ Click here for Web Info

Figure 16-7: General Eisenhower's scribbled announcement to be released in the event of failure was rescued from the trash by one of his aides.

Early on the morning of June 6, 1944, Allied troops landed on the beaches in France. Operation Overlord was underway. The future of the Allied effort hung in the balance. If the landings failed, it would be years before the Allies could assemble the men and equipment to try again. The Germans would have more time to prepare and the Allies might never be able to force the Nazis from Europe.

Resistance on four beaches—Utah, Gold, Juno, and Sword—was lighter than expected. British, Canadian, and American soldiers overran the beach defenses and quickly moved inland. The American GIs landing at Omaha Beach were less fortunate. Unknown to the Allied commanders, the defenses at Omaha Beach were manned by the elite German 352nd Division. The German soldiers fought fiercely and the Americans suffered severe casualties. The battle raged for hours.

For a time it looked like the Germans had repulsed the attack. A German observer reported, "the enemy is in search of cover...vehicles...stand burning on the beach...the boats keep farther out to sea...a great many wounded and dead lie on the beach."

Despite German resistance and the carnage on Omaha Beach, the American, British, and Canadian soldiers resolutely pressed on, driving the Germans from their heavily fortified positions on every beach.

★ Click here to watch video

Figure 16-9: The D-day invasion was a crucial step toward the defeat of Nazi Germany.

Estimates of Allied casualties for the first twenty-four hours after D-day range from 10,000 to 12,000 men. Some 6,603 U.S. soldiers were killed, wounded, missing, or captured during D-day operations. It was a costly victory, but a victory nonetheless. The Allies had established a foothold on the continent.

Back in Ishpeming, Art's sister Eleanor wrote:

> It's D-day! We heard it on the radio at work. They also stopped the machines to make the announcement. The first shock wave of news made us delighted as we realized a major step had been taken toward ending the war. Then it was followed by fear when we heard the casualties were heavy. No one talked for the rest of the day. Many heads were bowed in prayer, mine included. I know for certain that Art was in it, as that is what he trained for, for that time he spent in England. I know George is in it as they said the paratroops were in the initial lines of the invasion. This has been the longest day of my life. Today seems like a thousand years.
>
> Dear God, please take care of the souls of those who died for their country today!
>
> As for me, I think it is too early to celebrate. We still have a long way to go. No one denies it is a big step toward winning the war, but as Churchill said it will be and is a time of blood, toil, and tears for us all. I'll feel a great deal better about things when I find Oscar, George, and Art are safe. That may not be for a while.

★★★ Ordinary Heroes: Six Stars in the Window ★★★
17. You know it's no picnic

May, 1944: Almost a year after graduating from high school, Johnny walked into the Koski house and saw his father sitting in the kitchen. An official-looking envelope was propped up on the table in front of him. From the solemn look on his father's face, Johnny could tell the letter did not contain good news.

Johnny asked, "Father, what is it?"

His father just glanced down at the envelope. Johnny picked it up and saw it was addressed to him, from the War Department. He tore open the envelope and hurriedly read the letter. The letter informed him he had been reclassified and was ordered to report to the induction center in Milwaukee at the end of June. The letter did not mention the fact that he had previously been classified as physically unfit for service.

As Johnny read the letter, a large smile spread over his face. When he finished reading the letter, he looked at his father and said, "They want me, Father! The Army wants me!"

In his enthusiasm, Johnny failed to notice the apprehensive look on his father's face. Alfred Koski was not pleased to have yet another son in the military. Johnny, on the other hand, desperately wanted to do his part in the war. His biggest worry now was that the war would be over before he finished his training.

The other Koski brothers were upset when they heard Johnny had been drafted into the infantry. They knew the sort of casualties suffered by infantry units in combat. They knew that many young infantry soldiers were not going to survive the war and they didn't want anything to happen to their little brother.

Al was particularly worried about Johnny. He kept telling himself the war would be over before Johnny reached the front. After all, he reasoned, the Germans couldn't possibly hold out much longer against the combined might of the Allied forces.

Eleanor wrote to her fiancee, "Johnny received his induction papers. Lil and I are just sick about it. He is as happy as a lark. Not only that, but Lil found a letter he had addressed to the U.S. Marines. Good grief! I know the rigors of training there can make or break even the strongest of men. Although Johnny is physically frail, he has the courage and maturity of a person much older."

The last week of June, Alfred Koski drove his youngest son to the Ishpeming train station to catch the "Old 400." As the train clacked its way toward the induction center in Milwaukee, Johnny avidly watched the countryside from the train window. This was the first time he had traveled out of the Upper Peninsula, and he found everything new and exciting. Finally, he was following in the footsteps of his older brothers. Finally, he was on his way to join the Army.

After a short stop at the induction center, Johnny traveled by train to Camp Croft, near Spartanburg, South Carolina, for basic training. Upon arrival, the recruits were lined up and marched to a large building. They stood outside in the heat,

★ Click here to watch video

Figure 17-1: Morning came early for the recruits at Camp Croft.

entering as their names were called. Each recruit was given a uniform, three blankets, two sheets, and a pillowcase. Arms filled with equipment, they marched to the barracks and were assigned to bunks.

Most of the recruits at Camp Croft were draftees, so they were given little choice in selecting their specialty or unit. The recruits were assigned to a Rifle Company, Heavy Weapons Company, Cannon Company, Antitank Company, Headquarters Company, or Service Company, depending on the needs and whims of the Army.

Rifle Companies always sustained heavy losses, leading to significant demand for more riflemen, so ten of the companies at Camp Croft were Rifle Companies. Johnny was assigned to Company D of the 30th Infantry Training Battalion of the 9th Infantry Training Regiment.

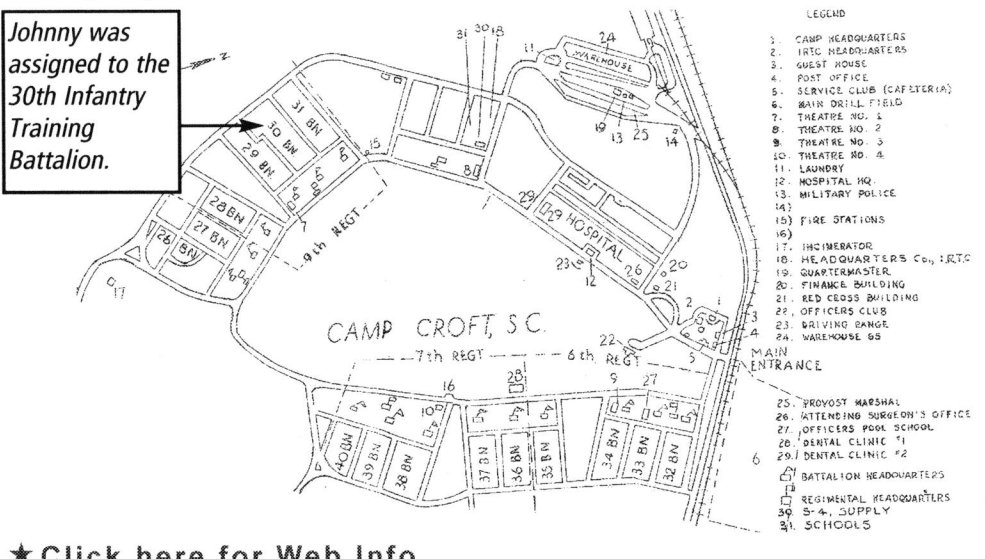

★ Click here for Web Info

Figure 17-2: As many as 75,000 soldiers per year trained at Camp Croft during the war.

In the middle of Johnny's first night at Camp Croft, the sergeant burst into the barracks yelling, "Get up! Get your asses out of those bunks!"

The day went downhill from there. The recruits lined up in the predawn darkness, marched to breakfast, then marched to the parade ground for calisthenics. All the while, the sergeant kept yelling at anyone who did anything wrong. And, if by some miracle, the recruits managed to complete an exercise without anybody doing anything wrong, the sergeant yelled at them anyway.

Johnny soon figured the only way to get through training was to listen up and try to do exactly what the sergeant said. Personal initiative was clearly not high on the sergeant's list of desired behaviors as he instantly pounced on anyone who tried to be a wiseguy.

On the first day, one of the new recruits made the mistake of saying, "Yes, sir!" to the sergeant. The sergeant's face turned red. He stepped up to the man, so close their noses almost touched, and yelled, "Don't call me sir! I'm Sergeant to you!" The trainee rocked back on his heels with the force of the shout. That was the last time any of the recruits called the sergeant "Sir!"

Figure 17-3: A young soldier named James Winterbottom sits on his cot during basic training at Camp Croft. They did not meet at Camp Croft, but Johnny was destined to meet James Winterbottom later in the war.

The days at Camp Croft were filled from the time the recruits were rudely awakened to the time they dropped, exhausted, into their bunks. If they weren't lining up for something, they were marching, exercising, training, or policing the grounds. Almost every day, the recruits crawled around the parade ground, picking up cigarette butts and other small pieces of litter. "Asses and elbows, that's all I wanna see!" the sergeant loudly reminded them.

By the end of the first hot day, Johnny's enthusiasm for the Army had waned considerably. By the end of the first sweltering week, he was wishing he was back in the cool Upper Peninsula of Michigan. During the day he sweated while eating, sweated while marching, and sweated even more while training. At night he lay sweating in his skivvies atop his bunk in the non-air-conditioned barracks.

Boot camp consisted of seventeen weeks of training: physical conditioning, marching, weapons training, and basic infantry tactics. By the start of the second week, Johnny knew these were going to be the longest seventeen weeks of his life.

Figure 17-4: Photo of John Koski and buddies in basic training at Camp Croft. Back: Hartnett, Karchner, Kitts. Front: Johnny, unidentified soldier.

Most of the men in Johnny's barracks had last names starting with H, I, J, or K. Johnny soon made the acquaintance of Privates Hartnet, Karchner, and Kitts. The first Sunday they were allowed to leave the base, they went into town and had a photo taken of themselves in uniform.

On July 16, 1944, Johnny sent the following letter to his sister Ann:

```
Dear Ann:

Received your letter yesterday. Was very surprised to
hear about cousin Ted being wounded. Now you have some
idea how heavy casualties are in the infantry. As you
might know, 50% of all battle casualties are infantry-
men, so you know it's no picnic. The officers told us
they expect at least 4% of us to get killed while in
training. That's a very cheering statement, isn't it?

Was very surprised to hear that brother George was home
on a furlough. The lucky guy! I got to wait sixteen
weeks before I can hope to even get one. And when I
do, it won't be a furlough, but a delay enroute.

You should see the guys that pass out from the heat.
Everyday guys are dropping while we are drilling.
Saturday during inspection, four guys fainted from our
platoon.
```

> Sometimes a guy wonders if it's any use staying here. One guy cut his throat with a razor. Another tried to shoot himself through the foot and is to be tried by court martial. You can't blame guys for things like that when they make you doubletime with a full field pack weighing sixty pounds in the sweltering heat.
>
> I'd give anything just to be home again, so would a lot of these other fellows. All they talk about after our day is over, is about their wives, kids, and sweethearts back home. They show everyone pictures of their kids and wives. You can tell how it hurts them to be parted.
>
> In your letter, you mentioned Art and a certain red headed girl. I wish you'd enlighten me by giving me her name.
>
> Well that's all for now. So long, good luck, and God Bless you and yours.
>
> Johnny

★ Click here for Web Info

Figure 17-5: Letter from Johnny to Ann.

Like most Americans, the Koski sisters worried constantly about their soldiers. During the long summer of 1944, Eleanor wrote:

> Do you remember Bill Richards who used to come to our house a lot? He was friends with Art and Al, in the Engineers with Art. Art feels terrible about him getting killed on D-day. The thing I remember most of all about his is him singing "The Girl I Left Behind Me." He was so enthusiastic about the military and planned to make a career of it. The Lowecke brothers from Ishpeming were both killed in action. How can their parents endure the anguish of a double loss? Robert Hart from National Mine is missing in action. He was on a submarine.
>
> It doesn't look good. There is so much anguish in the world and I feel so badly for those families who have sustained these horrible losses of loved ones.

★★★ Ordinary Heroes: Six Stars in the Window ★★★
18. Red dust and pasties

1944: By late summer, Allied troops were driving the Germans back in Normandy, Italy, and southern France. Soviet troops were forcing the Germans from Russian territory. In the Pacific, Allied troops had returned to Guam and the Philippines. Casualties were high, but the war had clearly turned in favor of the Allies.

Not all Americans who served their country wore a uniform. Men performing jobs considered essential to national defense were given six-month deferments from the draft. For those six months, they continued to work at their essential civilian jobs. At the end of the six-month period, the draft board reviewed the deferment for each man and either extended it for six months or selected that man for the draft.

Essential civilian workers included steel mill workers, agricultural workers, and factory workers building ships, tanks, planes, and other military goods. Production of guns, tanks, and ships requires massive quantities of steel. Steel is made from iron ore, so the Ishpeming iron mines and the men who worked in them played an essential role in wartime production.

Like his father, Reuben Koski worked as a hard-rock miner. Each day in the "dry" or changing room, he donned his red-stained mine clothes: leather boots, shirt, pants, and a helmet with a little light on top. He walked down to the entrance of the mine and picked up a numbered brass tag called a "check" used to track men as they moved into and out of the mine. If Reuben didn't make it back to the surface, the missing check would indicate that he was still somewhere down in the mine.

Reuben walked down a sloping tunnel to the top of the mine shaft and waited. After a few minutes, the crude elevator "cage" appeared, carrying miners from the previous shift. They jostled their way out of the cage, then Reuben and the incoming miners crowded in for the clanking ride into the depths of the mine. As the cage dropped down the shaft, an occasional glimmer of dim light reflected inside the cage from the upper levels of the mine.

The cage slowed, then stopped, almost half a mile below ground. Reuben stepped out of the cage to a scene of organized chaos. Miners moved in all directions, those from the previous shift heading for the cage and home, while the next shift headed to their work sites. Lights flickered on the rough surface of the rock walls and timber braces. Everything underground was dimly lit and tinged with reddish dust.

Huge water pumps constantly sucked water out of the mines, providing a constant background noise that forced the miners to talk in loud voices. The distant echo of air hammers and clanking machines hinted at the activity elsewhere in the mine.

★ Click here for Web Info

Figure 18-1: Reuben Koski and hard-rock miners. Reuben is in the center (4th from left) with his hand on the next man's shoulder.

From the base of the shaft, Reuben walked through a set of double doors that controlled air pressure and ventilation within the mine. He walked almost a quarter of a mile through the tunnel called the "main drift." It was a place of shadows, the only light coming from the miner's helmet lamps and widely spaced light bulbs strung along the ceiling. Small trains, heavily laden with ore, periodically rattled along the narrow tracks in the middle of the drift, bringing ore back to the shaft for the trip to the surface.

The next eight hours consisted of back-breaking work. The tools were primitive: compressed air drills, shovels, and dynamite. Reuben and the men in his crew laboriously drilled a precise arrangement of holes six feet into the solid rock. When the holes were deep enough, they inserted sticks of dynamite, lit the fuses and ran for cover.

The explosion echoed loudly in the rocky drift. The debris settled. Reuben and his crew returned to load the broken rock into little ore carts for transport to the surface. As they cleared the fallen ore, they braced the new section of tunnel with heavy timbers. When the broken ore had been removed, they repeated the process, drilling, blasting, and clearing another section of tunnel. In a good week, Reuben and his crew could finish two "rounds," extending the drift six feet further on each round. Each week, they blasted and loaded some 200 tons of ore.

Periodically Reuben and his partner heard, and sometimes felt, the explosions as other teams blasted rock elsewhere in the mine. Reddish clouds of dust from the closest explosions spread through the drift, coating everything with dust. The miners did not leave the mine for lunch. Reuben often heated a "pasty" on a shovel held over a flame. Originally introduced by Cornish miners, the pasty developed into a unique regional all-in-one meal, consisting of a pastry shell filled with meat, potatoes, onions, and rutabaga. It was "stick to your ribs" food, ideal for the long, grueling days of the underground miner.

The mines were infested with large rats, chronically hungry and waiting for the opportunity to steal an unattended lunch. To keep his lunch away from the rats, Reuben carried his lunch in his jacket pocket or hung it from the ceiling on a piece of wire.

It was dirty work. Reuben's mining clothes acquired a permanent reddish tinge that could not be washed out. The red dust worked its way into his pores, his hair, and his lungs.

It was dangerous work. Many men were injured or killed by falling rock, cave-ins, dynamite explosions, or other accidents. It simply wasn't possible to put that many men, that much heavy equipment, and that much dynamite in a confined area deep underground without occasional accidents.

Underground mining was grueling and dangerous, but the work was steady and the pay was good. America needed all the iron ore the miners could produce, so the miners kept at it, day after day, week after week, excavating an extensive network of tunnels and large chambers or stopes beneath the towns of Ishpeming and Negaunee.

The iron miners of the Lake Superior region, including the miners from Ishpeming, contributed an astounding 85 percent of the iron ore used by the Allies during World War II. Tanks, ships, and guns produced with iron ore from the Lake Superior region went into battle around the world, with British and American troops in the Pacific, in Europe, and in the Mediterranean. Weapons and vehicles produced with Lake Superior iron ore went into combat with Russian troops, who were equipped with massive quantities of American-made weapons, vehicles, supplies, and ammunition through the Lend-Lease program. It would be an exaggeration to say that the iron miners of the Lake Superior region won the war, but it is not an exaggeration to say that they played a crucial part in the Allied war effort. Without that iron, the Allies would have had a much more difficult time and the war could well have ended differently.

★ Click here to watch video

Figure 18-2: American workers were urged to help win the war by out-producing the Axis powers.

The underground miners were not the only residents of the Upper Peninsula to contribute to the war effort. Many women from the Upper Peninsula served with the U.S. military, performing essential tasks and freeing men for combat duty. Many women in uniform served as office workers, clerks, and nurses, but some served in less typical female occupations, including female pilots who delivered military aircraft around the country.

Particularly in lower Michigan, women moved into the American workforce in record numbers, building ships and tanks and airplanes. Rosie the Riveter may have been a fictional character, but she was based on millions of women working in the war effort.

Housewives and children also participated in the war effort. Government posters encouraged the public to "save your tires," "use it up, wear it out, make it do," and "turn off the lights." Children participated in recycling drives for everything from aluminum to rubber. Some of the collected material was of questionable value for the war effort, but most collection efforts did make a meaningful contribution to the war effort. One of the more successful collection efforts was the drive to collect excess household fats. Housewives saved leftover fat and brought it back to the butcher where it was was processed and used to make explosives.

Not every American supported the war effort. Some men attempted to evade the draft or simply refused to respond to their induction. Draft evaders were brought to trial and subject to stiff penalties, including several years in Federal prison.

Conscientious objectors refused to participate in the war effort for a variety of religious, ethical, and moral reasons. Some agreed to serve as unarmed medics and worked courageously to save the lives of wounded soldiers in combat. Others were put to work in government civilian public service camps, one of which was located in the Upper Peninsula.

★ Click here for Web Info

Figure 18-3: All Americans were urged to recycle and avoid purchasing new goods.

Civilian Public Service Camp 135 in Germfask was temporary home to approximately eighty conscientious objectors. These were not run-of-the-mill conscientious objectors. They were "incorrigibles"—conscientious objectors who had caused trouble at other camps around the country and were brought to Camp Germfask for close supervision. These COs or "conchies" as they were called, were supposed to work on government projects, but many refused to work on the grounds that their ethics did not allow them to contribute to the war effort in any way.

The COs in the Germfask camp were particularly troublesome, prone to work slowdowns, civil disobedience, and sabotage. Some of the sabotage was minor, more on the order of juvenile vandalism. In February of 1945, conchies broke into the camp pantry, breaking gallon jars of mustard and smearing the contents on the walls, spilling juice into baking powder, spilling one hundred pounds of kidney beans on the floor, and stealing twenty pounds of coffee. Other sabotage was more significant, including attempts to wreck the water and sewer systems at the camp. The most extreme COs believed that it was their responsibility to be as uncooperative as possible, thereby forcing the government to expend maximum resources to restrain them, resources that the government would otherwise expend on the war effort. These extreme COs also harassed any COs who were inclined to cooperate and perform useful work.

Senseless vandalism did not do much to enhance the status of the COs in the eyes of the guards or the civilian population of the Upper Peninsula. The COs were allowed to leave the camp for periods of time, but found themselves unwelcome in most of the surrounding towns and communities. Most of the local residents did not look kindly to "conchies" living in their midst while their own sons and fathers risked their lives in combat in faraway places.

Conscientious objectors were not the only unwilling workers in the U.P. The U.S. Army operated five prisoner-of-war camps in the Upper Peninsula. The POW camps were located in sparsely populated forests. The German prisoners were paid 80 cents a day to cut wood, which was primarily used to make paper and shipping crates.

The residents of the Upper Peninsula were not entirely happy to have Nazis in their midst. They were understandably worried that some prisoners might escape. Those fears were confirmed at the end of May 1944 when two German prisoners escaped from Camp Sidnaw. Fortunately the two were captured several hours later.

Two weeks later, three German prisoners of war escaped from Camp AuTrain. The next day, still wearing their German uniforms, they were spotted and recaptured near The Pines roadside resort between Shingleton and Seney. Three more prisoners escaped on June 27. A few days later, state police found footprints leading into the woods. They searched the woods and recaptured the Germans.

Aside from the spate of escapes in June of 1944, escape attempts were uncommon. The prisoners were treated well and realized they were a very long way from German-held territory.

Most of the prisoners also understood they were much better off in a prisoner-of-war camp in Michigan than in war-torn Europe. They knew they would be repatriated to Germany after the war. They would lose a few years, waiting for the war to end, but eventually the war would end and they could get on with their lives.

★ Click here to watch video

Figure 18-4: One of the POW camps in Upper Michigan was featured in this Universal Newsreel.

★★★ Ordinary Heroes: Six Stars in the Window ★★★
19. On borrowed time

July 1944: After graduating from navigation training, Flight Officer Oscar H. Koski went home on furlough. George went home on leave at the same time and the two brothers proudly stood at attention in their uniforms for a photo.

The six Koski sisters were very proud of their brothers in their handsome uniforms, showing them off to their envious friends.

Oscar and George spent time at Dead River and the Flat Rock hunting camp. They enjoyed the time away from the military, but knew this was only a temporary respite. Their was a war to be won and they could end up in the thick of it at any time.

Oscar tried to get George to talk about his experiences in the Army, but George would only say that he "couldn't talk about it." It was unusual for George to be so tight-lipped, so Oscar figured George must be involved in some sort of intelligence work. His sister Ann kept asking George for details about his military service and he finally admitted to her that he had "seen plenty of action in foreign countries." He said he had been to Puerto Rico, Trinidad, New Guinea, and Australia, but wouldn't or couldn't provide additional details.

Figure 19-1: Oscar Koski (left) and George Koski (right) when they were home on leave at the same time during the summer of 1944.

All too soon, their leaves were over. George left first, Oscar a few days later.

After his furlough, Oscar was sent to the 223rd Combat Crew Training School at the Army Air Field in Dyersburg, Tennessee, where he was assigned to a flight crew. There he met the men he would fly with in combat. The pilot was William Skillings from Michigan. The copilot was Clifford Ronk from South Dakota. Robert Spice from Indiana would be their bombardier. Oscar was the navigator, the fourth officer in the crew. Six enlisted men would later join the crew to serve as engineer, radio operator, right waist gunner, left waist gunner, ball gunner, and tail gunner.

During their training at Dyersburg, the crew learned how to fly as a team, each man using his specialized skills to help get the plane to the right place, drop the bombs on target, then get back to base. They flew a variety of training missions designed to develop and test the skills of the crew in formation flying, navigation, bombing, and gunnery. After each mission, their performance was carefully reviewed and critiqued.

Formation flying proved to be a difficult and dangerous business. The young pilots fought bad weather and turbulence as they maneuvered the heavy bombers in close formation. Near-misses were common and some crews were killed when their planes collided or crashed during training missions.

Oscar trained on the Celestial Navigation Tower, a sophisticated mechanical simulator designed by Edwin Link. This complex mechanical simulator included an overhead star display and a Plexiglas floor to simulate movement over aerial photos of the ground. Oscar discovered that the simulator even allowed for changes in elevation, cloud cover, and visibility.

Oscar's crew took its turn in the "ditching pond," which consisted of a B-17 fuselage sitting in a man-made pond. The crew buckled up in their usual crew positions throughout the plane. Somebody blew a whistle and they scrambled to get out of the plane and into the life rafts. They repeated the drill over and over again until the officer in charge decided they might be fast enough to get out of a ditched plane before it sank beneath the waves.

Oscar and the other airmen closely monitored news of the air campaign in Europe, including the first thousand-bomber raid on Cologne. The men in the Army Air Forces were keenly aware of the heavy loses during those raids. It was clear from the news reports that the Luftwaffe fighters and antiaircraft guns were taking a terrible toll on U.S. bomber squadrons.

Some nights, Oscar would lie awake on his cot and think about the crews flying missions from bases in England or Italy. Those crews were going to keep flying, day after day and week after week, until they completed their required twenty-five missions or until they were shot down. They would be replaced by another crew, and another, and another.

Someday, all too soon, Oscar and his crew would take their place on the flight line. Then they would fly until they completed their missions or until they were shot down. Oscar and his crewmates were just one more crew on a military assembly line that, too often ended in the flaming wreckage of a B-17 or a German POW camp.

One night Oscar and his roommates were discussing their immediate future. One of his roommates said, "Twenty-five missions! That's not so bad! Even if we're only flying three missions a week, we should be back in the states in three or four months."

Oscar shook his head and laughed ruefully, "It's not going to be that easy!"

"What do you mean?" asked his roommate.

Oscar explained: "Look at the numbers. Losses are currently averaging almost 5% per mission. On your first mission, you have a 95% chance of coming back. For your second mission it's more like 90%, close to 85% for your third. By your tenth mission, you're getting close to a fifty-fifty chance of coming back. Every mission after that, you're living on borrowed time."

His roommate looked uncomfortable, but Oscar continued, "Didn't you wonder why they made such a fuss about the Memphis Belle? Other crews started flying almost a year before the Memphis Belle. The crew of the Memphis Belle was just the first to beat the odds and complete twenty-five missions. No, I'm afraid many of us are going to end up dead or in a German prison camp long before we complete our twenty-five missions."

His roommate mumbled, "That's depressing!"

"Don't sweat it," quipped Oscar. "If you're dead, you won't really care."

After they turned out the lights and went to bed, Oscar lay awake for some time, wondering what life might be like in a German POW camp.

★ Click here to watch video

Figure 19-2: The crew of the Memphis Belle was the first crew to successfully complete its missions.

★★★ Ordinary Heroes: Six Stars in the Window ★★★
20. Someone's son

June 1944: D-day came and D-day went. The Allied troops consolidated their foothold on the coast of Normandy and threw back the German counterattacks. Art and the men of the 332nd were on standby in England, ready to leave at a moment's notice.

On June 22, Art and the men of the 332nd Engineers were awakened at 3:30 a.m. and told to pack their bags for the move to France. They ate a hearty breakfast while a convoy of trucks assembled outside, collected their gear and climbed into the back of the trucks for the trip to Yellowham Camp near Dorchester.

Five days later, they boarded ships in Portland Harbor. Most of the men from H&S Company boarded the *Prince Henry*, a Canadian ship which had previously sailed in Alaskan waters. Art boarded an LCT (Landing Craft Tank), which was essentially a floating metal platform with an engine.

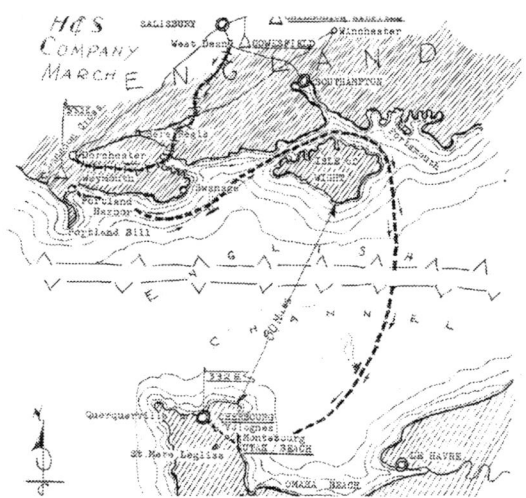

Figure 20-1: Route of the 332nd Engineers to Utah Beach.

Each LCT carried up to six vehicles, lashed to the metal deck so they wouldn't roll around. Art's job was to drive a truck off the LCT and onto Utah Beach.

Late that night, the LCT crossed the channel, anchoring off Utah Beach. As dawn came, he could see the litter of wrecked ships and landing craft. Some of the ships had been wrecked during the D-day assault, but others had been damaged during the fierce storms that slammed into the coast the week after the D-day landings.

Art and the Engineers were builders. They fixed things. But war was about destruction. As he watched the bombers flying overhead, heard the thunder of artillery in the distance, and viewed the wreckage on the beach, Art started to understand the scope of the job ahead.

Before the LCT could be unloaded, a major storm kicked up heavy waves, making the water too rough to safely unload the trucks and heavy equipment. For three days, the LCT rolled miserably in the waves. Art and the Engineers could see the beach, but could not land. Sergeant Jones issued each man a "vomit bag, one," but the seasick men soon found that one bag was not nearly enough.

★ Click here to watch video

Figure 20-2: A major storm struck the coast a few days after D-day, trapping Art on a ship for several days.

Stuck on that tossing ship, Art had time to talk to the English crew of the LCT. The young captain was just 19 years old, but the last three weeks had aged him significantly. His boat had gone in with one of the first waves during the D-day landings. Of the twelve boats in his group, only two had returned from that first trip to the beach.

The D-day landings were over and the beaches had been won, but the ship's loudspeakers constantly reminded Art that he was entering a combat zone. One announcement repeatedly warned, "Be sure you're wearing your dog tags. We're burying too many unidentified bodies. You don't want to be buried without your dog tags."

Every time he heard that announcement, Art tapped his chest to reassure himself he still wore his dog tags. If anything happened to him, he wanted Jenny to know. If he was killed, he didn't want her waiting in the forlorn hope that he might someday return.

After what seemed like a lifetime aboard the wallowing ship, waves finally subsided to the point where vehicles could be safely unloaded. The water was too shallow for the LCTs to reach the shore, so the vehicles were driven off the ramps in about four feet of water.

Art and the other drivers were apprehensive about piloting the vehicles through some 600 yards of surf from the LCT to shore. They'd waterproofed the vehicles and tested them in a water-filled ditch, but had never driven off a ramp and into the ocean.

Art watched closely as the first truck drove off the ramp. The engine stuttered, but kept running, and the vehicle slowly moved towards shore. That truck was followed by another, then another.

Art started the engine of his truck while another soldier stood in the machine gun mount, a circular opening in the roof of the truck. That soldier grasped a rod attached to the carburetor. His job was to manipulate the rod, feathering the choke to keep the engine running while Art drove the truck to the beach.

When Art received the signal to move out, he shifted into low gear and drove off the edge of the ramp. With a terrific splash, the truck dropped off the end of the ramp into four feet of water. The soldier standing beside him feathered the choke while Art carefully steered the truck towards the beach. The engine stuttered a few times, but the truck kept running and they made it safely to the beach.

Following hand signals from an MP, Art parked the truck and turned off the engine so he could remove the waterproofing and prepare the truck for operation on land. Sergeant Babcock and his crew had done an excellent job waterproofing the H&S Company vehicles and only one truck had to be towed to shore.

As Art stepped down from the truck and looked about the beach he had a strong feeling of déjà vu. He wasn't a superstitious man, but he wondered if that feeling meant this was where he was going to die. He tried to shake the feeling by telling himself that the place seemed familiar because he had thought about landing in France so many times over the past year. But try as he might, he couldn't quell that uneasy feeling.

The Germans had concentrated their heaviest defenses at the most logical points of attack along the coast of Europe. The beaches of Normandy were not ideal for an invasion, but were selected by the Allies because the Germans were less likely to expect an attack on that section of the coast. Through clever misinformation, the Allies convinced Hitler that the main attack would take place at the Pas de Calais, the narrowest part of the English Channel and a logical place for attack. The deception worked. Weeks after D-day, Hitler held back his reserves, convinced that the Normandy invasion was a just a diversion and that the real attack was yet to come.

★ Click here to watch video

Figure 20-3: Utah Beach was crowded with wreckage from the storm as well as vehicles, men, and supplies

One of the major problems with the Normandy invasion site was the lack of a harbor suitable for landing large quantities of men and supplies. The Allies partially countered this deficiency by constructing two artificial harbors, Mulberry A and Mulberry B, which were towed from England in pieces, then assembled off the beaches of Normandy. These artificial harbors played a major supply role in the days immediately after D-day. But the fierce storms that kept Art on the LCT destroyed Mulberry A and seriously damaged Mulberry B.

The Allies needed massive quantities of equipment and thousands of replacement soldiers to hold and expand the beachhead. With the loss of the artificial Mulberry harbors, Cherbourg became critical to the success of the invasion as the only deep water port available to the Allies.

Unfortunately the Germans still held Cherbourg and most of the Cotentin peninsula. U.S. troops moved across the base of the peninsula, isolating the German defenders. In fierce fighting they moved up the peninsula, slowly tightening the noose around Cherbourg.

★ Click here to watch video

Figure 20-4: The capture of Cherbourg was essential to the success of the invasion.

As the Allies moved up the peninsula, more French towns and villages were liberated. Most of the French people welcomed the Allies and many rose up to help the Allies. But some French men, and even some French women, fought alongside the Germans. One soldier told Art about a French woman sniper who had been wounded and captured by the Americans. She wasn't the only one. Apparently many French men and women in Normandy did not want to be "rescued" from Nazi oppression. This came as a surprise to the American GIs, who thought they'd be welcomed with open arms as liberators.

The Allies knew Cherbourg was essential to the success of the invasion. Unfortunately, the Germans knew it as well. When the Allies moved to seize Cherbourg, the German defenders fought valiantly to hold off the attack while German engineers sabotaged the harbor. On June 28, a German radio broadcast announced Cherbourg had been taken by the Allies but had been rendered unusable with "everything that distinguished Cherbourg's harbor as man-made rather than natural being completely wrecked. Then, important harbor basins and passages were blocked by sunken ships and by extensive sowing of mines."

The first Allies to reach Cherbourg agreed with that assessment. After viewing the destroyed harbor, Col. Albert Viney, responsible for devising the Allied plans for rehabilitation of the harbor, ruefully remarked, "The demolition of the port of Cherbourg is a masterful job, beyond a doubt the most complete, intensive, and best planned demolition in history."

Figure 20-5: GIs walk past a bulldozer clearing the road to Cherbourg.

By July 1st, Cherbourg had been taken, except for "pockets of snipers," so the 332nd was ordered to Cherbourg to begin reconstruction. Art was a member of the survey crew, but there wasn't any surveying to be done yet, so he drove a 2 ½-ton, or "Deuce and a Half," cargo truck when the regiment moved to Cherbourg. He stayed one night in the barracks at Les Ingoufs, then followed the convoy as it headed through Montebourg and Valognes towards Cherbourg.

The going was slow. Bulldozers busily pushed piles of rubble, wrecked tanks and other vehicles to the side of the road. Dead German and Allied soldiers lay unburied along the route.

When Art finally reached Cherbourg, he drove the truck to the motor pool in a partially wrecked airplane hanger near the docks. It was late and he was exhausted from the stress and the long drive so he ate some cold stew from a C-ration can, then stretched out in the back of the truck to get some sleep.

The next morning, Art noticed German soldiers milling around outside a hospital down the hill. In a moment of panic he thought the Germans might have retaken the city while he slept. He asked a Sergeant about the Germans, but was told not to worry, Cherbourg was still in American hands. The hospital was being used to treat wounded German prisoners and was staffed by captured German doctors and nurses.

Reconstructing Cherbourg harbor was a massive task, requiring the combined effort of three Engineer Regiments. The 332nd worked on the western end of the harbor, the 333rd worked on the center of the harbor, and the 342nd worked on the eastern end of the harbor.

Soldiers from the 332nd Engineers started the dangerous task of clearing mines and booby traps from the Digue du Homet, a concrete wharf extending into the harbor. The men repaired craters in the wharf and removed wreckage from the water so ships would be able to tie up at the wharf.

As the 332nd Engineers started repairs, Art was reassigned to his primary job with the H&S Company survey crew. The crew examined the damaged facilities, measuring the elevations and distances. The architects used those measurements to create plans and generate lists of required materials. When the construction crews arrived, they'd refer to the plans and start the reconstruction while the survey crew started the next project.

Lieutenant Fritz from H&S Company found a disabled boat powered by two Model A engines. The boat was in bad repair, but looked like it would float. Unable to resist the challenge, he tinkered with the boat and soon got the engines running. He took a few men for a quick tour around the harbor, but they were soon flagged down by a Navy patrol boat and warned that the harbor was heavily mined and was "no place for a joy ride."

Lieutenant Fritz hadn't thought about mines. He carefully motored back to the docks, keeping a wary eye on the water. They made it safely back and tied the boat up for good.

Because of the variety of mines the Germans had used, it wasn't possible to sweep the harbor once, then open it up to traffic. Mine sweeping was an ongoing process.

The Germans used at least four kinds of mines in the harbor. Pressure mines exploded when a passing ship caused a change in water pressure. These were located rather quickly, exploding when a minesweeper or ship passed near

Figure 20-6: Lieutenant Fritz by the old German boat at Cherbourg.

them. Contact mines were moored to the bottom and rose to just below the surface a variable number of days after they had been laid. New contact mines still rose to the surface months after the Allies took control of Cherbourg, requiring constant resweeping of the harbor to locate and remove newly risen mines. Magnetic mines lay on the bottom. A counter was incremented each time a ship passed over a mine. After the counter reached a specified number, the mine exploded when the next ship passed over it. "Katy" mines were moored to the bottom with a pole sticking up from the top of the mine. When a ship happened to hit the pole, the mine exploded.

More than 500 mines were removed from Cherbourg harbor, but not all mines were successfully removed. In one disastrous sequence of events, a tugboat going to assist another tug was blown out of the water by a mine. A short time later, a dredge, anchored about sixty yards away, was sunk by an explosion. About a half-hour later, a barge was destroyed by yet another explosion.

An investigation revealed the first tug had been sunk by a mine knocked loose from the mud. That explosion had released another mine, which drifted until it hit the dredge. The third explosion occurred as the tide went out and the barge settled on yet another mine buried in the mud.

Even aside from the mines, Cherbourg remained a dangerous place. German snipers regularly took pot shots at the GIs. On July 7, Art joined a party of enlisted men assigned to hunt down twenty German soldiers reportedly hiding in the hills around Cherbourg. They spent the day tramping up and down the hills, but found no German soldiers. That night, the sniping continued.

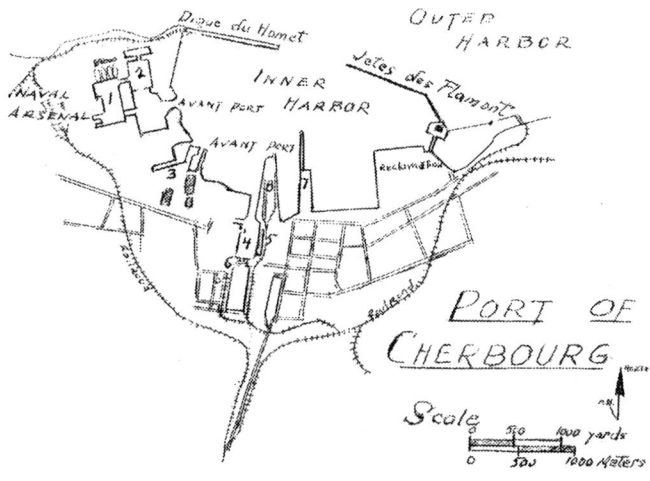

★ Click here for Web Info

Figure 20-7: Sketch of Cherbourg harbor drawn by 332nd Engineers.

The commanding officer decided the snipers were hiding in tunnels during the day, sneaking out at night to take shots at the GIs. A squad of specially trained Rangers were brought in to resolve the problem. The Rangers searched the area, located several tunnel entrances, poured a mixture of gas and oil into the tunnels, then set them on fire. That either killed the snipers or scared them off, because the sniping dropped off dramatically.

Art noticed most of the Jeeps sported a tall steel pole welded to the front bumper. The pole reached above the top of the windshield and had little notches in the leading edge. He asked one of the men from the H&S Company motor pool about the poles. The man replied, "The damn Jerrys like to string piano wire across the road at neck height. You can't see the wire. If you're riding in a Jeep with the window folded down, it'll catch you in the throat and take your head off. So, we started welding these poles on the front of the Jeeps. The pole catches the piano wire and breaks it."

The Germans created many tricky engineering problems when they sabotaged Cherbourg harbor. They blew up a lattice girder bridge, 130 feet long and weighing 230 tons, at the entrance of the Basin Napoleon. One end of the bridge had fallen into the water, the other end was hanging in the air. Five loaded freight train cars stood on the bridge. To further complicate matters, the Germans had mined the bridge and the surrounding waters.

The men of the 332nd began this seemingly impossible assignment by carefully removing the mines and railroad cars. Working sixteen to eighteen hours a day, they attached a complicated set of lines to two trucks and a floating crane. As they lifted the bridge into position, some of the lines fouled and broke, dropping the bridge back into the water. After reattaching the broken lines, they lifted the bridge a second time and moved it back into position, completing the entire repair in just fifteen days.

After more than a month of grueling work, Art wrote to Jenny, "As for expecting me home, don't even think I'll get home until some time after the war has stopped and most everyone else has returned. Engineers usually are the first to leave the country and the last to return. Well, I don't know whether it'll be that way or not, but if the situation requires it may turn out so. I'll bet you have a heck of a time training me to be like a civilized creature again. I'll promise to be good to you though, so don't worry much."

★ Click here to watch video

Figure 20-8: As the last of the German troops in Cherbourg surrendered, the engineers started working on the harbor.

Like most of the soldiers at Cherbourg, Art grew exceedingly weary of Army rations. Late one afternoon, a few soldiers disappeared with a box of German hand grenades and a piece of fish net. They returned just after dark with a net full of fish. Their fishing method was simple: tie two or three German hand grenades together with a rock, twist the fuse on one grenade, then toss the whole assembly into the water. The grenade sank and exploded beneath the surface, creating a shock wave that killed or stunned the fish in the surrounding water. The men used the net to scoop up the floating fish, which they proudly presented to the company cook. The taste of fresh fish was a real treat to men who had been living on Army rations, and so grenade fishing became a regular supplement to the menu.

Figure 20-9: Ship in Normandy harbor.

The Engineers worked long, hard hours, aware that Cherbourg was crucial to the success of the Allied offensive. The hard work paid off. On July 16 four Liberty ships docked at the finger wharves built by the 332nd off the Digue du Homet. The men continued to build docks, clear sunken ships, and remove other debris from the water near the docks. By the end of July, up to fourteen Liberty ships could dock at the same time, delivering vast quantities of urgently needed supplies. In recognition of their valiant efforts in the reconstruction of Cherbourg Harbor, Master Sergeant Tom Jones and Technical Sergeant Richard L. Leversen of the 332nd Engineers were awarded the Legion of Merit.

As more of the port was repaired, the flow of supplies through Cherbourg increased steadily from 2,000 dead weight tons per day in July, to 8,500 in August, to over 10,000 dead weight tons per day in September. Troops also began to land at Cherbourg in record numbers, with over 67,000 men disembarking in August alone.

The Engineers continued clearing debris from the harbor. One day, a work crew from the 332nd discovered the body of a German soldier. They examined the body and found his identity papers.

A dead German soldier wasn't all that unusual. Over the past six weeks, they had seen hundreds of dead soldiers near Utah Beach, on the roads as they traveled up the peninsula to Cherbourg, and in the ruins of the battle-scarred bunkers surrounding Cherbourg. But this dead German soldier seemed somehow different. He had died alone. He wasn't a nameless soldier, lying dead on the side of the road. His name was Richard Bohm. He was a man, someone's son, maybe a father, maybe a husband.

★ Click here to watch video

Figure 20-10: Since the rail lines from Cherbourg had not yet been repaired, supplies were moved from the harbor on a continuous stream of trucks known as the Red Ball Express.

In a simple gesture of respect, the men of the 332nd carried the body of this German soldier to the top of a hill overlooking the town. There, they dug a grave and buried Richard Bohm, marking the spot with a crude wooden cross.

Figure 20-11: Many German soldiers, including this one, died while defending Cherbourg.

★★★ Ordinary Heroes: Six Stars in the Window ★★★
21. Six blue stars in the window

July, 1944: As millions of men before him had discovered, Johnny found that basic training was not very much fun. Growing up in a cool northern climate, he suffered terribly in the stifling heat and humidity of a South Carolina summer. He tossed in his bunk at night and often dreamed of jumping into the cool waters of Dead River or Cooper Lake.

Much of his time at boot camp seemed to be spent waiting in line for one thing or another. For chow, he joined the line outside the barracks, marched to the mess hall, then waited some more. When he entered the mess hall, he'd stand in line again moving his tray through the food line. After a hurried meal, he'd line up again and march to some other place, usually to stand in line yet again.

Johnny and the rest of the recruits were given repeated physical exams and inoculated against all kinds of diseases, including some they couldn't even pronounce. Some days, he was sore in both arms and buttocks after receiving multiple shots. Many of the shots caused low-grade fevers or other reactions, so Johnny was hurting somewhere almost all the time.

Of course there wasn't any use complaining about the heat, the shots, the food, or anything else. The PX sold packages containing small souvenir photos of Camp Croft. This package included a "T.S. Ticket." As far as Johnny knew, no recruit had ever been so dumb as to try to "get his ticket punched by his platoon sergeant."

One memorable day, Johnny's platoon received a lecture on grenades. The sergeant explained they should never run from a grenade. Instead, they should pick it up and throw it back at the enemy. As they talked, the sergeant showed them how to pull the pin from a grenade. Suddenly he fumbled and dropped the grenade on the ground, yelling, "Live grenade!"

The recruits scattered, leaving the sergeant standing alone over the grenade. When the grenade didn't go off, the recruits sheepishly moved back into position. The sergeant gave them a good chewing out. "What did I just finish saying?" he shouted. "NEVER run from a grenade! How many of you listened? Not one—not a single one!"

Training at Camp Croft included time on the pistol, rifle, machine gun, mortar, antiaircraft, and anti-tank firing ranges. Johnny spent hours learning how to assemble, disassemble, clean, and shoot the .45 caliber pistol, .30 caliber M1 rifle, M1 carbine, Browning Automatic Rifle or BAR, .30 caliber light and heavy machine guns, .50 caliber machine gun, 60 mm and 81 mm mortars, bazooka, 37 mm anti-tank gun and 105 mm infantry howitzer.

★ Click here to watch video

Figure 21-1: At Camp Croft, Johnny was trained on all standard infantry weapons.

Like most GIs, Johnny took an immediate liking to the M1 Garand rifle. With an 8–round clip, semiautomatic firing, and adjustable rear sights, it was one of the most advanced rifles of its day. Like most GIs, Johnny caught himself a case of "M1 thumb" when he didn't move his thumb fast enough and the bolt slammed shut on it. Once he learned how to avoid M1 thumb, he came to trust and respect the M1, although by the end of a long hike he found himself wishing it weighed just a few pounds less.

Johnny also learned how to wear a gas mask. That training culminated with the gas mask test. He donned his gas mask and followed the other soldiers into a small building filled with tear gas. The first part of the test was easy—they stood in the gas-filled room to verify that their gas masks did not leak. The second part of the test was much harder. To train them not to panic if faced with gas, the men were ordered to remove their masks and forced to stay in the gas-filled room. After some of the longest minutes of his life, Johnny stumbled out of the room, gasping for breath and barely able to see.

Figure 21-2: Camp Croft trainees leaving the gas mask test.

On July 23. 1944, Johnny described this experience in a letter to his sister Ann:

> Dear Ann,
>
> Received your letter today and decided to answer it while I have the time.
>
> It kind of surprised me to hear that "Art" was in France. That's the kind of luck he always had. Also interesting to know that George has visited all those places.
>
> I might have written and told you about it before, but I sure was tortured last week. Tuesday I had six teeth pulled and a half an hour later I went through the gas chamber. Boy! That was something putting on your gas masks while standing there with your mouth full of blood and the tear gas burning your eyes. Wednesday we went out and were forced to jump in fox holes as tanks came bearing down on you. One big tank ran right over the hole I was in. The whole ground just shook, I had all I could do to stay in the hole. A person just feels like jumping up and you wish that fox hole was a lot deeper than three feet. When that thing went over I almost choked because of the dust.
>
> Thursday night we went on a night problem and it rained all the while. We had to hike with full field packs and pitch our tents. Friday we had to parade in front of Maj. General Hester. Saturday I had two more teeth pulled and fifteen minutes later I got two shots, one for typhoid and the other for tetanus. So Saturday night I had sore arms and a sore mouth.
>
> Today, Sunday, I am just lounging around wishing I was back home spending time out in the woods where it's a little cooler at least. Tomorrow we hike out to the rifle range and practice aiming and firing with blank cartridges. We also will fire the bazooka that you hear so much about. We also will fire machine guns and mortars, learn to drive jeeps, tanks, and half-tracks. Of course if you didn't drive in civilian life they won't start teaching you at all. This bazooka is quite an outfit, although it fires a big projectile it has no recoil.
>
> From what I hear, sister Martha, Jack, and her family have bought Ruuska's house. I suppose they still aren't satisfied.

```
Is Eleanor on her vacation yet? I bet she doesn't fully
realize how lucky she is to be that free. Around here the
guys look at a bird and think how lucky that thing is,
nothing to worry about.

Don't mind all this griping that I do, it's just a natu-
ral thing among soldiers. That's their way of blowing off
steam.

Well so long Ann and may God Bless you and Christine.
                                                  Johnny
```

★ Click here for Web Info

Figure 21-3: Transcript of Johnny's letter describing basic training.

This was the first time that Johnny and most of the soldiers had been away from home. They eagerly read and re-read letters from home and wrote letters at every opportunity. Since there often wasn't enough time to write before lights out, many men would take a seat in the latrine and write their letters there.

Johnny occasionally received letters from some of the girls back home. One of his buddies grabbed a few letters and ran off with them. He later brought the letters back, telling Johnny he'd written his own replies to the girls. Johnny wrote a letter to Ann, asking her to tell the young ladies that if they received any strange letters, they should just ignore them as they were probably written by his buddy.

Johnny's buddy apparently did send those letters to the girls. Some weeks later, Ann wrote to Johnny, "Both Pearl and Jane read those letters and boy were they mushy! Carol stated that she knew right away that it wasn't from you as you weren't the sentimental type. However, she showed me a card that she received later and said that was the real McCoy."

In the same letter, Ann wrote, "Oscar was home on a brief furlough and does he look grand. He seemed a little nervous probably worrying about his assignment in near future which will most likely be in the Pacific."

Johnny's training included a number of realistic combat courses. One course consisted of a replica of a landing ship. The men climbed down a cargo net with their full pack and clambered aboard a landing craft floating in a pool of water. Other training courses included a course with a mock tank, a street fighting course, amphibious training on Duncan Park Lake, and even a simulated Japanese village. After training in the Japanese village, many of the men were convinced they would fight in the Pacific, possibly in China or perhaps the invasion of the Japanese homeland.

As the training became more realistic, the sergeant repeatedly warned them, "You ARE going to see combat. If you don't pay attention here, you're going to screw up over there and you WILL get yourself killed. Even worse, you might get somebody else killed, maybe even me. Nobody wants to go into combat with a screw-up, so listen up and learn to do this right."

On August 6, 1944, Johnny wrote another letter to his sister Ann, in which he shyly informed her that he had been rated an expert on the M1 Garand.

```
Dear Ann,

Received your letter last week, but as you can guess
I was so busy I didn't have time to answer.

Last week we were out on the rifle range with the
Garand. Now that really is a peach of a rifle and if
I can, I'm going to take one home when this blows
over. As you might know I rated an expert with this
same gun. If you ask me, brother Rube would make at
least a score of 190 out of a possible 210. That
score has never been shot on this range.

How is Nestor Korpi getting along? I also heard that
"Art" Koski from Humboldt has got himself into a jam.
Too bad that some guys can't behave themselves.

Is Christine behaving herself, or does she still
sneak out to Cooper Lake for a swim without your per-
mission?

It seems funny to think that already five weeks of my
basic are past and it seems only yesterday that I
left home.

According to what one guy said over the radio,
Germany will be out of the war by Labor Day. I sure
do hope it would be over with the Japanese too, maybe
then I could be home in time for deer season.

Well Ann, so long, good luck, and God Bless you and
Christine.
                                                 Johnny
```

★ Click here for Web Info

Figure 21-4: Transcript of a letter from Johnny to Ann.

The recruits at Camp Croft didn't receive much official information on the progress of the war, but like everybody else, they read the newspapers and listened to the radio. Stories, purportedly from returning veterans, also circulated the camp—stories of Japanese atrocities, the casualties on D-day, and the fighting in Normandy, Anzio, and Monte Cassino. Depending on the news of the day and the latest story to make the rounds, the recruits were sometimes afraid the war would be over before they could get to the front and at other times were—at least privately—afraid it wouldn't end soon enough.

Eleanor Koski worried about Johnny in the Army in a letter to her fiancee,

```
Johnny's letters are so cheerful. He would like me to
believe that the infantry was one great ball. Yet I know
he is putting on a good front. Two of his buddies were
killed when they were practicing use of heavy weapons.
The tripod collapsed and they were using live ammo.

It kills me to think children have to go to do a
man's job. I thought it was such a great tragedy when
Mom died and left so many young children. Now I know
God loved her very much and took her away before she
had to see all six of her sons go to war. She could
never have endured it.
```

Johnny wrote another letter to his sister Ann, enclosing a photo of himself in uniform.

```
Dear Ann:

I don't recall whether I answered your last letter.
As you know I always received a letter from you on a
Sunday and answered it right away, but I must have
slipped up one day.

Things around here are running pretty smoothly as you
can see when I'm writing in the middle of the week.

I heard Toivo Laitinen was wounded and died as a
result. That's tough luck but that again is one of
the fortunes of war. This army doesn't figure things
in terms of a man's life, they think more of the
equipment.

Well I guess my hopes for getting in on the invasion
of the Philippines are shot. That will happen before
I finish my basic but I might make it in time to get
in when we begin pushing into China.

Ann, don't tack this picture up anywhere, just tuck
it somewhere. You can see it isn't any good. It was a
warm day and you can see the perspiration on my chin
and the stain on my cap.

Well that's all for now so, so long, good luck, and
God Bless you and Christine.

                                            Johnny
```

★ Click here for Web Info

Figure 21-5: Transcript of a letter from Johnny to Ann.

Figure 21-6: The photo that Johnny Koski sent with the letter to Ann.

★ Click here to watch video

Figure 21-7: Reuben Koski was drafted into the Navy in September, 1944.

On September 28, Reuben Koski, the last Koski brother still at home, left for basic training at the Great Lakes Naval Base near Chicago. All six of the Koski brothers were now in the service of their country.

That night Lilly sewed a sixth blue star on the bottom of the "son in service" flag that hung on the door of the Koski house. Each blue star represented a soldier from the family serving in the military. As she sewed, Lilly reminder herself to be thankful that the Koski flag did not have any gold stars, representing a house hold member who had been killed in action.

Early the next morning, Johnny's friend, Bobby Emmanuelson, rode his bicycle past the Koski house as he delivered the morning papers. When he saw the new star on the bottom of the flag, Bobby stopped and stood by his bicycle at the side of the road, thinking about the six brothers represented by the six stars on that flag.

Six Stars in the Window: By the fall of 1944, the flag by the door of the Koski house bore six blue stars, one for each of the six Koski brothers serving in the U.S. military.

★ *Frank Alfred "Al" Koski was with the 213th AAA in Seattle, WA.*

★ *Carl Arthur "Art" Koski was with the 332nd Engineers in Cherbourg, France.*

★ *George Harold "Jiggs" Koski was with the 587th Signal Corps in Orlando, FL.*

★ *Oscar Henry Koski was with the 223rd Combat Crew Training School in Dyersburg, TN.*

★ *Reuben Arnold Koski was at the Great Lakes Naval Training Station in Chicago, IL.*

★ *John Leslie Koski was with the 30th Infantry Training Battalion at Camp Croft, SC.*

★★★ Ordinary Heroes: Six Stars in the Window ★★★
22. Bridges and buzz bombs

July, 1944: While Art and the men of the 332nd worked to open the port at Cherbourg, the German and Allied solders were locked in bitter combat in the hedgerows of Normandy. In late July the Allies broke through the German lines at St. Lo and swarmed into France. But the rapid advance quickly outreached the supply lines. Fuel supplies ran critically low and General Patton's tanks were brought to a standstill—not by Germans, but by a shortage of gasoline.

On a sunny day in August, the famed General Patton strode into the office of General Lee. General Patton reportedly picked General Lee up by the shoulders, sat him on a nearby desk, and emphasized the desperate need for tank fuel. Whatever Patton said must have been effective as the Engineer Regiments were on the move within twenty-four hours. The 332nd Engineer Regiment received orders to move out at 3:00 a.m. on the night of August 13. Just two hours later, they were on the road. They camped the next night in a hayfield two kilometers south of Mayenne, France. The men of the 332nd traveled through areas that had seen heavy combat, including the towns of Carentan and St. Lo.

★ Click here to watch video

Figure 22-1: The rapid Allied advance eventually slowed, not because of German opposition, but because it ran out of essential supplies, particularly gasoline.

Near Isigny, the men of the 332nd repaired the first of many railroad bridges. They were just twenty miles behind the front lines and could hear artillery barrages in the distance as they worked.

Figure 22-2: American soldiers march through the ruins of Mayenne France in August, 1944.

A few days later, Art and the men of the 332nd found bunks in the abandoned Casserne German Army Barracks high on a hill in the town of Mayenne. Art joined a group of engineers as they took a quick evening swim in the nearby Mayenne River. Art thought it felt great to rinse off the accumulated grime from days of hard work and sleeping in the field.

When H&S Company arrived at La Hutte, they commandeered an engine and fifteen French railroad cars as a traveling headquarters. This greatly improved efficiency since it allowed the Headquarters Company to stay close behind the letter companies as they repaired the tracks and bridges, working their way across France.

Art traveled with the survey crew, ranging far ahead of the rest of the Regiment. They'd examine the damaged bridges and compile a list of materials and equipment needed for each repair. Master Sergeant Tom Jones and the other draftsmen then drew up the plans for the reconstruction.

Because they worked far ahead of the rest of the Regiment, Art and the other members of the survey team paid particular attention to their personal weapons. With the help of a soldier from Wyoming, Art painstakingly adjusted the aim of his M1 Garand rifle. He even reshaped the wooden grip on the barrel so it wouldn't bind if the barrel got hot from rapid firing.

★ Click here to watch video

Figure 22-3: 332nd Bridge Survey group. Left to right: Keith E. Vigent, Royal G. Sneed, and Frank E. Whitley. Art Koski could be one of the men on the bridge.

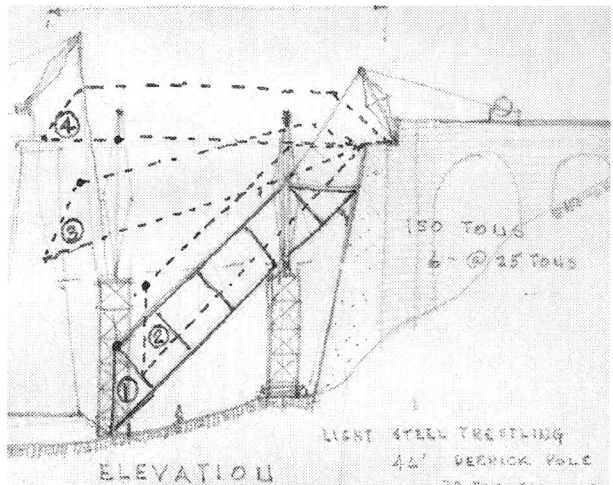

★ Click here for Web Info

Figure 22-4: Sketch for repair of a damaged bridge, drawn by Sgt. Tom Jones from Art's survey squad.

For additional protection, the survey crew typically rode in the H&S Company half-track. They carried their surveying equipment and personal weapons inside the truck and the armored sides protected them from snipers. That half-track became the survey crew's home away from home.

The Engineers raced to keep up with rapidly advancing Allied armies. When the HQ train moved to Dreux, France, Art found himself once again working just behind the front lines. General Patton's 3rd Army Headquarters was four miles off the main road and 1st Army Headquarters was fourteen miles west of Dreux. The 332nd worked furiously to repair the Dreux River bridge, and watched with pride as the first train passed over the bridge on September 9th.

Material was always in short supply, so the men scavenged timbers from bombed buildings and removed track from other railroad lines. Sometimes they even scavenged from their own supply depots.

Figure 22-5: Carl "Art" Koski posing by the half-track used by the H&S Company survey team.

Sergeant Warren Babcock, the man in charge of vehicle maintenance for the 332nd, warned Lieutenant Fritz that he wasn't going to be able to keep the heavy equipment running if he didn't get more spare parts and supplies.

The next day, the irrepressible Lieutenant Fritz drove up with a truck and told Sergeant Babcock to ride with him to collect some parts from the supply depot. The lieutenant had an official requisition for one set of gaskets. Sergeant Babcock thought it a little strange they were taking two men and a truck to pick up one set of gaskets, but he decided not to say anything about it.

Figure 22-6: Men of the 332nd watch a train pass over a recently repaired bridge.

When they arrived at the supply depot, the lieutenant showed the guard the requisition for gaskets and said, "We know where they are. We'll just go back and get them ourselves."

They drove into the supply depot. Lieutenant Fritz told Sergeant Babcock to collect whatever parts and supplies they needed to keep their equipment functioning. The two men proceeded to fill the back of the truck with an assortment of parts, including spare motors and transmissions. They closed the canvas top and the lieutenant handed Sergeant Babcock the set of gaskets.

When they reached the gate, they showed the MP the requisition and Sergeant Babcock held the gaskets up in one hand to show that he had them.

The MP asked the lieutenant, "Did you get anything else?"

Sergeant Babcock couldn't believe his ears when Lieutenant Fritz laughed and told the guard, "Hell yes! We filled the back of this truck with everything we could haul away!"

The guard looked at them in surprise, then laughed, handed back the requisition, and waved them through the gate. As they drove away from the supply depot, both men burst into laughter. Sergeant Babcock couldn't believe that such audacity could actually work. But it had worked and Sergeant Babcock and his mechanics were able to keep the heavy equipment running with the unofficially requisitioned parts.

In early September, Art wrote in a letter to Jenny, "I do hope I'll be home by next year this time. I'll be almost like a total stranger. It would sure be a joke to have to introduce myself to you, but being away from each other as long as we have might show a bit of changes that we don't realize. Anyway, I still think there's no one like my honey." He mentioned he had received a letter from his Cousin Ted Honkala. Apparently their outfits had been camped in the same town for a while, but they didn't run into each other and didn't know they had been so close to each other.

In another letter to Jenny, Art wrote, "I have a hard time thinking of anything but the woods back home. I wonder who'll be lucky enough to do any hunting this fall, since everyone is in the Armed Forces."

Art had resigned himself to missing yet another hunting season, so in a grand romantic gesture, he told Jenny, "Say, if you intend to go out by yourself this fall, you're welcome to use my shotgun."

A city girl might not have understood, but Jenny was from the U.P. She knew this meant their relationship had entered a new phase. Letting her use his shotgun was a serious step for a guy like Art.

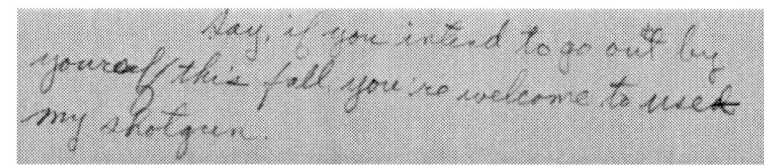

★ Click here for Web Info

Figure 22-7: Art's offer to Jenny to use his shotgun.

As the Regiment worked its way through France, the French people became friendlier, perhaps because they finally decided the Americans were in France to stay. In many towns, the French people would line the roads yelling, "Viva les Americaines! Viva la France!" They tossed fruit, flowers, and bread into the trucks. Pretty French girls sometimes ran up to the trucks to to give wine or pastries to the soldiers.

By mid-September, the 332nd Engineers had repaired bridges and railroad tracks from Cherbourg, south through Fourgeres, east to LeMans, north through Dreux and Paris, and then on to Charleroi, Belgium. Massive quantities of supplies and equipment were being unloaded at Cherbourg harbor, placed on trains, then shipped to supply depots located just behind the front lines. The German Army continued to fall back under the relentless pressure.

The Allied air force dominated the skies, but the German Luftwaffe was still a constant threat. Each time the train stopped at a new location, Art and the other enlisted men jumped out and dug new foxholes so they'd have somewhere to hide if the Germans strafed the train. Then they'd set up their pup tents and try to get some sleep.

★ Click here to watch video

Figure 22-8: In some towns and villages, the French people expressed their appreciation to the Allies for rescuing their country from the Nazis.

One night, most of the men were exhausted and dug rather shallow foxholes. About 10:00 p.m., antiaircraft guns started firing. Somebody yelled, "Take cover!" and everyone scrambled out of their tents and dove into their foxholes.

★ Click here to watch video

Figure 22-9: The Engineers weren't the only ones racing to keep up with the rapid advance across France. At times the entire Army advanced "right off the map."

Three German planes flew low overhead. They were followed by waves of German planes, strafing and dropping bombs. Fortunately most of the planes missed their targets in the darkness. When the noise died down, Art picked up his shovel and started to dig a deeper hole. In the darkness all around him, he could hear the sounds of shovels and picks as the newly motivated GIs worked in the dark to make their foxholes deeper.

When Art went back to his tent, he discovered that someone had moved the halftrack to hide it under the trees. Unfortunately they had run over his tent and his carefully "accurized" M1 Garand rifle was now just a twisted piece of metal.

He brought the ruined rifle to the supply sergeant, who handed him a Browning Automatic Rifle, or BAR, and said, "Use this, Koski." The BAR was a heavy gun, weighing almost twenty pounds. It was essentially a machine gun designed to be carried by one man. It had a 20-round magazine and featured a rate-of-fire selector switch that could be set to slow (330–450 rounds per minute) or fast (500–650 rounds per minute). Even at the slow speed, it would empty a 20-round magazine in a few seconds. As Art hefted it, he decided it could come in very handy the next time the survey crew came under fire.

★ Click here to watch video

Figure 22-10: The Allies stopped just outside Paris and allowed French troops under Charles DeGaulle to be the first to enter the city.

And the survey crews often did come under attack. On September 16, Lieutenant Bayless led a crew to examine the railroad tracks leading from Aubel, Belgium to Aachen, Germany. He didn't realize the Germans still held Aachen. As the crew walked along the tracks just outside Aachen, a German machine-gun crew in a switch house opened fire on the lead members of the crew. The tracks ran through an open plain, so the men dove for the only available cover: between the steel rails. The rails were only 6 ¾ inches high, but the men crawled to safety between them, keeping their heads and their butts low as machine gun bullets ricocheted off the steel tracks.

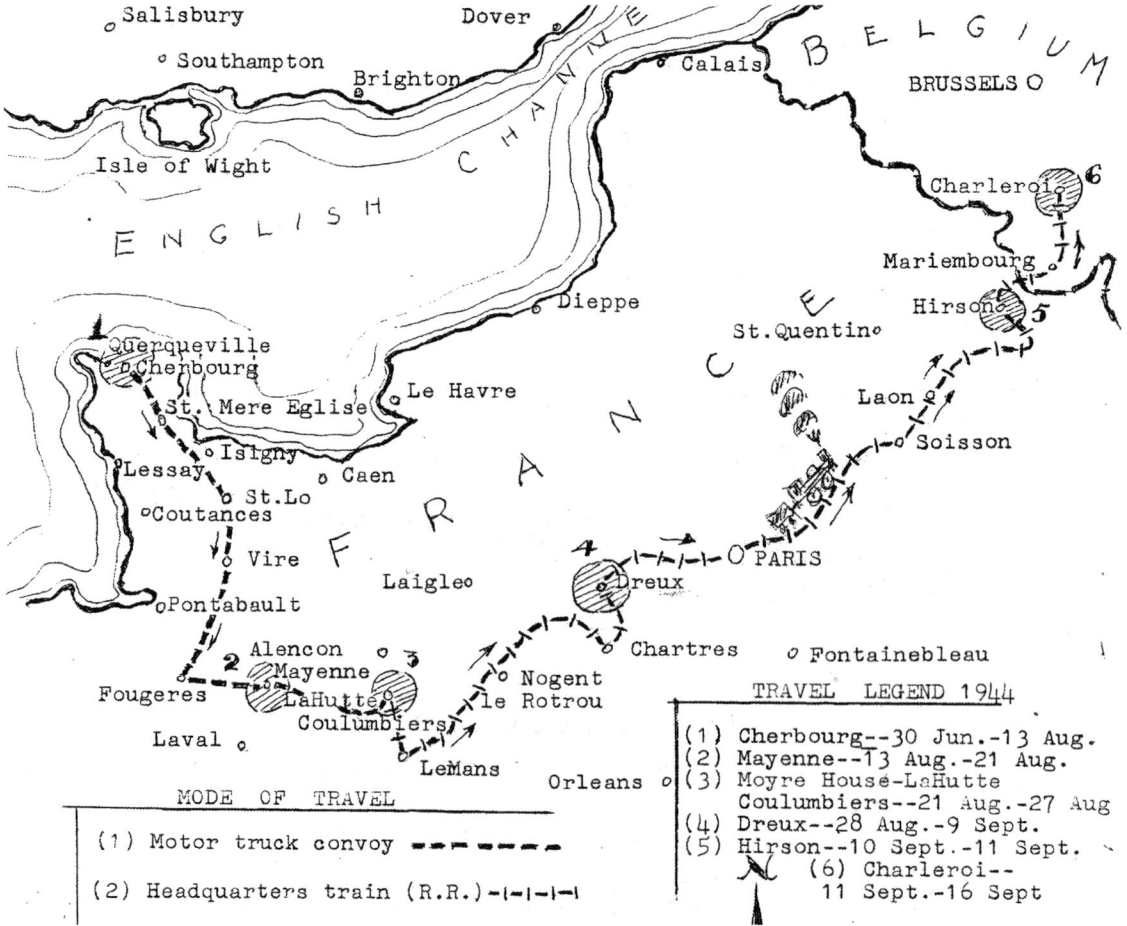

Figure 22-11: The route of the 332nd Engineers from Cherbourg, France to Charleroi, Belgium.

Private Carney Matheny had been following some distance behind the lead crew and had not yet crossed into the open area. He saw what was happening, took position behind a tree and fired into the switch house with his M1 Garand. The Germans fired back at him, almost severing a small tree behind him, but Matheny continued firing, distracting the Germans while the rest of the crew crawled to safety.

Finally the survey crew reached a point where the tracks were raised up on a small embankment. As the machine-gun bullets whizzed overhead, the survey crew rolled over the rail to the comparative safety of the embankment. Lieutenant Bayless and Private First Class Henry Levy were wounded as they rolled over the rail. As they carried the wounded men back to H&S Company, one of the men said, "I never knew I could stay so low and crawl so fast!"

The Germans weren't the only source of danger. During the Pepinster Bridge project, the men of B Company were loading timbers onto a flat car. The flat car broke loose and picked up speed as it rolled downhill from Dolhain towards Verviers and Pepinster. Two men jumped in a Jeep and raced alongside the tracks, trying to catch the speeding runaway. At the train station in Verviers, soldiers from the First Army yelled that a flat car full of timbers had just flown through the train station "like a bat out of hell!" The men gunned the Jeep in hot pursuit.

Figure 22-12: Railroad tracks, twisted by bombs.

The tracks ran downhill from Verviers to the heavily damaged Pepinster bridge. The supporting arches had been completely demolished, but the tracks and attached ties hung in a twisted loop.

The men working on the bridge heard something coming towards them down the tracks and were already running for cover when the runaway flat car burst into view. The flat car sped across the bridge, leaving the tracks partway across the span, spewing heavy timbers on the ground below. Luckily, no one was injured by the runaway car or the flying timbers.

Some of the Engineers couldn't stand the stress of the mines, snipers, and strafing. One surveyor, a big strong guy who seemed "tough as a rock," snapped, stole a jeep, and headed for the rear. The men heard later he had been caught by the MPs near Le Havre and placed in a psychiatric ward.

Other men took refuge in alcohol, which they found stashed all over France and Belgium. One day, when the survey crew came under fire from a German sniper, Art and the survey crew took cover behind a large wooden vat. A bullet hit the vat and liquid started to spray out.

One of the men dipped his finger in the liquid, tasted it, and yelled, "Hey, this is brandy!" He pointed his rifle at the vat, shot another hole it, and then filled his canteen with the leaking brandy.

After the sniper was eliminated, other men rushed over and filled their canteens with brandy streaming from the bullet holes. Art shook his head in disbelief. From his point of view, drinking was stupid in any context. He'd seen how people behaved and how much trouble they got into when they were drunk. But drinking near the front was more than stupid. If you didn't get caught and court-martialed you could get yourself killed.

As fall turned into winter, the Allies relentlessly pushed the Germans back into Belgium and the 332nd Engineers moved with them, building major bridges at Maastricht and Gemmenich, Belgium. Two more Engineers were killed and two were injured by mines left by the retreating Germans.

Dreaded V1 and V2 "vengeance" rockets fell to earth with increasing frequency. The V1 rocket, also called the buzz bomb or doodlebug, was a rocket with stubby wings, weighing just over two tons. Its engine made a distinctive warbling sound that soldiers and civilians soon came to fear. When the engine stopped, the rocket fell to earth and exploded. The V2 rocket was an improved model, an early ballistic missile carrying a one-ton payload that could flatten an entire city block.

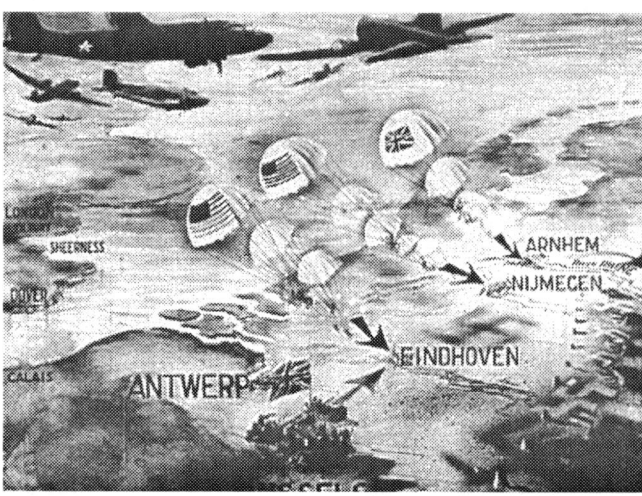

★ Click here to watch video

Figure 22-13: In late September of 1944, the Allies gambled that a daring airborne operation could capture crucial bridges across the Rhine and help bring a swift end to the war. The mission was not successful and Operation Market Garden became one of the costliest mistakes of the war.

The night the H&S Company train moved to Ans, Belgium, a V2 rocket landed only a hundred yards away, blowing out the windows on that side of the train and gouging a crater over seventy-four feet in diameter.

Several units of the 332nd built and operated a gasoline plant near Liege. This was one of the most important and dangerous projects completed by the 332nd. German buzz bombs landed regularly in and around the plant. During the worst of the bombing, the Belgian civilian employees refused to enter the plant, but the Engineers of the 332nd continued to operate the plant despite the constant danger of explosion.

On November 20, Warren Babcock heard the sound of a buzz bomb and looked up to see one flying overhead. He asked the man working with him, "What would you do if that thing stopped now?"

Just then, the motor cut out and the buzz bomb fell, exploding just a few blocks away. That was the first of a barrage of buzz bombs. In just two days, twenty buzz bombs landed in and around Liege. Three men from the 332nd were injured, but none were killed.

One buzz bomb landed on the tracks and skittered towards the 332nd Headquarters train. Nobody knew what to do as they watched the bomb slide along the tracks towards them. The men let out a breath of relief when it stopped before reaching the train and did not explode. George Stone, the Regiment's best demolition and booby-trap man, was called in to disarm it.

★ Click here to watch video

Figure 22-14: A V1 rocket or buzz bomb falls toward the 332nd Engineers.

For Thanksgiving, the cooks of H&S Company prepared a traditional turkey dinner with gravy, peas, and cranberry sauce. But the Thanksgiving holiday was repeatedly interrupted with twenty buzz bombs landing in Liege that day alone.

On November 24, 1944, a buzz bomb hit the 15th General Hospital in Liege. The building was heavily damaged and the men of the 332nd rushed in to help. They reached the hospital and started searching for survivors in the rubble. They rescued many patients, some of whom had been wounded at the front, then wounded again by the buzz bomb as they lay in their hospital beds.

While the Engineers cleared debris, another buzz bomb hit the hospital. The explosion broke a steel light pole and threw debris high into the air, injuring one man from the 332nd. The dazed and bleeding man staggered past Sergeant Babcock, muttering, "It was buzz bombs, Sergeant! buzz bombs!"

Art and other members of the 332nd spent the entire day clearing debris and searching for survivors. All of the patients survived, but fifteen hospital workers were found dead in the debris.

A few nights later, the hospital was hit by yet another buzz bomb. The bomb hit the damaged part of the hospital and no one was injured.

The captain became convinced the Germans had a spotter directing the attacks from the hills above Liege. He sent a squad to search the hills. They returned with a German soldier equipped with binoculars and a radio.

The captain took the German into a building for interrogation. The German refused to cooperate. The captain pulled out his pistol to encourage the German to talk. The German still refused to talk. The Engineers waiting outside heard a shot. A short time later the captain called for a couple of men to drag the German soldier away and bury him.

Nobody made a fuss about the dead German soldier. Everybody understood that this was war. People were dying. Terrible things were happening—things that in another context might seem horrendous, but that in this time and this place, were all too understandable.

★★★ Ordinary Heroes: Six Stars in the Window ★★★
23. Who fears?

September, 1944: Oscar and his crew had finished their training. The next step was an overseas combat assignment. Oscar didn't know where he was going or when he would leave. The only thing he knew for sure was that he would leave soon and that he would be stationed somewhere within flight distance of the enemy.

At the end of the month, Oscar and his crew boarded a train to Hampton Roads, Virginia. A few days later, they boarded the SS Athos and headed out to sea. On the second day at sea, they were told the ship was headed to Naples, Italy.

After the ship landed in Naples, the air crews were trucked to their assigned bases. Oscar and his crew were sent to a small air base known as Lucera 8, located about thirty miles from Foggia near the "spur" of Italy.

On November 8, Oscar reported for duty with the 352nd Squadron of the 301st Bomb Group Heavy of the 5th Wing of the 15th Army Air Force. The 301st was a typical bomb group, consisting of four squadrons: the 32nd, the 352nd, the 353rd, and the 419th. Each squadron consisted of nine to twelve airplanes, but not all of those planes flew every mission. On a typical mission, seven planes flew from each squadron, for a total of about twenty-eight planes from the 301st Bomb Group. With a typical crew of ten men on each plane, some 280 men ventured over enemy territory each time the 301st participated in a mission.

★ Click here for Web Info

Figure 23-1: Location of Lucera 8, near Foggia, Italy.

The emblem of the 301st was a blue shield, with three ravens impaled by a spear. Underneath was the motto: "Who fears?" It wasn't clear to Oscar what the three impaled ravens meant, but it seemed rather ominous. Some men said it referred to the three main Axis powers: Germany, Japan, and Italy. Others said the ravens represented Hitler, Mussolini, and Tojo. Still others said the three ravens and the one spear represented the unit number 301. Oscar didn't really care what the ravens meant. He was more concerned about that motto: "Who fears?" He knew he was afraid. Everybody was afraid, even though some didn't want to admit it.

★ Click for Web Info

Figure 23-2: 301st emblem.

The conditions at Lucera 8 were primitive at best. Oscar and the other crewmen slept in pyramid tents. Showers and dining area were located in more tents. Open trenches served as latrines. The only real buildings were the Squadron Headquarters, the Officer's club, and the NCO club. When the wind blew, it picked up the red dust, which covered everything in sight. During one wind storm Oscar asked, "Is it always this dusty?"

The other man thought for a moment, then replied, "No, it's not always this dusty. In the winter it snows. Then it's the snow that's blowing into your tent. When the rains come, there isn't any dust. Of course, then you're up to your knees in mud. No, I guess it's not always this dusty."

Even the landing strips were clearly temporary affairs. Instead of paved runways, interlocking steel mats lay over the dirt. The dirt had been graded before the mats had been laid down, but as the heavy planes landed and took off, they formed bumps and ridges the length of the runway. After training on smooth paved runways in the States, those metal-covered gopher pits proved a challenge for rookie pilots.

Figure 23-3: Tents on a muddy field at an airbase in Italy.

The skies were overcast for days after Oscar arrived, so the 301st didn't fly any combat missions on November 8, 9, or 10. While waiting for the skies to clear, Oscar heard other crews talking about the mission of November 7, when bad weather forced the planes to the alternative target, the marshaling yards at Maribor, Yugoslavia.

Twenty-eight planes from the 301st that flew that mission. Eighteen were damaged and one was lost. Only five or six chutes were seen leaving the plane. Nobody knew what happened to the crew members who bailed out of the crippled plane. If fortune had smiled on them, perhaps they landed safely and somehow escaped the German soldiers sent to capture them. Otherwise they were dead or in a POW camp.

Oscar and his crew also learned of the recently revised mission rules. Through October, 1944, 15th Army Air Force bomber crews had to accumulate a total of fifty combat mission credits before rotation home. Each combat mission was worth at least one mission credit. Missions flown over two or more areas controlled by German fighters, were worth two mission credits. Each crew member had to fly twenty-five to fifty combat missions to complete his tour of duty, depending on how many missions were given double credit.

Two days before Oscar joined the 301st, the mission policy was changed. All crews had to complete a total of thirty-five combat missions, with each flight over enemy territory counting as one mission. This change caused some grumbling among those airmen who had almost completed their required tours under the old system. Four days later, the system was revised again. Airmen who had arrived on or before September 1, 1944 continued to fly under the old system. Those who arrived after September 1, including Oscar and his crew, flew under the new system, completing at least thirty-five combat missions.

On November 11, 13, and 16, Oscar's crew flew training missions over friendly territory. The first two missions lasted two to three hours and were designed to give the crew practice flying in formation. The third mission was very short, just a thirty-minute mission to certify them as ready for combat.

Oscar was quiet as he climbed out of the plane after that last training mission. His training was finally over. The next time he climbed into a B-17 he would be headed for enemy territory.

There was just one more requirement before the crew flew in combat. Their pilot, Bill Skillings, had to fly as copilot on an actual combat mission. Assuming he survived that flight, the entire crew would then be added to the flight roster.

On November 11, the 301st sent thirty-six B-17s to join a formation of more than 200 bombers sent to Brux, Czechoslovakia. Oscar and his crew watched the planes leave in the morning and waited for them to return at the end of the day.

Most of the planes were recalled due to bad weather but one-hundred and sixteen B-17s hit the alternative target at Salzburg. The 15th Army Air Force lost twenty-two bombers and eight fighters on that mission, but none of the missing planes were from the 301st.

Because of heavy overcast, no missions were sent out from November 12 through 15. On November 15, pilot Bill Skillings was informed he'd be flying as copilot on the mission scheduled for the next day. This would be his final test before taking his own plane into combat.

On November 16, the planes from the 301st were given orders to attack German troops near Novi Pazar, Yugoslavia. Oscar and the rest of the crew stood at the flight line and watched as the plane carrying Bill Skillings left the ground. The planes disappeared into the distance as the sun rose over the horizon. Oscar turned and walked silently back to his tent.

Oscar's entire crew found themselves drawn to the runway that afternoon, to wait anxiously for the planes and Bill Skillings to return. The assembled airmen counted the returning bombers, "thirty-four, thirty-five, thirty-six." Everyone breathed a sigh of relief as the last of the bombers touched down. On this day at least, every plane from the 301st returned home safely.

When Skillings returned to the tent after his debriefing, Oscar and the other crew members pumped him for information on the mission. Skillings shrugged and said, "There's not really too much I can tell you."

He busied himself rummaging through his footlocker for a pack of cigarettes. The tent was quiet. Skillings looked up to see everyone else watching him and realized he had to tell them more. "We took off and assembled into formation, just like a practice mission. When we got over the target, it was covered with clouds. The lead plane decided to return to base, so we turned around and here we are."

"Any flak?" pressed one of the crew.

"There wasn't much in the way of antiaircraft fire and we didn't see any German fighters. I was sweating all the way," he admitted, "but it was a milk run really. I don't think every mission's going to be that easy. If you want to know what combat is like, you're just going to have to wait. I have a feeling you'll find out for yourself soon enough. Now I'm dead tired and I'm going to sleep."

Oscar and his crew had been checked out and the pilot had flown on a combat mission. It was clear they would fly a combat mission very soon. Some of the men would have been happy to delay their first mission as long as possible. Oscar felt they might as well get on with it, thinking, "We're not going home until we've flown thirty-five missions, so we might as well get started on them."

That evening, Oscar checked the flight list for the next day. Partway down the list, he saw the name Skillings. The waiting was over. He and the crew were on the list for the mission the next day.

That night, the crew went to bed early, but Oscar tossed and turned on the hard Army cot. He was asleep for only moments when he felt someone shaking his arm. It was the "wake-up guy," the man sent to make sure the flight crews did not oversleep.

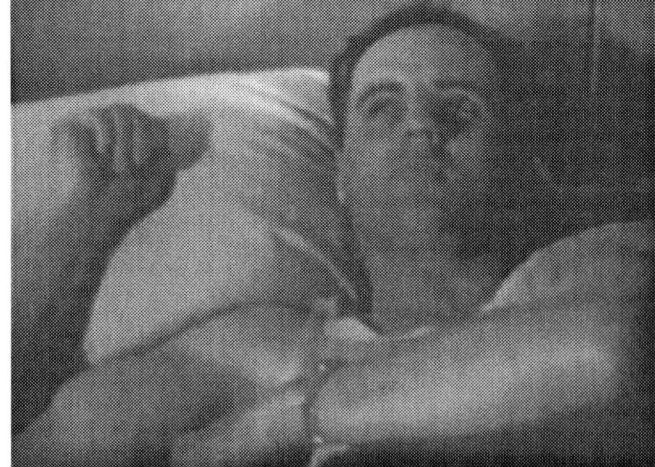

★ Click here to watch video

Figure 23-4: The night before a mission, air crews did their best to get some sleep before the wake-up guy burst in the door to roust them out of bed.

Oscar groggily looked at his watch. It was 3:00 a.m. The wake-up guy told them breakfast was in thirty minutes and the mission briefing at 4:00 a.m. Oscar pulled on his uniform and stumbled to the mess tent in the chilly predawn air. He found the crews eating a hearty breakfast of coffee, bacon, toast, and real eggs—the first they'd had since they arrived in Italy. As Oscar was to find, flight crews needed that hearty breakfast. Except for a sandwich and a thermos of coffee, he wouldn't eat again until they got back from the mission, ten or twelve hours later.

At 4:00 a.m. they assembled for the initial briefings. The men sat on benches in a Quonset hut, staring at a large map covered by a curtain in the front of the room.

★ Click here to watch video

Figure 23-5: The crews gathered for mission briefings where they would learn where they were headed that day.

Most of the men were smoking and the room soon filled with a haze of tobacco. The Group commanding officer entered the room. Someone yelled, "Atten-hut!" and everyone stood at attention. The commander told them, "At ease!" then pulled the curtain up, slowly revealing a map of southern Europe with red string outlining a route from their base to a city in Czechoslovakia. He looked at the men and said, "The target for today is the oil refinery at Brux, Czechoslovakia, northwest of Prague." Some men groaned. They'd been to Brux before and knew it had heavy antiaircraft defenses.

The CO emphasized the importance of the Brux oil refineries to the German war machine. He rapped the map with his pointing stick and said, "We're going to hit them hard and we're going to keep hitting them until we put this refinery out of business. If you don't complete the mission, or if you miss the target, you're going to have to go back again and again."

The CO surveyed his men gravely, then continued, "The best thing is to do it right, take out this refinery, and shorten the war. If the Germans don't have fuel, they can't put up fighters against you, they can't run their tanks, and they can't get supplies to their troops in the field. Good luck, and may God go with you."

Figure 23-6: Brux, Czechoslovakia, target for Oscar's first mission.

After the initial briefing, the crews went to separate briefings for pilots, navigators, bombardiers, and gunners. Oscar headed to the navigators' briefing where he memorized the route, waypoints, the initial point (or IP) at the start of the bomb run, and the target. A meteorologist discussed visibility and projected weather conditions along the route, including wind speeds at various altitudes.

As they exited the briefings, the flight crews crowded into a small room filled with shelves. The men removed any personal items, including wallets, photos, letters, and jewelry, that might prove helpful to enemy interrogators. They put those items in canvas bags and placed them on shelves. The room was quiet and the men were thoughtful as they carefully placed their personal effects in the little bags. Each airman knew that if he didn't come back from the mission, that little bag of personal effects would be the last thing his family would receive from him.

★ Click here to watch video

Figure 23-7: The 15th Air Force had been directed to focus on destroying oil fields, oil refineries, and synthetic oil production facilities.

Oscar walked with his crew to another room where they put on special flight clothing designed to keep them warm in the minus-fifty-degree temperatures they'd endure as the unheated plane flew some 30,000 feet above sea level. Oscar removed his uniform, then pulled on underwear with electric heating elements. Over this, he pulled on insulated pants, jacket, and an insulated flight helmet. He picked up an oxygen mask, a pair of electrically heated gloves, a steel helmet, a flak vest with heavy metal plates, a parachute, a yellow inflatable life preserver, and a .45 caliber pistol.

Each airman was issued a special survival kit to be used only if he was forced to bail out. Rumor had it that the survival kits included a silk map, compass, water purification tablets, morphine, sulfa tablets, energy bar, and money or a gold certificate to buy supplies or bribe people for help. But nobody seemed to know for sure. Each survival kit was sealed and had to be turned in after the mission. The men were warned of serious consequences if the seal on the kit was broken.

Oscar shoved the survival kit deep into his pocket and hoped he wouldn't have to use it.

By 5:00 a.m., Oscar and the crew were hanging onto Jeeps headed to the dispersion point where their B-17 stood silent in the predawn darkness. Nobody talked as they headed toward the planes. Most of the men smoked, some chewed gum, and others looked thoughtfully into the darkness.

When they reached the plane, the pilot and copilot walked around it for a visual inspection. The rest of the crew loitered near the plane, talking quietly and smoking. None of them were in a hurry to climb aboard the plane. They knew they'd be flying for many hours. Subconsciously at least, they all understood this could be the last time they would stand on this earth.

A soldier drove up in a Jeep and handed out thermoses of hot coffee, saying, "Here Joe, this will keep you awake."

Oscar quipped, "Thanks bud! Although I don't think I'm going to have trouble staying awake!"

★ Click here to watch video

Figure 23-8: The crews rode to dispersal areas where they clambered aboard their planes.

All too soon, the pilots finished their inspections and Skillings told the crew to get on board. Oscar entered through an emergency hatch near the navigator's station. He stood under the open hatch, with both hands on the edges of the opening. Then he pulled up on his arms and flipped his legs up and through the hatch, twisting to land on the floor inside the airplane. At least that's how it was supposed to work. He'd heard how bulky clothing could catch on the hatch, leaving an unlucky crewman hanging upside down halfway from the hatch while the rest of the crew commented on his lack of agility.

Inside the plane, Oscar settled into the navigator's position, just behind the Plexiglas nose of the plane. He crouched in front of a small desk and spread out his maps and instruments. A window in front of him showed the left wing of the plane. The handle of a machine gun stuck through a hole in the window. This was his "cheek gun." When the plane came under attack by fighters, Oscar was supposed to use that gun to help defend the plane.

A few feet ahead of Oscar, the bombardier sat behind the bombsight in the Plexiglas nose of the plane. After the plane reached the initial point, the bombardier would use the bombsight to control the plane, guiding it over the target and releasing the bombs at the appropriate time. When not guiding the plane on the bomb run, the bombardier manned a pair of .50 caliber machine guns mounted in the nose of the plane to defend against attacks from dead ahead.

Oscar strapped on his throat mike, then double-checked his maps and compass. He made the first entries in the navigator's log book, marking the location for the start of the flight. Above and behind him in the cockpit, he could hear the pilot and copilot as they completed the preflight checklist:

"Controls and seats?"

"Checked"

"Fuel transfer valves and switch?"

"Off"

"Intercoolers?"

"Cold"

The entire plane vibrated as the powerful engines roared to life. The first rays of the sun reached the airfield and a signal flare rose into the air near the end of the runway. It would only be moments now. One by one, the planes pulled onto the runway and laboriously climbed into the sky. The roar of the engines was deafening, even muffled by Oscar's earphones and leather helmet.

Once airborne, the lead plane flew in an oval, as if around a race track, slowly gaining altitude. The next two planes pulled into position below the lead plane, one to the right and one to the left. A fourth plane pulled in below, just off center so it wouldn't get hit when the lead plane dropped its bombs. Two more planes pulled into position to the right and left of that plane. Finally, the lowest plane pulled into the bottom position, behind and below the other two planes. The plane in this position was called "tail end Charlie." It was the least desirable position, exposed to enemy fighters and the plane most likely to be hit by antiaircraft fire.

Similar formations assembled to the right and left, and another set of formations formed just behind them. Four squadrons of seven planes merged into a group formation of twenty-eight planes. Those group formations joined planes from other groups to create even larger formations, all based on the same diamond pattern.

The idea was to fit the planes into a compact formation, so their bombs would land in a concentrated area for maximum damage to the target. The tight diamond formation allowed the gunners to share the job of defense against German fighters. No matter which angle a fighter approached from, he would face the concentrated fire of .50 caliber machine guns from almost every plane in the formation.

Tighter formations made for more effective bombing and better defense against fighters. But flying in close formation created its own hazards. If a plane wandered out of position, it could crash into planes above, below, or to the side. That plane could then hit another plane, causing a cascading collision, resulting in the loss of two or three planes. If any of the lower planes wandered out of position, they would be hit when the upper planes dropped their bombs.

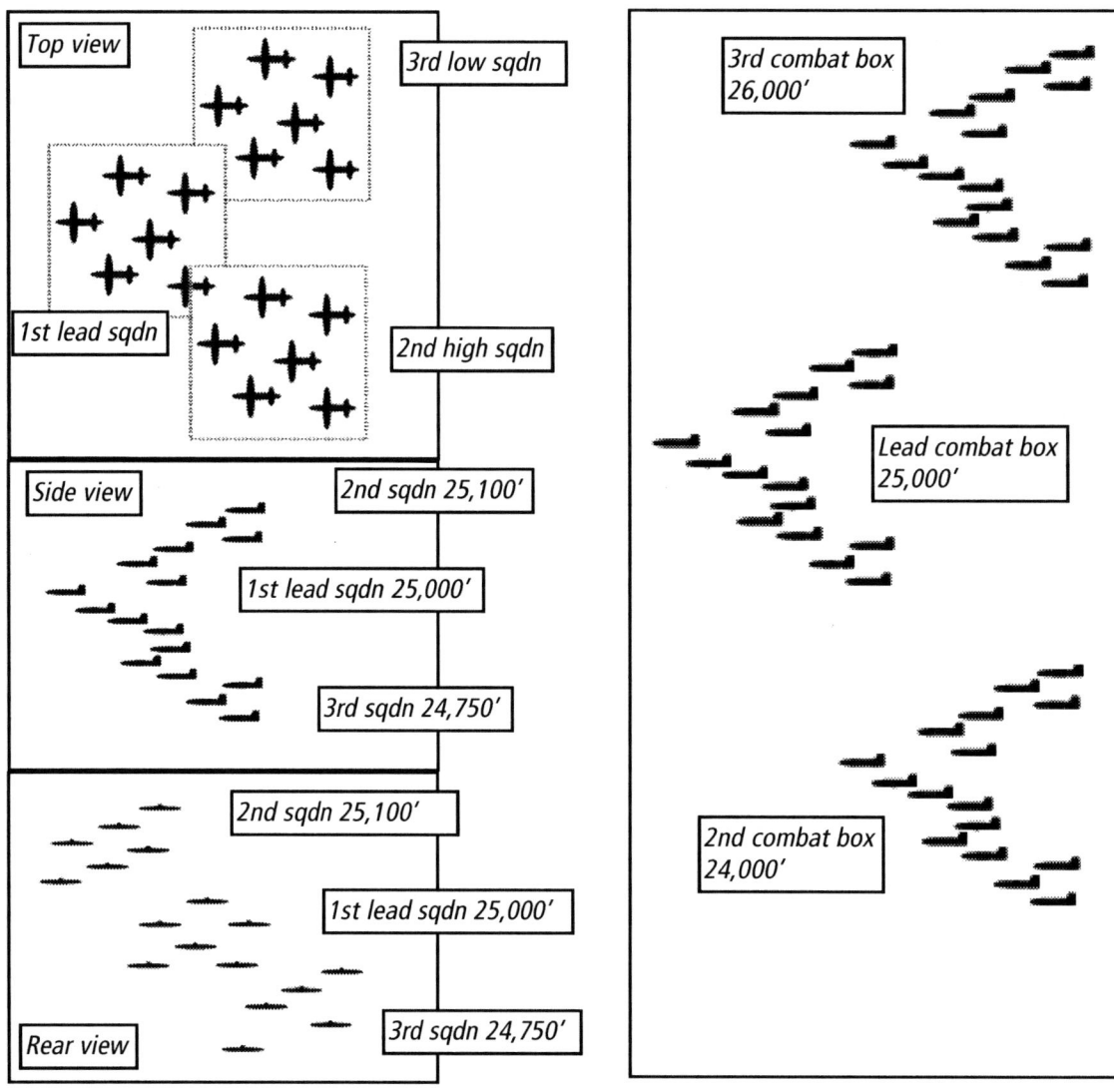

Figure 23-9a: Diagram of a B-17 combat box formation.

Figure 23-9b: Diagram of a larger formation consisting of three combat boxes.

On this mission, all the planes joined the formation without incident. They circled to gain altitude, then flew north toward German-occupied Czechoslovakia. As they passed 10,000 feet, the pilot told the crew to switch to oxygen.

Since the planes were flying in formation, the navigator in the lead plane had primary responsibility for the course. However, Oscar and the navigators in each plane continually plotted and verified the course on their own charts, carefully noting their location, changes of direction or altitude, and other relevant information in their log books. It was essential for every navigator to know where he was at all times so he could plot a course back to base if the plane became separated from the rest of the formation.

Some time later, the pilot told the crew members to test their guns. Each of the gunners shot off a few rounds. The bombardier tested the chin guns and Oscar test-fired the cheek gun. Every gun position was responsible for enemy fighters attacking from a specific angle. The navigator and bombardier were responsible for fighters attacking from the front. The turret gunners were responsible for planes coming from above and below, while the waist gunners covered the sides of the plane. The tail gunner, crammed into a tiny space at the very rear of the plane, was responsible for planes attacking from the rear.

As they passed over northern Italy, Oscar called on the intercom, "Navigator to pilot, we are about to cross enemy lines."

The pilot replied, "Okay everyone, stay alert. This is the real deal."

Periodically the copilot requested a response from each of the crewmen. "Check in, check in." One by one the crew members responded:

"Navigator okay."

"Bombardier okay."

"Tail okay."

"Left waist okay."

"Right waist okay."

"Radio okay."

"Ball turret okay."

"Top turret okay."

If the copilot didn't get a response from one of the crew, he'd send someone to make sure he hadn't lost his oxygen supply. Without oxygen, a man would lose consciousness and would die in a matter of minutes. Lack of oxygen could sneak up on a man. Most didn't even realize they had a problem until they awoke to find another crew member holding an oxygen mask over their face.

As the plane droned on, Oscar thought one of the engines seemed to be making an unusual sound. The pilot and copilot suddenly seemed to be very busy in the cockpit, flipping switches and talking to each other. A few minutes later, pilot Skillings announced the #2 engine was running erratically. He decided to abort the mission and return to base. Oscar quickly prepared a return flight plan and passed it on to the pilot.

It took a lot of guts for a pilot to abort, particularly on his first combat mission. Bill Skillings knew the plane would be checked very thoroughly when it returned to base. If the mechanics couldn't confirm the problem, or if the commanding officer didn't agree that it had been serious enough to abort the mission, he would be blamed for "lack of moral fiber." But the #2 engine could stop running at any time. He and the co-pilot agreed it would be foolhardy to start the mission with only three functioning engines. If anything happened to one of the other engines, they'd lose the plane and the crew.

After they crossed back into friendly territory, the radioman tuned to the Armed Forces Radio station in Foggia and the crew listened to the latest hit records over the intercom.

As they neared the base, Bill Skillings' decision to abort was confirmed when the #2 engine quit completely. He quickly feathered the prop to reduce drag and continued flying on the remaining three engines. Fortunately, the B-17 was able to fly reasonably well on three engines. But even veteran pilots agreed that "things got a bit dicey if you lost two engines."

★ Click here to watch video

Figure 23-10: A B-17 takes off for a mission.

After what seemed like an eternity, the landing strip came into view. Skillings set the plane down and taxied off the runway. The crew piled out of the plane, happy to be safely back on solid ground. They hadn't come under enemy fire, but they had flown over enemy territory, so it counted as their first combat mission, the first of thirty-five.

On the ride back for debriefing, the crew joked and pretended they hadn't been worried. But they all understood that next time they couldn't abort. Next time they had to go all the way.

Oscar was relieved to have made it back, but also felt strangely disappointed. He had tried so hard to prepare himself for this first combat mission. He thought that today, one way or another, he would have experienced combat. But his first combat experience still loomed ahead of him. If he couldn't avoid it, he'd just as soon get it over with as soon as possible. "Surely," he thought, "combat can't be as bad as I've imagined."

Figure 23-11: A B-17 navigator, wearing flight gear and oxygen mask, plots a course.

★★★ Ordinary Heroes: Six Stars in the Window ★★★
24. Ready for duty

October 1944: As Oscar sailed to Italy, Johnny continued his basic training at Camp Croft, South Carolina. He and his buddies often walked past the German POWs held in a large fenced enclosure. Most of the captured Germans were older than the recruits, but they didn't seem as tough or as nasty as expected. Many of them smiled and tried to wave the GIs closer to the fence. Johnny figured they just wanted cigarettes, so he stayed away from them.

Training continued with support weapons such as the 60 mm and 81 mm mortars. A mortar crew typically set up behind a ridge or hill where they could not see the target directly. A spotter relayed firing instructions to the mortar crew, telling them to adjust the angle and side-to-side position of the tube. The crew added or subtracted increments of powder on the base of the shell to control how high the shell would fly. When everything was adjusted, the first gunner dropped a shell into the tube and quickly stepped out of the way. If everything worked right, the shell flew out and landed somewhere near the target. If the first shell missed the target, the crew adjusted the angle of the tube or the number of increments on the next shell and tried again. With just two or three shots the crew could almost always "walk the shells" in to the target.

An 81 mm mortar could drop a lot of explosives on an enemy position in a very short period of time. The largest HE (high explosive) shells weighed up to 15 pounds and could hit targets from 100 to 3,290 yards away. The typical rate of fire was 18 shells per minute, but a skilled gunner could fire as many as 30–35 rounds per minute.

★ Click here to watch video

Figure 24-1: At Camp Croft, Johnny was trained in the operation of the 81 mm mortar.

Unfortunately, the 81 mm mortar was a very cumbersome weapon. The three main components—the tube, the bipod, and the base plate—each weighed almost 45 pounds. In a typical seven-man squad, one man carried the tube, one carried the base plate, and one carried the bipod. Three other men carried ammo in vests with pockets sewn on the front and back. The typical load was four to six shells, each of which weighed from seven to eighteen pounds.

The squad leader was the only man not carrying a heavy load. He carried a mortar sight, compass, firing tables, aiming post, binoculars, pistol, and firing pin, plus a screwdriver used to remove the firing pin when it needed replacement.

Although most of the recruits complained about the food, Johnny managed to chow down large plates of meat and potatoes at every meal. Between the food and the exercise, he gained weight for the first time in his life. After months of hard training and solid food, he was in the best condition of his life and, like many young recruits, felt ready to take on any enemy.

As Johnny adapted to Army life, he learned some old soldier's tricks such as making himself scarce to avoid undesirable duty. One of his buddies, a private named Kitts, joked that back in Roman times some Centurions probably got out of chariot–cleaning duty by pretending to be sharpening spears or something.

On October 8, 1944, Johnny wrote the following letter to his sister Ann:

> Dear Ann:
>
> It's some time ago since I received your letter. I started to answer it last Sunday the 1st, but they came looking for guys to clean machine guns so my friend Kitts and myself went for a walk in the woods. Well we came back in time for supper and after that I didn't have time to finish it because all last week we were on night problems. One of them included going through the infiltration course. We also went through a number of other battle courses. In one case we took a village using live ammunition on silhouette targets. It's all very interesting, but also can end very sadly if everyone isn't on the alert.
>
> Well now this week we fire the .45 automatic pistol plus driving jeeps and trucks. This coming Saturday we go out on maneuvers for a two week period. After that we stay in camp for an indefinite period.
>
> I spent two days on K.P. last week. And of course I got enough to eat. Boy, it really is good to tie into meat, butter, and all of that rationed stuff and not worry about ration points.
>
> How is Christine coming along? I bet she's cute as the dickens seeing she's almost a year old. I suppose you bought a small game license and you're bagging your limit of birds and rabbits every day.
>
> Well that's all I can think of for now so I'll say so long, good luck, and God Bless you and Christine.
>
> Johnny

★ Click here for Web Info

Figure 24-2: Transcript of a letter from Johnny to Ann.

In the final weeks of basic training, Johnny faced one final hurdle, the physical fitness test. This last test was a grueling physical ordeal that included running with full gear and backpack and a four-mile timed march. The recruits sweated and grunted and groaned, but very few dropped out.

Johnny pushed himself hard, determined to pass this final test. He knew there were only two options: successfully complete the test, or drop out and repeat all seventeen weeks of training. Johnny refused to quit. He wasn't going to go through basic training a second time. Once had been more than enough.

Johnny passed that final test. By the end of October, 1944, his basic training was over and Private John Leslie Koski was ready for active duty with the United States Army Infantry. But it wasn't clear if he would ever see combat. The German army was being pushed back by the Brits, Canadians, and Americans on the west and by the Russians on the east. Everyone expected the war in Europe to end soon, perhaps by Christmas. If Johnny was going to see combat it would most likely be somewhere in the Pacific, possibly in the invasion of Japan.

Figure 24-3: Private John Leslie Koski on graduation from basic training, wearing his Expert medal for marksmanship with the M1 Garand Rifle.

★★★ Ordinary Heroes: Six Stars in the Window ★★★
25. Two down

November, 1944: Oscar and crew were on the mission list again for November 18. When they crossed into Austria, Skillings warned the crew to keep a sharp eye out for German fighters. Cliff Ronk, the copilot, said he saw about a dozen dots off to the left. Skillings replied over the intercom, "Those are German fighters. As long as those dots keep moving, don't worry about them. But if any of those dots stop moving, call out right away. Any dot that's not moving is coming right at us."

Figure 25-1: 301st Mission to Vienna, Austria on November 18, 1944.

The crew anxiously watched the distant dots, but the fighters kept their distance and did not attack the formation of B-17s. As the fighters disappeared over the horizon, Oscar said thoughtfully, "Maybe they were low on fuel or ammunition."

Robert Spice, the bombardier replied, "I don't care what the reason was, I'm just glad they didn't come after us."

The target was the Florisdorf Oil Refinery near Vienna, Austria. During the briefing they learned that heavy flak was expected, starting about nine miles from the target. As they approached within four miles of the target, they would come within range of sixty antiaircraft guns. Over the target, as many as 150 antiaircraft guns would be firing at them.

The planes reached the Initial Point and Skillings turned control of the plane over to Robert Spice. As bombardier, he would guide the plane from the IP to the target and release the bombs. From their seats in the plane's Plexiglas nose, Oscar and Spice saw hundreds of clouds scattered over the target area. They were small, but very dark, like baby thunder clouds. New clouds suddenly appeared, then gradually faded away.

At first, Oscar didn't realize what he was looking at. Then he understood. Those were clouds of flak from exploding antiaircraft shells.

"We can't fly into that," he told himself. "We'll lose the whole formation. I better check the route to the alternative target so I'll be ready when they abort this run."

He checked the route to the alternative target, but the order to abort did not come and the bombers did not turn away from the clouds of flak. The lead pilot held the course and the other planes followed in unwavering formation.

"Can't they see it?" Oscar thought with growing alarm. "Don't they know what that is?"

★ Click here to watch video

Figure 25-2: Bombers of the 301st Bomb Group fly through clouds of flak.

The bombers did not turn away, steadfastly maintaining their course, flying directly into the clouds of flak. They had started the bomb run. Until they dropped their bombs, the crews could not take evasive action of any kind.

Through the Plexiglas nose of the plane, Oscar watched the lead planes of the formation fly into the flak clouds. One by one the other planes followed them. Then it was their turn.

As Oscar's plane entered the flak clouds, it was rocked by near-silent explosions. To Oscar, many of the explosions seemed far too close for comfort. He'd hear the muffled "Whuff!" of the exploding shell, accompanied by a flash of red light.

"This can't be right!" Oscar thought. "Somebody's screwed up and sent us on a suicide mission. Oh God, this can't be right!"

Occasionally, a shell exploded under a wing, tossing the giant plane upwards like a toy. Other shells exploded around the plane, briefly illuminating the inside of the plane with an eerie red glow. Shrapnel from the closest shells pelted the plane like hail. Oscar was surprised the shrapnel didn't make much noise. It didn't even sound dangerous, kind of like gravel being tossed on a tin roof, but instead of bouncing it punched right through the thin aluminum skin of the plane.

Some of the shrapnel came in one side of the plane and went out the other, leaving little jagged holes in the skin of the airplane. The pieces that passed completely through the plane were bad, but the pieces that hit something on the way through the plane were worse. Bits of shrapnel bounced off supports and other heavy metal objects and ricocheted around inside the plane, shredding wires, hydraulic lines, instruments, and any airmen who happened to be in the way.

To Oscar, it seemed like every gunner in Germany was shooting right at them. But the German antiaircraft gunners weren't shooting at individual planes. They set the shells to explode at the same height as the bombers, then threw up a continuous barrage of exploding shells in the path of the formation and waited for the bombers to fly into them.

The aircrews could not affect the outcome. They could only pray that the plane and an exploding antiaircraft shell would not occupy the same place at the same time.

After what seemed like an eternity, the bombardier released the bombs, calling, "Bombs away!" into the intercom. The plane lurched upwards and the formation turned away from the flak. The focus of the mission changed from hitting the target to getting back safely. As some men put it, "Until we drop those bombs, we're flying for Uncle Sam. Once we let them go, we're flying for ourselves."

Gradually, the flak eased off as the bombers flew away from the heavily defended target. They weren't out of danger yet. They could still run into flak and fighters on the long trip out of enemy territory. But defenses focused on stopping the bombers before they reached the target. Once the bombs were dropped, the damage for that mission had been done. German fighter pilots followed, ready to finish off any bomber that fell out of formation, but the most ferocious opposition was usually encountered on the way to the target or during the actual bomb run.

★ Click here to watch video

Figure 25-3: German propaganda films documented German antiaircraft crews successfully downing Allied bombers.

Surprisingly, no one on Oscar's plane was hit by flak. Oscar found finger-sized holes through the fuselage of the plane above his navigator's desk. He picked a small piece of shrapnel off the floor and blew some little bits of debris off of the charts on his navigation desk. Aside from small shrapnel holes scattered around the plane, they had come through without serious damage.

The bombardier smiled a tight smile, gave Oscar the thumbs-up sign and said, "That's two down. Only thirty-three to go!"

Oscar smiled ruefully and thought to himself, "That's two down—but thirty-three more to go? We're supposed to do that thirty-three more times? We can be lucky once or twice, but we can't expect to be lucky thirty-three more times!"

Just then Skillings came on the intercom and warned the crew to be extra alert for German fighters. "That fighter group we saw on the way in has had plenty of time to land for fuel and ammunition, so there's a good chance we'll run into them on the way back. Stay alert and sing out if you spot any enemy planes."

The entire crew scanned the horizon for enemy fighters, but none appeared.

About an hour after they left the target, Skillings muttered uneasily, "That plane ahead is in trouble. It's throwing oil from the #2 engine."

Moments later, the crippled B-17 lurched upwards into the propellers of another plane. The lower plane broke away from the upper plane, then went into a spin, narrowly missing one of the other planes in the formation.

Oscar called out, "I see three chutes!" Moments later, one of the gunners yelled, "I see two more chutes!" Finally, the tail gunner added his report, "It's in a spin, heading towards the ground. I don't see any more chutes."

The intercom went silent. As the last chute disappeared into the clouds below, Oscar thought about the five men who had parachuted into enemy territory and the five crewmen who apparently went down with the plane.

★ Click here to watch video

Figure 25-4: A crewman parachutes from a B-17 over enemy territory.

Oscar continued to monitor their position as the B-17 lumbered south toward their base. Two hours later, everyone breathed a sigh of relief when Oscar informed them they had crossed back into friendly territory. A hundred things could still go wrong, but at least they could stop worrying about German antiaircraft crews.

As they passed over the Adriatic, the formation dropped to a lower altitude so the crew could warm up and take off their oxygen masks. Oscar ate a half-frozen Spam sandwich and drank lukewarm coffee from his thermos.

Returning bombers approached the runway and went into a holding pattern as individual planes peeled off for a landing.

The engine of a B-17 flying ahead of them suddenly burst into flames. It lost altitude and the crew began to bail out. "Eight, nine, ten!" yelled the bombardier, counting the men as they jumped from the burning plane. Moments after the last man jumped, the burning engine fell off, taking the fire with it. The unmanned plane glided towards the ground and crashed.

During the debriefing, Oscar learned the last plane had been piloted by Captain William Ludwig, the former commander of the 352nd Squadron. Captain Ludwig had requested permission for an immediate landing due to an engine malfunction, but had been ordered to keep circling the airfield and to land in turn.

When he found himself unable to control the aircraft, Captain Ludwig ordered the crew to bail out. The rest of the crew jumped and landed safely. Captain Ludwig was the last to jump. By that time, the plane was too low. His parachute did not open and he was killed on impact.

Like the rest of the crew, Oscar was unsettled by this first combat mission. As he lay in his bunk that night he thought, "Men died today. I could have died. How can they ask a man to go through that thirty-five times?"

He knew he would have to do it again.

As he dropped off to sleep, he wondered if he could do it again.

★ Click here to watch video

Figure 25-5: After landing, the crews went through a lengthy debriefing process.

★★★ Ordinary Heroes: Six Stars in the Window ★★★
26. I'm going to come back

November, 1944: Like most soldiers, Johnny received thirty days leave after basic training. When he got on the train heading north from Green Bay, he found a recent copy of the *Mining Journal* someone had left on the seat. In it, he read about the Lukkarinen family from Negaunee. They had two sons, both in the service. One son, Sergeant Arthur Lukkarinen, was killed in a bombing raid over Bremen Germany in 1943. Now the second son, Private Fred Lukkarinen, a rifleman, had been killed while fighting in France on September 15, 1944.

Johnny dropped the paper to his lap and looked out the window at the passing trees. "Those poor folks," he thought. "To have two sons, then lose them both. Their family is gone. With their sons in different branches of the service, they probably figured at least one of them would make it home."

His thoughts turned to his own brothers: Al in Washington, George in Florida, Art in France, Oscar headed overseas, and Reuben near Chicago. He thought about his own uncertain future as an infantry replacement. "I guess there's no guaranteed safety for any of us. All we can do is trust in the Lord to see us through."

The train arrived in Ishpeming. Johnny climbed out and looked around expectantly. There was Lilly! Johnny swept her up in an enthusiastic bear hug. His father stood nearby, wearing an uncharacteristic smile. He and Johnny looked at each other for a moment, then solemnly shook hands.

Lilly said Johnny looked very grown up in his uniform. She could hardly believe this fit young man in uniform was her little Johnny, the boy she had raised since the age of five. Johnny threw his bag in the back of the car and they headed home.

Johnny dropped his duffel bag in the boy's bedroom, then said he was going to take a walk around West Ishpeming to see what had changed. Still wearing his uniform, he headed down the hill, thinking West Ishpeming seemed much smaller than he remembered.

His friend Bobby Emmanuelson saw Johnny walking towards the school in his uniform. "Johnny!" he cried, running across the street to slap his friend on the back and shake hands. "I'm so glad you're back. Tell me all about the army!"

Johnny told him a bit about basic training, emphasizing the machine guns, bazooka, and the day they drove a tank over his foxhole. After a while Johnny said he had some things he needed to do. Bobby asked if he could tag along, but Johnny said mysteriously, "No, I need to do these things myself."

Johnny went home, changed into his camp clothes, and announced he was going to Flat Rock hunting camp. He explained to Lilly, "I don't have much time. I figure I'd better go to camp while I have the chance. Besides, deer season is starting in a couple of days. I ain't gonna miss that!"

Johnny walked out to Flat Rock with his deer rifle and a pack full of supplies. It felt strange to be at camp alone. It was so very quiet without the rest of his brothers. During the day, Johnny walked through the woods alone, checking for deer sign. In the evenings he sat by the fire and thought about years past.

The night before deer season opened, Johnny cleaned his rifle and thought about how busy the camp had been in previous years, with all the Koski brothers checking their rifles and reminiscing about previous hunting seasons.

Johnny got his deer that year. He dressed it, dragged it back to camp, and hung it up like his brothers had taught him. The last night he stayed at the camp, Johnny sat on a log overlooking the little pond called Koski Lake. It was a cold, crisp night and there seemed to be a billion stars in the sky. Johnny thought, "I love this place so much. I don't think there's anything better than a night at camp. I think I'd stay here forever if I could."

Although he loved his time at camp, Johnny decided he'd better spend his last few days of leave with his family in West Ishpeming. As he locked up the Flat Rock camp, he took one more look around and mentally said goodbye to his favorite place in the world. He hoisted his pack, laden with venison, and started the long walk back home.

In the following days, Johnny often walked around West Ishpeming, stopping for a neighborly cup of coffee with friends and neighbors. He visited his sister Martha, who was married and lived on the other side of West Ishpeming. On one visit, he found Martha's daughter Nonny sitting on the curb outside her house, crying to herself.

"What's the matter, Nonny?" he asked.

She replied that her older sister Jackie had been teasing her.

Johnny sat down next to her on the curb and said, "Don't worry Nonny, if she picks on you again, I'll come back from the war to get you."

That made a huge impression on the little girl. From then on, whenever Nonny felt alone or afraid, she'd think, "It's all right. If it gets too bad, Uncle Johnny will come back for me."

For Thanksgiving, Lilly borrowed ration tickets from the neighbors and purchased two chickens from Kallatsa's store. She roasted the chickens and made mashed potatoes, two of Johnny's favorite dishes. After an hour in the oven, the chickens looked like they were done. Lilly tugged on a chicken leg to see if the meat was tender, but the leg snapped back as if held by rubber bands.

Lilly cooked the chickens for another half-hour. They got darker, but still felt like rubber. Finally, Lilly gave up. She took the chickens from the oven and served them. Nobody complained about the tough chickens, but they didn't say anything good either. They just chewed and chewed and finally swallowed as best they could.

After the meal, Lilly quietly slipped out the back door. When she didn't return, Johnny stepped outside and found her sitting on the steps, sobbing. He sat down next to her, put his arm around her and said, "Don't cry, Lilly."

Lilly replied, "This is one of your last meals at home. I wanted it to be special for you, but those chickens were terrible. I don't want you to remember me for such a horrible meal."

Johnny replied comfortingly, "Oh Lilly, I know you tried. You've always tried. You've cooked so many good meals and done so much for us over the years. Two tough chickens won't make any difference!"

"Someday," he continued, "maybe I'll get married and have a little girl. If I do, I think I'll call her Lilly after you." Then he grinned and his brown eyes twinkled. "Of course, that's assuming my wife agrees."

Lilly smiled through her tears at the thought of little Johnny with a wife and children of his own. It warmed Lilly's heart to know that Johnny appreciated what she had tried to do. She'd worked so hard for so many years, yet the family rarely thanked her. Johnny hugged Lilly close, she dried her tears, and they went back inside to visit with the rest of the family.

★ Click here to watch video

Figure 26-1: Unidentified customers outside Kallatsa's store, which carried everything from meat to shoe polish.

The next morning Johnny woke early. As he packed his duffel bag in the boys' bedroom, Edna Mae tiptoed in and watched. When he pulled the drawstring tight, she shyly asked, "Johnny, why do you have to go to war?"

Johnny knelt and put his hand on her shoulder. "Do you see these empty bunks Edna Mae? The other brothers have gone to war. If I didn't go, how do you think I'd feel when they come home?"

Johnny continued reassuringly, "I need to know I did everything I could to help win this war. I need to know I did my part. Don't worry Edna Mae, I'm going to come home. I promise. The war will probably be over before I get there anyway."

Edna Mae bit her lip and tried not to cry.

Taking off his graduation watch, he slipped it around her wrist. "You keep this watch safe for me, Edna Mae. I'll be back to get it when the war is over."

"Ah-oogah! Ah-oogah!" Their father was outside, blowing the horn in the old Model A.

Johnny shouldered his duffle bag. "Come on! Father is waiting!"

They didn't talk much on the drive to the Ishpeming train station. There wasn't anything left to say. The "Old 400" waited on the tracks at the station. Scattered clumps of people hugged and said goodbye to handsome young men in uniform. Johnny hugged Edna Mae and Lilly and shook hands with his father.

Johnny climbed up the steps of the train. He turned, smiled, then waved goodbye. Then he was gone.

As the train rolled away from the Ishpeming train station, Edna Mae held the watch to her heart and whispered, "I'll keep this watch safe for you Johnny. I promise!"

★ Click here to watch video

Figure 26-2: Johnny Koski standing on the snowy street outside the Koski house, possibly when he was home on leave in November, 1944.

★★★ Ordinary Heroes: Six Stars in the Window ★★★
27. We could'a been killed

December 10, 1944: Art ate breakfast in a large building near the railroad tracks in Plombiers, a small Belgian town just a few miles from the German border. The town was so close to the border that the train station sign identified it as both Plombiers and Bleiburg. Plombiers was its Belgian name, Bleiburg was its German name.

There was optimistic talk at breakfast. The Germans were being steadily pushed back by the British, Canadians, and Americans in the west and by the Russians in the east. Most of the soldiers at Art's table believed the Germans would surrender "any day now."

Art wasn't so sure. It was one thing to push the Germans out of France and Belgium. It was another thing to pursue them through the heavy fortifications of the Siegfried Line and into the heartland of Germany.

★ Click here to watch video

Figure 27-1: As 1944 drew to a close, the Allied armies tried to prepare for a winter at war.

After breakfast, Art followed Sergeant Donald Stark and Private First Class Wilbur Vreeland out the door. He fell in step with a group of men walking back to the H&S Company headquarters train, nodding to Sergeant Babcock as he passed.

As his feet crunched over the gravel railroad bed, Art gradually became aware of plane engines thrumming in the sky. As the sound grew louder, one of the men said, "Don't those planes sound awfully low?"

Figure 27-2: Men of H&S Company posing before the train used as mobile headquarters.

Another man replied, "Yeah, why would they be flying so low? There aren't supposed to be Germans around here."

A group of planes flashed into sight. Everything happened at once. The men saw flashes from the wings of the planes. Machine gun bullets pelted the ground. Someone yelled, "They're Germans!" Everybody ran for cover.

Art dove down a shallow embankment and rolled into a muddy ditch. Other men rolled into the ditch around him.

Within moments, it was over. Art could hear someone moaning nearby. He waited a few moments to make sure the planes were not circling around for another pass, then crawled out of the ditch to see if he could help.

Somebody yelled, "Those were American planes! Why were they shooting at us?"

Sergeant Babcock replied, "One looked like a Messerschmitt. The others were American planes. But those weren't American pilots. They were so low I could see their blue Luftwaffe uniforms."

Sergeant Donald Stark and Private First Class Wilbur Vreeland emerged from under the train where bullets had hit so close the men were sprayed with bits of gravel. Vreeland exclaimed, "That was damn close! They almost got us! We could'a been killed!"

Cries of "Medic! Over here!" rang out and the men of the 332nd spread out to assist the wounded.

★ Click here to watch video

Figure 27-3: Gun cameras recorded attacks on ground targets, such as this attack on a supply train.

Art saw a soldier looking down the embankment near the engine of the train. Art ran over to him. The soldier glanced at Art, then just pointed down the embankment where two men lay unmoving, riddled with bullets. Ona Miller and John Woodward had been killed. Three other men were wounded.

As Art helped carry the bodies of the men who had been killed, he wondered, "Can it get much worse than this?"

Figure 27-4: Carl "Art" Koski with his rifle in a ditch with the H&S Company train in background.

★★★ Ordinary Heroes: Six Stars in the Window ★★★
28. Who will sleep here next?

★ Click here to watch video

Figure 28-1: Oscar found that even the unthinkable can become routine. By the end of November, life had become a blur of early morning briefings and hazardous missions in the skies above Europe.

November 19, 1944: At 3:00 a.m. Oscar was rudely awakened for the third morning in a row. At first he thought someone had made a mistake. They'd just flown two combat missions, one yesterday and one the day before. Surely they weren't going to be sent out again today.

But it wasn't a mistake, Oscar and his crew were flying again. During the briefing, he learned they were going back to Austria, this time attacking the Winterhafen Oil Storage Depot near Vienna.

They donned their heavy flight suits, then clambered onto Jeeps for the drive to the plane. For Oscar, climbing into the plane was much harder than it had been the day before. Yesterday, his fear had been somewhat balanced by his naive excitement about his first combat mission.

Today, he knew what lay ahead. He could envision planes flying into clouds of flak. He remembered the sound of shrapnel passing through the thin aluminum skin of the plane. He knew planes would be lost and men would die. He knew he could be killed today. He knew that once he climbed into that plane, there was nothing that he could do to change his fate.

Oscar grabbed the edge of the hatch and hoisted himself into the plane. As he forced his shaky hands to arrange his navigation instruments, Oscar could tell the others felt the same stress. The bombardier's eyes were unnaturally bright and the pilot's voice was tense as he read through the preflight checklist. They were all afraid. But they were going anyway. They knew what they were flying into, but they were determined to do their duty. Oscar felt proud to be part of this crew.

With a deep breath, Oscar tried to put his fear out of his mind and focused on plotting the course to the target.

The mission went easier than Oscar expected. Twenty-six B-17s from the 301st joined a formation of 164 B-17s. Everything went well. All planes dropped their bombs on target and no planes were lost.

After the plane landed, Oscar found two new shrapnel holes over his navigator's desk. He thoughtfully ran his finger over the raised edges of the holes in the skin of the plane, then searched for the exit holes to see where the shrapnel had exited the plane. One piece of shrapnel had missed him by several feet. He couldn't find the exit hole for the other piece of shrapnel. It must have bounced off a strut or embedded itself in something. He surreptitiously felt his arms and legs to make sure it had not hit him.

The next day Oscar flew again, his fourth mission in a row. His plane joined a formation of 509 heavy bombers headed for the Blechammer Oil Refinery in Germany. Before they reached the target, all thirty-six planes from the 301st were diverted to an alternative target, the marshaling yards near Brno, Czechoslovakia. They encountered light resistance and suffered no losses. The planes that attacked the main target were not so lucky, losing sixteen B-17s and two fighters to fierce resistance. Over 160 men were lost.

Figure 28-2: A stricken B-17 goes down, smoke billowing from at least two engines.

On November 21, heavy cloud cover forced cancellation of all missions. After four combat missions in a row, Oscar got a day off. He read a book and chatted with some of the other men, trying not to think too much about the last four missions or the thirty-one missions that lay ahead.

On November 22 the weather improved. Oscar and his crew did not fly, but 549 bombers from the 15th Army Air Force attacked the marshaling yard at Regensberg. The mission went fairly well. One bomber from the 301st suffered minor damage and one crew member was injured when his plane went into a spin.

When the crews returned from Regensberg, they couldn't stop talking about the super-fast German fighters that had streaked past them. After the debriefings, intelligence determined the aircrews had spotted two Me 262 jet fighters and one Me 163 rocket-powered plane. These were the first jet-powered or rocket-powered planes any of the airmen had seen. The airmen excitedly discussed the flight characteristics of those German planes, trying not to mention the obvious fact that the Allies had no such planes.

Bad weather returned and the 301st was grounded again. After a few days on the ground, Oscar's natural ebullience returned, as demonstrated in a letter that he wrote to his brother Al. Al was serving with the 63rd Coast Artillery Anti-Aircraft and his wife had recently given birth to their daughter Karen.

```
November 24, 1944

Somewhere in Italy

Dear Al:

I've been meaning to write for six months but writing
requires an amount of mental effort which of course
gives me an excellent alibi.

I also wish to congratulate you on the birth of your
daughter. I do hope the mother is making out well.
```

I'm having a bull session with a fellow navigator about human psychology, good places to hunt rabbits and Polaris landfalls (please differentiate between windfalls) & started writing this letter 3 hours ago & I'm still at it.

I suppose you heard from the DNB that American terror fliers raided Vienna on Nov. 19. Well it may please you to know (at least as much as it displeases me) that I was there bouncing flak fragments off the instrument panel.

In case you don't know---the F/O stands for Flight Officer (quite a special case as it is generally understood to mean something else). In the case of the Air Force is synonymous to anything & everything which aids this most commendable organization. I don't want you to think I am belittling my rank for after all we can call P.F.C.'s subordinate.

I thought Hitler would certainly surrender as soon as he heard I arrived here, but obviously he's crazier than I thought. If you happen to correspond with the gentleman mentioned will you please convey unto him the hopelessness of any further resistance as General Marshall told me the other day. "We consider you a sufficient reply to all of the German High Commands V1s, V2, V3, V4 & etc."

Of course that's not going to bust the buttons on my blouse. I bought it four sizes too large.

I suppose as morale officer you'd be interested in putting your outfit in exuberant spirits.

Suggestion: Issue of all day suckers and a handful of steel painted, double pointed roasted toasted peanuts encased in an ermine diamond studded case guaranteed not to rip, slip, or show rag sag, or bag in the knees, not to mention a fur lined jock strap with twin exhaust stacks or for those jet propulsion fans a side pocket for the 8-ball and a turbo supercharger. Some of the more cautious might even add a bottle of insect repellent to keep the First Sergeant away.

It's getting late & I'm afraid somebody has to lock the tent fly shut so I'll close.

So long. Good Luck and God Bless you.

Oscar

★ Click here to watch video   ★ Click here for Web Info

Figure 28-3: Transcript of a letter from Oscar to Al.

As November, drew to a close, Oscar had been with the 301st for about three weeks. He had flown four combat missions, leaving thirty-one missions to complete his tour of duty. In those three weeks, the 301st had lost six B-17s, each carrying a crew of ten men. Sixty men from the 301st had either gone down with their planes or parachuted to an unknown fate in enemy territory.

After each mission, Squadron staffers stripped the beds of the men who had been lost and boxed up their personal effects for shipment back to the states. By the next morning, no trace of the missing crews or planes remained, except in the memories of the men who had flown with them. It was as if the lost fliers had never existed.

Replacement crews arrived regularly, moving into tents that had been occupied just days before by crews who had been shot down. As he watched one new crew settle in, Oscar thought back to the first day his crew had arrived at Lucera 8 and had been assigned to this tent. Somehow, he'd never thought about the crews that had lived in that tent before him.

That night, Oscar lay awake on his cot, thinking about the men who had slept in this tent. Were they dead or alive or in a German POW camp? Had any of them completed their thirty-five missions and gone home? How long would it be before yet another crew moved into this tent? Who would sleep in this cot after he was gone?

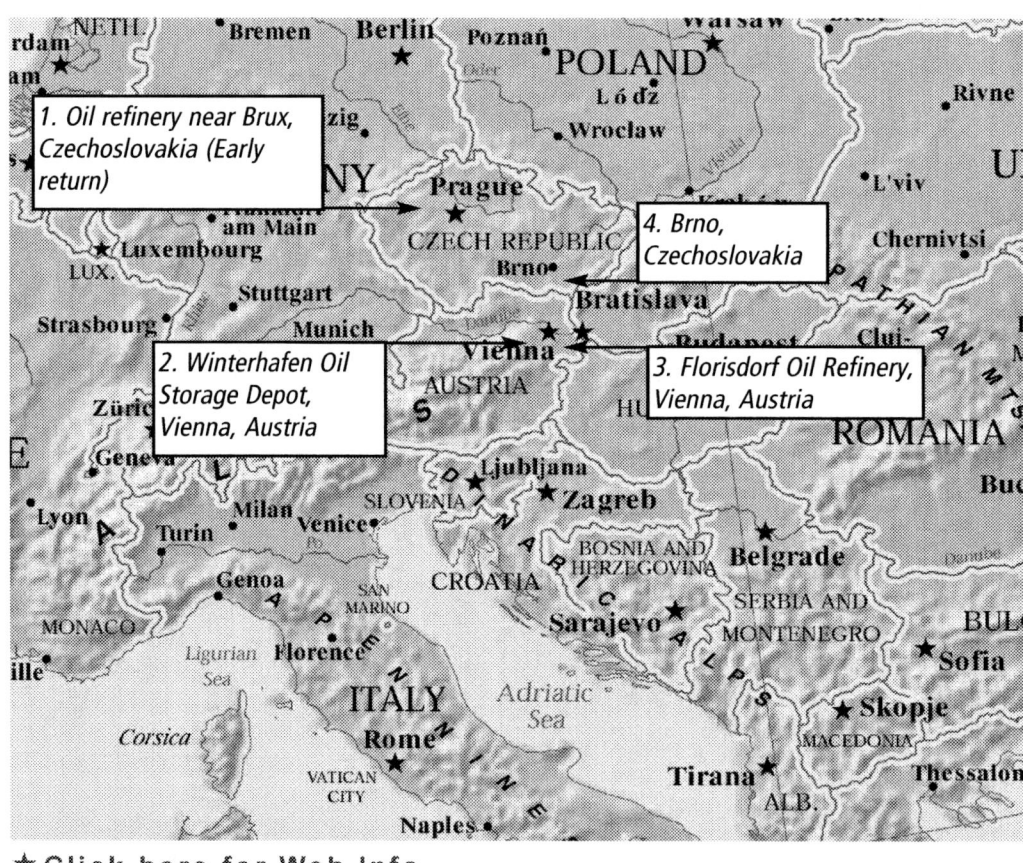

★ Click here for Web Info

Figure 28-4: Oscar's combat missions during November, 1944.

★★★ Ordinary Heroes: Six Stars in the Window ★★★
29. You'd better finish up

December 17, 1944: Art had been in Plombiers, Belgium for less than two weeks when he was awakened in the middle of the night by the sound of men and equipment. He stepped outside and saw a steady column of infantry, trucks, and half-tracks moving through the village. All other traffic was forced to the side of the road as the military police made way for the column.

A soldier standing nearby said, "Something's up! It looks like we're mounting a major attack on the Germans."

Art gestured to the column and replied, "But why are they headed west? Germany's the other way."

The men stood there, uneasy about the massive, inexplicable movement of combat troops back to the west, away from Germany. After a few minutes, they decided someone would eventually tell them what was happening. In the meantime, they'd better get ready to move out.

The next day, German Me 109 fighter planes attacked D Company of the 332nd. A fragmentation bomb hit a truck, wounding six men. Two men from C Company were wounded by mines while clearing a tunnel entrance. Later that day, the HQ train was strafed by German fighters. Two men were killed, one man lost his leg, and one man was slightly injured.

The men of the 332nd didn't know it yet, but an entire German Army was headed their way.

★ Click here to watch video

Figure 29-1: On December 16, the Germans launched an unexpected, major counter-offensive.

On the morning of December 16, the German Army had launched operation Wacht am Rhein. In the predawn darkness, German artillery bombarded American positions in a quiet sector of the line in the densely wooded Ardennes forest near the Belgian-German border. As the artillery shells stopped falling, overwhelming numbers of German tanks and infantry appeared out of the fog, quickly overrunning the American positions.

The 106th Infantry Division bore the brunt of the attack. The 106th was a new division and had been in Europe only ten days, stationed in this supposedly "quiet sector" of the Ardennes to gain some frontline experience before being thrown into battle. Within hours, the 422nd and 423rd Regiments of the 106th Infantry Division were surrounded. The men fought hard, but they were severely outnumbered and outgunned. One of the last radio transmissions from the 423rd was a terse request: "Can you get some ammunition through?" Then all contact with the regiment was lost.

Within days, 6,697 men of the 106th were taken prisoner. As they were marched into Germany, some members of the 106th picked away at the threads holding the Golden Lions patch to their sleeve, ashamed that their unit had surrendered so quickly. The officers in charge of the 422nd and 423rd Regiments had faced a difficult choice. The regiments were surrounded by overwhelming forces. They were out of ammunition and could not be resupplied. If they continued to fight, they would be slaughtered.

★ Click here to watch video

Figure 29-2: Thousands of Allied soldiers were taken prisoner during the early days of the battle. Among those prisoners were black GIs from the Engineer Regiments who had every reason to worry about their treatment at the hands of the Nazis.

Surrender was a bitter choice, but the commanders of the 422nd and 423rd had no other option.

Ten Panzer divisions drove through the American lines, attempting to take supply depots and drive a wedge between the northern and southern armies. Three armies participated in the German attack. The 7th German Army attacked in the south through Luxembourg. The 5th SS Panzer Army attacked in the middle, passing through Bastogne. The largest group, the 6th SS Panzer Army, was ordered to take Liege, then move northwest to Antwerp.

At first, the Allied commanders didn't realize what was happening. Heavy clouds and fog kept most American airplanes on the ground. As the Germans overran front-line units and drove deep into American-held territory, communication was cut off. Days after the 422nd and 423rd infantry surrendered, as they marched into Germany as prisoners of war, the commander of the 106th kept trying to reach them on the radio.

To the GIs on the frontlines, the massive German advance seemed unstoppable. Only the German commanders knew what a desperate gamble they had taken in launching the offensive. The German tanks did not have sufficient fuel to complete the attack. Their only hope was to capture the American fuel depots like the one near Liege, Belgium, which was operated by the 332nd engineers.

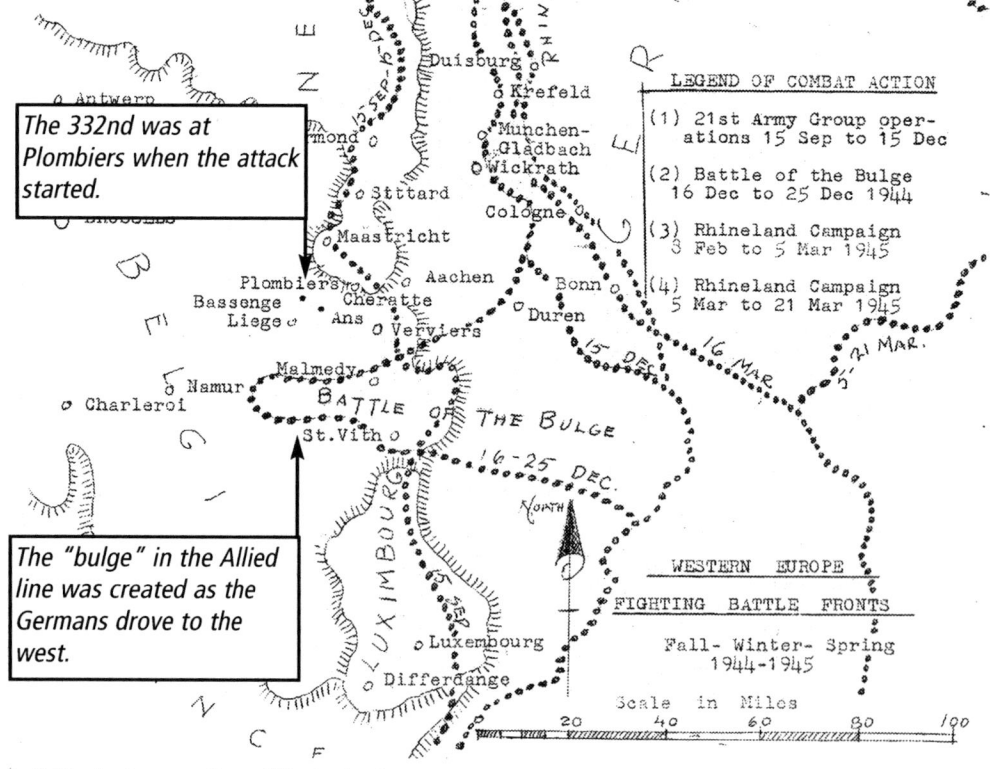

★ Click here for Web Info

Figure 29-3: Map showing the German advance during the Battle of the Bulge. When the Germans attacked, the 332nd Engineers were stationed in Plombiers, just north of Liege, very close to the German border.

Liege was a primary target for another reason, the bridges over the Meuse River, west of the city. If the Germans could capture the fuel depot and the bridges over the Meuse, they hoped to be able to drive all the way to Antwerp on the coast. This maneuver would split the American and British forces and deprive the allies of Antwerp as a port of supply.

Rumors ran rampant. Some said the Germans had reached Antwerp. Others said thousands of German soldiers, dressed in American uniforms, had parachuted behind the lines. One rumor claimed the Germans had perfected some sort of death ray, a weapon that harnessed the energy of the sun and could vaporize an entire city. Not too many soldiers believed that—nobody had a weapon that could vaporize an entire city.

Hundreds of thousands of men on both sides were rushed into the area as a battle of epic proportions got underway, a battle that later became known as the Battle of the Bulge because the German penetration created a massive bulge in the Allied lines.

★ Click here to watch video

Figure 29-4: The Germans quickly overran the surprised Americans in the Ardennes, penetrating deep into Belgium.

As the extent of the German attack became known, the Allies responded. The 332nd Regiment was ordered to move back to the relative safety of Liege. Men and equipment took to the roads in a convoy of seventy vehicles, including heavy equipment, jeeps, trucks, and the H&S Company half-track. The men driving the vehicles were issued M15 thermite grenades. If the Germans overran the slow moving vehicles, the men were ordered to put the thermite grenades on the engine blocks and pull the pin. The device would ignite and burn at very high temperatures, destroying the engine block and making the vehicle useless to the enemy.

As they approached Liege, the 332nd convoy was ordered to pulled to the side of the road to let a British convoy pass. Someone was moving in the right direction, east, toward the Germans. As the Brits moved past, the Americans learned it was General Montgomery and his men, moving forward to try to stem the German attack.

Along the way, one company from the 332nd was left to repair a critical bridge the Germans kept hitting with buzz bombs. Their orders were ominous: stay at the task until the American forces returned or until the Germans drove them from the bridge.

Axis Sally, the English-speaking German propaganda reporter, warned American soldiers in Liege that 2,500 V1 and V2 rockets were aimed at them. A rain of rockets fell on Liege. One landed on a fuel truck driven by a soldier from the 332nd, obliterating the truck and the driver in a massive explosion. As they waited for the burning debris to be pushed off the road, the other truck drivers tried not to think about what would happen if their truck was hit by a rocket.

The 332nd received orders to place demolition charges on all bridges along the Meuse from Liege to Namur. After placing the explosives, the men were told to take up defensive positions at each bridge. If German troops or tanks approached, they were to hold them off and blow up the bridge. Their orders were simple: stop the Germans at any cost.

Just as the men of F Company finished placing demolition charges on the railroad bridge at Namur, they heard the sound of an approaching plane. Remembering the strafing incidents from the past week, they dove for cover. A German plane flew low over the bridge, dropping a bomb, which landed near the bridge.

The explosion set off the demolition charges and the entire bridge was destroyed, much to the surprise of the GIs and probably to the surprise of the German pilot who wouldn't have expected such a massive explosion from a single bomb.

Having completed their assignments, Art and the weary enlisted men of H&S Company were treated to a Christmas Eve dinner in the dining car usually reserved for officers. Art marveled at the generous portions of turkey, mashed potatoes, and stuffing. After months of lousy food, hard work, stress, and cold, it was a rare evening of warmth and good food.

As they finished eating, someone snapped a photo, preserving the moment. It was 10:35 p.m., Christmas Eve, 1944. Sergeant Tom Jones sat under the clock at the end of the table, enjoying a drink and a fine cigar. Carl "Art" Koski is just barely visible, on the right side of the photo, fourth person from the front.

The convivial evening abruptly ended when Captain Towne burst into the dining car. "You'd better finish up! We've just received orders to establish blockades on all roads leading to Liege. S2 (intelligence) figures the Germans need fuel and are headed here. It's our job to stop them. Everyone outside, pronto!"

Figure 29-5: Enlisted men of H&S Company eat dinner in railroad car, 10:35 p.m., Christmas Eve, 1944. Sergeant Tom Jones is sitting under the clock. Carl "Art" Koski is seated on the right side, fourth person back, his head just partially visible. Seated on the left side, front to back, are Waltz, McGilvray, Spicer, Hepner, Leverson, and Behrens. Seated on the right side, front to back are Vigeant, Whitley, Webb, Koski, Gruber, and Whitcomb.

★★★ Ordinary Heroes: Six Stars in the Window ★★★
30. Don't they know they're the bad guys?

December 2, 1944: After being grounded for almost two weeks due to bad weather, Oscar found himself crouched in front of his navigator's bench once again. The original target was Blechhammer, but the planes were diverted and instead attacked a bridge near Gyor, Hungary.

The first part of the mission went well. On the return flight, 1st Lieutenant Eugene Tillotson from the 419th Squadron radioed that his #2 engine was leaking oil and requested permission to land on an island in the Adriatic. A newly assigned major denied his request, ordering him to stay with the formation. A short time later, the lieutenant radioed that the leaking engine had caught fire.

★ Click here to watch video

Figure 30-1: The Germans used radar and coastal defenses to identify and neutralize bombing missions flying north from Italy.

The fire soon spread to the inside of the plane and Lieutenant Tillotson ordered the crew to bail out. Six crewmen managed to parachute out of the plane. The other four went into the Adriatic with the plane. Four of the six crewmen who bailed out were picked up by British ships. Six of the crew did not survive.

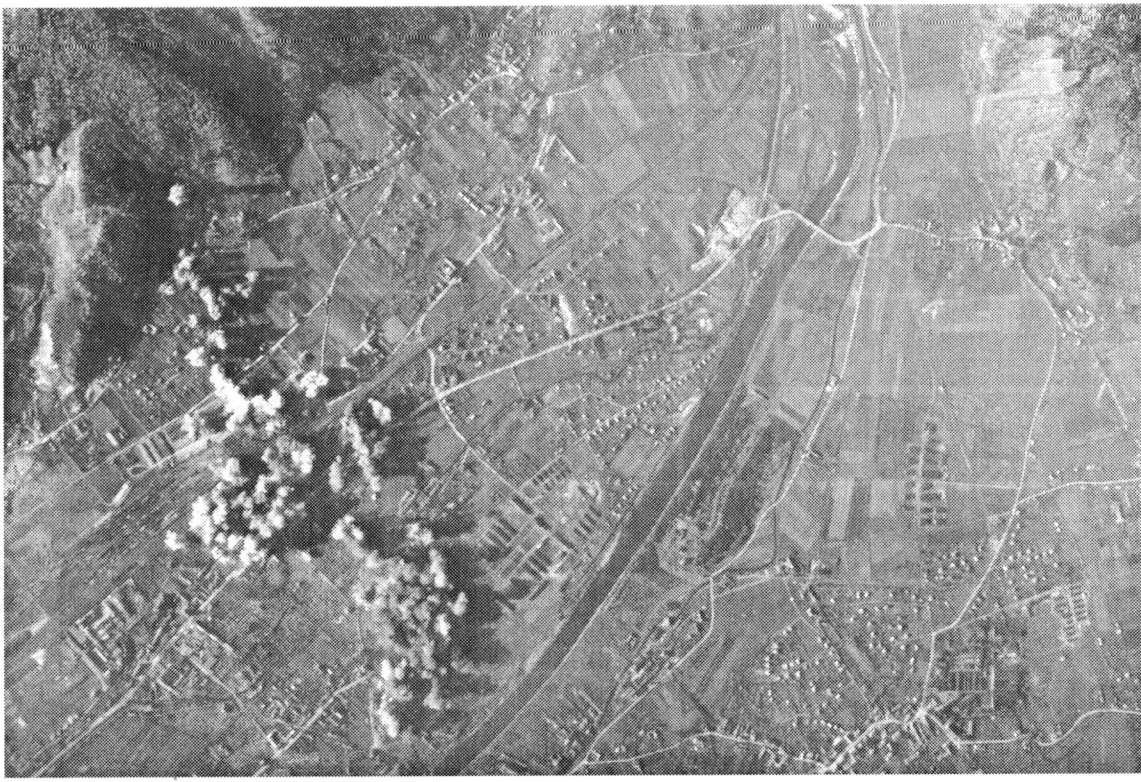

★ Click here for Web Info

Figure 30-2: Bombs from the 301st explode near Graz, Austria.

On December 6, Oscar flew with a different crew against the Brux Oil Refinery in Czechoslovakia. Heavy clouds covered the target area, so they dropped their bombs on a secondary target near Zagreb, Yugoslavia and headed home. All planes made it safely home.

Oscar preferred flying with his original crew, but some officer up the chain of command had decided it would be psychologically healthier if the airmen occasionally flew with different crews. Oscar didn't like that policy. None of the men did. They all preferred to go into combat with men they knew and trusted. But this policy did encourage airmen to mix with members of other crews.

Oscar became good friends with a pilot by the name of Ralph Stueve. Oscar and Ralph both loved jokes, perhaps part of the reason they became such good friends. Stueve's crew often sat with Oscar's crew in the mess hall. At dinner, Stueve would set his tray on the table, fold his hands, and ask "Isn't anybody going to say Grace?"

Somebody would shout "Grace!," the men would groan at the stale joke, and they all would dig in. The joke wasn't that funny, at least not after the fourth or fifth time they heard it. But they kept it up because it brought continuity to their lives. No matter what they might have been through on that day's mission, the men knew that Ralph Stueve would set his tray on the table, grin, and ask "Isn't anybody going to say Grace?" As long as he did that, everything was going to be okay.

Some missions were less than successful. On December 11, Oscar flew on a mission against the Moosbierbaum oil refinery near Vienna, Austria. It was a large formation consisting of 253 heavy bombers and 159 fighters. Unfortunately most of the bombs missed the target. Some landed in fields as far as two miles from the target area. After the mission, one crewman joked that German farmers "preferred to do their own plowing and didn't need help from the 301st."

But bombing those fields had cost lives. Two B-17s were lost. The B-17 flown by Lieutenant Cliff Morris of the 32nd Squadron of the 301st was hit by flak just after the bomb release. The #1 prop ran away, the #2 engine cooler was damaged, and the #3 engine started to run erratically. Lieutenant Morris decided he could not make it back to base and landed at a Soviet-held airfield near Debrecen, Hungary.

One other bomber from the 301st sustained major damage and nineteen others sustained minor damage.

Oscar flew again on December 16 as 526 B-17 and B-24 bombers flew against targets in Brux, Czechoslovakia. From his position in the nose of the plane, Oscar saw fireballs blossom in the sky below as heavy flak tore into the low-flying B-24s. Twelve B-24s were shot down on the Brux mission. Another hundred and twenty men did not make it back to their bunks that night.

Flying back from the target, several crews noticed a B-17 with markings from the 2nd Bomb Group attempting to join into the formation. That was odd, since the 2nd Bomb Group was not flying that mission. The gunners kept the B-17 in their sights while the lead plane attempted to make radio contact. The unknown plane refused to respond. The squadron leader decided it must be a captured plane, flown by Germans, so the gunners were ordered to fire on the unidentified plane. As soon as they opened fire, the plane left the formation and headed back towards German territory.

The missions started to blur together in Oscar's mind. Most of the missions seemed the same: the early morning briefing, the long, cold flight to the target, the bomb run, sometimes lurching through heavy flak, sometimes strangely unopposed, then the long, cold flight back to base, always alert for approaching fighters or the sound of a faltering engine.

If all went well, they'd get back to the base before dusk, go through the long debriefing session, then try to get some rest. They might fly again the next morning, maybe in a few days, or maybe not until the next week.

On each mission, the target area far below them looked like an elaborate toy train set with roads, train tracks, bridges, farms, and miniature toy buildings scattered about. As the bombs hit, small plumes of smoke and debris rose into the air, but from 30,000 feet, they didn't seem that destructive. Sometimes, when the flak and the fighters weren't too heavy, it seemed more like a game than a war.

The bombardiers always tried to drop the bombs on military targets, but from 30,000 feet, it was difficult to distinguish civilians from soldiers.

Sometimes, as he fell asleep on his cot, Oscar would once again see the bombs falling on the target, and for a moment—just for a moment—he'd imagine what it was like on the ground when those bombs hit. In his imagination, he'd feel the earth shake and see buildings collapse in clouds of debris as the heavy bombs rained down from the sky.

Figure 30-3a: Bombs from the 301st fall near Wiener Neustadter, Austria.

Sometimes he felt guilty about his role in the war and the destruction they were causing, but he would try to remind himself that the world was locked in a fierce battle for the future of civilization. If there ever was a war between good and evil, this was it. Yes, there probably were civilian casualties, but the bombing was necessary. It could shorten this terrible war and save countless lives on both sides. It was just best not to think too much about what might be happening on the ground below.

Some missions were not at all like games and would never be forgotten by the men who flew them. On December 17 the 15th AAF sent 527 heavy bombers against the oil refineries at Blechhammer and Odertal in Germany. On this mission, the bombers came under heavy fighter attack before they reached the target. The intercom crackled as the gunners tracked the incoming fighters: "Bandits, 6 o'clock high! Bandits, 6 o'clock high!"

Oscar gripped the handle of his machine gun and scanned the horizon. Twelve Me 109s flashed past, firing at the lumbering bombers in their tight formation. Two B-17s were hit and fell behind the rest of the formation. The fighters closed in on the straggling bombers, like wolves after a struggling deer. The rest of the formation droned on towards the target, leaving the stragglers to their uncertain fate.

Figure 30-3b: Dust rises as the bombs strike targets on the ground.

Between Brno, Czechoslovakia and Vienna, the B-17s were attacked again, this time by eighty to a hundred German fighters. The intercom went wild as crewmen called out the positions of the incoming fighters: "Bandits, three o'clock high! Bandits, 6 o'clock level! He's gonna ram us! That was close!"

Oscar couldn't see the fighter as it flew in from the side, but he felt the big bomber dip as the German fighter whizzed overhead.

Then, "Bandit 12 o'clock level!" That meant a fighter coming in from dead ahead. Oscar's knuckles were white as they gripped his machine gun. With both planes on an apparent collision course, the fighter raced towards them at an incredible speed. Robert Spice, the bombardier, fired, his gun spewed .50 caliber bullets and tracer rounds stitched a path to the oncoming fighter.

★ Click here to watch video

Figure 30-4: By the end of 1944, the German air force was running low on planes, pilots, and fuel, but German fighters could still provide fierce opposition to Allied bombers.

Oscar saw flashes from the machine guns mounted on the wings of the German fighter plane as it hurtled towards them. Just as a collision seemed inevitable, the fighter dove out of sight, so close that they could see the pilot's grim face in the cockpit.

His mouth dry, Oscar whispered in his microphone, "Did you see that?"

No one answered. They were all too busy firing at the German fighter planes swarming around them like angry wasps. The American fighter escorts gamely dove after the German fighters that swooped through the bomber formation. Everybody was firing: German fighters, American fighters, and gunners on the bombers.

The air battle continued all the way to the target area. As the American bombers entered the clouds of flak over the target, the German fighters pulled back, not wanting to get hit by their own flak.

The German fighters attacked again when the American bombers emerged from the flak cloud. American fighter pilots and gunners in the B-17s struggled valiantly to hold them off.

South of the target, a B-17 flown by 2nd Lieutenant Michael Kearns fell out of formation. He radioed that his #3 engine had been knocked out by flak and his #2 engine was failing. He was going to try to make it to Soviet-held territory. Over Bielsko, Poland, the plane was hit by more flak, knocking out the #4 engine. With only one engine remaining, the crew was forced to bail out.

Twenty bombers and six American fighter planes were lost on that mission. Over 200 American airmen did not come back. American fighters claimed twenty-two German fighters.

After the debriefing, the officers trickled into the Officer's Club. Many were visibly shaken by the fierce fighter attacks. Oscar's friend, Ralph Stueve, said, "Where the hell did they get those fighters? I thought we'd bombed their fighter factories!"

Oscar quipped, "I guess they've been saving up!"

He leaned back in his chair and continued more seriously, "The thing that bothers me is how good those German pilots were. They were in and out like bats. And they wouldn't quit. Spice poured fire into that one that came at us from the front and he just kept coming. I thought he was going to ram us."

Oscar shook his head and said thoughtfully, "Don't they know they're the bad guys? Don't they know they're supposed to be stupid and scared?"

Nobody responded. That was part of the problem. The Germans weren't stupid and they weren't scared.

★★★ Ordinary Heroes: Six Stars in the Window ★★★
31. Why go for 40?

December 18, 1944: Oscar flew again on December 18, his third mission in three days. The 301st sent thirty-three bombers to attack an oil refinery near Odertal, Germany, running into heavy resistance.

Along the way, the turbocharger malfunctioned on First Lieutenant Ted Keiser's plane. He dropped his bombs to lighten the load, but still couldn't keep up with the formation. His plane fell further and further behind. East of Vienna, he lowered his landing gear and left the formation. When last seen, his #2 engine was smoking. Nobody knew what happened to him or his crew after that.

As the bombers neared the target, some fifty German fighters attacked, about half going after the fighter escort and the other half attacking the bombers. As the battle raged, fighters criss-crossed the sky, some passing right through the closely packed bomber formation. Falling planes, debris, men, and parachutes dotted the sky. Oscar saw one man, tumbling through the air, arms flailing as he tried to stabilize himself in flight.

Below, a crippled B-17 slowly rolled over. As the plane rolled onto its back, Oscar saw the belly gunner, trapped in his turret beneath the plane. The doomed man waved a sad farewell, then was lost to view as the plane fell into a steep dive and disappeared into the underlying clouds.

The American fighter pilots put up a fierce fight. Many of the fighter escorts were P-51 Mustangs with distinctive red tails, flown by black pilots from an outfit known as the Tuskegee Airmen. The Tuskegee Airmen were determined to prove that they could fly as well as any white man and they swarmed after the German fighters with a vengeance.

Odertal was covered by clouds, so the bombardiers used a secret new electronic device to locate the target area. They dropped their bombs, but since they couldn't see the target, they had no idea what they hit. Maybe the results had been worth the loss of four bombers and forty airmen. Or maybe not.

On December 20, Oscar flew on a mission against the Regensburg Oil Refinery. Little resistance was encountered and no planes or men were lost. It was the first "milk run" that month.

The 301st held a Christmas party on the night of December 24. The men were treated to a traditional Christmas dinner with turkey and all the trimmings. Afterwards, many sang, danced, and drank too much. Many of the men opened presents from home, presents that often contained prized food items such as Vienna sausages, pineapple, or fruit cocktail. Oscar and his crew left the party early as they were scheduled for another mission on Christmas day.

On Christmas Day, Oscar flew as part of a formation of 171 B-17s and 189 B-24s that attacked the oil refinery at Brux, Czechoslovakia. They'd hit that target before, but intelligence reports indicated the Germans had repaired the facility so someone had to hit it again. It was one of the least effective missions of the war.

The formation came in from the wrong angle and had to make two 360-degree turns over the target to make the bomb run. They were still off target. Bomb damage assessment showed the bombs from the first wave fell two and a half miles from the target. The bomb damage assessment photos showed no sign of craters from the second wave. No one knew where those bombs had fallen.

The flak was heavy, damaging twenty-one of the thirty-one bombers from the 301st Bomb Group. Six bombers from other bomb groups were lost.

So ended Oscar's second month of combat. According to his flight record, he flew ten combat missions on the 2nd, 3rd, 6th, 10th, 11th, 16th, 17th, 18th, 20th, and 22nd of December, but he received credit for only eight combat missions.

As 1944 drew to a close, Oscar and the men of the 301st continued to fly into harm's way on a regular basis. Planes—and men—continued to fall from the sky. Before each takeoff, Oscar tried to convince himself, "We've gone out before. We've always come back. There's no reason why we can't get back today. God alone will decide when my time has come, not some German gunner."

The Army Air Forces knew that all men would eventually break under the stress of combat. Air Force psychologists initially estimated the average man should be able to complete twenty-five missions before suffering a nervous breakdown. Of course, some men broke much earlier. An Army Air Forces survey of returning airmen revealed that forty percent admitted to being afraid every time or almost every time they flew. An additional forty-four percent admitted they were afraid one-half to three-quarters of the time. Being afraid was not a sign of weakness, it was a logical response to the danger and losses of the missions.

When asked how they felt about men who quit flying after a few missions, over half said, "one should not judge as it might happen to anyone." They understood the tremendous psychological stress of repeated combat missions, they realized they themselves were hanging on to their sanity by the thinnest of threads.

Surprisingly few men cracked under the strain. Some requested removal from flight status. They were temporarily assigned to ground duties, but in most cases returned to flight status after a short break. A few men never recovered and did not fly again. Those airmen, described as people whose "wheels won't touch the ground anymore," were either assigned to undesirable ground duties such as KP or were transferred to other units.

The young airmen tried to deal with the stress through jokes. One night as they sat in the Officer's Club, one of the old-timers told a story from the time when the 301st had been part of the 8th Air Force in England:

> The control tower received a call: "Calling Lazy Fox, calling Lazy Fox. This is G for George 311, G for George 311. I need assistance. The pilot is dead and the copilot is unconscious. Two engines are feathered, the vertical stabilizer has been shot off and we have no hydraulics. I'm the bombardier and have taken over the controls.
>
> The navigator is wounded, but is guiding us in. I believe the rest of the crew has bailed out. I think I can make it to the airfield, but I don't know how to land. Please advise, please advise."
>
> There was a long pause, while the man in the tower tried to think of some way to save the plane. Then the tower called back, "I read you G for George. Here are your instructions. Repeat slowly please, repeat slowly. Our Father who art in heaven..."

The men burst out laughing. Oscar laughed along with them. Deep down, they all knew the same thing could happen to any of them on any mission. But they also knew they could not afford to let the fear take control. They had to laugh, they had to make fun of the things that scared them, or they wouldn't be able to go up in those planes again and again and again.

Oscar's friend and fellow navigator, Danny Moore, often quipped, "Why go for 40 when you can make it in 20?"

He meant that if you could do everything important in life by the time you were 20 years old, you shouldn't worry about living to be an "old man" of 40.

Some of the jokes were even less tasteful. Each morning, the men lined up for roll call. Too often, the CO would call the name of someone who had been lost in the previous day's raid. After a short pause, someone would inevitably call out, "KIA!" and the rest of the men would chuckle.

It wasn't a joke and it wasn't even funny.

It was just a group of young men trying to deal with the stress. They couldn't let it get to them. If they could laugh, they could shrug it off and they could do their job for yet another day.

They knew that somewhere nearby, officers were planning another mission and all too soon they would be climbing into their planes for another mission over enemy territory.

★ Click here to watch video

Figure 31-1: Planning a mission was a sizable task, requiring the efforts of many men, including intelligence officers, meteorologists, supply officers, and ordnance officers.

★ Click here for Web Info

Figure 31-2: Oscar's missions in December, 1944.

★★★ Ordinary Heroes: Six Stars in the Window ★★★
32. Last-ditch defense

Christmas Eve, 1944: As the door of the railroad car slammed shut behind Captain Towne, Art and the enlisted men of H&S Company drained their glasses, grabbed their jackets, and hustled outside.

Sergeant Tom Jones ordered them to line up. Their breath hung in little clouds in the still air. They stamped their feet in the cold, waiting for the captain to return with their orders.

The captain's manner was serious as he explained that the engineers had been ordered to blockade the secondary roads heading toward Liege. "The main roads are already guarded, but headquarters thinks the Krauts might send scouts down the secondary roads looking for a way into Liege. We don't have enough men, so you'll be posted in two man teams. We don't have enough radios either. If your team is attacked, one of you will delay the attackers, while the other runs back with a warning."

★ Click here to watch video

Figure 32-1: Carl "Art" Koski was stationed by the side of a snowy road with one other soldier.

Nobody explained exactly how an engineer with a rifle was supposed to delay a column of German troops or Panzer tanks.

The engineers shuffled their feet in the snow. They all understood that the man left behind was as good as dead. He would sacrifice his life to buy a few minutes of lead time for the runner.

The men were warned to watch for German soldiers pretending to be Americans: "Be on the lookout for any suspicious behavior. Don't be afraid to ask questions to determine if they really are Americans." That warning proved useful. Later that day, a squad of engineers guarding a bridge over the Meuse was approached by two men wearing American uniforms. When asked what state they were from, one of the soldiers answered, "Chicago!" The wary GIs took the men prisoner and turned them over for interrogation. Questioning revealed that the men were Germans. The men were dressed in American uniforms, presumably taken from American soldiers. The Germans were interrogated, then lined up and shot as spies.

After Captain Towne finished giving his orders, Art and the other enlisted men climbed into the back of a truck. After bouncing along for a few miles, the truck came to a spot where a rough trail joined the main road. The truck stopped. Two men were handed rations and told to take up positions down the trail.

The truck continued to a spot where another rough road led off into the dark pine forest. Art and a short, dark-haired soldier were dropped off and told to hike up the road and take up defensive positions. The other soldier had an M1 Garand rifle and two grenades. Art had given up the BAR, but he had an M1 and four clips of ammunition.

The truck drove off, leaving Art and the other soldier standing alone in the snow-covered forest. The weather was bitterly cold—barely above zero during the day and much colder at night. They hiked down the little road, eventually finding a spot where the road went down a steep hill, making a sharp turn at the bottom of the hill.

Art said, "This looks good. They'll have to slow down to make that turn, then gun their engines to get up that hill. We should hear them before they come over the top."

They tried to dig a foxhole near the side of the road, but the ground was frozen solid. After chipping at it for a while with their entrenching tools, they agreed it was futile. Scouting up and down the road they found a culvert where a small creek ran under the road. The culvert was large enough for a man to crawl into. It was probably filled with water in the spring, but now, in the middle of winter, there was just a bit of ice in the bottom. They took up positions in the ends of the culvert and took turns on watch, two hours on, then two hours off for each man. The man on watch sat with his legs in the culvert, peering down the road for any sign of German troops and listening for vehicles. The man who was not on watch huddled in the culvert, out of the wind, trying to keep warm.

As they waited, they talked in soft voices. Art learned the other man's name was Ron. He was from Duluth, Minnesota, not too far from the Upper Peninsula of Michigan. He and Art had a lot in common. Both loved hunting and fishing and both had girls back home they planned to marry as soon as they got out of the service. Ron carried a photo of his girlfriend in his pocket, along with several letters from her. Art always carried a photo of Jenny and one or more letters from her.

Art asked Ron, "If the Germans come, one of us is supposed to hold them off while the other runs to alert headquarters. How are we going to work that out?"

Ron thought for a minute, then said, "Well, I was thinking we'd flip for it. But then I'm thinking, you're the corporal so it seems to me, that if some Germans come, maybe you'd better hold them off while I run back for help. How's that sit with you?"

Art cleared his throat and said, "I'm not too keen on staying here, but I'm the corporal so if they come, I'll hold them off as long as I can. But you'd better run like the dickens because I'm not going to be able to hold them back for long by myself."

While Ron tried to sleep, Art sat on the edge of the culvert. As the shadows lengthened into night, he took the photo of Jenny out of his pocket. He looked at it and thought, "Well, I've got myself into it now Jenny. If I don't get out of this, I hope you forgive me. Forgive me, but don't forget me." He tenderly kissed the photo and placed it back in his chest pocket.

Art knew about cold weather, but even by Upper Michigan standards, that night got cold, very, very cold. He figured it had to be at least twenty below zero. The snow squeaked and his breath hung heavy in the air. They didn't have proper winter gear, just their leather two-buckle boots, wool mittens, and an overcoat.

Neither of them slept that first night. They just huddled in the culvert, moving their arms and legs and rubbing their gloved hands under their armpits to keep warm. By morning, Art and Ron realized they had to do something or they were going to freeze to death.

Art remembered passing a few ruined houses on the main road, not far from where they were dropped off. Through chattering teeth, they agreed that Ron would stay at the culvert while Art walked back to the houses to see if he could find something that might help them stay warm.

Art walked back to the ruined houses just off the side of the road. Almost everything usable had been stripped from the houses, but he found two dirty cot mattresses and an old curtain, which he brought back to the culvert.

Art and Ron agreed that one man would stay on watch, while the other man tried to sleep in the culvert between the two light mattresses, like a "man sandwich." The man on watch would wrap himself in the curtain, sit in the end of the culvert, and scan the road for approaching Germans.

Later that morning, Art was shivering in the culvert while Ron was on watch. Ron heard the sound of an engine coming up the hill and hissed, "Something's coming! Better get up here Art!"

Art poked his head out of the culvert. He heard the sound of an engine. Then, he saw a vehicle come over the crest of the hill. At first, he couldn't tell what it was, but as it came closer he recognized the distinctive shape of a German scout car headed right towards them. Two German soldiers sat in the car, rifle barrels visible beside them.

Art propped his rifle on the edge of the snowy road and took aim at the Germans.

On the other side of the culvert, Ron carefully placed two grenades in the snow in front of him.

Neither man said anything as the German scout car moved towards them.

Figure 32-2: This rather blurry photo shows Carl "Art" Koski standing guard around the time of the Battle of the Bulge. He appears to be wearing some sort of scarf or hood under his helmet as protection from the bitter cold and is holding an M1 rifle with a bayonet attached.

★★★ Ordinary Heroes: Six Stars in the Window ★★★
33. We thought you were dead!

January 8, 1945: After almost two weeks on the ground, Oscar flew another mission against the main train station in Linz, Austria. One hundred and twenty-one B-17s dropped 326 tons of bombs on the target. Heavy flak from as many as 194 antiaircraft guns hit ten planes from the 301st, causing heavy damage to three and minor damage to seven.

Figure 33-1: Bombs fill the sky as B-17s from the 301st attack a target.

As Oscar's plane headed for home after the bomb run, he noticed the airspeed dropping. Oscar overheard the copilot, Clifford Ronk, talking on the radio, apparently unaware that anything was wrong. Oscar called the pilot on the intercom: "Hey! Watch that airspeed!" but didn't get a response.

The airspeed continued to drop and the plane suddenly fell into a dive.

Oscar struggled back to the flight deck, a difficult task in the diving plane. Bill Skillings was slumped in his seat, unconscious. Clifford Ronk was wrestling with the controls, trying to pull the plane out of the dive. Ronk noticed Oscar and yelled, "He passed out! Check his oxygen!"

Oscar traced Skillings' oxygen line. It was unplugged, rolling around on the floor. Oscar plugged the oxygen line back in and helped Skillings recover. Gradually Ronk regained control and the plane leveled off. By that time, the rest of the formation had disappeared into the distance and their plane was skimming the tree tops.

Skillings mumbled, "Wha' happened?"

Oscar replied, "Your oxygen line was unplugged. You lost consciousness, but we're okay now."

Skillings was breathing normally inside his oxygen mask. "I must have knocked it loose when I adjusted the superchargers after dropping the bombs."

The immediate danger was over, but a larger problem now loomed before them.

This was the situation they all feared. B-17s relied on the combined firepower of the formation to fend off attacking fighters. When flying alone, only one or two guns could be aimed in any one direction, making a lone B-17 easy prey for German fighters.

The only chance the crew had now was to fly low and head back to base, hoping not to be spotted by German fighters. Oscar quickly plotted a course back to base. To reduce the chance of encountering fighters, he plotted a course to the Adriatic, avoiding cities and military targets. On the way back, they spotted a formation of B-17s under attack by German fighters. Fortunately none of the fighters seemed to notice the low-flying bomber.

When they reached the Adriatic, Bill Skillings brought the plane even lower, just skimming over the tops of the waves. Suddenly a German speed boat appeared right in front of them. Skillings pulled up on the controls. Oscar and the bombardier, Robert Spice, had a clear view of the Germans sailors, as they looked up in astonishment, then dove for the deck as the huge B-17 thundered just a few feet overhead.

Ronk worked the radio, but was unable to contact the base. No one knew they had survived. No one knew they were on the way in.

They got back to Lucera 8 well after dark. The rest of the formation had landed and had already been debriefed.

As they taxied off the runway, the ground crew ran out to meet them, smiling and waving. The ground crew had maintained a lonely vigil on the deserted runway, hoping for their safe return. As Skillings dropped out of the plane, he grinned and teased the ground crew, "I can't tell if you guys are happier to see us or the plane."

The crew chief patted the belly of the plane and said, "We're happy to see you too. Now, get out of here while we see what you did to our baby!"

After debriefing, Oscar and his crew walked back to their tent, dead tired. Inside, the lantern was glowing and several figures were silhouetted against the walls of the tent. Ronk said, "Look! Somebody's stealing our stuff!"

Skillings brusquely yanked the tent flap open and Oscar's crew pushed their way into the tent. "What's going on here?" Skillings demanded.

Three airmen slowly straightened up. Footlockers lay open on the bunks in front of them, personal items sorted into little piles. Ronk stepped towards them, fists clenched. "Put that stuff back. Put it all back now." he said in a threatening voice.

The scavenging crewmen backed away from the open footlockers with their hands up, "Hey, we thought you were dead! The last we saw, your plane was in a steep dive heading into the undercast. No one heard from you after that. You gotta understand, we thought you were dead!"

Skillings replied, "Well, we hate to disappoint you, but we ain't dead yet. So put our stuff back, get the hell outta here, and let us get some sleep!"

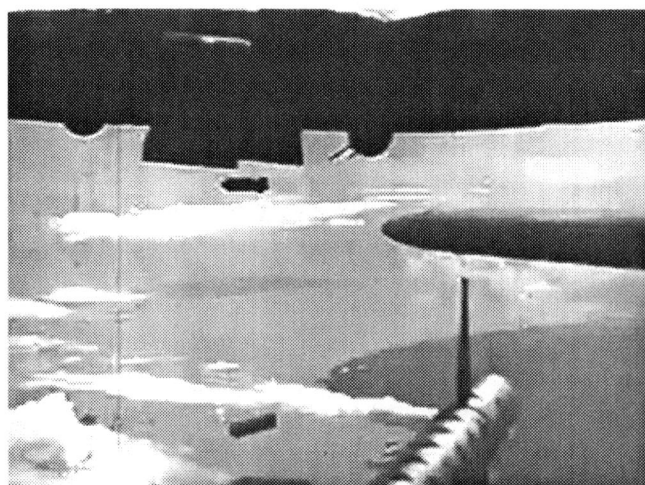

★ Click here to watch video

Figure 33-2: Oscar and his crew were late, but they did return from that mission over Linz.

★★★ Ordinary Heroes: Six Stars in the Window ★★★
34. I can't think of any other way

December 26, 1944: Art barely breathed as the German scout car bounced up the rough road toward the culvert where he and Ron were crouched.

Art found himself muttering, "Go away! Go away!"

Suddenly, inexplicably, Ron hopped up on the road and walked nonchalantly towards the Germans, his rifle still slung over his shoulder. Art whistled urgently at him, but Ron just kept walking up the snowy road toward the oncoming Germans.

Art couldn't believe what was happening. The German scout car slid to a stop some distance away. The driver stared at Ron. The other German was yelling something at the driver while Ron casually walked towards them. Art took aim at the driver.

Suddenly, the German driver threw the car into reverse, spun it around, and drove off. As the scout car disappeared around the curve, the German soldier in the passenger seat peered anxiously back at Ron.

Ron walked back to the culvert, smiling. Art yelled at him, "Why the heck did you go and do that? You could have been killed."

Ron just smiled and said, "I don't know. It didn't seem right to just start shooting at them fellows without any warning. I thought I'd go up and ask them to go away. I didn't particularly want to shoot them and I was kind of hoping they didn't want to shoot me either."

Later, as they crouched in the culvert, Art chuckled and said, "When you walked up to them like that, you looked like you were going to give them directions or something! Doggone if that's not about the most incredible thing I ever saw anybody do."

"Yeah?" Ron replied, not knowing if he was being congratulated or ridiculed.

Art continued, "I think I know why they left. When you walked up to them like that, without even having your rifle ready, they must have thought you had a lot of men behind you and were coming to tell them to surrender. Let's just hope they go back and report that this road is held by a strong force."

Ron pulled some ice crystals out of his stubbly beard, then smiled and replied, "Yeah, I think we'd be in real trouble if they knew this road was held by two Engineers huddled in a culvert."

Art and Ron continued to keep watch from the culvert. One of them always stayed awake, anxiously watching the road and hoping the Germans would not return. They did their best to stay warm for another day, another night, then another day and yet another night. Each day and each night seemed colder than the last.

On the third night, while he shivered between the two thin mattresses, Art's right foot worked its way out from between the mattresses. His entire body was so cold he didn't realize that one foot lay unprotected from the cold. When Ron woke him up to take his turn at watch, Art couldn't feel anything in his right foot. He hopped around and tried to stomp on it to get the circulation going, but nothing seemed to help.

Art carefully removed his boot and massaged his foot. The skin was cold and white and he couldn't feel anything from his shin down. It felt like he was rubbing somebody else's leg. "Well," he thought, "there's nothing to do about it now."

Art and Ron both wondered what was happening in the larger battle. Where were their reinforcements? Had the Americans pulled back? Had they been abandoned in the forest? Who were they going to see next, a column of German tanks or American GIs?

They decided that regardless of what was happening in the larger battle, their only option was to sit tight. They had been ordered to hold this position until relieved, so they would just stay put and hope their men arrived before the Germans.

As the afternoon shadows lengthened into night, Art heard vehicles approaching down the road behind them. He and Ron turned and peered nervously from the ends of the culvert, hoping those weren't German tanks. They saw movement through the trees, then a beautiful sight: a squad of GIs leading a Sherman tank down the snowy road.

Art and Ron climbed onto the road and Art hobbled over to greet the GIs. "We're sure glad to see you guys! We've been here alone for three nights! What's going on out there? Did we stop the Germans?"

One of the soldiers replied, "They hit us hard. Bastogne was cut off for almost a week. We lost a lot of good men, but we're pushing them back."

Later that day, a truck from the 332nd came by to bring Art and Ron back to H&S Company. Art asked them to drop him off at the medical tent. He limped in and told the medics his leg had been frozen the previous night. After examining his leg, the medics told him, "You've got severe frostbite. We have to amputate."

★ Click here to watch video

Figure 34-1: In December of 1944, cooks, musicians, clerks, and engineers found themselves engaged in desperate struggles to slow the German advance.

Art exploded: "Amputate! You're not gonna amputate nothing! I've got a lifetime of hunting and fishing ahead of me! I'm not going through the rest of my life as some kind of cripple."

The medics tried to explain, "If we don't amputate, you could die from gangrene."

Art replied forcefully, "Well, I guess that's a chance I'm going to have to take! I'm getting out of here and I'm taking both of my legs with me!"

★ Click here to watch video

Figure 34-2: Trench foot was a very serious problem during the winter of 1944–1945.

Art laced up his boot, hobbled out of the aid station, and headed back to H&S Company. He figured he wasn't the only soldier who would be walking on frozen feet that winter. He warmed the leg as best he could, changed his socks frequently, and massaged the frozen flesh at every opportunity, trying to bring some circulation back into the damaged limb. Slowly, painfully, the leg began to recover.

As the Allies pushed the Germans back, the 332nd advanced with them. The weather stayed bitterly cold, hindering both sides. Tank crews built small fires under their tanks to keep the oil from thickening. GIs urinated on the frozen mechanisms of their M1 rifles to thaw them. Rubber tires froze to the ground during the night, trapping vehicles in place. Warren Babcock ordered the men to drive the trucks and Jeeps onto pieces of wood each night so they wouldn't have to chop them loose from the ice in the morning.

A few days later, as the trucks drove along a snowy road, the men of H&S Company came to a sharp curve at the base of a steep hill. A squad of GIs had tried to stop the Germans at that curve, ambushing them when they slowed down to make the tight turn. But on this road, the Germans hadn't turned and fled. The frozen bodies of the German soldiers stacked along the side of the road provided mute testimony to the savage fighting that had taken place as the GIs fought to hold the Germans back. As his truck chugged past the frozen Germans, Art thought, "I probably wouldn't be alive today if these guys had come down the road towards our culvert."

The trucks rounded the curve and started up the steep hill. The first truck slowed, then started to slip. The men got out and pushed, but the heavy truck just couldn't get enough traction on the slippery snow. One of the engineers remembered the frozen German bodies stacked by the curve. He told the driver of the truck to back down the hill, then got a few men to help him to lay the frozen bodies across the road like logs. They gunned the engine and powered the truck up the hill. This time, with the extra traction from the bodies on the road, the truck made it up the hill. The rest of the trucks followed, the weight of the heavy trucks grinding the bodies into the snow.

Art looked back at the trucks as they drove over the frozen bodies and thought, "Those were men. They were somebody's sons, brothers, husbands, and fathers. Now they're just something to throw on the road for traction. Their families will probably never even know what happened to them."

Art shook his head in disgust, "This is one God awful dirty business. And the worst of it is, I can't think of any other way to deal with somebody like Hitler, I just can't think of any other way."

As the news of the unexpected German offensive reverberated around the world, millions of Americans worried about their loved ones. A letter written to one of the Koski sisters said, "I am thinking your brothers George, Art, and Oscar have all partaken of what they now call 'The Battle of the Bulge'. Casualties are heavy and I am hoping to hear they are all right. I was glad to turn the calendar on 1944. It was not a good year."

★ Click here to watch video

Figure 34-3: 1944 had been a very difficult year, but even with setbacks such as the Battle of the Bulge, the tide seem to be turning in favor of the Allies.

★★★ Ordinary Heroes: Six Stars in the Window ★★★
35. A little bit of good

January 1, 1945: Art drove a truck as H&S Company moved from Plombiers to Bassenge, Belgium, about fifteen miles north of Liege. For much of January, most of the 332nd Engineer Regiment worked on the Ilse de Monsin bridge over a small island between the Meuse River and the Albert Canal.

Figure 35-1: In January of 1945, the 332nd Engineers repaired the Ilse de Monsin bridge on the Meuse River.

Equipment poured into Belgium as the Allies rushed to replace the vehicles, weapons, and men lost during the Battle of the Bulge.

Almost every outfit was desperately short of men. In the Battle of the Bulge, over 8,000 Americans had been killed, 48,000 were wounded, and 21,000 were captured or missing in action. All those men had to be replaced.

The Engineers were repeatedly asked for volunteers to join infantry outfits. Many volunteered—so many that the 332nd had to hire civilian laborers to make progress on its construction and repair projects.

Art was thankful that he didn't have to decide if he would volunteer to join the infantry. He had a hard time walking with his bum leg. There wasn't any way he could keep up with the infantry as they advanced through the snow.

Art was often assigned to drive a truck back to the supply depot for food and equipment. Those were cold, lonely drives, nursing the big "deuce and a half" truck along the narrow, icy roads. Despite the cold, he kept the window partly open so he could hear approaching aircraft and try to get off the road before they strafed him. The days were short, getting dark by 4:00 p.m. and not getting light again until 8:00 a.m. If he ran late, Art tried to resist the urge to drive a little faster. He knew that if he put the truck in the ditch, he'd be stuck there through the bitterly cold night.

Art knew that Jenny had probably heard about the Battle of the Bulge. He had sent her many letters written "somewhere in Belgium," so she would know that he had been close to the fighting.

It wasn't until February 4 that Art found time to scribble a short letter to his Jenny. He didn't mention the Battle of the Bulge or his frozen leg. He only alluded to the cold weather: "Those days in France weren't bad at all now when I recall the nice warm sunny days. Quite a contrast with that and these gloomy towns in Germany where most buildings are shattered or burnt and have that dead smell. I did dream I was out trapping beaver. Doggone I was having good luck, I had a stack of beaver hides two feet high and then of course I have to wake up and find it was only a dream. I sure wouldn't mind if that dream came through some day."

★ Click here to watch video

Figure 35-2: Retreating Germans planted booby traps and mines to slow the advancing Allies.

After completing the Ilse de Monsin project, the 332nd started work on a six-span masonry bridge over the Roer River near Baal, Germany. The bridge had been heavily mined, forcing the engineers to cautiously remove hundreds of box mines, Schu mines, stick mines, and regal mines. Two privates detonated over sixty mines by throwing a grapple over them and dragging it back over the mines. Another squad deactivated 150 Schu mines. A mine hidden under a railroad tie killed a sergeant from F Company and wounded two Belgian civilians and four engineers.

As the Allies pushed the Germans back into Germany, Art was shocked at the extent of the destruction in German cities such as Herzogenrath, Eschweiler, Julich, and Geilinkirchen. Aachen had been reduced to blocks of rubble, barely recognizable as having been buildings. Few buildings remained intact in the badly damaged German towns, so the enlisted men often slept on the floor in the H&S Company railroad cars. When the survey crew was in the field overnight, they tried to find an undamaged basement or schoolhouse in which to sleep.

Germany was a ruined nation, an apocalyptic nightmare. Almost all civilians were homeless. Some German civilians worked to clear the debris, but others wandered around in a daze or sullenly watched the invading GIs from gutted buildings.

Refugees wandered the roads, straggling back to their homes in France, Belgium, or Holland. Many had been forced to work for the Nazis. They had escaped or been left behind as the Germans retreated. The refugees wore all the clothes they owned and carried their possessions in old sacks, old suitcases, or crude carts built like wheelbarrows. They traveled alone or in small groups, picking through the rubble for scraps of food or valuables.

So many refugees crowded the roads that military traffic often slowed to a crawl. Civilians and soldiers stayed alert for the sound of approaching airplanes as German fighters sometimes swooped over the crowded roads, spraying machine gun bullets at military vehicles and refugees alike.

In Aachen, Art was adopted by a scrawny German Shepherd puppy. He gave it some Spam—the universally despised over-processed meat in cans—and took it along as his little "Kraut dog."

★ Click here to watch video

Figure 35-3: Hundreds of thousands of refugees filled the roads, trying to find a safe place in war-torn Europe.

A few nights later, Art and the survey crew were sitting near a burned-out building. Some were eating C-rations heated over the fire. Others were smoking, resting up from the grueling day. Art was feeding the dog bits of leftover Spam. A passing lieutenant stopped, looked at Art and asked, "Soldier, why are you feeding that dog?"

Before Art could reply, one of the other Engineers gestured at the bombed-out building and answered, "Well sir, we can't do much about a lot of this mess. But we can give a stray dog a piece of Spam from time to time."

The Engineer scratched the dog's chin thoughtfully. "It's not much, but it's something."

Another Engineer grinned and added, "Besides, there's one thing we've got enough of, and that's Spam!"

The lieutenant just chuckled, shook his head, and walked away.

On February 15, Art wrote another letter to Jenny. This was the first and only time he mentioned the Battle of the Bulge in his letters.

```
Feb 15, 1945

Dearest Sweetheart,

I'm very happy today 'cuzz I got three letters from
you and one from sis El. I'm glad you got around to
writing, it improves my morale greatly every time I
hear from my honey.

What's the matter with the folks back home? They all
seem to think just 'cuzz a few Germans got back into
Belgium that the war was almost lost. Heck, that burns
me up, besides the Armies over here are the best in
the world, no matter what Adolf might try to tell the
world. It didn't worry any of us guys anyway.

Say, I hear you're trying to learn to speak Finnish.
My, my, it should really amuse me to hear you,
although Al's wife learned enough to speak to my Dad
and carry on a short conversation.

So you haven't been out skiing this winter. You'll
soon forget how. Well as long as you're doing fine
with that cooking you speak of. I'll be back to sample
some of it before the year is out, I hope. Anyway,
that's what everyone is telling me in their letters.

I got a touch of rheumatism the last few days, my neck
and shoulders are stiff and sore just as if I had
worked hard. It's just a sign of old age creeping up
on me. Can't stand the wet mud and the cold like I
used to when I was young.

I hope I get to see George if he comes this way.
Wonder what he's with now, he used to be with the
Artillery, then he was with a Signal outfit, then an
Ordnance unit. He never did stay long in one place.

Well must sign off for this time honey.

Goodbye and lots of love and kisses from "Art"
```

★ Click here for Web Info

Figure 35-4: Transcript of a letter from Art to Jenny.

Art didn't mention his frozen leg to Jenny. To his way of thinking, "There's no point making her worry about that. I can explain it to her when I get home. If I don't get home, it won't matter."

Art did not get gangrene and he was able to get around well enough to do his work. He worried that his leg might never heal properly, but he still had two legs. He could walk, and, when he finally got back home, he'd be able to hunt and fish. That had to be good enough.

Figure 35-5: German cities such as Aachen and Julich suffered heavy damage during the war.

★★★ Ordinary Heroes: Six Stars in the Window ★★★
36. My mother loved me

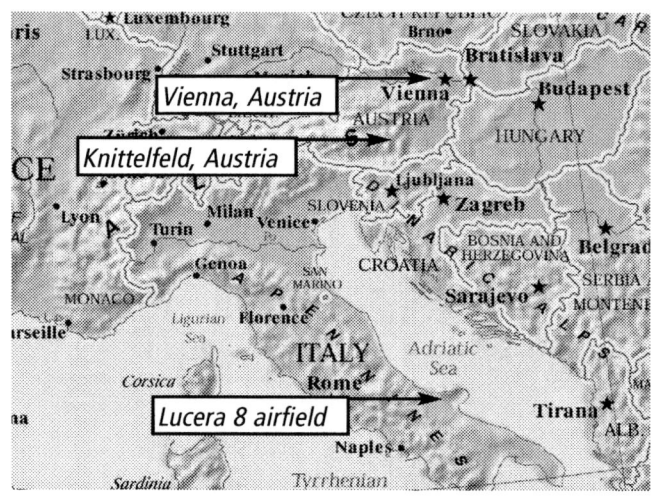

Figure 36-1: Map of the Vienna mission.

January, 1945: Bad weather grounded the 301st for most of January. Oscar flew on the 9th, but the flight was aborted after an hour and a half in the air. On the 15th, the weather cleared and he flew on a successful attack against railroad targets in Vienna. He took off again on January 19, but that mission was also aborted due to bad weather.

On January 21, Oscar was temporarily assigned to a different crew. The pilot was a friend of Oscar's by the name of David, or "Davey," Mills, who came from Texas. He was a superb pilot, able to hold a B-17 in close formation with a delicate touch on the controls. The copilot was Norbert F. Moore and the bombardier was Morris Bogrow. Their regular navigator was a fellow by the name of Koch, but Oscar took his place for that day.

Oscar's plane joined a formation of 208 bombers attacking the Schwechat Oil Refinery in Vienna. Intelligence reported over 300 antiaircraft guns in the Vienna area, but flak was fairly light and no planes were lost. The target was completely obscured by heavy cloud cover, so the bomb run was aborted and the formation headed back without dropping their bombs. Oscar thought to himself, "That was an easy one!"

That's when things started to go wrong.

Just a few minutes after leaving the target area, the #4 engine started to act up. Davey Mills eased up on the throttle to nurse it along.

Oscar kept telling himself, "We're okay. We're okay. Plenty of B-17s have come home on three engines."

A short time later, Mills called on the intercom, "The #2 engine just quit. I think we took some flak over the target. Koski, we gotta drop these bombs or we're not going to make it back. Find me a place to drop 'em!"

Oscar checked his maps against the occasional features he could identify through gaps in the clouds below. A small town lay ahead, partially visible through a gap in the clouds. Oscar thought it might be Knittelfeld, Austria, but he couldn't be entirely sure because most of the landmarks were obscured by the thick clouds.

Oscar didn't have anything against Knittelfeld, but they needed a place to drop their bombs. That little town was on the way and it was enemy territory.

★ Click here to watch video

Figure 36-2: Without sophisticated instruments, B-17 navigators were sometimes reduced to looking out the window, trying to match ground features with their maps to determine their location.

Over the intercom, Oscar reported to the pilot, "See that little town up ahead? I think that's Knittelfeld, Austria. That should be a good place to drop them."

Davey responded, "Are you sure that's Knittelfeld? I don't want to bomb some Swiss village."

Oscar replied, "I'm pretty sure it's Knittelfeld, but with this undercast, I can't be absolutely sure."

Oscar glanced at his map again, "I think this is Austria. We can either drop the bombs here, where they might do some damage, or drop them in the mountains where they won't do any good."

Davey Mills grunted in displeasure but brought the plane down to 20,000 feet and flew over the town. They spotted a train in the marshaling yard and Mills turned towards it. As they flew towards the train, German antiaircraft guns fired on them. The train had flak guns on it and they were flying right over it!

Ignoring the flak from the train below, Morris Bogrow dropped their bombs pummeling the train and stopping the flak. But the last shots from the flak train struck home.

Thinking the worst was over, Oscar tried quipped, "At least we know that wasn't Switzerland!"

Then they got the bad news as Davey Mills yelled over the intercom, "The #3 engine's been hit! I gotta shut her down!"

Mills barely managed to trim the propeller before the #3 engine stopped.

The situation was not good. They were down to one good engine and one that was acting up and they were still a long way from home.

The intercom was silent as the entire crew tried to think of some way out of this jam.

Oscar could envision many endings to this ride and none of them were good. The bomber could lose altitude and crash in the mountains. Davey Mills could decide they weren't going to make it and could order the crew to bail out. Somebody at Knittelfeld could have alerted the Luftwaffe and German fighters could already be on an intercept course.

Oscar didn't want to die. No one does, particularly not a 21-year old who has the rest of his life yet before him.

Oscar tried to turn his mind from the things that could go wrong. He tried to think of all the things that had made his life worth living: his friends, his family, and his faith. The thought that proved most comforting to Oscar, was a simple one: "My mother loved me!"

Oscar's mother had died when he was just seven years old, but somehow, as that crippled B-17 struggled to make it over the Alps, he knew his mother was still watching over him. Over the years, his memory of her face had dimmed, but as long as he knew his mother had loved him, he felt that everything would be all right.

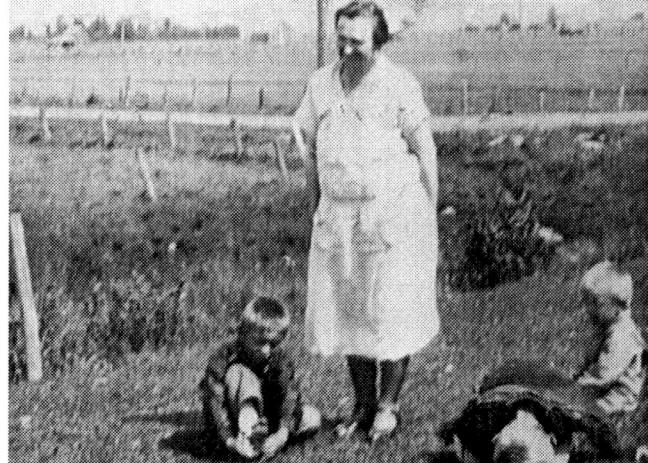

★ Click here to watch video

Figure 36-3: Oscar's mother, Elizabeth Koski, watching over two of the boys as they play in the yard.

★★★ Ordinary Heroes: Six Stars in the Window ★★★
37. Don't be in a rush to leave here

December, 1944: After a short stay at Fort Patrick Henry, Johnny took the train to Newport News, Virginia to await shipment overseas. In late December he boarded an old Italian liner that had been converted for use as a troop ship. The men were crammed below, with bunks stacked five high. Because there were so many men on the ship, Johnny rarely got up on deck, spending much of each day below decks waiting in line for the two meals served each day. When they weren't standing in line, most of the men played cards, read, or wrote letters.

★ Click here to watch video

Figure 37-1: The GIs packed on the troop ships were not told where they were going.

When the ocean was calm, being stuck below decks wasn't so bad, but when the waves got rough, almost everyone got seasick. Those few men who weren't affected by the motion got sick from the smell of unwashed men, diesel oil, vomit, and backed-up toilets.

Johnny was on the ship for almost two weeks. He could tell they were sailing east, but didn't know where the ship was headed. It wasn't until after they passed into the Mediterranean that he and the other men were told they were being sent to a replacement depot in northern Italy.

As the ship neared Naples, Johnny saw ominous clouds of dark smoke billowing into the sky from a cone-shaped mountain on the outskirts of the city. The wind shifted and Johnny caught a whiff of sulfur. One of the men standing nearby muttered something about Vesuvius and surreptitiously made the sign of the cross over his chest. Johnny was glad to see that he wasn't the only one made uneasy by the brooding volcano.

As the ship moved closer to the dock, Johnny saw that the port and the city had taken a tremendous beating from Allied bombing, artillery, and deliberate destruction by the retreating Germans.

★ Click here to watch video

Figure 37-2: Mount Vesuvius erupts over Naples, 1945.

When the ship pulled into port, Johnny realized that what he thought was a dock was actually an overturned ship. The ship had sunk and turned turtle. No one had time to pull it out of the way, so a crew of welders had secured walkways to the upturned hull and it had become a dock.

Like many GIs, Johnny was surprised by the desperate situation of the Italian people. Children, dressed in rags, begged the GIs for food, candy, clothing, or cigarettes. Johnny had seen poor people before, but had never seen anyone desperate enough to beg and he'd never seen children begging for scraps from a man's plate.

Johnny knew that his brother Oscar was stationed near Foggia, just over a hundred miles from Naples and thought, "It sure would be swell to see Oscar!"

The next day, Johnny boarded a landing craft for the trip to Liverno, a city that most GIs called Leghorn. For a day and a night, the boat sailed north along the beautiful Italian coast, its small fishing villages barely visible. The landing craft rolled heavily in the seas. Most of the men got violently seasick, but the rolling seas didn't bother Johnny.

A sailor pointed out the beaches at Anzio where Allied troops had landed the previous January, but most of the men were too seasick to care.

★ Click here to watch video

Figure 37-3: Allied troops and equipment being unloaded in Naples Harbor.

Large barrage balloons floated gracefully over the Liverno harbor. The balloons were tethered to steel cables, creating deadly obstacles for any low-flying German planes that might try to strafe the harbor.

After landing at Leghorn, the men were herded onto trucks and bounced along the road, heading east towards the center of the Italian peninsula. The trucks finally stopped at the 8th Replacement Depot located in an olive grove just outside Empoli. Empoli was a modest town with cobblestone streets and old stone houses. Johnny noticed that everyone seemed undernourished and the people, mostly old men and old women, all wore black.

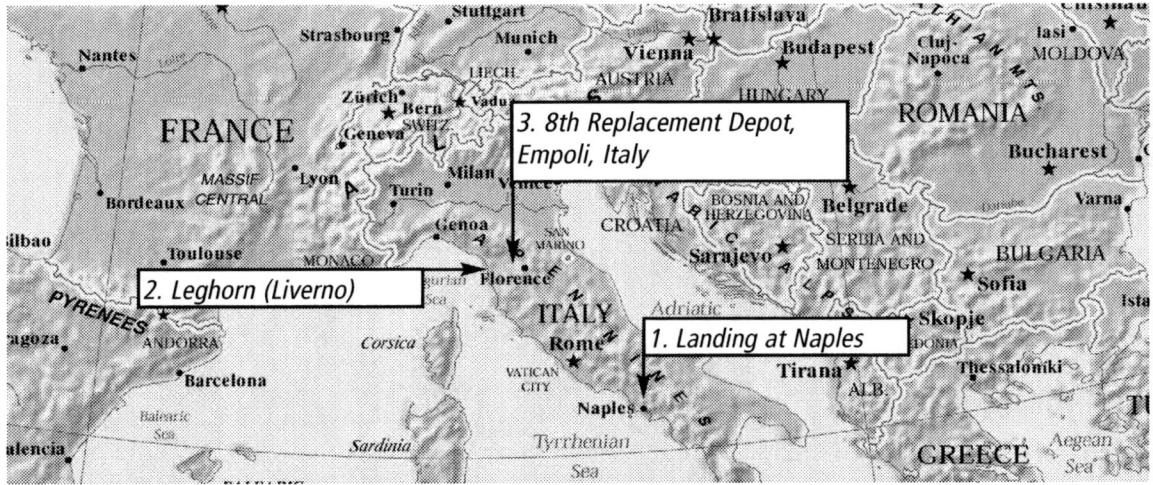

Figure 37-4: Earlyi in 1945, Johnny Koski landed at Naples, then traveled to Liverno and Empoli.

The 8th Replacement Depot wasn't much to look at. A patch of bare ground used as a drill area was surrounded by mess tents, administrative tents, and pyramidal sleeping tents arranged in rows between irrigation ditches. Johnny lined up with the other new replacements, was assigned to a platoon, then headed off to his tent.

In mid-January, Johnny watched a large convoy of trucks carrying new troops as it passed the replacement depot, heading towards Florence. One of the men next to him said, "I saw that outfit when I was in Pisa. They're the Mountaineers—the guys who were in *Life* magazine some time back. I guess somebody finally decided to send them here to see what they could do."

The war in Europe was once again going well for the Allies. The Germans had surprised everyone with the attack in the Ardennes, but they had been pushed back and had lost troops and tanks they could not replace. By mid-January, the Russians moved into Poland and American and British troops were on Germany's eastern border. It seemed only a matter of time before the Allies won the war.

★ Click here for Web Info

Figure 37-5: These GIs were at the 8th Replacement Depot about the same time Johnny was there.

Action at the Italian front was mainly confined to patrols, so relatively few replacement soldiers were needed. The men at the 8th Replacement Depot in Empoli kept busy with calisthenics, drills, and combat training. Every week or so, another group of replacements joined them. Rumor had it the big offensive would start in the spring, after the mountain roads were clear of snow, but no one knew for sure.

The tents at the replacement depot were cold and snow blew in at the corners where the sides were laced together. To warm the tents the men cut the tops off jerry cans and burned twigs and sticks in them. The improvised heaters were forbidden because of the fire risk, so the GIs hid the cans in the bushes behind the tents every morning before inspection.

None of the men at the replacement depot had any idea when they might be assigned to a unit or which unit they might join. Most replacements were trained as infantry, so they assumed they'd be joining one of the infantry divisions fighting north of Florence.

When the men had a chance to leave the base, they discovered there wasn't much to do. Johnny visited the nearby city of Florence, also called Firenze. He tried to describe the beauty of Florence in a letter to his sister: "I went to 'Firenze La Bella' and saw some of the art works by Michelangelo, Leonardo da Vinci, Celline, and Galileo. Those names seemed mythical when studying them in school. I can hardly believe I've seen them for myself."

Johnny became friends with a quiet, thoughtful young man with the rather unlikely name of Shapley Haines. While the other men argued about one thing or another, Shapley Haines would often just lean back, close his eyes partway, and listen. Because he was so quiet, some of the other men started to call him "Sleepy Haines." But Shapley Haines wasn't sleeping, he was listening. He was one of those rare individuals who was content to spend more time listening than talking.

When Shapley Haines did talk, he usually had something to say. One day as they watched another load of new replacements get off the trucks, Shapley turned to Johnny and said, "I get a bad feeling about all these replacements. Everybody thinks the war is almost over, but the Generals wouldn't send all these men here if they

★ Click here to watch video

Figure 37-6: Children are not spared from the hardships of war.

weren't darn sure they were going to need them. We're getting ready to fight somebody. If the Germans in Italy are about to surrender, we must be getting ready for something else."

A group of Italian kids hung around the gate of the replacement depot, begging for food or candy. Several GIs were adopted by a little boy called "Kanuch" whose mother and father had both been killed. He spent all of his time near the camp and spoke English "just like a GI." Somebody gave him some sergeant's stripes and helped him sew them on the sleeve of his jacket.

One day, Johnny noticed a young Italian girl standing back while the other kids asked the GIs for food or gum. She reminded him of his niece Christine, so he worked his way around to her, knelt down and held out a chocolate bar. Her dirt-smudged face broke into a huge smile, then she grabbed the candy bar and ran down an alley, shouting excitedly. He didn't understand her words, but he didn't need to know Italian to see she was very happy with that candy bar.

Figure 37-7: Photo of Italian orphan called "Kanuch."

In the days that followed, Johnny often noticed that young girl standing shyly at the edge of the crowd of kids who waited outside the camp. She'd wave at him and he often gave her some food or candy. She didn't talk much, but he finally found out that her name was Maria.

One sunny day, Johnny saw Maria waiting by the gate, holding the hand of an older Italian man. She pointed at Johnny and shouted something in Italian. The man stepped over to Johnny and, with a large toothless smile, extended his hand. Maria called the Italian man "Papa," so Johnny figured he must be her father. Talking excitedly in Italian, the two guided Johnny down an alley to a small stone house near the edge of the village.

As they walked, Johnny noticed the man had a limp, but he thought it would be too nosy—and too difficult—to ask if the limp was from an accident or a war wound. The man could have fought with the Italian Army against the Allies, or he could have fought with the Italians against the Germans after the Americans arrived. It didn't really matter to Johnny either way. Whatever had happened in the past, they were not enemies now.

When they reached the house, Johnny could smell something cooking that definitely wasn't Army chow. With gestures, Maria's father made it clear he wanted Johnny to come into the house and join them for dinner. They didn't have much—a little pasta and a few vegetables—but they shared what they had. Johnny was grateful for the home-cooked meal.

Johnny knew only a few words of Italian and the family knew even fewer words of English, but they laughed and gestured as they ate. By the end of the meal, Johnny felt at home with them. When he left, he shook hands with the father and hugged both Maria and her mother. As he walked back to the camp, he couldn't help wondering what his own mother would have thought about that family. He decided she would have liked this simple Italian woman who had shown such kindness to her youngest son.

During his stay at the replacement depot, Johnny saw men from many different units, including the Brazilian Expeditionary Force, the 1st Armored Division, and the British 8th Army. He saw troops from India and even some men from the 92nd Infantry, one of the few all-black U.S. combat units. He heard rumors of troops from many other countries, including Great Britain, New Zealand, Canada, South Africa, and Poland. There was even a Jewish Brigade composed of some 5,000 Jewish soldiers dedicated to defeating the Nazis.

One day Johnny thought he saw a Jeep full of Japanese men wearing U.S. Army uniforms. He asked around and learned they were Japanese-Americans from the 442nd Nisei Regimental Combat Team who were on the line to the east. Although many of their families were being held in internment camps in America, these second-generation Japanese had volunteered to fight for America. Many Americans and many soldiers hated the Japanese for the sneak attack on Pearl Harbor and the atrocities they had committed in the Far East, but the soldiers of the 442nd earned the respect of other combat soldiers through their professional, courageous performance in combat.

Another day Johnny saw a group of soldiers, with full beards, turbans and vicious-looking swords. Shapley Haines said he'd heard they were Sikhs. Supposedly a group of them once crept behind enemy lines and killed an entire platoon of Germans. They'd cut off the German soldiers' heads and placed them in a circle.

Johnny wasn't sure if he believed the story, but he thought those Sikhs looked mean enough to have done that. As Johnny stood watching the wild-looking Sikhs march by, Shapley whispered, "It's good to know they're on our side."

On January 26, Johnny wrote a letter to his sister Lilly. In the letter, Johnny mentioned Al's recent furlough. Apparently Al had spent most of his furlough doing chores and hadn't gone to the hunting camp at all.

```
                              Jan. 26, 1945
                              Somewhere in Italy

Dear Folks:

Received a few letters from home this past week so
decided to drop you a line. There isn't much doing
here now as you already know. The Russians are steal-
ing the show and by the time this letter reaches you
their purpose will have been accomplished. How do the
people back home take the news of all this success?

As yet I have not had a chance to see brother Oscar,
but hope to do so in the near future.

I knew Alfred's visit would be just like it turned
out. Why didn't he spend his time like I did mine?
He's not independent, the poor sucker. Someone gave
him a bum steer. Would he ever like to read this.

Do you hear from "Art" very often or does he spend
all his time writing to that red head? Let's hope he
gets over those silly ideas.

What is brother George's address or do you have it? I
also would like to know Roy Honkala's address.

It sure is hard to write around here. No tables, no
light except for a candle. And not only that but
you're interrupted every once in a while and so you
forget everything you had in mind and the letters are
jerky.

How is dad getting along? Give him my regards and
tell him everything is O.K.

Well there isn't much more to write about so I'll say
so long, good luck, and God Bless you all.
                                          Johnny
```

★ Click here for Web Info

Figure 37-8: Transcript of a letter from Johnny to Lilly.

The Koski sisters worried constantly about their brothers as indicated in this letter from Eleanor:

```
A very bad news blackout from the brothers. Dad is
worried. The only one we hear from is Johnny. I have
had terrible reccuring nightmares lately. It is
always the same. It is a snow covered mountain and
the trees are cut down to stumps. A solder is run-
ning. In my dream I know it is Al or Johnny. Suddenly
he falls forward and the large pack he is carrying
falls to the side. I scream because I see he is
bloody and his helmet rolls down and down the hill. I
am afraid to go home from work lest there is a
telegram with the usual "We regret to inform you."
```

Early each morning the soldiers waiting at the 8th Replacement Depot lined up for roll call. They stood in formation in the cold wind and listened intently as the sergeant read the names of those men who were being assigned to combat units. After all the names were called, the men who'd been selected fell out of formation to collect their gear. They met at the assembly area, climbed into trucks, then drove away. The soldiers who remained behind at the replacement depot didn't know where the other men were sent and they never heard what happened to them.

During his first weeks at the replacement depot, Johnny was convinced that each day would be the day he would be assigned to a unit. But, as the weeks dragged on, he began to think he might spend the entire war in the replacement depot. "That would be lousy!" he thought. "Everyone else will be telling their war stories and I'll have to say I spent the whole war waiting in a replacement depot."

One night, the men watched a film called *The Battle of San Pietro* which featured combat footage of the 143rd Infantry Regiment of the 36th Infantry Division. During that battle, the 143rd suffered over 1,100 casualties, many of which were shown in the film as they were carried off in body bags. After the film, Johnny wondered why the Army had shown it to the replacements. It certainly wasn't going to boost anybody's morale.

★ Click here to watch video

Figure 37-9: The GIs were shown the rather brutal film, The Battle of San Pietro.

One of the men in Johnny's tent, a veteran who had been wounded and was waiting to be reassigned to a unit told them, "Don't worry about that movie. Things can get rough out there and men get killed, but no matter how bad it gets, some men are going to get through it. You just have to decide you're going to be one of 'em. Remember, not everybody dies in a war."

On February 21, the GIs at the 8th Replacement Depot began hearing reports of the battle of Riva Ridge and Mount Belvedere. They learned the 10th Mountain Infantry Division had successfully mounted a surprise night attack, climbing a cliff with ropes to catch the Germans by surprise. With Riva Ridge under Allied control, other units were able to take and hold Mt. Belvedere, Mt. Gorgolesco, and Mt. della Torraccia.

By mid-afternoon, trucks and ambulances started to arrive at the medical unit located near the replacement depot. Truck after truck drove into the camp, each carrying a load of wounded soldiers. The men of the replacement depot grew somber as they realized what this meant. With so many casualties, the Army was going to need a lot of replacements.

For several days, Johnny and the other replacements watched the trucks come into the camp, bearing wounded men from the front. Each morning, the sergeant called out the names of more men who had been assigned to units at the front. The trucks, loaded with replacements, then headed back to the front.

★ Click here to watch video

Figure 37-10: The men of the 10th Mountain Infantry Division got their first real combat experience during the attacks on Riva Ridge, Mount Belvedere, Mt. Gorgolesco, and Mt. della Torraccia.

The mood at the replacement depot became increasingly grim as more and more replacements were assigned to units and shipped to the front. It seemed pretty clear that somewhere near the front, some units were going through a lot of men.

One of the men in Johnny's tent had been at the front with the 34th Infantry Division. He'd been hit in the leg by shrapnel and spent almost a month out of the line. When the other men asked him what combat was like, he just looked into the distance and said, "It's not something you can really explain. You're so afraid that you piss your pants. You feel sick. You see your friends get killed, and you just try to make it through the next few minutes without screwing up and getting yourself killed."

He took a puff on his cigarette, "You try your best, but you know that it doesn't always matter how hard you try. If a shell's got your name on it, it's gonna get you no matter what you do. When it's over, you're too tired to spit. You eat some lousy food, sleep in a wet hole, then get up the next morning and do it all over again."

After a short pause, the man went on, "Don't be in a rush to leave here. This replacement depot might not seem all that great, but it's a hell of a lot better than a foxhole. Nobody's shooting at you, you get hot food, a cot, and regular showers. No, don't be in a rush to leave here."

★★★ Ordinary Heroes: Six Stars in the Window ★★★
38. Some uncertainty exists

January 21, 1945: Oscar and his crew bounced in their seats as Davey Mills manhandled the crippled B-17, trying to find his way over the Alps and back to Allied territory. They'd lost two engines to antiaircraft fire and the #4 engine was only running at half power, so Davey Mills was having a hard time keeping the plane at its current altitude of 20,000 feet.

Ominous thunder clouds stretched across the horizon. They didn't have enough power to climb over those clouds, so they'd have to weave a path between them. The entire crew understood their chances of getting back to base were slim to none. Even if the crippled plane made it through the thunder clouds and turbulence, they'd have to get over the Alps, then somehow keep the plane in the air until they could find a friendly airfield.

As Davey Mills wrestled with the controls of the B-17, Oscar rechecked his charts and feverishly worked his E6B computer. He thought he knew where they were, but he couldn't confirm it through the heavy clouds below. Without more data, he just couldn't be certain of their exact location.

Davey Mills called back to Oscar on the intercom, "Do you know where we are?"

Oscar replied, "I'm doing what I can. I think I know where we are, but we're weaving all over the place and I can't see anything through that undercast." He added ironically, "Some uncertainty exists as to our exact location."

Davey Mills yelled, "Dammit Koski! Can you get us back or not?"

Oscar replied, "If you can get us over these mountains, I'll get us back. Somehow."

"Okay then," said Davey Mills with determination. "Listen up men." The intercom crackled and the crew waited to hear what he had to say. Davey cleared his throat then continued, "We're going to need every foot of altitude to make it. Jettison everything you can get out the doors and I mean everything."

The crew opened a hatch and threw out everything that wasn't attached, including the machine guns, ammo, and flak jackets. They threw out Oscar's little navigator's bench even though it only weighed a couple of pounds. The crew even unbolted the ball turret and let it drop.

In short order, the crew removed everything that wasn't needed to fly the plane. Without machine guns and ammo, they were completely defenseless. One of the crewmen quipped, "If we run into German fighters, about all we can now do is spit at 'em!"

Oscar hoped German fighter pilots wouldn't be foolish enough to fly in this kind of weather. The crew already had more than enough problems.

Oscar thought, "It's up to God—God and Davey Mills—to get us home."

To keep his mind occupied, Oscar started to doodle in the remarks column of his navigator's log book. One thing led to another, and he found himself scribbling a bawdy limerick in the margin. Oscar then proceeded to add other nonsensical notes, including a fanciful entry: "Dropped bombs on Swiss village. Bomb caused avalanche, burying the town."

That hadn't happened. Those notes were just the nervous scribblings of a young officer trying to keep his mind occupied until the crippled bomber either fell from the sky or made it over the Alps.

Davey Mills coaxed the plane higher and somehow threaded a path through the Alpine peaks. After flying for a while, Davey Mills called Oscar on the intercom. "Koski, we're low on fuel and I can't see anything. You gotta tell me where we are."

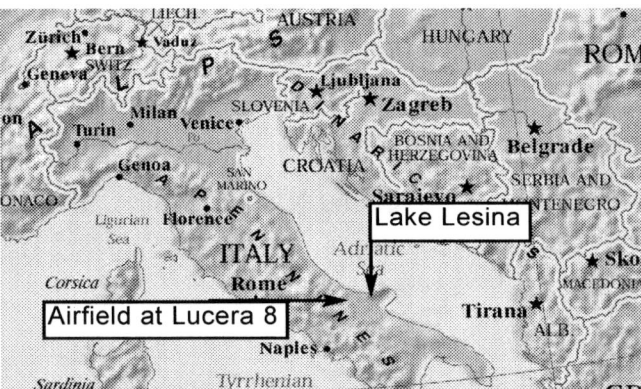

Oscar still wasn't certain of their exact location, but he knew Davey Mills didn't want to hear that. They all needed some good news, so he guessed and said, "Roger that! See that hole in the clouds up ahead? If my calculations are right, Lake Lesina should be right under that clear spot."

The pilot dropped the plane through the hole in the clouds and to everyone's vast relief they saw Lake Lesina below them.

Figure 38-1: Lake Lesina and Lucera 8.

Now that he knew their location, Oscar plotted a course back to base. As they approached the runway, they saw a group of airmen standing in formation, with officers handing out medals. Babying the remaining one and a half engines, Davey Mills brought the plane in for a perfect landing.

The assembled airmen and officers rushed across the runway towards the B-17 to see if they could assist the crew.

Now that they were safely on the ground, Oscar became worried about his scribbles in the navigation log. He grabbed the logbook and told the rest of the crew, "I gotta skedaddle." In the commotion Oscar managed to slip away from the plane without being noticed.

Oscar couldn't delete those entries from the log book and he couldn't remove the pages. His only plan was to stealthily return the logbook and hope no one looked at it too closely. His plan didn't work. At the briefing the next day, the squadron operations officer, Othmer Kemper, said, "We got some damn good men in this outfit. One guy, I call him Shakespeare 'cause of his poetry."

Kemper looked directly at Oscar and waited. Oscar looked down and pretended to take notes. After a short pause, Othmer Kemper moved on to other topics.

To Oscar's surprise and great relief, that was the last he heard about those scribbles in the navigator's logbook.

★ Click here to watch video

Figure 38-2: Oscar and his crew managed to return from the mission to Vienna.

★★★ Ordinary Heroes: Six Stars in the Window ★★★
39. Maybe they were going to be all right

February 28, 1945: Early that morning, Johnny found himself standing in line once again, listening as the sergeant at the 8th Replacement Depot called out the names of the men who had been assigned to combat units:

"Gray, Donald"

"Guidry, Dallas"

"Haines, Shapley"

Johnny perked up when he heard his friend's name. "Shapley!" Johnny thought. "He gets assigned to a unit and I'm still stuck here."

The sergeant continued calling out names:

"Kintner, Mancle"

"Klopfer, Adolph"

"Koski, John"

Johnny could barely believe that his name had been called. He wasn't going to spend the entire war at the replacement depot after all! The sergeant droned on, "Kovach, George, Kraft, Robert, Manse, Leroy," but Johnny didn't hear him. All he could think about was that he had finally been assigned to a combat unit. This was what he'd trained for, this was what he'd been waiting for, this was the reason he and these other young men were camping in this wind-swept olive grove in the middle of winter.

The sergeant told the men whose names had been called to collect their gear and report back in thirty minutes. Johnny hustled back to his tent, packed his gear into his duffel bag, and hurried back to the assembly area to join a group of enlisted men.

Johnny saw his friend Shapley Haines, so he walked over to chat with him. Shapley was counting the enlisted men and officers. As he finished his count, Shapley whistled and said, "That's thirty-eight enlisted men, eight Sergeants, and a couple of 2nd lieutenants. A full company only has about two hundred men. I don't know which outfit we're joining, but it looks to me like they just lost an awful lot of men."

Several trucks pulled up. Somebody said, "Hey! Those drivers are negroes."

One of the truck drivers, a huge black man, leaned out the window and said, "Hiya boys! We drives the new soldiers up the mountain. We drives the wounded and the body bags back down. You guys ready to take a ride?"

Aghast, the soldiers all took a step back. The truck driver broke into a broad grin, obviously enjoying his little joke.

A few minutes later, a sergeant from the replacement depot appeared. "Listen up! You men have been assigned to the 10th Mountain Infantry Division, 85th Mountain Regiment, F Company at Campo Tizzoro. When you get there, the first sergeant will assign you to platoons. Good luck!"

★ Click here to watch video

Figure 39-1: John Koski was assigned to a mortar squad of the 85th Regiment of the 10th Mountain Infantry Division.

As they lined up to get into the trucks, Johnny said to Shapley, "I always wanted to be in the Mountaineers, but I would have liked some of that special training on skis and stuff. It looks like we missed that part."

Shapley chuckled and said, "Yeah, I guess we missed that part. But, if you have to go into combat, you might as well go with the best. If those *Life* magazine articles got it right, those 10th Mountain guys are supposed to be the best."

Another soldier piped up, "I have a brother who volunteered for the Airborne. He says when the shooting starts, you're better off if the man beside you knows his stuff."

The men were quiet on the ride to Campo Tizzoro. Some smoked, some looked out at the rugged mountains, but most sat lost in thought. This was it. After weeks of waiting, they were finally going to find out what it was like in the front lines. Johnny, like the rest of the men, fervently hoped he would be up to the challenges that lay ahead.

One of the men sitting on the other side of the truck pulled his cigarette out of his mouth and said, "The 10th Mountain Division... that's the outfit that took Riva Ridge and Mount Belvedere last week. It was some kind of night assault up a sheer cliff. That's where all those wounded men have been coming from."

He flicked the ashes from his cigarette, then continued, "It was supposed to be a great victory, but it seems they lost a lot of men taking those hills. If you need this many replacements after winning a battle, I'd hate to see what happens after you lose one."

Johnny looked thoughtfully at the men bouncing on the seats across from him and wondered how many were going to make it through the coming months. He had no way of knowing that during the next eight weeks, nine of these replacements would be wounded and four would be killed in action.

Many of the men were thinking back to the circumstances that had brought them here, to a truck bouncing up a muddy road on the way to the front lines. One of the men in the truck remarked, "I was trained as a B-17 tail gunner. I don't know what I'm doing up here."

Another man added, "Yeah, I'm an antiaircraft gunner. One day someone drives up and tells us the Luftwaffe is done for and we're being sent to the replacement depot. Next thing I know, here I am, in a truck on the way to join the infantry!"

After hours of winding up narrow mountain roads, the trucks pulled into Campo Tizzoro, a small village comprised of rustic stone houses. The trucks worked their way through narrow streets towards an array of pyramidal army tents in a field at the edge of the village.

As they passed through the town, Johnny reviewed what he knew about the structure of an infantry regiment. The 85th Mountain Infantry Regiment would consist of approximately 2,400 men in three battalions. Each battalion had four letter companies, one Service Company, one Medical Company, and one Headquarters Company. The 1st Battalion included A, B, C, and D Companies. The 2nd Battalion consisted of E, F, G, and H Companies. The Third Battalion included I, K, L, and M Companies. The last letter company in each Battalion—D, H, and M Companies—were heavy weapons companies equipped with heavy machine guns and large mortars. The other three companies in each battalion were rifle companies.

Rifle companies typically consisted of four platoons. The 1st, 2nd, and 3rd platoons were Rifle Platoons, consisting of squads of about a dozen men armed with M1 Garand rifles and Browning Automatic Rifles, as well as a few snipers and bazooka squads. The 4th platoon, the Weapons Platoon, typically consisted of three mortar squads and two machine-gun squads. Johnny had been trained as a rifleman, so he figured he'd be assigned to a Rifle Platoon. He'd earned an Expert rating on the M1 rifle, so he thought they'd use him as a rifleman, or maybe even as a sniper.

As Johnny climbed out of the truck and took his place in line, First Sergeant William Ballek, F Company's highest-ranking non-commissioned officer, took charge. He called out each man's name and squad assignment. To Johnny's surprise, he was assigned to the 1st mortar squad of the 4th Platoon. Two other new replacements who had ridden up with Johnny, Adolph Klopfer and Robert Kraft, were assigned to the same mortar squad. Together, they set out to find the rest of the squad—the men they would serve with in combat.

As they walked over to find the mortar squad, Johnny said, "A mortar squad! I was hoping for a rifle squad. I don't want to be lobbing shells from behind the front lines."

Figure 39-2: William Ballek, First Sergeant of F-85.

Robert Kraft replied, "Think about it Johnny. They need three replacements for this one mortar squad. It doesn't sound to me like they were too far behind the lines."

From somewhere in the distance Johnny heard a phonograph playing "Oh, What a Beautiful Morning." That incongruous reminder of civilian life just made him feel further away from home.

They walked past a tall soldier standing outside a tent. Bobby Kraft asked him if he knew where they could find the 1st mortar squad. The soldier replied, "You found it. Just duck behind that tent right there."

Behind the tent, they found the men of the 1st mortar squad. The squad leader, Sergeant Bernard Carney, was a short, red-haired man who didn't seem to have any doubts about his role or his ability to fill it. Private First Class James Messier, the 1st gunner, was a short man from Massachusetts. Private First Class Edward Smieska, the 2nd gunner, was a thin fellow from Lansing, Michigan. Private First Class James Winterbottom—the soldier who had directed them to the tent—and Private First Class George Armstrong, the ammo bearers, were both from upstate New York. Winterbottom, also called "Summertop," was a very tall man, Armstrong was short and Smieska was only a little taller.

★ Click here to watch video

Figure 39-3: Some of the men from the 4th Platoon. Left to right: James Winterbottom, James Messier, George Armstrong, Ed Smieska.

As the newest members of the team, Johnny, Adolph Klopfer, and Robert Kraft were assigned as additional ammo bearers. Sergeant Carney gave them the scoop. Their lieutenant had just been transferred, so the platoon was under command of Platoon Sergeant James Orwig. With the new replacements, the platoon was now close to full strength with thirty-four men serving in two machine-gun squads and three mortar squads. Sergeants Tustin Ellison and Robert Ellis were in charge of the machine-gun squads. Bernard Carney, Oliver Eyer, and John Dempsey ran the mortar squads. All five of the squad leaders were newly promoted, the previous squad leaders having been killed or wounded the previous week.

Sergeant Carney explained what he wanted them to do. "Your main job is to carry mortar shells. The gunners can't do much if they're out of ammo, so you gotta carry a full load: four shells in the front pocket of this vest and four more shells in the back."

He paused and the new men nodded to show they understood. "Your hands will be free, so you'll also carry your M1 rifle or carbine. The Germans just love to take out our mortar crews, so when we deploy the mortar, you'll pass your ammunition vests to the gunners and take up defensive positions. Stay there unless I tell you to go back for more ammo. When we pack up, grab your ammo vest."

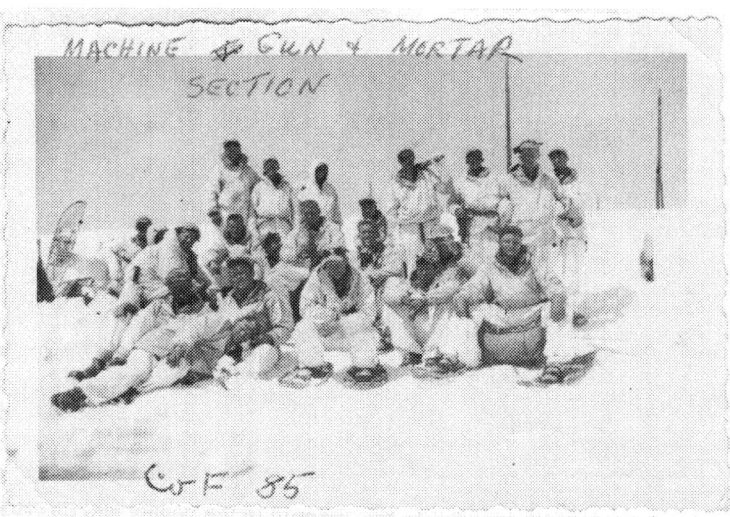

Figure 39-4: The soldiers of the 4th Platoon of F-85 during winter training at Camp Hale, Colorado, before deployment to Italy.

Lt. Jenkins (34)

M.G.
Norton
Ellis
Krusell
Mofford
Manse
Ch'Frson
Kintner

Ellison
Cantin
Coldham
Kovach
Miller
Cooke

O'Brien
Nelson
Canham
Orwig
Serjak

Mort
Carney
Messier
Legassey
Weiskar
W'Botom
Kraft
Kupfer
Koski

Eyer
Good
A'Strong
Boyajian
Babcock
McDaniel

Dempsey
Burkhart
Hart
Wentzler
Blasius
Hall

★ **Click here for Web Info**

Figure 39-5: This page from Sergeant James Orwig's notebook dated March, 1944, lists the men in his mortar and machine-gun squads. Johnny Koski is listed in the 1st mortar squad in the right column

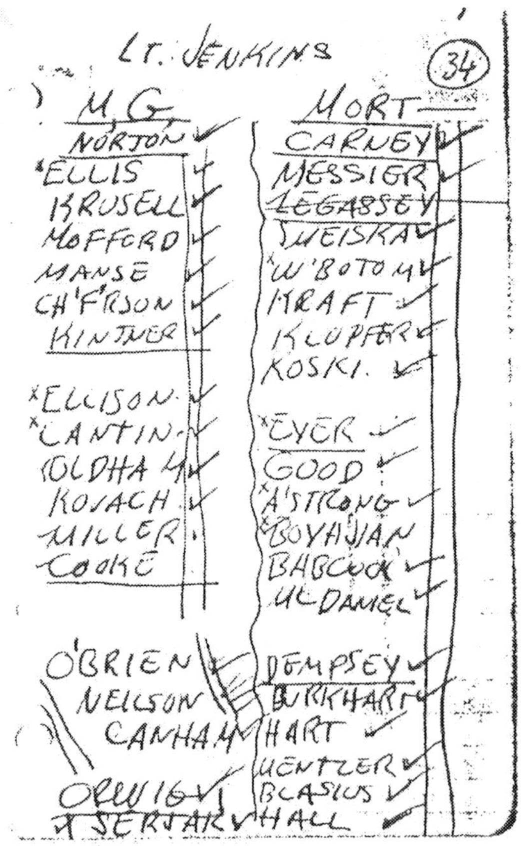

Sergeant Carney momentarily locked eyes with Johnny. "Sounds easy enough, doesn't it? Well, you'll find it's tough going, humping ammo up and down these mountains. You gotta stay sharp. We're gonna be focused on the targets. You're responsible for squad security. If a German with a grenade gets within throwing distance, we're all dead. You got it?"

"Yes, Sergeant!" the new men yelled together.

"Jeezus! You guys are green as grass. Don't go yelling 'Yes, Sergeant!' around here. I don't want every German sniper in the valley looking at me. And, remember, no saluting anybody when we're at the front. Those snipers just love to pop an officer."

The new replacements looked at each other and nodded solemnly. This man seemed to know what he was doing. Maybe they were going to be all right.

★★★ Ordinary Heroes: Six Stars in the Window ★★★
40. The ones who weren't so lucky

January 27, 1945: Flight Officer Oscar Koski was promoted to the rank of 2nd lieutenant. He was just one month shy of his 21st birthday, but he had flown and returned from nineteen combat missions. Like most of the other young airmen, he didn't expect to live to see another birthday.

On January 31, the 15th AAF sent 805 bombers against the oil refinery at Moosbierbaum. The 301st led the mission over the target. The target was covered by clouds, but the lead plane used one of the new electronic navigation systems to locate the target area.

As the planes started on the bomb run over the city, they found themselves flying into 120 mile-per-hour-headwinds. The meteorologists of the time knew little about the jet stream and had not predicted those headwinds. Oscar called on the intercom, "With this headwind, we're just crawling over the city. I estimate no more than 90 miles per hour groundspeed. This is going to be tough!"

The German antiaircraft gunners seemed to have been taken by surprise or maybe they were confused by the slow-moving planes. In any event, the planes from 301st experienced only sporadic flak as they flew over the target and dropped their bombs.

The squadrons following them were not so lucky, flying directly into some of the worst flak they had ever experienced. The German gunners couldn't see the bombers through the heavy clouds, so they threw up a heavy barrage of flak over the target and the slow-flying bombers flew right into it.

Oscar listened as the tail gunner described the scene behind them: "Jeez! Planes are going down all over the place! I never seen it this bad. Heavy losses! There goes another one—three engines smoking and the wing on fire!"

Oscar closed his eyes and said a silent prayer of thanks for whoever decided to put the 301st in the lead on this mission.

Thirty bombers were lost that day, taking 300 crewmen with them.

That night, Oscar sat in the officer's club. The room filled with smoke and a group of airmen at a nearby table began recounting legendary tales of narrow escapes and incredible luck.

★ Click here for Web Info

Figure 40-1: Oscar's missions in January, 1945.

One member of the ground crew told them about a mission to Greece in January of 1944. "Two B-17s from the 97th Bomb Group ran into engine trouble. For some reason, instead of turning to the right, away from the group, they turned left, into the group. Both planes collided with other B-17s, sending pieces of B-17s raining down. A B-17 from the 353rd Squadron of the 301st was hit by one of the other B-17s, cutting off the tail and trapping the tail gunner in his position. The tail was cut off just right, so it spun around and around like a seed from a maple tree. The tail hit a clump of pine trees, softening the fall. The gunner opened his hatch and climbed out. Until he climbed out, he hadn't realized that the rest of the plane was gone."

The other men were incredulous. "That's ridiculous! You can't expect us to believe a man survived a landing in the cut-off tail section of a B-17!"

The storyteller replied, "Hey, I know this happened. The tail gunner's name was James Raley and I heard the story directly from him. It happened on January 11, 1944 and the tail number of the plane was 42–3098 if you want to check it out for yourself."

After a few more drinks, one of the men asked, "Did you hear about the B-17 that was almost cut in half in Africa? An Me–109 attacked from above. The German pilot was killed by the gunners, but his plane flew into the fort, knocking off the left horizontal stabilizer, almost cutting the fort in two. The pilot shouldn't have been able to keep that plane in the air, but somehow he managed to keep it flying for over an hour. He reached the base and put it down for the softest landing possible. He landed okay, but when they opened the hatch to get out, the plane broke in two on the runway. The plane was scrap, but the crew survived."

Skillings said, "You're putting me on! B-17s are tough, but I don't think anyone could fly one home without the horizontal stabilizer. And if the frame was that weak, it would have fallen apart on landing, if not before."

The other guy said, "I've got five bucks that says it happened."

Skillings said, "You're on!"

They both slapped five dollar bills on the counter. Then the other man reached into his pocket and pulled out a photo that showed a B-17 in flight. The left horizontal stabilizer had been blown off and the plane was cut almost in two. As everyone stared at the photo in disbelief, the man reached over and pocketed both of the five dollar bills. "I told ya' so!" he said.

★ Click here for Web Info

Figure 40-2: Photo of a B-17 that was almost cut in half, but still made it home.

One of the airmen piped up with another story: "Do you remember that mission of December 29th, when we hit the marshaling yards at Innsbruck, Austria?"

A number of the men groaned to indicate they remembered that mission all too well.

The airman continued, "You probably remember we lost two B-17s on that mission, but I bet you don't know what happened to Lieutenant Pearson and his crew. 1st Lieutenant Lyle Pearson from the 419th Squadron was flying a new plane on its first combat mission. Both the pilot and the copilot were on their final mission, the last time out before they got sent home."

A 2nd lieutenant interrupted: "Lousy luck! To get shot down on your last mission!"

A pilot remarked, "I don't know. Is it worse to get shot down on your first mission or your last mission?"

The first airman thumped his glass on the table and glared until they quit talking. He continued, "As I was saying, before reaching the IP, their plane was hit by flak in the lower turret and the bomb bay. The plane caught fire and went into a steep dive. The right wing and the tail tore off the plane. Crews from other planes didn't see any parachutes, they just saw the plane hit the steep side of a mountain and explode."

One of the other guys said, "I remember. They all got killed."

"Nope!" said the airman, "They didn't all get killed. Somebody just got a letter from Lieutenant Pearson. He's in a German POW camp. He wrote that he was blown through the Plexiglas nose of the plane and was knocked unconscious. He awoke just in time to deploy his chute and landed safely."

The airman paused for dramatic effect before he continued, "But, that's not the end of the story. The copilot, Sam Wheeler, was blown out of the plane without a parachute. As he tumbled through the air, he remembered hearing that a man could stabilize his fall if he flattened out his body. There didn't seem to be any point to it, but he thought he'd try it, since he didn't have anything else to do at the time."

"So Wheeler was falling through the air, lying face-upwards, when a chestpack parachute hit him in the face. He grabbed it and fastened it to his harness. He pulled the rip cord and landed safely."

The men groaned in disbelief.

The airman held his hand up to indicate that he wasn't finished, "But they weren't the only lucky men on that plane. The navigator, Arthur Frechette, was blown from the plane without a parachute and regained consciousness just before he hit the ground. He hit the side of a snow-covered, 45-degree slope and bounced and rolled down the hill. He ended up with a broken right arm, a sprained right ankle, a smashed left knee cap, and friction burns on his right side, but he survived. Six of the ten-man crew survived and were taken prisoner by the Germans."

Tapping the table for emphasis, the airman finished, "You gotta admit, that is one lucky crew!"

The other men just shook their heads in amazement. They'd never heard of so many miraculous escapes from a single plane.

After a few minutes, a captain, who had been sitting quietly by himself, climbed rather unsteadily to his feet. He raised his glass and said in a slurred but serious voice, "You know, whenever I hear about men with such good luck, I can't help but think about the other men, the men who didn't make it back to tell some incredible story. I can't help but think about the guys who fell and couldn't grab a chute, the guys who couldn't bail out, the men who rode their plane all the way down."

He stopped for a moment, then held up his glass, "Here's a drink to those poor souls, the ones who weren't so lucky."

★★★ Ordinary Heroes: Six Stars in the Window ★★★
41. What was it like?

March 1, 1945: When Johnny and Bobby Kraft lined up for breakfast on their first morning with F Company, they ended up behind an unusually tall GI. Johnny had known some big men, but this guy towered over the other GIs. Later, as the men sat eating, Johnny saw the big man carefully spooning his food into the back of his mouth and chewing only with his molars.

He asked one of the other GIs about the big guy. The GI replied, "Oh, that's Wally Krusell. Up near Belvedere, a shell landed just in front of him. The concussion blew his front teeth back into his mouth. He just reached in and pulled them back down. He didn't want to go to the medics and get sent to another unit, so he's just hoping they'll heal by themselves. Sure, he eats funny, but if I was you, I wouldn't mention it again. He's kind of sensitive about it and you can see for yourself how big he is."

The F Company soldiers ate quietly. They'd smile occasionally and sometimes laugh at a joke, but they didn't participate in the kind of rough horseplay, boasting, and teasing normally found in a group of young soldiers.

The soldiers of F Company had just been through some tough times and they were still trying to come to grips with that experience. They had met the enemy, and in their first major action, had handed the Germans a stunning defeat. They knew the war wasn't over yet, but they had survived their first combat experience and helped win a decisive battle that opened a gaping hole in the last heavily fortified defensive line in Italy. Many of them had been wounded, many had lost good friends. Most of them knew they had come close to being killed once, if not numerous times. Those experiences were enough to make even exuberant young men take life a bit more seriously.

Even the Italian civilians noticed a change in the young soldiers after their return from the front. Two elderly Italian women watching a group of F Company soldiers, talked to each other in hushed voices. Carl Cossin, a rifleman with F company, asked an Italian interpreter what the women were saying. The interpreter said, "They said when those young boys left here last month, they were cheerful, they had a bright gleam in their eyes. Now their eyelids are half closed. Even when they laugh, they have a frown on their faces. They do not act like children anymore."

Johnny noticed many new replacements wandering through the camp. It wasn't just the 4th Platoon—every platoon in F Company seemed to have a gaggle of nervous replacements wearing new uniforms and unsuccessfully trying to blend in with the old timers.

Johnny and the other two new replacements in the 1st mortar squad, Klopfer and Kraft, stuck together during their first days at Campo Tizzoro. The other men in the squad weren't really unfriendly, but they didn't go out of their way to make the new men feel at home. Johnny thought he understood how they felt. Those men had trained together for years, at Camp Hale and Camp Swift. They had shared the dan-

★ Click here to watch video

Figure 41-1: All GIs trained with the bayonet. Few expected to use one in combat, but some did.

gers of the previous weeks in combat. They knew they could rely on each other when the going got rough. They didn't know the replacements and didn't know if they could depend on them.

There was another reason for the squad's cool attitude towards the new replacements. The new men were replacing old friends who had just been killed or wounded. Making friends too soon seemed just a bit like betrayal of their fallen comrades. Johnny figured things might change once they got into combat, but for now, they'd just have to live with the gulf between the veterans and the new replacements.

Johnny noticed that most of the veterans bore some marks from their time in combat. Many men limped. Many had difficulties moving their arms, or bore cuts and bruises on their faces or hands. Many wore bandages under their shirts or trousers. These men had won a battle, but they had clearly taken some punishment in the process.

After breakfast, the men lined up for close order drill and calisthenics. The veterans grumbled and some of them moved stiffly, but the first sergeant kept them at it anyway. Minor wounds were no excuse.

While waiting in line for lunch, Johnny heard the veterans talking about the men who had been missing since the attack on Mt. Belvedere, Mt. Gorgolesco, and Mt. della Torraccia the previous week. Each day more missing men were confirmed as killed in action. Michael "Bony" Pliscek, Edward Stepnowski, Lorin Carson, William Brown, Leonard Pierce, Warren Steiner, Richard Elmer, William Watson, Leonard Paddock, William Bridges—the list of men who had been confirmed dead continued to grow. The men of F Company received word that some of the missing men had survived and had been sent back for medical treatment. But some men were still listed as SUD, or Status Undetermined. No one knew what happened to them. Maybe no one ever would.

Johnny, Klopfer, and Kraft took their mess kits to a half-empty table where they were greeted with a half-hearted nod from its other occupants. After an uncomfortable pause, one of the soldiers stuck out his hand: "Tustin Ellison, 1st Machine Gun Squad."

John solemnly shook his hand: "John Koski, 1st Mortar Squad. This is Klopfer and Kraft."

Tustin gestured at the men sitting next to him. "You already know Messier. That's Boyajian over there."

A soldier from the next table asked Tustin Ellison, "Did you hear about Al Wiedorn?"

Ellison replied, "No, I haven't heard anything about Wiedorn since he was transferred to H Company. How's he doing?"

The other soldier replied, "Well, here's the way I heard it. The Germans counterattacked and his platoon was being overrun. Wiedorn grabbed a .30 caliber machine gun, stood up, and mowed down the advancing Germans, cradling that machine gun in his arms. That broke the attack. His platoon regrouped and they drove the Germans back."

Ellison replied, "That crazy son of a gun! Did he make it?"

The other man replied, "Yeah, he made it. Somebody said they put him up for a Silver Star."

Ellison replied, "Well, I guess you never know who's gonna come through in combat. I remember at Camp Hale, we were hiking up the mountains with full packs. We got to the top and the lieutenant gave us a twenty minute rest. Most of the men crawled to the side of the path, but Wiedorn plopped himself down in the middle of the trail, still wearing his ninety pound pack. A major came up that trail and told Al to move out of the way. Wiedorn told that major that he wouldn't move off the trail 'if Jesus Christ himself came up the path.' I thought that major was gonna explode! I wouldn't have bet Wiedorn would still be in the Army, let alone up for a Silver Star."

A few minutes passed in silence. Then, inexplicably, Larry Boyajian started chuckling and said to James Messier across the table. "Jimmy, I hear the medics found Tom Condon. I guess your flag worked."

"Yeah," Messier replied. Noticing the puzzled expressions on the faces around the table, he explained, "They were pounding us with those 88s. I crawled into a shell hole. Tom Condon was lying there and he said 'I've been hit, I've been hit.' I checked him out and found a little hole in his right chest and a 6-inch star-shaped wound in his back. It wasn't bleeding, it was just steaming in the cold. I poured powder in the wound and covered it with a pad. Just about then, Boyajian slides into the hole. We decided we'd better try to hook up with the rest of the Company, but that meant leaving Tom in that shell hole."

Messier took a long drink of coffee, then continued, "I wanted to make sure the medics found him, so I stuck a couple of sticks in the dirt near the edge of the shell hole, then wound toilet paper back and forth between them. I figured the medics would see it and find him in the hole. Then Larry and I took off. I guess the medics saw the flag and found him after all."

A few minutes later, a corporal from another company stopped by the table and asked hopefully, "I'm looking for a friend of mine. He's with F Company, but I don't see him anywhere. Do any of you guys know where I can find Tommie Creel?"

Johnny and Kraft looked at each other and shrugged. They'd never heard of Tommie Creel.

Several of the men at the table looked uneasy, but no one said anything.

The soldier said, "Well? Do you know where I can find him or not?"

Finally, Tustin Ellison replied, "Yeah, we know where Tommie Creel is. He ain't here. He got killed, he was one of the first guys that got hit up near Belvedere."

The soldier just stood there for a bit, clenching and unclenching his fists. Then he turned, and shuffled away. The men at the table just stared down at their plates and continued eating. They didn't dare think too much about their missing comrades. For now, they just wanted to enjoy these few days at the rest camp. They knew they'd be back at the front all too soon.

That afternoon, the platoon ran some tactical problems, giving the new men a chance to practice working as part of the team in a combat situation. The replacements soon learned this wasn't going to be easy. The rest of the squad—Carney, Messier, Winterbottom, Armstrong, and Smieska—had been training together for years. They worked together like cogs in a watch, and could deploy the mortar and start dropping shells on target in a matter of minutes. Johnny and the other replacements found they had to stay sharp to keep up.

As they waited in line for supper that night, Klopfer said, "Those guys are good! This is like trying to join a championship ball team the night before the big game."

Kraft responded, "Yeah, and the other team is going to be shooting back."

Klopfer continued, "We only got a couple of days to get this right before they send us back to the front lines. If we don't stop making mistakes, the Germans are going to kill us. Of course, that's if Sergeant Carney doesn't kill us first!"

All three chuckled, but they knew it wasn't that funny. In a few days, they were going into combat as part of an elite team. If they didn't learn how to work smoothly as part of that team, they were going to get somebody killed.

After supper, Johnny ran into Nesbur Brandt, who had come up with him from the 8th Replacement Depot. They walked over to the Red Cross wagon to get some coffee and donuts. While Johnny and Nesbur stood in line they talked about some of the men they knew and tried to act nonchalant about moving to the front lines.

Nesbur said, "Back in basic, we had a drill sergeant who gave us this big talk about how the Army had invested so much in us, so they wouldn't let anything happen to us. He said if we just did what we were told, we'd be all right."

Johnny replied, "Our drill sergeant gave us the same speech. But then I heard Sergeant Orwig talking about those mules coming down Mount Belvedere. The Army didn't take such good care of those guys."

Nesbur continued, "Yeah, I keep hearing stories about what it was like up on Riva Ridge and Mount Belvedere and how many men got killed. It makes me wonder if that drill sergeant ever went through anything like that."

They stopped talking and just kicked at the dirt as they waited in line for a donut and coffee.

★ Click here to watch video

Figure 41-2: An Italian Alpini, wearing his distinctive cap, leads a supply mule up Mount Belvedere.

Later that night, Johnny walked past the Red Cross shack again and spotted Nesbur waiting in line again. "Hey!" he teased, "You must really like coffee and donuts!"

Nesbur grinned sheepishly, but didn't say anything in response.

Johnny knew Nesbur wasn't standing in line again just for the coffee and donuts. The Red Cross shack was operated by girls, honest-to-goodness American girls. To the homesick GIs, they looked like angels. It was definitely worth standing in line for a while to have one of them smile as she handed you a cup of coffee and a donut.

Over the next few days, the men had a chance to attend recreational shows. One night they watched a performance of the play *Blithe Spirit* by Noël Coward, a comedy that gave them a welcome break from the stress of the battlefield. Another night, they watched a magician named BerMar. After the usual magic tricks, the magician looked deep into his crystal ball and solemnly announced the war would end on April 15.

Johnny turned to Kraft and said, "Wouldn't it be something if the war ended on April 15th?"

Kraft answered, "I certainly wouldn't complain if this war ended by mid-April. Maybe this guy should put on a show for the Germans and tell them the same thing. Then on the 15th, we could all just stop shooting, pack up, and go home. Yes sir, that would be just fine with me."

Johnny replied, "Boy, wouldn't that be sweet! I could be hunting at Flat Rock this fall. Yeah, that would suit me just fine."

The replacements were all anxious to know what combat was like. One night, as the men sat in their tent checking their gear, Klopfer finally got the nerve to ask James Winterbottom the question that all of the new replacements had been dying to ask: "What was it like up near Belvedere?"

Winterbottom thought for a while, then said, "Okay, I'll tell you what it was like."

> The Germans were dug in along the top of Riva Ridge and Mount Belvedere. Riva Ridge overlooked the approaches to Belvedere. The Army had tried to take Mount Belvedere three times, but was forced back every time under heavy fire from Riva Ridge. We couldn't take and hold Belvedere if we didn't take Riva Ridge first.
>
> The problem was, the face of Riva Ridge was a sheer cliff, some 1,500 feet high. The Germans didn't think anybody could climb it, not in force anyway. Sure, a few guys could probably find some way up that cliff, but a couple of Germans standing at the top with grenades could easily wipe them out as they climbed. That's why nobody else had tried to take Riva Ridge.

Well our men did it. They climbed that cliff at night, with ropes, without making any noise. To make sure no one fired an accidental shot, which would warn the Germans, the men were ordered to unload their rifles before they climbed the cliff. So, up they went, climbing a sheer cliff at night, with unloaded rifles, hoping to take the Germans by surprise.

That part worked. They caught the Germans off-guard. Most of them were still asleep and didn't get a chance to man their guns. That attack cleared the way for the main assault on Mount Belvedere, Mount Gorgolesco, and Mount della Torraccia. That's where we came in.

It was still dark when we started hiking uphill, somewhere near Mount Belvedere or Gorgolesco—in the dark one hill looks a lot like another. I remember we were part way up the mountain, winding back and forth on a little trail, joking as we walked. We could hear explosions up the hill, but we didn't realize what was going on.

Then we saw a mule train coming down the road towards us. Each mule had a dead GI hanging over its back, head on one side, legs on the other. Those dead men wore the same uniforms we were wearing. That's when we realized what we were in for. Nobody laughed after that.

We started to see dead GIs and bright red splotches in the snow. We finally got to the top and dug in. The Germans launched a vicious counterattack like they always do, but we beat them off.

Then they pounded us with mortars, 88s, and Moaning Minnies. You don't hear those 88s until they hit, but you hear those Moaning Minnies howling as they fall. Each one sounds like it's coming just for you. We huddled in foxholes all night while German shells tore up the trees and ground around us. It was a long cold night! Every time the shells stopped falling for a few minutes, you could hear men praying and the wounded screaming for help.

The next morning, we were supposed to advance up the next hill, Mount della Torraccia. The day started badly. A group of officers from H Company went to an observation post to plan the attack. They got hit by German 88s. Only one officer survived, the rest were killed or wounded.

We were supposed to move out at 7:00 a.m. Just as we were getting ready to leave, the damn Germans counterattacked. We fought them off, reorganized, then headed up della Torraccia about 8:00 a.m. Hell of a way to start a day!

There was only one way up della Torraccia, a narrow trail that wound back and forth up the steep slope. We didn't know it, but the Germans had 88s covering that trail. They waited until the 4th Platoon moved well within their fire zone, then started to fire. When we tried to move back, they fired on the rear. When we tried to move ahead, they fired on the front. They had us where they wanted us, trapped on that trail. Some of the men found a way up the mountain. The rest of us scrambled for whatever cover we could find.

Winterbottom paused and looked at the ground for a moment. "Snow doesn't give you much cover from shrapnel."

One shell hit right behind my squad. I was hit in the back and fell face-first down the hill. When I came to, I was lying in the snow, with blood running down my back and over my head.

I wasn't in a lot of pain. I remember thinking I was going to die, and somehow it didn't seem so bad. I lay there fading in and out of consciousness for most of the afternoon—maybe five hours—while the Germans shelled that hill. By the time I came to, it was getting dark and the shelling had stopped. I heard German voices, so I held my breath, pretending to be dead. I heard a German walking towards me. He bayoneted the guy who had fallen to my right. Then he stepped over me. All I could do was lie there and wait for the bayonet.

He said something in German and then he stepped away. I heard him thrust his bayonet into the man lying to my left. I just lay there, trying not to breathe. I must have passed out, because the next thing I remember it was very dark and I heard voices, American voices, speaking softly nearby.

I don't know why those Germans didn't bayonet me. I can only figure they saw all the blood on my head and thought I had such a bad head wound that I had to be dead. Maybe holding my breath convinced them I was dead. Maybe passing out saved my life.

When I heard those American voices, I managed to roll over so I could see what was happening. I saw that some of the other men had somehow survived. I ordered the men to pull the firing pins out of the mortars. We bent the pins so the Germans couldn't use them. Five of us then crawled down the hill and hid under a haystack for the night. When we got back to Battalion the next day, they poured sulfa powder on my wounds, bandaged me up, and sent me back to the squad.

F Company started up that mountain with just over 200 men. Before it was over, seventeen men were dead, forty-six were wounded, and one is still missing. That's sixty-four casualties—almost a third of the company killed or wounded. That's why you see so many new replacements. The three of you are replacing good men who got killed or wounded on that hill.

Winterbottom stopped talking and looked down at the dirt floor of the tent, lost in thought. The new men sat and waited.

After a minute or two, Winterbottom swallowed, looked up, and continued, "We held our positions until the 28th, when we were relieved by the Brazilians and pulled back here to Campo Tizzoro. They cleaned us up, paid us, and fed us a hot meal. That's when you joined us. Is there anything else you want to know?"

The new replacements sat in stunned silence. There wasn't anything they could say to that, so they silently went back to checking their gear.

★ Click here to watch video

Figure 41-3: Sergeant James Winterbottom told the new replacements about his experiences in the area near Mount Belvedere, Mount Gorgolesco, and Mount della Torraccia.

★★★ Ordinary Heroes: Six Stars in the Window ★★★
42. Not your burden

February 1945: February started inauspiciously. Oscar flew again on the 7th as the 301st sent nineteen B-17s with a 5th Wing raid on the Lobau Oil Refinery in Vienna, Austria. The planes flew as two groups. In one group, 1st Lieutenant George Fischer from the 419th Squadron of the 301st was flying a B-17 that developed engine problems. The plane left the formation and dropped its landing gear. Three chutes were seen leaving the plane. The plane crash-landed and the remaining crewmen were taken prisoner.

In Oscar's group, the oxygen system on the lead plane malfunctioned and the top turret gunner and navigator lost consciousness before reaching the target. The entire group missed the bomb release point, so they continued to the alternative target at Pola, Italy, which they bombed, but missed.

As the Allies continued to pound the German industrial and military infrastructure, and as U.S. and Soviet troops moved closer to the heart of Germany, some missions became easier. There were occasional "milk runs," such as Oscar's mission to Graz, Austria on February 8—missions where flak was light and no planes were lost. But other missions encountered heavy resistance. There was no way of knowing ahead of time what kind of resistance they might run into, so every mission was stressful. The increasingly superstitious crews didn't dare breathe a sigh of relief until the wheels touched down on the landing strip.

The strain of the missions was evident in the faces and behavior of the airmen. Almost everyone smoked, even those who hadn't smoked before they got to a combat zone. Many developed nervous tics. Some became moody and withdrawn. Some couldn't sleep, while others spent most of their off hours lying motionless in their bunks. Some wrote a constant stream of letters home. Some developed a passion for poker or craps.

The night before a mission, their feelings often went beyond fear. As Howard Jackson, a bombardier with the 15th Air Force put it, "The terror starts the night before the mission. This should not be confused with fear. Fear is when you have to ask a girl to dance who might say no, or when waiting in class to be asked a question you don't know how to answer. Terror is anxiety, dreams, rationalization of excuses not to fly, headaches, loose bowels, shaking, and silence."

When a plane was shot down, the surviving airmen didn't spend a lot of time mourning the lost crew. It wasn't that they didn't care, it was more that they couldn't care. It was a matter of protecting their own sanity. If they spent too much time thinking about the missions or the men who were lost, they would not be able to cope. It was better to forget, to just get on with the job. Grief and stress would be dealt with, somehow, after the war was won.

On February 22, the 15th AAF sent 774 bombers and 334 fighters against fifty different targets in Germany as part of Operation Clarion. The planes flew at low altitudes, hitting railroad, communication, and transportation targets. Many targets were German towns that had escaped previous bombing. The goal was to "spread the impact on the population" and cripple German morale.

Operation Clarion took place only a week after the British and American bombers attacked the German city of Dresden. Dresden had not been previously bombed and was crowded with refugees trying to escape the Soviet advance. The incendiary bombs started huge fires and the resulting firestorm decimated the city center, killing an estimated 35,000 to 200,000 people. Germany was being hit hard, but despite the massive attacks and devastation, the Germans refused to surrender.

On February 25, Oscar waited on the runway for twenty-four bombers from the 301st to return from a mission to Linz, Austria. He saw his friend and fellow navigator, Danny Moore, also waiting for the bombers to return.

"What are you doing here?" Oscar asked. "I thought you guys were flying today."

Danny replied, "Yeah, I was supposed to be flying, but I had to get a tooth pulled. So, Burnstein is navigating in my place."

They turned as they heard the first planes returning. The formation was ragged. Some of the planes were obviously damaged. It looked like it had been a tough mission.

Someone counted the planes as they landed: "Twenty-one, twenty-two, twenty-three. Oh, oh, we're missing one."

Oscar turned to see Danny Moore peering anxiously into the distance. Danny said, "505 didn't land. Oh God, I hope they're all right."

Oscar said, "Hey, maybe they're just late or had to make an emergency landing somewhere. Don't assume anything until we find out what happened."

★ Click here to watch video

Figure 42-1: Support personnel and off-duty combat crews waited for the return of each mission.

They waited a while longer, straining to catch sight of one more approaching plane. But nothing came. After almost two hours, they slowly walked to the officer's club.

As the crews finished their debriefing, they trickled into the officer's club. It had been a tough mission and it showed on the faces of the crewmen. One of the men said, "The flak was heavy. Somebody screwed up and most of the bombs missed the target. They landed in a fenced area. I think it might have been a prisoner-of-war camp. We lost four bombers all together. Eight of ours were badly damaged, fifteen had some damage, and one didn't make it back."

Danny spoke up. "Stueve was flying 505. Was that the plane that was lost?"

The man looked down at his drink, then replied, "Yeah, Stueve's plane went down. We were getting hammered by flak as we approached the target. His #4 engine caught fire. Then it spread to the right wing. He fell out of formation, then the plane exploded. He hadn't dropped his bombs yet, so the plane just disappeared. One minute it was there, then it was just a cloud of smoke with some bits and pieces falling down. Someone said they saw two chutes, but I didn't see any."

Danny turned and walked away. Oscar walked silently with him back to his tent, the tent where all four officers from Stueve's crew had slept. Three of them would not be coming back. Danny sat on his cot and stared at the three empty cots.

After a while, Oscar told Danny, "The first sergeant's going to come to collect their personal effects. We'd better sort through them now."

One by one, they opened the three officers' footlockers, removing snacks and cigarettes, and looking for any pinup photos or other items that shouldn't be sent home to the dead flier's wives or mothers. When finished, they sat and looked at the footlockers with the last names stenciled on front: Stueve, Varns, Kock.

Danny buried his face in his hands and mumbled, "I hope they didn't suffer."

Oscar tried to comfort his buddy, "You don't know they're dead. Somebody saw two chutes and there could have been more. They could be safe with the resistance. Or, if the Germans caught them, they could be on their way to a prison camp. Who knows? You might see them again after the war."

Danny just sat there, brooding.

Oscar stood up in front of him and said, "Listen Danny. I've thought about this a lot–every time my crew goes up without me. If my crew got shot down when I wasn't with them, I know I'd feel relieved that I was still alive. Then I'd feel guilt, guilt that I wasn't on the plane with them, guilt that I was still alive. But you have to remember, you didn't shoot them down. It wouldn't have made any difference if you were with them. You couldn't have saved them."

Oscar sat on the bunk across from his friend, "Danny, you can grieve for them, you can remember them, you can even name your children after them. But you can't carry any guilt for what happened to them. It wasn't your fault. It's not your burden to bear."

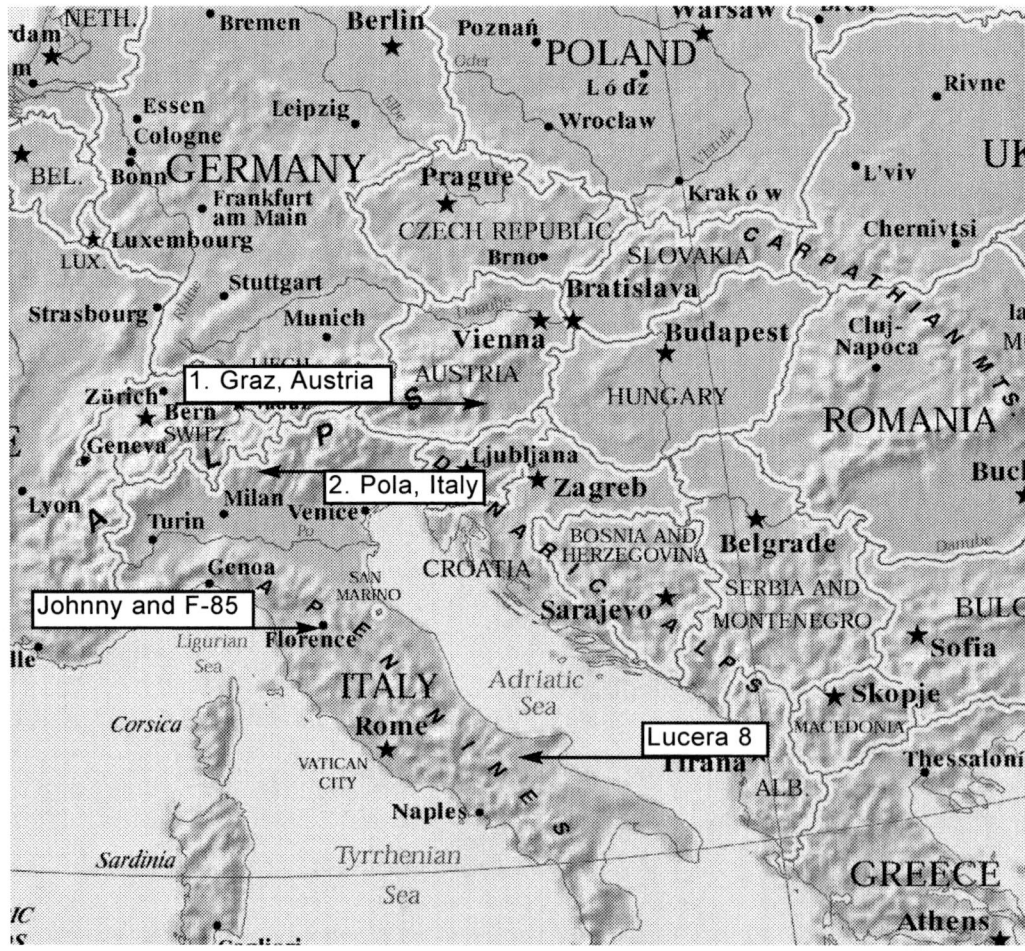

Figure 42-2: Oscar's missions in February, 1945. He flew fairly close to the mountains where Johnny Koski was serving with F-85. Unfortunately, the page from Oscar's records listing his flights for February of 1945 was missing from his folder. The flights have been reconstructed from his overall mission record and unit histories of the 301st.

★★★ Ordinary Heroes: Six Stars in the Window ★★★
43. Just scared kids in uniform

March 2, 1945: Private First Class James Winterbottom disappeared for a few hours, then returned to the squad carrying an unusual weapon that looked like the cut-down barrel from an 81 mm mortar. It had a shoulder strap, a small base plate, and a lanyard, but no sight and no bipod. The tube was just a little longer than an 81 mm shell.

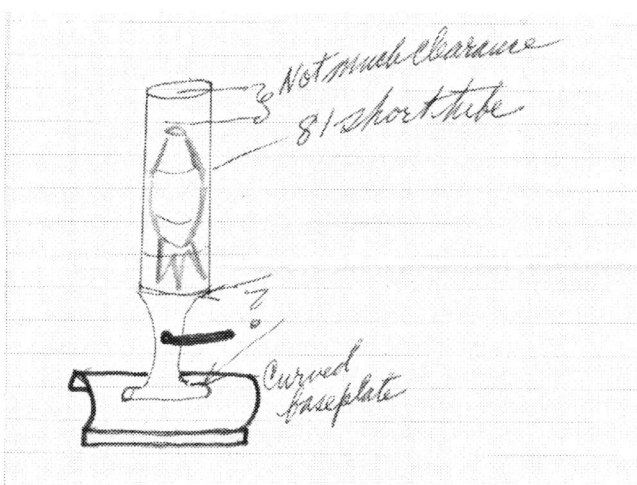

★ Click here to watch video
★ Click here for Web Info

Figure 43-1: Sergeant James Winterbottom's sketch of his knee mortar.

Some of the men in the platoon looked at it and started laughing. Sergeant Ellison, from the machine-gun squad teased him, "Hey SummerTop, where do you attach the bayonet?"

Winterbottom ignored the jibes and proudly showed the mortar to his squad. Short mortars were not new. The Germans, Japanese, and British troops used them. The U.S. Army had equipped some units with the portable M19 mortar, based on the M2 60 mm mortar. But those mortars fired the much smaller 60 mm shell. This knee mortar could be carried by one man, but used 81 mm shells the size of bowling pins that packed a heck of a punch.

Private Winterbottom's unusual mortar appeared to be a very unofficial modification of a standard 81 mm mortar. Winterbottom said he thought someone in Ordnance made it by cutting down the barrel of a damaged 81 mm mortar.

Using an imaginary shell, Winterbottom demonstrated how he could slide a shell into the barrel, then carry the mortar around by the strap. He explained that it was essential to keep the barrel pointing slightly up, or the shell would slide out of the tube. He then demonstrated how he could place the base plate against the ground and fire by pulling the lanyard attached to a trigger at the base of the mortar.

Since the mortar had a short barrel and no sight, it wouldn't be as accurate as a full-sized mortar. But it had some real advantages, one man could carry the entire mortar, brace it against the ground, and fire in a matter of seconds.

Winterbottom explained that the Japanese were using a similar device called a knee mortar. But he said, "Don't get confused by the name knee mortar. If you ever place one of these things against your knee or thigh and fire, it will break your leg for sure. It's got a kick like a mule."

The squad got some shells and experimented with the knee mortar. Winterbottom soon convinced them of its usefulness in mountainous terrain. Next they had to convince Sergeant Orwig, the platoon sergeant and acting 4th Platoon leader, to let them take it into the field.

Winterbottom demonstrated the device to Sergeant Orwig, emphasizing the portability and instant setup. Sergeant Orwig was skeptical at first, but when Winterbottom demonstrated how quickly he could advance and start dropping shells onto enemy positions, the sergeant decided to let them give it a try. Winterbottom would carry the knee mortar on a strap over his shoulder, while the rest of the squad carried the regular mortar and ammunition. If the knee mortar didn't work as well as they hoped, they would abandon it and switch back to the standard mortar.

F Company was ordered to prepare to move back to the front that evening. The men carefully checked their weapons and equipment. Ammunition was issued to each soldier and the platoon sergeants made lists of needed equipment, such as boots, jackets, packs, and sleeping bags.

A final round of transfers brought the squads up to full strength. James Winterbottom was promoted to first gunner for Johnny's mortar squad.

That afternoon, the men were gathered in an old factory building when someone announced that the move had been postponed for another day. A great cheer filled the large room when the men heard they would not return to the front lines for one more day.

The next day, as they prepared once again to move to the front lines, one of the old-timers told the new men in the squad, "Don't ever buckle the chinstraps on your helmet. If an artillery shell hits nearby, the concussion will blow the helmet right off your head. If your chinstrap is buckled, it'll take your head with it. I've seen it happen and it ain't pretty."

The new men looked around and noticed for the first time that none of the veterans had fastened their chin straps. As one, they reached up and unbuckled their chin straps.

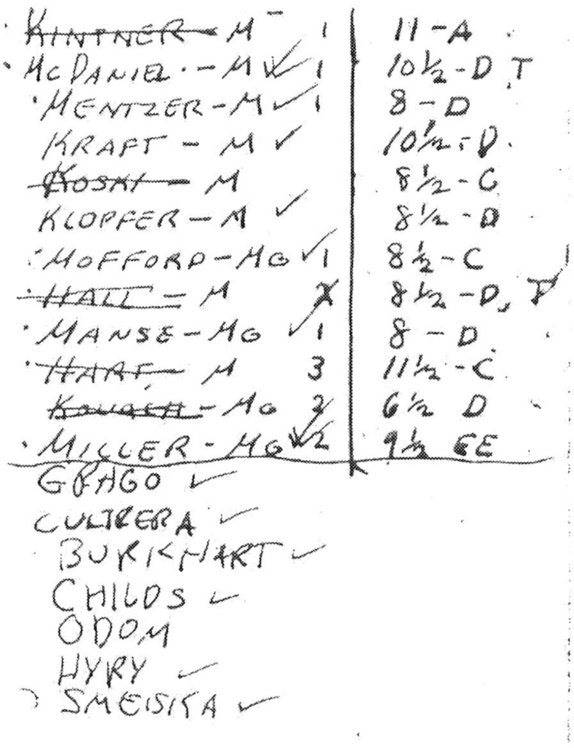

★ Click here for Web Info

Figure 43-2: A page from Platoon Sergeant James Orwig's notebook showing boot sizes for 4th Platoon members. The left column lists last name, M or MG indicating a mortar or machine-gun squad, and the squad number. The right column lists the boot size. Johnny Koski is listed as wearing an 8 1/2 C. We don't know why some names are crossed out, but it could be that they had already received their new boots.

The new men were all thinking about the move to the front lines. The veterans also seemed quieter than usual. Many of them seemed to be thinking back to the combat on Mount Belvedere, Mount Gorgolesco, and Mount della Torraccia.

That afternoon, a story spread through the camp—a story about a grenade, a crowded room, and a courageous staff sergeant by the name of Maurice E. Murphy.

Johnny heard the story when one of the men from F Company came by and asked Ed Smieska if he remembered Sergeant Murphy. Ed Smieska chuckled, "Sure, I remember him. He's with G Company. We used to call him 'Speed' Murphy because his legs were so short and he had to move them so fast to keep up with his men."

The other man said:

> Well, Speed had some trouble today. His entire platoon, almost forty men, was crowded into a hallway to collect ammunition before moving to the front. Somehow—we don't know how—a live grenade got dropped on the floor. Sergeant Murphy grabbed the grenade and dove with it into a small room off the hallway.
>
> But there were soldiers in that room too. Sergeant Murphy raised his arm to throw the grenade out the window. Just as he was about to let go, he heard voices in the street outside. Murphy found himself with a live grenade and three very bad choices—toss it into the hallway with forty soldiers, keep it in the small room with himself and a few other soldiers, or toss it out the window onto the people in the street.
>
> Then he did something—something really incredible. He switched the grenade to his left hand, stuck his arm out the window, and held that grenade firmly against the stone wall of the building. The guys with him in that little room said he just pressed his cheek against that rough stone wall and waited.
>
> He didn't have to wait long. Moments later, the grenade exploded. Fortunately the sturdy stone wall absorbed most of the blast and deflected the shrapnel. No one was injured. No one, except of course, Sergeant Murphy. He lost his left hand.

The men of the squad were stunned and proud, proud to be serving in the same outfit with a man like Sergeant Murphy. Each of them wondered if he would be able to think so quickly or act so courageously if faced with a similar situation. The men were still thinking about Sergeant Murphy as they climbed into trucks shortly after 6:00 p.m. They bounced along the rough mountain roads to a village called Gaggio Montano, then climbed out of the trucks, pulled on their heavy packs, and started hiking up into the hills.

Part of the time they hiked through a large cloud of oily smoke that was being generated to help hide their movement from the Germans. As the smoke thinned, they found themselves moving towards the top of a rocky ridge. Finally, after 9:00 p.m., they were told to drop their packs and dig in.

Johnny had dug a lot of foxholes in basic training, but the digging seemed much harder here than back at Camp Croft. He and Kraft were already tired from the march with full packs and equipment. They chipped away at the frozen ground with their

Figure 43-3: The men of F Company march toward the front lines.

entrenching tools, slowly gouging out a shallow hole. They noticed most of the other men quit digging once they had a hole just deep enough to get their bodies below ground level. Johnny and Kraft kept digging for a while longer, but eventually stopped and lay in the shallow hole to get some sleep.

This was Johnny's first night in a foxhole in the Italian mountains. He was cold and miserable, lying in that hole with the rocky frozen soil as a mattress. But he figured he could deal with it. He'd spent a lot of cold hours crouched beside deer trails at Flat Rock and he tried to tell himself that if he just took this one day at a time, it might not be so bad. Then it started to rain and their shallow foxhole filled with cold, muddy water. Later that night, the rain turned into a mix of light rain and snow. It was impossible to sleep or stay warm. Johnny shivered uncontrollably, wet and miserable in the shallow foxhole.

As dawn broke, the squad leaders checked their men once more, making sure everyone had ammunition, grenades, rations, flares, and all the other equipment needed on the line.

In the morning light, Johnny got a better look at the area around Gaggio Montano as he ate a biscuit for breakfast. The company was dug in on a hill overlooking a small village, with snow-covered mountains rising in the distance. A large rock sprouted from the middle of the village, with a tiny chapel perched improbably on top of it.

Johnny's squad spent March 4 trudging up one hill and down the next. Other companies were in the lead, and F Company followed along in reserve, ready to move into action if needed. From time to time, they could hear heavy fighting in the hills and valleys around them, but for the men of the mortar squad those days were one grueling march, up and down the hills carrying heavy pieces of the mortar and ammunition.

★ Click here to watch video

Figure 43-4: The chapel on the rock in Gaggio Montano, 1945. These are the mountains where Larry Burrows got his nickname "Jaggers."

They saw a lot of other soldiers, trucks, and even some tanks moving into position for the attack. Clearly, F Company was just one part of a much larger attack. It was good to know they were not attacking the Germans alone.

On the night of March 4, they dug in again on the flanks of another frozen mountain. It didn't rain that night, so they were got a few hours sleep, huddled under blankets in the cold foxhole.

As they settled in for the night, one of the riflemen by the name of Larry Burrows mistook a snow-covered thorn bush for a rock. He sat down on it, then jumped up with a yelp. "Those damn jaggers stuck me again!" The men in the nearby foxholes started chuckling and Larry Burrows earned himself a new nickname: "Jaggers."

The next day dawned clear and cold. The men were issued more ammunition. One of the men ahead of Johnny in the line grumbled, "Great, more ammo. You always know something good is coming when they issue more ammo!"

The ominous feeling was reinforced when they weren't ordered to march again that day. The men figured they weren't marching because they were already close enough to the German lines.

There had been a lot of good-natured grumbling and teasing while they marched the day before. But now that they weren't marching, the men were quiet. Veterans and replacements alike checked their equipment and tried not to think too much about what lay ahead.

Johnny could hear the sounds of combat from the hills ahead of them, but so far F Company hadn't come under fire from the Germans. For most of the day, they stayed near their foxholes and waited for orders. Late in the day, one man was wounded by a sniper. A rifle squad searched the area, but couldn't find the sniper.

Late that afternoon, the men were briefed about the attack planned for the following day, March 6. The 85th, 86th, and 87th Mountain Infantry Regiments would sweep four miles forward over steep ridges and mountain meadows to take Mount della Spe, the little town of Castel d'Aiano, and the hamlet of Iola. These areas were held by German forces in entrenched positions, so fierce fighting was expected.

On the evening of the 5th, the men quietly moved into positions overlooking Upper Canolle. Seeing how seriously the veterans checked their weapons and equipment, the new replacements double, then triple-checked their own gear. Rifles were cleaned, then cleaned again. Bayonets and knifes were sharpened to a keen edge.

Just after midnight, the men of F Company moved forward. At 3:30 a.m., they paused and then held position until dawn. At 8:00 a.m., F Company moved out, heading southeast, following E Company over hills 838 and 866. E Company advanced toward a group of houses at Tora, but was halted by heavy machine-gun fire from Mount Spicchione and Mount della Castellana.

Captain King, commanding officer of F Company, watched the advance through his binoculars and concluded, "We can't take Tora with those German machine guns at our backs. We have to take Castellana first."

The officers of E Company must have reached the same conclusion, because the soldiers of E Company soon changed direction and surged up a gully on the west side of Mount della Castellana. A few men were hit by automatic weapons and light machine-gun fire, but by 3:00 p.m. the Americans had taken the top of Mount della Castellana.

From the top of Castellana, the Americans were able to fire on German positions on Hill 998 to the south of Mount della Castellana. Those Germans realized they had been cutoff from the main German lines and soon surrendered. The German prisoners were escorted down the hill, past the men of F Company as they climbed up the slopes of Castellana. Many of the Germans were wounded, and one was being carried on an improvised stretcher made from sticks and a German overcoat.

Johnny looked at the German prisoners walking past and said, "They don't look so tough. They're just dirty, scared kids in uniforms."

Ed Smieska smiled and said, "They kind of remind you of us, don't they?"

Johnny flashed a lopsided grin and agreed. "Now that you mention it, I guess they do."

★ Click here to watch video

Figure 43-5: Wars are fought by soldiers, but those soldiers are sometimes just kids in uniform.

★★★ Ordinary Heroes: Six Stars in the Window ★★★
44. God is with us

March 6, 1945: Having forced most of the Germans from Mount della Castellana, E Company turned northwest toward Tora and Montesinistro. The men of F Company moved up to secure the rest of Mount della Castellana.

Johnny trudged behind Kraft and Klopfer, but kept a hunter's eye on his surroundings, mapping out the terrain in his mind and always watching for the nearest cover. As they advanced over the crest of a hill, he saw a grim reminder of the seriousness of the business that lay ahead. A dead American soldier sat propped against a shattered tree trunk. His shirt had been cut open, he had bandages on his arm and chest, and a needle stuck in his arm where someone tried to give him plasma.

One glance told the whole story. The GI had probably been hit within a few feet of where he now sat. The other men of his squad had pressed onward, leaving the wounded man in the care of a medic. The medic had propped him up against the tree and worked feverishly to save the man's life, bandaging his wounds and even giving him plasma. But those efforts had failed and this young man had died. Everything he had been, everything he had hoped to be, had ended in the mud of Italy.

Now the battle had moved on and the dead man was left alone, staring sightlessly over the valley. In a day or two, after the battle was over, the men of the Graves Registration unit would work their way over the battlefield, place him in a body bag and truck him down the mountain for burial.

John felt a chill as if he might have just glimpsed his own future. "May God be with you," he prayed, as much for himself as for the dead soldier.

Rifle squads fanned out over the summit of Mount della Castellana. At first, they ran into only scattered resistance from Germans hiding in bunkers and trenches. But as the GIs approached Hill 1003, the north peak of Mount della Castellana, they came under heavy machine-gun and rifle fire from a series of trenches at the top of the hill. Men were running and yelling, shells were exploding, and everything was happening at once.

★ Click here to watch video

Figure 44-1: A trained mortar squad could drop up to thirty rounds a minute on enemy targets over 3,000 yards away.

Sergeant Carney ordered the 4th Platoon to fire on the German machine-gun positions. Armstrong and Smieska set up their mortar behind a small knoll. Winterbottom crawled to the crest of the knoll and scanned Hill 1003 with his binoculars. He pinpointed a machine-gun nest near the middle of a trench system, then jammed an aiming stick into the dirt on top of the knoll. The aiming stick was a simple wooden stick with a metal nail on one end. The mortar crew couldn't see the target from behind the knoll, so they used the aiming stick as a horizontal aiming point.

Winterbottom lay near the crest of the knoll, estimating the angle and distance to the target through his binoculars. He then gave the initial fire orders: "HE, heavy. Zero. Stake. 350. One round."

With a quick look at the firing tables, Smieska aligned the mortar with the aiming stake and adjusted the elevation while Armstrong removed increments of propellant from the bottom of an HE, or high explosive, shell. The squad ducked as Smieska dropped the shell into the barrel of the mortar. With a sharp cough, the shell flew out of the barrle and arced toward the enemy.

Winterbottom watched intently through his binoculars. The first shell hit to the right and slightly below the machine-gun nest. He yelled adjustments to the mortar squad, "Left one turn. Up two turns. One round."

Smieska adjusted the mortar and dropped another shell into the barrel.

Winterbottom watched that round land in the German trench just to the right of the machine-gun nest, then ordered the squad to fire again, "Left two turns, two rounds."

Smieska turned the traversing hand wheel two turns to the left, then dropped a shell into the mortar barrel. The shell dropped to the bottom of the tube, then flew out of the barrel with a loud "Whuff!" As soon as the first shell flew out of the barrel, Smieska dropped in the second shell.

Winterbottom watched the shells hit, then called back adjustments for additional shots, guiding the mortar team as it dropped shells along the German positions.

Winterbottom yelled back to his squad, "They've got a machine gun inside a stone house near the top of that hill. I don't think we can drop a shell into it from here. I'm going to move a little closer to see what this knee mortar can do. Smieska, take over here and keep the pressure on those Germans."

Winterbottom crouched and ran. Carrying his knee mortar and a couple of shells, he worked his way to the side, then started up the hill, trying to stay out of the line of fire of the machine guns.

Smieska and Armstrong continued firing the mortar, while Johnny and Kraft took positions on the sides of the knoll, watching for Germans who might attack the mortar squad.

The ground in front of them was littered with the debris of battle: shell holes, a helmet, a bloody boot, and a German soldier lying face up in the dirt. The stink of gunpowder and the smell of blood lay heavy on the hills. It was clear the Germans hadn't given up this ground easily.

The sound of mortars, machine guns, and grenades drifted down from the hill. Occasional bullets whined overhead. Men shouted. Some screamed for help. Off to the right, someone was calling pitifully, "Mama! Mama!"

As he peered around the sides of the knoll, Johnny saw the tops of German helmets moving in a trench system near the edge of the mountain. He and Kraft fired and the helmets disappeared. Moments later the Germans returned fire and bullets sprayed the knoll. Johnny and Kraft continued to fire. They couldn't see any Germans. They were firing to keep the Germans pinned down in their trenches. Johnny peeked out over the edge of the knoll and squeezed off a few shots, then ducked behind the knoll before the Germans returned fire.

Suddenly Johnny saw movement in a trench to his right. Three German soldiers jumped from the trench and rushed towards the mortar squad. Two of them carried submachine guns. The one in the lead carried an old bolt-action rifle.

Johnny saw the Germans, pointed his M1 rifle at the closest German and pulled the trigger. He didn't have time to think about it, he instinctively aimed and fired just like he had been trained.

The bullet struck the German in the chest. As if in slow motion, he collapsed backwards on the ground, kicked, then lay still, one hand outstretched as if reaching for something.

Kraft started shooting and the other two Germans fled back to the trench. Johnny clutched his rifle tightly in his hands. He'd seen the German jerk backwards when the bullet hit him and he knew with sick certainty that he had killed him.

Kraft yelled, "Good shot, Koski!"

Johnny bent over and vomited in the dirt.

Kraft looked over in concern, "Are you hit?"

Johnny shook his head and lay back down in firing position. His hands were shaking, and the bitter taste of vomit burned his throat, but he was there to protect the squad and he was determined to do his duty.

Figure 44-2: A German soldier hunches down as he runs along a defensive trench.

This was Johnny's first combat experience. It wasn't as bad as he had expected. It was worse, much worse.

He had been prepared to be afraid. He hadn't been prepared for the smell, the chaos, or the noise. He hadn't known that some men could die so hard, their life slowly slipping away in the mud of a hill that didn't even have a name. He hadn't really thought he would have to kill someone, and he'd never, ever thought it would feel so very wrong.

Gradually, the sound of combat on the hill started to fade away. Except for an occasional shot, the firing had stopped. The Americans had overrun the Germans. A few GIs started to walk slowly down the hill. John saw Winterbottom walking back down the hill, the knee mortar slung over his shoulder.

Winterbottom flopped to the ground next to the squad, breathing heavily. Smieska asked him, "What happened up there?"

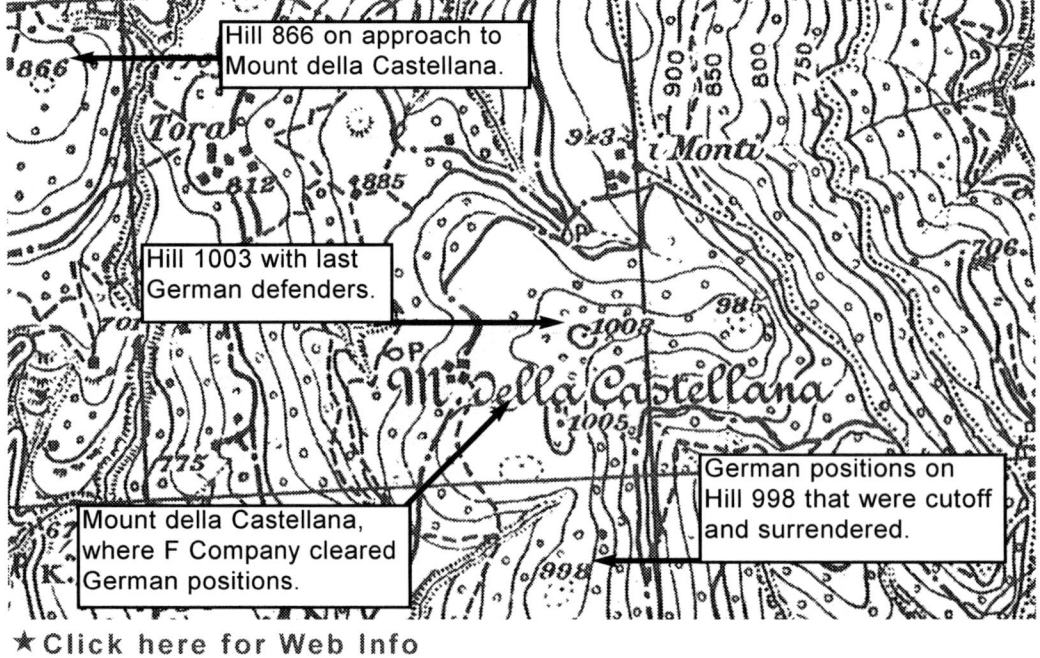

★ Click here for Web Info

Figure 44-3: Map of Mount della Castellana.

Winterbottom replied, "That machine gun was well positioned. All the approaches were covered. I worked my way up as close as I could and dropped a round right in the window." He patted the cut-off knee mortar, "Yeah, this little baby is gonna come in mighty handy."

F Company settled in for the night, taking over German foxholes and trenches around the perimeter of the hill. Many of the foxholes were still occupied by dead Germans who were unceremoniously dragged out and deposited on the hillside. They didn't need protection anymore. The GIs' first priority was to establish defensive positions against a German counterattack. They'd bury the dead when time allowed it.

By the night of March 6, the Americans controlled all of Mount della Castellana and had outposts on Casella, San Cristoforo, and Hill 864. Johnny and the mortar squad took positions on the north side of the hill, looking towards Mount Spicchione and Montesinistro. Other platoons mined the road at San Cristoforo and established a roadblock to stop the Germans from moving in supplies or reinforcements. The Americans had fought hard to take those hills and they meant to keep them.

When Johnny went back for rations and ammo, he heard that Private Kintner, one of the men who rode up with him from the replacement depot, had been wounded and sent back to the evacuation hospital. "Lucky dog!" he thought. "At least one of us is going to get out of here alive."

Johnny also heard that Torger Tokle, the famous Norwegian ski jumper, had been killed by an artillery shell. Johnny had seen Tokle jump in ski tournaments in Upper Michigan. He'd also heard tales about Tokle from the old Camp Hale veterans. Tokle apparently had legs of spring steel. In one story, he stood next to a dining table wearing a light pack. From a standing position, he jumped up and landed with both feet on the top of the table.

The Camp Hale veterans were disturbed by Tokle's death. Tokle had been a larger-than-life figure. If somebody like him could be killed by an artillery shell, it seemed an ordinary man didn't have much of a chance.

Figure 44-4: Mount Della Spe as seen from positions of the 4th Platoon on Mount della Castellana in March, 1945.

Throughout, the night John could hear the sounds of battle in the distance on Mount della Spe. The 1st Battalion had taken the hill, then fought off a series of four determined German counterattacks. Heavy artillery pounded Hill 920, just to the south of Mount della Spe. But, aside from the occasional artillery shell, things were relatively quiet for F Company during that first night on Mount della Castellana.

As Johnny sat in his foxhole, he thought about the events of that day. He wondered why he and the other men continued to move towards the enemy, running towards the bullets and the shells, when every instinct screamed for them to drop their guns and run the other way.

He finally decided it didn't have anything to do with patriotism or heroism. He kept going because that's what the men around him were doing. He just couldn't let them down. In this hellish place and time, these men were his family. They had eaten together, bunked together, and bled together. Johnny decided he would fight as long as they would fight and he would endure anything they could endure.

Figure 44-5: F Company First Sergeant William Ballek on Mount della Castellana.

F Company had been lucky, with only three men wounded in the attack. Later, Johnny heard that the first Battalion had heavy casualties from multiple counterattacks on Mount della Spe. One man said a lieutenant from B Company had been wounded in the arm, leg, chest, and had lost an eye, but still refused to be evacuated. Someone said Company B had suffered fifty percent casualties as it beat back the German counterattacks.

On March 7, the men were issued new socks and additional ammunition. Otherwise things were relatively quiet and they continued to "improve their positions," which to the enlisted men meant a lot more digging.

Later that day, Sergeant Orwig ordered the men to bury the dead. Johnny and Bobby Kraft carried the body of the German soldier—the one that Johnny had killed—to the other side of the hill to lay him in a shallow grave. As they put the man down, Johnny noticed the words engraved on the German's belt buckle. "Bobby, what does it say on his belt buckle?"

Bobby slowly read the words on the buckle: "Gott mit uns. It's been a few years since my German classes. Let me think—'with us', 'God with us'. Yeah, that's it. 'God is with us'."

★ Click here to watch video

Figure 44-6: Johnny's platoon sergeant, James Orwig, on Mount della Castellana, with his rifle and bayonet close at hand.

Bobby shook his head, then said, "It kind of makes you wonder, don't it? How can God be on their side when he's supposed to be on our side?"

★ Click here for Web Info

Figure 44-7: WWII German Gott Mit Uns Belt Buckle.

Johnny just shrugged his shoulders. That was just one more puzzling thing in a world that sometimes didn't seem to make too much sense.

Johnny reached into the soldier's chest pocket and pulled out a photo. It showed a young woman and a little girl, presumably the soldier's wife and daughter. Johnny sat back on his haunches and gazed at the photo. Tears came to his eyes as he thought of the young woman who would soon find out she was a widow, and the little girl who would grow up without her father.

He shook his head and said, "I didn't have anything against this man. If we'd met in another time and another place, we might have been friends. Maybe we'd go hunting or fishing together. I didn't know anything about him. I didn't hate him. Yet I killed him."

He looked down at the photo again. "His little girl is going to grow up, get married, and have children of her own. This man is going to miss all that. He's going to miss it, because I killed him."

Kraft, crouching by his side, tapped Johnny on the shoulder and said, "Hey Johnny, you did what you had to do. If you hadn't killed him, he and his buddies would have killed you, me, and the rest of the squad. Would you rather we were all dead?"

Kraft gently pulled the photo out of Johnny's dirty fingers and stuck it in his own pocket. "There are some things in this world you just can't fix. You just gotta do what you have to do and try not to think too much about the rest of it."

Johnny nodded glumly.

He knew Kraft was right, they were doing what had to be done. But he didn't have to like it. Like every combat soldier, he would just have to find some way to live with the memories of the things he had seen and the things that he had done.

Figure 44-8: Unidentified German woman and baby in front of a cafe with a swastika in the window.

★★★ Ordinary Heroes: Six Stars in the Window ★★★
45. Don't blame us

February, 1945: Art and the men of the 332nd Engineers continued to work their way into Germany, crossing the Siegfried Line and repairing bridges at Geilenkirchen and Baal. The Ninth Army ran short of infantry soldiers as it pushed deeper into Germany. More enlisted men from the 332nd volunteered for infantry duty, leaving the Regiment even more dependent on hired Belgian and German laborers.

The Germans were being driven back, but the work of the 332nd remained dangerous. While the Engineers struggled to repair a bridge above Geilenkirchen, the Germans shelled the site with 88 millimeter artillery. American artillery, dug in all around the work site, fired back on the German positions, adding to the din. One engineer drove his D-6 caterpillar bulldozer over a Schu mine. He was shaken, but not injured by the blast. A short time later, three artillery men were killed when one of them stepped on a mine.

German snipers stayed behind to harass and delay the Allied advance. The most troublesome snipers picked a hiding place with a view of a bridge or damaged section of road. When the Engineers arrived and started to work, the sniper would squeeze off a couple of shots. The Americans would take cover, then send squads to search for the sniper. Most snipers were chased away, captured, or killed, but each sniper could kill or wound several GIs and delay the project for precious hours. Snipers couldn't stop the Allied advance, but they sure could slow it down.

Near the end of February, while surveying a bridge over the Roer River, Art looked through the transit and saw a German sniper taking aim at him from across the river. He dropped to the ground and yelled, "Sniper!"

The sniper fired at other men in the survey party, including Corporal Williams of B Company and 1st Lieutenant James Birchette of H&S Company. As they dove for cover behind a bridge pier, they noticed Privates Thomas Hughes and Milton Yougken standing at the edge of the river, looking into the water.

They called out to the privates, "What are you guys looking at?"

Hughes replied, "Look at these splashes in the water! I wonder what kind of fish those are."

The lieutenant yelled, "Those aren't fish! Those are sniper bullets. Get the hell out of there!"

The men ran for cover. The survey team fired at the trees where Art had seen the sniper. Lieutenant Birchette carefully poked his head out from behind the bridge pier. The sniper didn't fire, so he sprinted to cover behind the half-track. The sniper still didn't fire at him. Convinced that the sniper had left, he ordered the team to get back to work and they proceeded to survey the bridge.

Later that day, as the survey team drove back in their half-track, Art yelled down to a GI sitting in a foxhole near the road, "Hey buddy, you got a German sniper on the other side of that river!"

The GI pointed to his foxhole and yelled, "The front line is right here! We haven't even gotten to the river. I don't know what you guys were doing out there, but don't blame us if you go past the front lines and run into a few Germans."

The next week, the survey squad spent the night in a little German village. It was a lot like every other village in Germany, but for some reason, this village hadn't been damaged as badly as most of them had. Even the little church on the main street stood pretty much intact.

German civilians still lived in the village, but they avoided the Allied soldiers and the GIs avoided them, in part because the GIs had been warned not to interact with German civilians and the Army had instituted a sixty-five dollar fine for any soldier caught fraternizing with German civilians.

As the men ate a breakfast of cold C-rations, they heard singing in the distance. They couldn't recognize the words, but the tune was hauntingly familiar. One of the guys muttered, "That's church music. Must be Sunday. Anybody want to go to church?"

Sergeant Jones swallowed and said, "Get your guns. I think we'd better check it out."

The men grabbed their guns and followed the sergeant up the street. As they got closer they could tell from the voices there were twenty or thirty people in the church. As they walked up the steps in their heavy boots, the singing stopped.

★ Click here to watch video

Figure 45-1: As they moved deeper into Germany, the GIs encountered many German civilians, but were warned not to fraternize with them.

Sergeant Tom Jones stopped outside the church door, looked down at the M1 carbine in his hands, and shook his head. This might be a war, but he wasn't going to bring his gun into a church. He carefully leaned the carbine against the wall, then opened the door and stepped into the church.

The rest of the squad followed suit, leaning their rifles against the wall before stepping into the church.

As Art stepped into the dark church he almost walked into the rest of the men, bunched up just inside the door of the church. He barely noticed the German villagers staring back at the American intruders. Like the other GIs he was mesmerized by the tall red banners hanging on the walls of the church. There were many of them—a half dozen or more. Each banner bore a name, presumably the name of a village boy who had been killed in the war. But the red banners bore more than names, on each banner was a large Nazi swastika.

Art couldn't tear his eyes from those banners. He just couldn't grasp that anyone would hang the hated Nazi emblem in a church.

Sergeant Tom Jones jerked his thumb over his shoulder, pointing back toward the door, and the GIs slowly backed out of the church. As they walked down the street, rifles in hand, the villagers started to sing in the church behind them.

★★★ Ordinary Heroes: Six Stars in the Window ★★★
46. This might be hell

March 8, 1945: Eight new replacements joined F Company and were assigned to squads. One of the new replacements told Johnny he'd seen piles of shells stacked for miles alongside the road. "What are they ever going to use that many shells for?" he asked.

★ Click here for Web Info

Figure 46-1: Although the men of the 10th had trained extensively for winter warfare, they used skis and snowshoes only a few times while in Italy.

Johnny just shrugged his shoulders. By this time, he knew the Army usually had some reason for everything it did. A large stockpile of shells meant heavy barrages. That meant a major attack. He figured they'd find out what those shells were for soon enough.

Things remained relatively calm at the front. On March 8, one man was wounded and one was killed. Two days later, a patrol ran into stiff resistance and another man was killed. Johnny found himself thinking like the old timers, "Three days. Two killed, one wounded. Things seem kind of quiet around here."

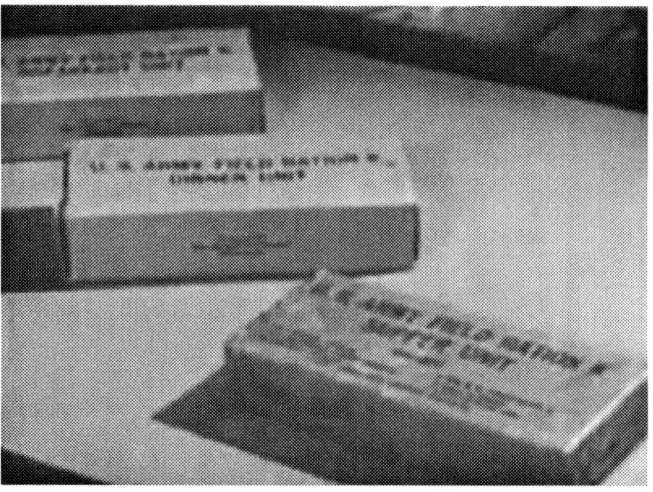

★ Click here to watch video

Figure 46-2: K-rations were easy to carry, but only nominally edible.

F Company moved to positions overlooking the ruined town of Castel D'Aiano. Once again, the men dug in, kept an eye on the Germans, and occasionally sent out patrols. Some of the patrols went out on skis, but as the weather got warmer, the snow developed an icy crust, so patrols trudged through the mountains on foot.

Johnny and Bobby dug a foxhole overlooking Castel D'Aiano, then slid into it. Johnny opened a box of K-rations. It was a little cardboard box about the size of a Cracker Jack box and contained a small can of meat, biscuits, cigarettes, toilet paper, chewing gum, matches, and coffee.

He picked up a hard biscuit, examined it disdainfully, and said, "You know, ever since I was a kid, I wanted to be a soldier. I thought soldering was about being brave in the face of danger. I was ready for that. But, I never thought we'd spend so much time sitting in a hole in the ground, hungry, tired, dirty, and cold."

Bobby snorted and replied, "Yeah, if anybody back home asks me what this was like, I'll tell them to take a shovel, a box of crackers, and a can of Spam. Dig a hole, climb in, and stay there for about a week. The middle of winter is best, but any cold, rainy week will do. Maybe they could get somebody to sneak up and throw firecrackers in the hole every now and then. By the end of the week, I think they'd start to have some idea what the more pleasant days were like."

"I think that might be more than they really want to know," said Johnny with a grin. They both shook their heads and chuckled at the thought of some guy trying to live in a foxhole in his backyard.

Sitting in his foxhole with Bobby Kraft, Johnny had time to think about how he felt about combat. Before he reached the front, he had worried most about getting wounded, but now that really didn't seem so bad. If he got slightly wounded, he'd get out of the line, at least for a few days. If he was seriously wounded, he'd get sent to the rear for treatment or maybe even sent home. Sure, he might lose a hand or a foot or an eye, but he'd be alive and he'd be off the line.

Even getting killed didn't seem so bad anymore. By this time, they'd all seen many soldiers killed. Most of them probably didn't even know what had happened to them. Most guys figured, "Once you're dead, you're dead. At least your combat days are over. Surely, whatever is waiting for you can't be any worse than this."

★ Click here for Web Info

Figure 46-3: 4th Platoon mortar squad positions on Mount della Castellana in March, 1945.

Spring was coming to the Italian countryside and the men became increasingly aware of the beauty that surrounded them. Platoon Sergeant James Orwig scribbled the following entry in his diary:

```
Days a succession of blue sky with hot sun. Weather
growing steadily milder. First spring flowers
appeared and the last drifts of snow disappeared.
Dawns colored by bird songs, all strange, but so
beautiful. Artillery thumping day and night with
overtones of air support. Surrounding country fantas-
tically beautiful. Wide valleys on all sides with
hills rising and a backdrop of snowcapped peaks to
the southwest. Hills and ridges all farmed and dotted
with stone barns and little hamlets as far as the
distant horizon. Our hill seems to be an island of
peace in a sea of bellowing lashing sound. Peace
interrupted infrequently by Kraut artillery. But
threat is always present and holes are deep and cov-
ered. Has been a good two weeks. But now I need a
bath and a shave and new clothes and a haircut and a
few days beyond the threat of German artillery. It
will be nice. But after that...
```

For the men of F Company, the war had entered a quiet phase. Spring had arrived. Nobody wanted to die, not now, not so close to the end of the war. Even the Germans seemed reluctant to escalate the violence.

Sometimes the Germans fired artillery shells filled with propaganda leaflets rather than explosives. Some leaflets ominously quoted the old saying "See Naples and Die." The last line was "Well, now you've seen Naples..."

Figure 46-4: A German propaganda piece fired in an artillery shell in Italy.

Most of the propaganda wasn't that subtle. Many leaflets tried to lay the blame for the war on politicians, Jews, and profiteers. Others encouraged the GIs to surrender, describing in great detail the comforts of the German POW camps, including live shows, sporting events, good food, and recreational activities. None of the GIs seemed to take the propaganda seriously, but it was usually good for at least two things: a laugh and use as toilet paper.

The U.S. Army had its own propaganda pieces. One of the most successful was a Safe Conduct pass which promised that any German soldier carrying the pass would be treated well, given food, provided with medical attention, and removed from the combat area as soon as possible.

That was American policy for all POWs, whether they were carrying the Safe Conduct pass or not, but many captured German soldiers carried a Safe Conduct pass, so it apparently meant something to them. The GIs were surprised by this. It was dangerous for German soldiers to carry those Safe Conduct passes. If a German officer caught a German soldier with a Safe Conduct pass, he could order the soldier shot for planning to desert.

Sometimes Germans tried to infiltrate American lines wearing uniforms stolen from dead GIs. U.S. troops were warned to be extra vigilant and to suspect anyone who didn't know the passwords. One night, James Winterbottom heard someone moving behind him. He knew it wasn't anyone from his squad, so he drew his pistol. Moments later a soldier with a General's star on his helmet crawled into his foxhole. "What company is this?" he demanded.

Winterbottom leveled his pistol at the soldier's head and asked, "What's the password sir?"

The soldier looked him in the eye and said, "Son, I don't know what the bloody password is."

Winterbottom swallowed, then made up his mind. "Well then, I'm sure you'll understand I'm going to have to bring you back to headquarters so they can figure out who you are."

The soldier grumbled, but let Winterbottom march him back to the command post. Winterbottom later found out that the soldier was a real general who had somehow gotten lost. Surprisingly, no one reprimanded him for marching a general back to headquarters at the end of a pistol.

On March 13, thirty-two enlisted men joined F Company as replacements. Johnny watched as the new men were assigned to squads. He was surprised to find himself thinking how innocent they looked, with their clean shaves, fresh uniforms, and new equipment. Sergeant Orwig assigned one of the new men to Johnny's foxhole so he could "learn the ropes." The new man slithered into Johnny's foxhole and just sat there for a while, nervously gripping his rifle. After a few minutes, he fished a pack of cigarettes out of his pocket, held them out towards Johnny, and asked if he wanted one. Johnny shook his head and said, "No, thanks."

After the man lit up, he asked Johnny, "When did you get up here?"

Johnny scratched his stubbly chin and said, "Let me see, I think it was the beginning of March."

The replacement looked at Johnny's dirty uniform, his sunken eyes, and his weary expression, then innocently asked, "What year?"

Johnny started laughing uncontrollably. After a few minutes, he managed to stop laughing long enough to reply, "This year. Two weeks ago!"

The new man obviously didn't believe him. "No offense buddy, but nobody can look that bad after just two weeks on the line. You look like you been here since the start of the war."

Johnny thought that was hilarious. He knew that in a few weeks that replacement soldier would look just as haggard as he did. After that, whenever Johnny saw the new guy, he teased him, asking, "Hey, what year?"

New replacements were always anxious to know about combat, though only a few of them were bold enough to came right out and ask. When one of the new men asked Johnny about combat he thought for a while, then replied, "It's kind of hard to describe. It's loud. It's confusing. You're scared spitless. Everything happens very quickly, and yet somehow you have time to notice things that you'd never pay attention to otherwise. You see the way the bullets kick up dust when they hit. You'll see a man get hit and as he falls, your eyes meet and you can tell he knows he's as good as dead. You know that the next moment, anything can happen and you'll either live or die. When it's over, you're exhausted, you don't have anything left. All you want to do is crawl into a hole and curl up in a ball."

While sitting in his foxhole, Johnny wrote several letters to Al, Oscar, and Art. In those letters, he wrote about the chaos of combat—the explosions, the screams, the sharply focused memories, and the dreams that would not go away.

The 1st mortar squad found a large cache of German mortar shells when they took over the German positions. The German shells were the same diameter as the American mortar shells, so James Winterbottom asked Sergeant Carney if he could try them out to see how they worked.

Sergeant Carney said, "Sure, just shoot at that abandoned farmhouse down there."

Winterbottom dropped a shell in the mortar and watched as it landed just outside the farmhouse. Moments later, several GIs dove out the door and windows of the farmhouse. Winterbottom and his squad quickly moved the mortar and pretended to be busy improving their foxholes.

Later that day, word got around that Captain King had been pouring coffee in a farmhouse in the valley. A German mortar round came out of nowhere and landed just outside the window. When he picked himself off the floor, he was holding just the handle of the coffee pot, the rest had been blown off by the shell. He sure was curious where that mortar shell came from because he thought they'd eliminated the German mortar positions on the surrounding hills.

When Winterbottom heard about Captain King, he gave each of the men in the squad a hard look. Bobby Kraft put his finger to his lips and said, "Mum's the word Sarge." Captain King never learned who fired that mortar shell.

One of the squad members found a supply of primer cord in a German bunker. Winterbottom showed the men how to put it to use, wrapping primer cord around a trunk of a tree, then lighting it. When the primer cord blew, it cut the tree as neatly as a chain saw. He handed lengths of primer cord to the men in the squad, telling them, "I want logs over the top of every foxhole."

★ Click here to watch video

Figure 46-5: Sergeant Winterbottom narrowly avoided disaster when he fired the German mortar shells at the "abandoned" farmhouse.

The men used the primer cord to fell the trees and cut them into manageable lengths. They dragged the logs over their foxholes and covered them with sandbags and dirt for protection from shrapnel.

Figure 46-6: Bill Kehres from F-85 digs a foxhole while under fire.

F Company didn't have enough men to secure the entire line. To fill the gaps, the mess sergeant, 1st cook, and 2nd cook were ordered to take positions in the line. Winterbottom checked on them, and found the three men squeezed into a foxhole barely large enough for two men. He told them to enlarge the hole, then cover it with logs and dirt.

The next day, he went back and found that the cooks had covered the foxhole with saplings. He yelled at them: "What good are those twigs gonna do? They won't stop shrapnel. You need logs, the bigger the better."

The cooks grumbled that there weren't many logs left, since the other men had already taken most of them. But they promised to hike back over the hill the next day to find some large logs to cover their foxhole.

That afternoon, the Germans fired a series of artillery shells. One of the shells scored a direct hit on the foxhole with the three cooks. The sticks didn't protect them from the explosion. Two were killed and the third was badly wounded.

A few days later, several men returned to F Company after recovering from wounds received on Mount Belvedere, Mount Gorgolesco, and Mount della Torraccia. Two of them, LeGassey and Canham, had been wounded in the buttocks by shrapnel during that extended shelling. That wasn't unusual. Experienced infantrymen hit the dirt as soon as they heard an incoming shell. They drove their face into the dirt. The rest of their head

Figure 46-7: Two Company soldiers huddled in a foxhole on Mount della Spe. Note the log roof designed to stop shrapnel from tree bursts.

was protected by their helmet, so the buttocks stuck up the highest, and was most likely to get hit. A hit in the buttocks wasn't usually fatal, so a lot of men ended up with Purple Hearts for buttock wounds.

Some of the young GIs couldn't resist teasing others about getting shot in the buttocks. Robert Ellis, one of the machine-gun squad sergeants, teased Canham and LeGassy about their wounds: "Did you hear about the new regulation? You have to pin your Purple Heart over the place where you got wounded." He'd then laugh while Canham and LeGassy rolled their eyes and tried to ignore him.

★ Click here to watch video

Figure 46-8: Soldiers seem to find humor in things that other people might not find so funny.

Most nights, some of the men crawled back over the hill after dark for a warm meal, brought up from the kitchen on Jeeps. One night, as they ate, Sergeant Messier started talking about an odd thing that happened to him in the mountains near Belvedere.

> I was dug in and it was just starting to get dark. I saw some papers blowing past my foxhole. I grabbed them and saw they were from a recent copy of the *Blizzard* [the 10th Mountain newsletter]. I started to read them and noticed the name of a Sergeant Hall. "That's odd," I thought. "I know a Sergeant Hall. He's a great football player from my home town." I started to read the article and found it was the same Hall that I knew. We used to call him "Midge." According to the article, he had been killed while on patrol in January. I knew he was here with the 86th Regiment, but that was the first I heard about his being killed. That really shook me up. It was like God was sending me a message or something.

Messier downed another spoonful of hash, then continued, "Since then, I've had this nightmare where I'm up on a mountain and a newspaper blows past. I pick it up and I see my own name, and read that 'Sergeant Messier was killed by an 88 and probably didn't even know what hit him'."

Messier chuckled. "I swear, sometimes I wonder if I'm not already dead and this might be hell. But then I wonder, what are you guys supposed to be?"

The other men laughed uneasily. Johnny thought their laughter seemed a bit forced. He figured he wasn't the only one who felt uneasy about that story. Probably all of the men at the front had troubled dreams. He knew he did.

In Johnny's recurring dream, he found himself at Flat Rock, walking back to the cabin after a long day of hunting. He saw his brothers Art and Oscar on the trail ahead. He waved and called out to them, but they didn't hear him. He tried to follow them back to the camp, but somehow he always lost them in the woods. He ran and ran, but he never could catch up to them, and never made it back to camp.

★★★ Ordinary Heroes: Six Stars in the Window ★★★
47. Rendezvous

March 20 1945: Johnny and the soldiers of F Company turned their positions over to another unit and marched back toward the rear. That night, they slept soundly, finally free from the constant danger of enemy counterattacks, sniper fire, and artillery.

The next day, the GIs mustered for inspection, then marched further toward the rear. Their spirits rose as they got farther away from the front lines. After three weeks on the line, the men were more than ready for a hot shower, a cooked meal, and a cot.

On the 22nd, John and his buddies climbed into waiting trucks. The same large dark-skinned driver waved at them and gave them a cheerful "Hiya boys!" as they climbed into the truck.

They bounced along in the back of the truck for several hours, through Passatore to the village of Montecatini. Someone started to sing the song *Over There* and the rest of the soldiers joined in an off-key chorus:

> *Over there, Over there,*
>
> *Send the word, Send the word, Over there*
>
> *That the Yanks are coming, The Yanks are coming,*
>
> *The drums rum-tumming everywhere.*
>
> *So prepare, Say a prayer,*
>
> *Send the word, Send the word, To beware*
>
> *We'll be over, We're coming over,*
>
> *And we won't come back...*

Instead of finishing the last line, they stopped after "And we won't come back," omitting the line "Til it's over, Over there." They all laughed at the morbid joke. After a few rounds of the truncated song, Shapley couldn't stand it anymore. When they stopped, he continued alone, singing the last line "Til it's over, Over there" in his high-pitched voice. The other GIs thought that was hilarious, so they laughed and kept singing the song without the last line, forcing Shapley to finish the last line by himself.

As the trucks drove closer to Montecatini, the GIs became more boisterous. They had survived, they were young, they had some leave coming, and they were feeling pretty spunky. One of the riflemen elbowed Johnny in the ribs and teased, "Hey Koski, I hear you found a Jerry wearing a 'Got mittens' belt buckle. I don't know why Jerry wears those things. Hell, we got mittens too!" The men in the truck roared with laughter at the old joke.

But not everybody was in a boisterous mood. Some, like Sergeant Orwig, sat quietly, remembering friends who had been killed or wounded. While the others laughed and joked, he closed his eyes and his thoughts turned back to the night he sat in the snow and had held his dying friend in his arms.

★ Click here to watch video

Figure 47-1: Soldiers like James Orwig do not forget—cannot forget—the things they have seen or the friends they have lost.

★ Click here to watch video

Figure 47-2: Soldiers of the 10th Mountain Infantry Division on leave in Montecatini, Italy, 1945.

The trucks pulled into Montecatini just after midday on March 22. A local band played Italian music and Johnny could smell hot food cooking nearby. The small village seemed like paradise after the war-torn front. The trucks stopped outside a barn that had been converted into a shower. Johnny stripped off his mud-caked boots and uniform, then soaped up under lukewarm water dribbling from a 50-gallon barrel punched full of holes.

One of the men standing in line outside yelled out in mock alarm, "Hey fellas! There's a general in there with you! I see stars on his helmet out here." He then added jokingly, "Of course you probably can't tell who he is without his uniform." Everybody laughed, including the general, who was the only middle-aged man in the shower.

After rinsing and drying off, Johnny searched through neat stacks of folded, clean uniforms and boots, finally locating the right sizes. Clean for the first time in weeks, the men of F Company were marched to a lecture on the dangers of venereal disease. Captain King warned them to stay away from certain establishments at the edge of town. After the lecture, one of the men quipped, "Same old story. The chaplain tells us what we shouldn't do, the doc tell us what will happen if we do it, and the captain tells us where to go to do it."

Johnny's squad was assigned to a cot-filled room on the top floor of a four-story house. The room was crowded, but the cots with clean sheets and blankets made it seem like a luxury hotel compared to a foxhole on the line.

Many of the men set out to find something to drink. Johnny didn't drink or gamble, so he and Shapley walked around the town, looking at the buildings. Horse-drawn carriages moved through the streets and American soldiers wandered aimlessly about, seemingly unsure how to behave now that no one was shooting at them.

Figure 47-3: A typical Italian grandmother in her kitchen during WWII.

The next afternoon, Johnny and Shapley talked with some soldiers from C Company. One of the men was from Finland. He'd been a crew member on a Norwegian freighter, but when the ship docked in New York, he'd been given the choice of spending the war in an internment camp as an enemy alien or volunteering for the 10th Mountain Infantry Division. He chose the 10th and ended up fighting in Italy.

Johnny said, "My Father is still a Finnish citizen. Earlier this year, some government men checked up on him. They didn't want an enemy alien working in the iron mines."

One of the Finnish soldiers asked, "What happened to him?"

Johnny replied, "I guess they decided he wasn't a threat. With six sons in the U.S. Army, he wasn't going to sabotage the mines or spy for the Nazis."

The Finnish soldier talked briefly about the fierce fighting between the Finns and the Russians near Lake Ladoga in the early years of the war. Johnny said his entire family had listened to the radio broadcasts of the Finnish–Russian war. "We paid more attention to the Finnish–Russian war than to what was happening in Germany or Japan. I never thought the war in Europe would affect me. But I guess you can say it's affecting me now, it's definitely affecting me and my brothers now."

When they went back for chow, Johnny and Shapley got their plates of food and joined a group of GIs sitting against the side of a house, eating. An Italian woman came out and gestured for the GIs to come into her house. On the table, she had one empty plate. As each GI came in, he put something from his plate on the empty plate. Soon, the Italian woman had a plate heaped with food. The men ate, and as they left, she gave each of them a little cake made from chestnut flour. They thanked her and walked out with the cakes. It was good they left with the cakes, because when they tried to eat them they found they were impossibly tough.

Spring had definitely arrived in the village of Montecatini. Trees were blooming and the sun felt warm on Johnny's face. It was strange to smell the sweet blossoms and feel the warmth of spring after the cold and death of the previous weeks. To Johnny, spring usually felt like the start of a new year, but after a few weeks at the front, he felt somehow disassociated from the promise of spring.

On their last day of R&R, Johnny and Shapley took another walk around the village. Johnny had been quiet during the entire stay in Montecatini. Like many of the soldiers, he was still trying to come to terms with the things he'd been through. Shapley was more cheerful, telling Johnny, "The Germans are on the ropes and they could surrender any day. We've spent some time on the front lines and we came through okay. Sure, some guys got hit, but if we keep your heads down and stay sharp, we can get through this. Besides, spring is here and nobody is shooting at us today. What more can you want? If you're not happy today, when are you going to be happy?"

Johnny smiled sadly at his optimistic friend and looked out over the valley below them. In a quiet voice, he began to recite *Rendezvous with Death*, the poem he had memorized as a boy just a few years before.

> *I have a rendezvous with Death*
> *At some disputed barricade,*
> *When Spring comes back with rustling shade*
> *And apple-blossoms fill the air—*
> *I have a rendezvous with Death*
> *When Spring brings back blue days and fair.*

> *It may be he shall take my hand*
> *And lead me into his dark land*
> *And close my eyes and quench my breath—*
> *It may be I shall pass him still.*

> *I have a rendezvous with Death*
> *On some scarred slope of battered hill,*
> *When Spring comes round again this year*
> *And the first meadow-flowers appear.*

God knows 'twere better to be deep
Pillowed in silk and scented down,
Where love throbs out in blissful sleep,
Pulse nigh to pulse, and breath to breath,
Where hushed awakenings are dear...

But I've a rendezvous with Death
At midnight in some flaming town,
When Spring trips north again this year,
And I to my pledged word am true,
I shall not fail that rendezvous.

Shapley listened, then said, "Sheesh Johnny! That gives me the willies. Cut it out, okay? Let's go back and get some supper."

Figure 47-4: Apple blossoms bloom near Mount della Spe in the spring of 1945.

★★★ Ordinary Heroes: Six Stars in the Window ★★★
48. I'm almost there

March, 1945: As the weeks dragged on, Oscar and the men of the 301st continued to fly mission after mission. Sometimes flak was extremely heavy, sometimes German fighters swarmed from all sides. On other missions, the bombers flew almost unopposed. Sometimes all the planes came home, other times they did not.

Strange things happened on some missions. On March 1, after the group successfully bombed the Maribor Marshaling Yard and Locomotive Depot near Moosbierbaum, Germany, a lone B-24 tried to join the formation. The crews tried to contact it by radio, but it would not respond. Suddenly the B-24 abruptly turned away and headed towards Germany. The crews assumed it was another American bomber, captured and flown by Germans. No one could think of a good reason for the Germans to try to join the formation. The best guess was that the Germans hoped to fly back to the base with the formation, then attack the base and any planes on the ground.

On March 4, Oscar's formation flew against the Florisdorf Oil Refinery in Vienna, Austria. The bombers of the 301st were diverted to a secondary target, the Marshalling Yard at Zagreb, Yugoslavia. Two fighters and five bombers went down with fifty-two airmen. Two of the downed bombers were from the 301st.

After hitting the target, Lieutenant William Brdzyk reported fire in the radio room and bomb bay. The plane went into a dive and broke in half. The other crews spotted only one parachute.

First Lieutenant Ralph Sommers was flying his plane named "Garbage Cannie" when it was hit by flak. He tried to make it to an emergency airfield but was forced to ditch in the Adriatic. The crew survived the landing, but waves swept three of them to their deaths as they struggled to deploy the life rafts. The rest of the crew managed to reach an island in the rubber rafts and survived.

On March 8, during an attack on the Marshaling Yard at Hegyeshalom, Hungary, Lieutenant Thomas Clancy of the 301st was doing his best to keep a failing engine running. He couldn't feather the prop and severe vibrations started to shake the plane. The plane fell out of formation and lost altitude. Suddenly, the prop tore loose, slicing through the tail of the plane. That stopped the vibration, but there was no way the crippled plane could make it back to base. Clancy headed for an emergency field in Zara, Yugoslavia where he managed to land the plane. The crew was loaded aboard a C-47 transport plane and flown back to base. As Lieutenant Clancy put it, "We hit the target, lost the plane, and almost made it back home with the squadron."

On a mission the next day, eight bombers were lost. Lieutenant O'Callaghan from the 352nd Squadron reported flak hits to the #3 engine, then the #1 engine. They dropped their bombs to lighten the plane, left the formation, and eventually bailed out just south of the German lines.

The drumbeat of missions and losses continued. On March 12, during the mission against the Florisdorf Oil Refinery in Vienna, three B-24s and one B-17 were lost. Second Lieutenant Atlee Gulley reported an engine out due to mechanical problems. Gulley's crew dropped their bombs and tried to make it home, but were forced to bail out just east of the Drava River in Hungary.

On March 16, two B-24s and one B-17 were lost on a mission to Vienna. First Lieutenant Ned Neidemir's B-17 started to lose oil. One engine quit. A second engine quit, then a third sputtered and died, forcing the crew to bail out south of Vienna.

New crews and planes were regularly sent to the squadron, to replace men and planes lost on previous missions. To veterans like Oscar, the new men seemed all the same: fresh faced, wearing new uniforms, trying not to show their fear, desperate to have someone tell them what combat was like, desperate to believe they would do okay when the going got rough.

Oscar tried to be patient with them, after all he'd been one of them just a few months ago. But he couldn't begin to describe what he'd been through over the last four months. There wasn't any way to tell them what it was really like. They were going to have to experience it for themselves. If they were lucky, they'd live through it. If they were strong-willed, they would find some way to deal with it.

As they survived more missions, the men got increasingly superstitious. Most developed their own peculiar good-luck rituals: wearing the same scarf, saying a little prayer before takeoff, carrying a good-luck pendant, kissing a photo of a girlfriend. They didn't relax until the plane rolled to a stop and they hopped out onto solid ground. They'd been through enough missions to know that everything could go well, right up to the end.

One plane, tail number 397, suffered a serious of mysterious mechanical problems and aborted missions. The flight crews decided that somebody was a jinx. They rotated various crew members on and off the plane and discovered that tail number 397 flew just fine as long as Oscar was not on board. Oscar didn't really think he was the cause of the problem, but everyone was happier when they arranged to keep Oscar out of that particular plane.

On March 20, Oscar was flying with a different crew as they returned from a mission. As they neared the base, the pilots were warned of strong crosswinds over the runway. The pilot angled the plane into the wind to compensate for the crosswind, but underestimated the strength of the wind. Oscar and the bombardier watched wide-eyed as the plane twisted in the air and dropped towards the ground, turned almost sideways to the runway. The pilot and copilot frantically wrestled with the controls, trying to straighten out the plane before the wheels hit the metal runway.

★ Click here to watch video

Figure 48-1: As they survived more missions, air crews tended to become increasingly superstitious.

Less than a hundred feet above the runway, the pilot managed to get the plane headed in the right direction. But they were too far down the runway to land. The pilot accelerated and took the plane around for a second attempt. When the plane finally rolled to a stop, the crew finally exhaled and scrambled out of the plane, happy to be alive.

As Oscar and the crew stood near the runway, smoking, joking, and trying to pretend that they hadn't been worried, they saw one of the other planes fire off a flare as it came in for a landing. That was the signal they had wounded men aboard.

Ambulances raced out to meet the plane at the end of the runway. Oscar watched the medics carry a wounded gunner from the plane and remembered that George Sarberg, Lilly's rejected suitor, was now serving as a medic with the 12th Air Force.

Lilly knew that George was an Army Air Forces medic, but Oscar didn't think she knew what that really meant. The folks back home didn't know what so many of their boys were really doing in the war. Maybe they didn't want to know, especially about the bad jobs like climbing into the blood-spattered fuselage of a battered airplane, crawling over spent shell casings and bloody bandages, to try to extricate wounded and dead crewmen from their stations. It wasn't heroic, it wasn't fun, and it wasn't the sort of job you'd want to talk about after the war. But somebody still had to do it.

★ Click here to watch video

Figure 48-2: Ambulances stood by to treat the wounded as the B-17s returned from their missions.

On March 22, Oscar flew on a mission against the oil refineries near Ruhland, Germany. The Luftwaffe hit them hard. More than thirty Me 262s savagely attacked the bomber formations. Thirteen B-17s were lost, along with eleven B-24 Liberators, taking 240 crewmen with them. No planes from the 301st were lost, although one sustained major damage and ten had minor damage.

Those were the heaviest losses of any mission that Oscar had flown. The men knew they were lucky to have survived and they all hoped it would be a long, long time before they had another mission to Ruhland.

Oscar was back in the briefing hut early the next morning. The commanding officer arrived, pulled up the curtain and announced that the target was Ruhland, the same target where they had been so savagely mauled just the day before. The men groaned, but knew they had to go. So they suited up, hoisted themselves into their planes, and formed up for the long flight.

As they neared the target, they spotted about fifteen German fighters. All the gunners anxiously tracked the German fighters with their machine guns, waiting for them to come into range.

But for some reason, the German fighters did not attack that day. Three bombers were lost to flak. Only one plane from the 301st suffered major damage and nine suffered minor damage.

On March 24, unusually favorable winds made it possible for 15th Army Air Force Planes to try for the "Big B": Berlin, the heart of the Third Reich. Oscar did not fly that day as 169 B-17s and 289 fighters attacked a German tank factory. Allied planes encountered an assortment of German fighter planes, including jets. Five American P-51 fighters and nine B-17s were lost in the raid, but mission photos indicated the bombers had heavily damaged the factory and the nearby marshaling yard.

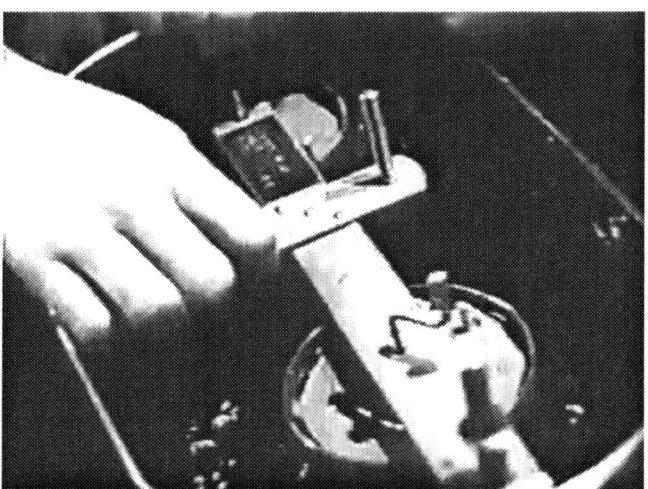

★ Click here to watch video

Figure 48-3: Photos taken on each mission were used to assess damage and plan future missions.

Oscar flew again the next day, this time to Kleby Airfield near Prague, Czechoslovakia. The flak was heavy, but no planes from the 301st were lost.

The mission to Kleby Airfield was Oscar's last mission for March of 1945. He had left the ground seventeen times in March, but bad weather forced cancellation of seven of those missions.

In three and a half months with the 301st, Oscar had survived twenty-nine combat missions—twenty-nine flights into enemy territory while enemy fighters and antiaircraft gunners did their best to knock his plane out of the sky. Hundreds of men had been lost, but somehow, he had survived.

As he lay in his bunk that night, Oscar tried to convince himself that he was going to make it after all. "Just six more missions," he thought. "I'm almost there."

He tried not to think too much about the German fighter pilots and the antiaircraft gunners who were going to do their best to shoot him down.

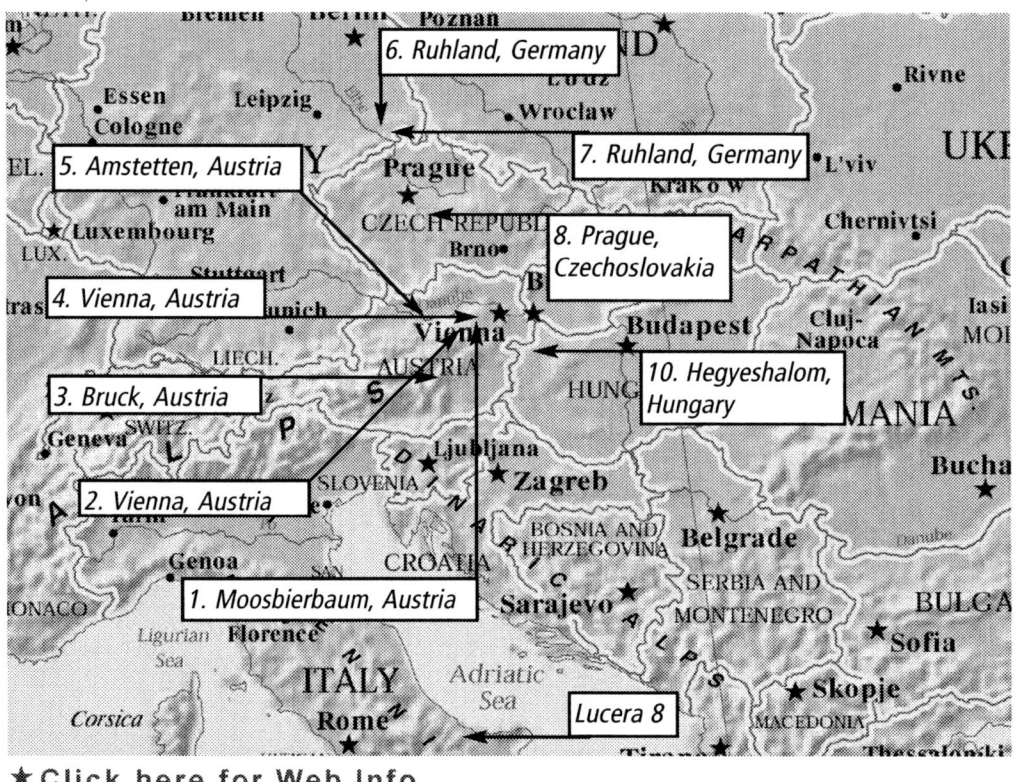

★ Click here for Web Info

Figure 48-4: Oscar Koski's missions during March, 1945.

★★★ Ordinary Heroes: Six Stars in the Window ★★★
49. Mountain of hope

March 22, 1945: Johnny and Shapley returned from their walk to find James Winterbottom and Sergeant Orwig discussing the knee mortar. Sergeant Orwig decided the squad could leave the standard mortar behind. From now on Winterbottom would carry the knee mortar and the rest of the squad would carry personal weapons and as many mortar shells as they could manage. The squad would give up some long-distance accuracy, but they'd be able to move quickly and carry a lot more ammo.

After only a few days in Montecatini, F Company got orders to move out. Strong, gusty winds blew in grim, gray clouds. As they prepared to return to the front, the mood of the men became more serious. Except for the newest replacements, the men now understood what combat meant. They realized many of them might not survive the coming weeks.

They rode in trucks for a while, then got out and walked. The soldiers of F Company trudged for miles up the winding mountain road, past shell-pocked hillsides and splintered trees. Scattered here and there, soldiers from both sides lay dead beside the road. The stink of death was in the air. The apple blossoms of Montecatini seemed a thousand miles away.

The talk turned to a discussion of religion and the morality of war. One of the recent replacements brought up the subject first: "I've heard you fellas talk about faith. From where I sit, it makes sense to believe in something. What is there to lose? If God doesn't exist, you've lost nothing by believing, but if he does exist, you've got a lot to gain. I guess that's why they say there aren't any atheists in foxholes—it just doesn't make sense to be one."

George Murray, a private from a rifle platoon, spoke up. "I believe faith can save a man. Up near Belvedere, I was pretty sure I was going to die. I took out my Bible and wrote goodbye messages to my family and my girl back home. I stuck that Bible in my shirt pocket. The next day I felt something strike me in the chest. I hit the dirt and felt that Bible in my pocket. Later I pulled it out and saw a bullet lodged in it. It was this bullet and this Bible."

He reached into his pocket and pulled out his pocket-sized Bible. Holding it out towards the men, so they could see the bullet hole, he said, "I think I can safely say this Bible saved my life."

Murray continued, "I've also scratched a line from Psalm 90 into the back of my helmet here." Taking off his helmet, he read to the men, "A thousand shall fall at thy side, and ten thousand at thy right hand, but it shall not come nigh thee." He paused, then concluded, "I figure that as long as I have my bible and my helmet, I'm going to be okay."

Another private, a devout Catholic, spoke up: "But do you really think we can get into heaven after killing so many Germans?"

No one answered. It was a question that weighed heavily on many of the men. Finally Johnny spoke. His voice was soft and hesitant as he tried to put his thoughts into words. "Killing people isn't usually considered a good thing. But when people are doing evil things, well, I guess stopping them has to count as a good thing."

He looked up at the looming hills. "What if you were on patrol and you came across a German about to shoot a child? You have two choices: kill the German or let him kill the child. If you kill the German to save the child, wouldn't you feel that was a good thing?"

Nobody said anything, so Johnny continued, "If it's a good thing to kill one German to save one child, then I figure it has to be a good thing to kill a hundred Germans to save a thousand children. At least it seems that way to me."

Johnny hitched his rifle up on his shoulder and continued, "I'm a Christian, but I believe I'll go to heaven when I die, even if I kill some Germans."

F Company arrived at Passatore just after 5:00 p.m. and stayed there through the evening of the 27th. One man was wounded by a lone artillery shell, perhaps a U.S. shell that fell short.

At 7:30 p.m. on March 27, the GIs of F Company moved out, hiking to their new positions. None of the men were happy about returning to the front. As they marched along under their heavy packs, one of the men grumbled, "I wonder where we're going now."

One of the other men pointed to the hill ahead of them. "I heard we're headed to that mountain. It's called Mount della Spe or 'Mountain of Hope' in Italian."

One of the other men muttered, "Yeah, Mountain of Hope. I hope it ain't the last place I see..."

★ Click here to watch video

Figure 49-1: Soldiers of the 10th Mountain Infantry Division advance past enemy dead lying beside a war-torn road.

After a couple hours of hiking, they reached their positions on Mount della Spe. In the darkness, the men slid into foxholes and positions held by the 3rd Battalion, which was being sent back to Montecatini for a break. A cold rain fell as the men tried to make themselves comfortable in the muddy foxholes and trenches.

The next morning, Johnny could see that Mount della Spe had been the scene of fierce fighting. The hillside was covered with shell holes and the thick limbless trunks of chestnut trees had been splintered by explosions. The ground was littered with debris: empty cans, shell casings, and pieces of blood-stained clothing.

The F Company GIs knew the Germans wanted to retake Mount della Spe, so they spent most of the next day improving their positions. They dug trenches connecting their foxholes, placed barbed wire in front of their positions, and sited their machine guns and mortars to cover the most likely approaches.

The rain stopped and the sun came out. Johnny took off his wet socks and shirt and spread them out near his foxhole to dry in the warm sun. From his foxhole, Johnny could see a small village in the valley between the hill occupied by the Americans and the hill occupied by the German troops.

Two American fighter planes swooped into the valley. They flew so low Johnny could see the paintings on their noses. The planes started with a strafing run, flying low over the village, pelting the ground with machine guns. They wheeled around and the first pilot skimmed the rooftops, then dropped his bomb. The second pilot flew right behind, disappearing in the smoke and dust from the first bomb. The pilots made one more strafing run, then headed back to base.

A few days later, Johnny and Shapley were on patrol when they discovered the wreckage of an American P38 fighter plane. Johnny and Shapley watched as two GIs carefully removed the mangled body of the pilot from the wreckage.

Shapley muttered, "I always envied those fighter pilots as they headed back to base, away from all this mud and blood. But I guess they die too. And when they die, they die alone."

In a low voice, so quiet Johnny could barely hear, Shapley added, "I'd hate to die alone like that."

The GIs buried the pilot in a shallow grave near his plane and stood one of the blades from the propeller as a marker. James Winterbottom scratched the man's name and the date into the propeller and attached his dog tags to it. When they returned from the patrol, they reported the location of the grave to Graves Registration, but they never learned if the body was recovered.

The platoon was assigned a new lieutenant, replacing Sergeant Orwig as platoon leader. He had been a window dresser in Chicago and the men soon decided he was entirely unsuited to a combat command. Behind his back, some of the men started to call him "The Turtle" for his reluctance to come out of his foxhole.

A few days later, Johnny was eating with some soldiers from one of the rifle platoons. Private Phil Lane was griping about one of the 2nd lieutenants: "One of the 2nd Louies—you know who I'm talking about—never got around to digging his own foxhole. So one day I hear incoming artillery and I jump in my hole. This lieutenant jumps in on top of me. Next day it happens again—twice! So we're getting up out of my foxhole and this lieutenant says to me, 'Son, I'd guess you're probably getting kind of tired of me jumping in on top of you like that.'"

Lane spat and continued. "Well, I looked him in the eye and said, 'No sir, that's just fine by me. I figure one of these days a shell is gonna land nearby and I'll be damn glad you're there on top of me.' I told him,'Just don't ever try to beat me to my hole.'"

The men gathered around him rocked with laughter. When they recovered, Lane continued, "I've noticed he spends a lot more time digging his own damn holes. And he hasn't jumped in on top of me since!"

Again the men roared with laughter. They knew foxholes and they hated them. Sometimes it seemed they spent most of their time in foxholes or digging foxholes. They ate in them, slept in them, and even went to the bathroom in them.

After a few minutes, one of the soldiers said, "Speaking of foxholes, I heard we're going to be here for a while. We might as well dig them a little deeper."

Figure 49-2: Soldiers of the 10th Mountain Infantry Division sitting near the trenches on Mount della Spe.

Johnny and Bobby Kraft headed back to their foxhole and started digging. Johnny's shovel clanged as it hit something metallic. He put his shovel down and started digging carefully with his hands, gradually revealing a German artillery shell that had failed to explode on impact. As he dug the shell out and carried it away from the foxhole, Johnny said, "I'm not complaining, but those Germans seem to have a lot of dud shells. If their factories are so great, why can't they get good shells?"

Kraft replied, "I heard it's sabotage. Most of the factory workers are forced laborers. The Germans watch them close, but those workers hate the Germans and do whatever they can to sabotage production."

John speculated, "If that's true, then there's more than a couple of us who owe our lives to some unknown factory worker. I guess we'll never get to thank those guys."

Kraft replied, "Yeah, probably the best thing we can do for them is to win this war as quickly as we can. Remember what that magician said: the war is supposed to end on April 15. Cheer up Johnny, this could be all over in just a few more weeks."

German artillery pounded the American positions with increased frequency. By the end of March, Johnny and Bobby were living in their foxhole. At night, one of them would crawl out to get food and water. During the day, one man rested while the other kept watch.

No one dared get too far from their foxholes, particularly during the day, because shells could start falling at any time. Sometimes the Germans would just fire a shell or two, maybe to remind the GIs they were still there or maybe to try to catch someone who had left his foxhole. But other times, the Germans bombarded the entire mountain. Those were the worst times. The earth shook, shrapnel whizzed through the air, and dirt and debris rained down on the men huddled deep in their foxholes. Sometimes Johnny prayed, sometimes he cried, sometimes he just curled into a ball at the bottom of the foxhole and tried very hard to believe what that veteran had told him, so very long ago: "Not everybody dies in a war." Sometimes it was hard to believe that anybody would live through it.

It didn't seem like either side was trying too hard to win the war. Patrols scouted enemy positions, using the cover of darkness to move carefully into the Pra del Bianco valley, which lay between Mount della Spe and the German positions on the opposing hills.

The Germans were doing pretty much the same thing—digging in and sending night patrols into the valley below.

By the end of March, 1945, most Germans knew they couldn't win the war. They were just trying to hold on as long as they could. Maybe if they held on long enough, they could negotiate an end to the war short of "unconditional surrender." Maybe, somehow, Germany could still have a future.

The Germans could settle for a stalemate in Italy. The Allies would not. They were determined to win, determined to crush the Nazi war machine once and for all. The war in Europe would not end until the last Germany army had surrendered.

The German soldiers on Serre D'Aiano and the American soldiers on Mount della Spe waited for the attack they knew must come. The soldiers on both sides of the valley knew that sooner or later, the Americans were going to have to leave their foxholes on Mount Della Spe, the Mountain of Hope. The Americans would have to cross the valley in between, then advance up the opposite mountains while the Germans fired down on them.

Both sides knew that many young American soldiers would not live to reach the other side. Both sides knew that once the Americans took those hills, the war in Italy would be all but over.

★ Click here to watch video

Figure 49-3: The soldiers of F Company held positions on Mount della Spe. Across the valley, German soldiers waited for the attack that both sides knew must come.

★★★ Ordinary Heroes: Six Stars in the Window ★★★
50. Until the day I die

March, 1945: The early months of 1945 brought continued success for the Allies. The U.S., British, and Canadian troops had broken the German attack in the Ardennes, destroyed most of their tanks, and driven the remnants of those German armies back into Germany. Soviet troops moved into Poland and captured Warsaw. In the Pacific, Allied troops recaptured Bataan and Manila and landing on Iwo Jima.

In the last weeks of March, General Hays, commander of the 10th Mountain Infantry Division, ordered combat patrols to capture German prisoners for interrogation. Those orders moved down the chain of command and in the weeks that followed, Lieutenant James Tippett of A Company, Lieutenant William Putnam of L Company, Lieutenant Robert Dole of I Company, and Lieutenant Carl Kerekes of B Company, led patrols into German territory.

On March 28, it was F Company's turn to send out a patrol. Lieutenant William Douglas led a fifty-eight man combat patrol to attack enemy positions in Serra Sarzana and attempt to capture German soldiers for interrogation. Johnny, Phil Lane, and Bobby Kraft went along as riflemen.

They moved carefully through the dark, probing constantly for mines. After several hours, they reached the outskirts of Serra Sarzana. Just after 1:30 a.m., they opened fire. The Germans fired back with rifles and machine guns. So far, everything was proceeding as planned.

Johnny heard the whistle of an incoming shell. Somebody yelled, "Incoming!" and everyone dove for cover behind a stone fence. More shells followed the first. The stone fence was tall at one end, but got shorter as it continued along the side of the road. The men at the head of the patrol had some protection, but the men at the end found themselves trying to take cover behind a wall that was only knee high.

The German mortar shells started to walk down the fence. As they came closer, Phil Lane said, "Dammit! Why do we have to be stuck here behind this crappy little wall?"

Johnny didn't answer, he just pushed his helmet down and buried his face in the dirt behind the low stone wall. Suddenly the shells stopped falling.

Johnny carefully turned his head to the side and asked Phil, "Why'd they stop shooting?"

Phil spit some dirt out of his mouth and muttered, "They musta figured no one would be stupid enough to try to hide behind a wall this low!"

The lieutenant ordered the men to withdraw. It was too late to try another attack, so the patrol headed back, anxious to get back to the American positions before dawn. They hadn't captured any Germans and they hadn't gathered much useful information. But as patrols went, it was modestly successful. They had reached the objective, made contact with the enemy, and everyone came back alive. At this stage of the war, that wasn't too bad.

Later that week, Platoon Sergeant James Orwig described the view from his foxhole and his feelings about the war in his diary:

```
...here on this blasted hill among the heavily
bunkered foxholes, the sun is hot and insects buzz
busily. With my shirt off, I am sitting in the mouth
of my hole with the hot, friendly sun full on my back
...the litter of C-ration cans and debris flows like
a glittering sea among the sand-bagged bunkers.

The air is absolutely still and the silence of the
scene is disturbed only by the grinding of Rover
Joe's (an artillery spotting plane) ceaseless plowing
overhead, the rumbling of our own artillery and the
voices of the occupants of nearby foxholes lured into
the open by the sun. They are staying close to their
holes though, for the threat of fire is always immi-
nent whether it be the zing of a sniper's bullet or
the full-throated crunching of mortar shells on the
hill. Shells whisper and whine overhead, their delin-
quent detonations returning as distant thunder...

We are on a chain of crests that enjoys enemy expo-
sure on three sides, but down to the left is the
plowed up little town of Castel D'Aiano, peaceful in
its bed of rubble, smoke innocently drifting from a
chimney where some Yanks have a fire. It is our town.

The nearby crests are pocked with burrows and dugouts
where a brother regiment sweats it out. Through the
glasses one can see the boys taking sun in the vicin-
ity of their holes.

Was just thinking here in this delectably treacherous
scene that this would be a nice day for the war to
end. Last night's delayed news was full of sensation-
al reports that western Germany is cut to pieces!
Some columns of our troops are well over 100 miles
beyond the Rhine. Nurenburg is surrounded and troops
are advancing on Munich. It is almost unbelievable.
And Russia is pressing hard on the flanks of Austria
in the north on the Oder. The doom of Berlin may have
already been unleashed.

It seems that it can't go on much longer—it's a mat-
ter of days and hours. That's why I think this would
be a nice day for the war to end. That's also why
(and a sniper's bullet just fizzled overhead) I am
infused with a profound feeling of caution. This is
no time to get hit! Today or tomorrow may be the last
day of the European War. So I sit in the sun at the
mouth of my hole like a gopher—only I have a little
more ahead of me in the future.
```

One significant advantage to staying in the same place for a while was that the food improved. The monotonous diet of K-rations and C-rations was relieved by deliveries of 5-in-1 and 10-in-1 rations. A 10-in-1 ration included enough food for one man for ten days, or enough for ten men for one day. But the best thing about 10-in-1 rations was the food you could actually cook. The most coveted item in the rations was the tin of bacon. The fried bacon tasted fantastic and the men soon learned to use the leftover bacon grease to fry almost anything they could find.

One day Shapley came by and pulled a handful of new potatoes from his pocket. Some of the guys had found the potatoes, lying exposed in the dirt where shells had plowed into a field. He and Johnny fried bacon from a 10-in-1 ration, then sliced the potatoes thin and fried them in the bacon grease. Their mouths watered as they hovered over the pan of potato slices, carefully turning them with their metal forks as they fried to a crispy brown.

"Boy that smells so good!" Johnny said, "My stomach is jumping in anticipation."

Shapley said, "Mmmm! It smells just like the breakfast my Mama used to make. Of course, anything's better than mystery meat in a can. You'd better enjoy this Johnny, it might be the best food you're gonna get until the war is over."

As they savored the crispy fried potatoes, Johnny grew quiet and finally asked, "Shapely, you ever shot anybody?"

Shapley glanced at Johnny to see if he was serious, then speared another crispy chunk of potato and replied, "I can't say for sure, but I don't think I have. When everyone else is shooting, I point my gun in the same direction and I shoot, but I don't think I've ever hit anyone. I kind of hope I haven't."

★ Click here to watch video

Figure 50-1: After weeks of eating cold K-rations and C-rations, 10-in-1 rations were a welcome luxury because they included bacon and other food that GIs could heat and eat.

Johnny nodded his head. He understood what Shapley was saying. Killing was serious business. It wasn't something that a good man should take lightly.

Johnny replied, "I only know for sure that I shot that one German. When I saw him running towards me, I didn't have time to think. I just aimed my gun and shot him. I've thought about that a lot since then, but I don't know what else I could have done."

Shapley didn't respond. He was focused on the last crispy bit of fried potato.

Johnny sat lost in thought, the stress of the past weeks evident on his dirt-smudged face. He swallowed his last piece of potato, then added, "At night, I still see the surprised look in his eye as he fell over backwards. He knew he was killed and I think he was surprised. He didn't think he was going to die in this war. He thought he was going to live. He thought he was going to go home to see his wife and daughter."

Johnny closed his eyes and leaned his helmeted head against the dirt of the foxhole wall. "I think that will haunt me until the day I die."

★ Click here to watch video

Figure 50-2: 10th Mountain Infantry soldiers advance past a dead German soldier in March, 1945.

★★★ Ordinary Heroes: Six Stars in the Window ★★★
51. Such happiness doesn't last forever

March 11, 1945: The H&S Company train chugged into Wickwrath, Germany just south of Muchen-Gladbach. A stream of freight trains followed, carrying supplies the 9th Army needed to support the troops that had crossed the Rhine into the German heartland. The Allies were deep into Germany, but the war was not yet over, not for Art, not for the Koski brothers and not for the millions of soldiers and civilians caught up in the death throes of the Third Reich.

Art's crew was surveying the Wesser River Bridge. They sky was clear and the sun was shining. It was the kind of day that made you feel maybe the war would actually end someday. Art leaned on the railing, looked down, and stiffened.

★ Click here to watch video

Figure 51-1: The near miraculous capture of the intact bridge at Remagen allowed the Allies to pour men and material into the heart of Germany.

There were bodies floating down the river. Some were trapped in the bushes along the edge, others floated serenely along with the current. Some were in uniform, but many were civilians. It was clear that death touched everyone: German soldiers, Russian soldiers, men, and women.

Then he saw the body that would haunt him for the rest of his life: a blond-haired baby drifting peacefully down the river. The baby's eyes were closed and he looked like he was sleeping as he drifted along with the current. Tears came to Art's eyes as he thought about that little baby, killed by an adult war. "That little guy didn't do anything to cause this war. Killing him didn't help anybody. How did we, how did God, ever let things go this far?"

As the Allies pushed deeper into Germany, Art saw what it meant for a country to be on the losing end of a war. Many cities were just piles of rubble with a few broken walls. Dazed survivors poked around in the rubble, like rats in a garbage heap.

Curiously, not every building had been destroyed. Scattered buildings stood virtually untouched. In Cologne, the great cathedral stood guard over the smoking ruins of the city. In Munster, Art was riding with Warren Babcock when they passed the cathedral rising proudly over the rubble. All the buildings around it had been pulverized by heavy bombers. Art turned to Babcock and asked, "Isn't it odd that the cathedral wasn't hit?"

★ Click here to watch video

Figure 51-2: GIs moving into Cologne were surprised to see the towers of the great cathedral still standing.

Sergeant Babcock replied, "I don't know if it's true, but I've been told that the bombardiers aim at easily recognized buildings like that cathedral. Even from 30,000 feet I bet that tower stands out like a sore thumb. They aim at that cathedral and let loose. The bombs drop all around, but the building at the aiming point, the one at dead center, often won't get a scratch on it."

Art shook his head and replied, "It figures don't it? The safest place to be is right where they're aiming."

A few blocks beyond the cathedral, Art saw two German boys playing by the side of the road. They had constructed small buildings out of twigs and sand. One of the boys held his arm out and dropped rocks as he walked along making buzzing sounds and intoning, "Das Amerikan Bomber! Das Amerikan Bomber!"

To those boys, Americans were the people who bombed their cities, killed their parents, and invaded their country. They certainly didn't understand that their country was being reduced to rubble because people like their parents let a madman take control.

On March 14, Art wrote to Jenny. As in many of his letters written that spring, he wrote fondly about the good things in life. "It sure would be nice to spend a few days at Mulligan Creek, teasing some of those overgrown trout. That trip we made out there before I left home is one of the pleasant memories I can look back at. I enjoyed that more than any other time in my life, but as life usually goes, such happiness doesn't last forever. Well anyway, a person can look forward to all that after this war ends and people can start living like they should."

On March 20, Art wrote again. In a previous letter, Jenny had teased him about his aches and pains, so he replied, "You must realize I'm getting up in years and starting to feel the beating that the elements are giving me. I'm getting old fast, like everyone else in this game."

On April 1, Art wrote yet another letter to his beloved Jenny: "I had a birthday a couple of days ago. Didn't remember it until I looked at the calendar. Reminds me I'm getting to be quite an old man, no wonder I'm getting stiff in the joints, old age creeping up on me. If I don't get out of this business soon, I'll be ripe to take a pension and live in the old soldier's home the rest of my days."

Carl "Art" Koski had just turned twenty-six years old. He had been in the Army for three long years.

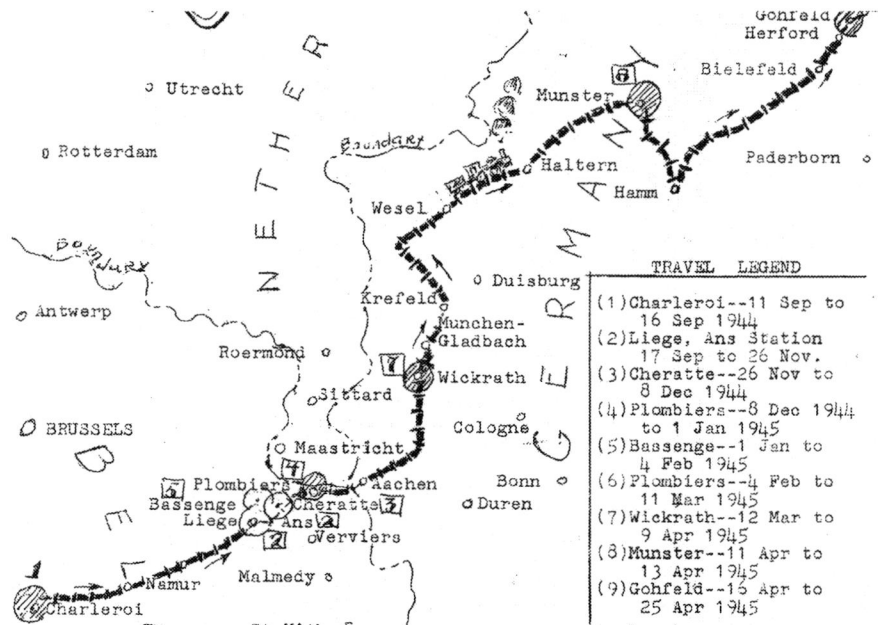

Figure 51-3: The 332nd Engineer's primary projects from Charleroi to Bad Oyenhausen.

★★★ Ordinary Heroes: Six Stars in the Window ★★★
52. Wrong place, wrong time

April 1, 1945: Bobby Kraft got hold of a heavily creased second-hand copy of the *Stars and Stripes*, the thin newspaper published for U.S. servicemen. Bobby excitedly scanned the paper, summarizing the headlines for Johnny: "The Russians are sixty-five miles from Berlin! Our guys are across the Rhine and moving towards the Elbe! The Germans are being squeezed from all sides. The show's almost over for the Nazis!"

Johnny listened with a growing sense of optimism. Maybe the war was almost over. Maybe they weren't going to have to cross that valley after all.

The *Stars and Stripes* did not reveal that General Eisenhower had established three primary goals for this last phase of the war:

1) Capture the industrial heartland of Germany.

2) Minimize the risk of Allied friendly fire incidents as the U.S. and British troops drew closer to the Russians.

3) Prevent fanatical Nazi troops from withdrawing to the Alps where they might engage in a prolonged guerrilla war.

That last goal was to have a direct effect on the men of the 10th Mountain Infantry Division. Plans were already underway for the Allied armies in Italy to punch through the heavily defended Gothic line, enter the Po River Valley, and cut off the lines of retreat to prevent German soldiers in Italy from retreating to the Alps.

There were only two main roads through the rugged mountains along which trucks and armor could advance. They were Highway 64 and Highway 65, both of which ran north to the crucial city of Bologna. Allied troops and armor could not advance along those highways until the Germans were forced from the mountains overlooking them.

The 10th Mountain Infantry Division, 371st Infantry, 365th Infantry, and Brazilian Expeditionary Force were assigned the difficult and dangerous task of taking the heavily fortified positions overlooking those highways. In the coming weeks, many young men would die to clear the way for the Allied advance up those roads.

Easter Sunday dawned clear and sunny. Scattered blades of new grass poked their way through the trampled mud and a few brave birds sang in the shell-shattered trees.

One man from each foxhole was allowed to attend Easter morning church services. After breakfasting on K-rations, Johnny crawled out of the foxhole he shared with Bobby Kraft. Staying low, he slowly worked his way over the hill to the back side of Mount della Spe, where he caught sight of his old friend Shapley Haines.

"Hey Shapley!" he said. "How ya' doin?"

Shapley replied, in his usual optimistic way, "I'm fine Johnny, just fine. Isn't this a beautiful day? I hear the Germans are about to surrender. We might not have to take those hills. Our war could end right here on this hill. I told you we were going to be okay!"

They walked together down the slope, to a shallow depression in the side of the hill. The chaplain had set up an altar on the hood of a jeep. The men kneeled on the ground with their rifles and helmets beside them.

The chaplain spoke.

> Where is God now?, you might ask. As you sit in your foxhole in the lonely hours before dawn, you might wonder if he is still with you. But surely you do not believe God would desert you here on the battlefield, here where your need is so great.

> God does not run away when the going gets tough. You have but to open your eyes to see him. You have but to open your heart to hear him.
>
> Where is God?
>
> He is where he has always been—in the sunshine, in your thoughts of home, in the hearts of your comrades, and in your own heart. God is with you wherever you go. He is with you today, and always.

Johnny listened to the service and gazed around at the soldiers sitting near him. Many of these men were rough around the edges. Most of them swore and many of them drank. They were definitely more worldly than the members of the Apostolic Lutheran Church back home. Just a few years before, he wouldn't have had anything to do with most of them. But now, having served with them in the most difficult of circumstances, he understood that deep inside, they were all good men. On this Easter morning, his heart was filled with affection for these tired, ragged soldiers. These were some of the finest men he had ever met and he was proud to serve with them.

The chaplain finished his sermon. As the men sang "Onward Christian Soldiers", they could hear artillery shells exploding in the distance. Johnny thought, "I'll never sing that song again without thinking of today."

Figure 52-1: Soldiers from F Company attend Easter Sunday church service on the slopes of Mount della Spe.

After the church service, Johnny walked with Shapley back to his squad. The men were sitting on the side of their trench, enjoying the beautiful weather. Bill Kehres and Neil Christie were laughing about some joke. After chatting for a bit, Johnny got up to head back to his own squad.

As Johnny said goodbye, Shapley looked up from his copy of the *Stars and Stripes* newspaper, and said, "Don't worry so much Johnny. Everything is going to be all right. This war is almost over. I can feel it."

Moments later the men heard the distinctive sound of an incoming shell. Johnny rolled into a shell hole and buried his face in the dirt. The men sitting on the side of the trench dove for cover. The shell passed harmlessly overhead, landing in the valley below.

Johnny lifted his face out of the dirt and looked back. The men from Shapley's squad slowly stood up and brushed themselves off. Shapley was still sitting on the side of the trench, newspaper in his hand, chuckling at the dirt-covered men. "I knew that one was gonna miss! I could tell by the sound!"

Another shell whistled towards them. Johnny dove for cover once again. This shell hit close by, showering Johnny with dirt and pebbles. The men back at the trench recovered a bit more slowly, warily crouching in the trench, yelling, "Is anybody hit? Is anybody hit?"

Johnny saw two soldiers working on a wounded man. He ran over to see if he could help. It was Bill Linscott. He'd been sitting near Shapley just minutes before and had been wounded by splinters when the incoming shell burst against the logs on top of one of the foxholes.

Johnny looked around to see if anyone else needed help. That's when he saw Bill Kehres trying to revive Shapley.

Shapley was lying very still. There wasn't a mark on him, he was just dead. Bill Kehres felt for a pulse, then looked at Johnny and shook his head. Shapley was gone.

Johnny was stunned. He could barely accept that Shapley was dead. They'd just been talking moments before. There hadn't been a big attack. The men felt safe today, safe enough to sit on the edge of their foxholes and enjoy the sun. Out of the blue, the Germans lobbed a couple of shells over the hill and now Shapley was dead. It didn't make any sense, it didn't serve any purpose.

Johnny wandered back to his own foxhole. He dropped heavily into his foxhole and sat there, staring at the dirt wall. A couple of times, Bobby Kraft asked him what was wrong, but Johnny didn't respond. Sometime later, he heard the distinctive whistle of more incoming shells. For hours, he and Kraft huddled in their foxhole while German artillery pounded the hillside. They couldn't talk over the noise. They just crouched in their foxhole, praying that no artillery shells would land in the hole with them.

★ Click here to watch video

Figure 52-2: F Company soldiers shortly before the shells hit on April 1, 1945. Left to right: Bill Linscott, Bill Kehres, Thomas O'Keefe, Neil Christie, Joe Escher, Henry "Hank" Schools, Shapley "Sleepy" Haines.

With every explosion, Johnny relived the moment when Shapley had been killed. He thought of his friend Shapley: soldier, optimist, always confident everything would turn out all right in the end. He remembered Shapley in the bouncing truck on the way to Montecatini, singing "Til it's over, Over there," in his high pitched voice. He thought of Shapley, killed by a German artillery crew that probably never even knew he was there.

That evening, after the artillery barrage was over, Johnny wrote a letter to his sister Lilly. Like most soldiers, he'd decided there wasn't any use telling the folks at home what was really happening. There was nothing they could do about it and it would only make them worry. So, he didn't tell them much about what was really happening, with the explanation that any details wouldn't get past the censor anyway.

```
                         April 1, 1945
                         Somewhere in Italy

Dear Lilly:

I've been with this new unit for a while now. We've
been through some tough times, but I think we're
going to be O.K. The newspaper says the Germans are
about ready to call it quits. By the time you get
this letter, it might all be over.

The food here is not great, but otherwise we're doing
fine. It's gotten a lot warmer and it seems that
spring is here. Some days, we even take off our
shirts to lie in the sun. That sure feels fine! Lying
in the sun with my eyes closed, it's almost like
being at Dead River camp.

I still haven't had a chance to see Oscar, but maybe
that will work out later on. I see trails from B-17s
flying overhead and I wonder if Oscar is in one of
them. They sure are up there, far from the mud and
such down here.
```

```
I can't imagine what it's like to fly. I guess I'll
have to give that a try after the war. Boy, I bet
that's something!

How is Dad getting along? Give him my regards and
tell him everything is O.K with me.

Well so long, good luck, and God Bless you all.
                                        Johnny
```

Later, he wrote another letter, a darker letter, to his brother Art:

```
                        April 1, 1945
                        Somewhere in Italy

Dear Art:

I've been with this new unit for a while now. We've
been through some tough times. We're all hoping the
Germans will surrender soon so we can all go home.

One of my buddies got killed today. An artillery
shell landed next to him. He was in the wrong place
at the wrong time. Sometimes it seems that's all it
is, random chance.

I try to hold on to my belief in God, but it's hard
to think that God could let this happen. Does he know
what's happening here? Does he even care?

As you can probably tell, I've been down some dark
paths lately. Sometimes I wonder if any of us will
see the end of this war. If we do, I wonder if we'll
ever be the same.

Maybe all I need is some time at Flat Rock, some time
with nobody shooting at me.

Well, I hope you guys are giving them heck there in
Europe and Hitler will quit soon, so we can all go
home.

                        Good luck and God Bless.
                        Johnny
```

★ Click here for Web Info

Figure 52-3: Click here for more information on both of the above letters.

★★★ Ordinary Heroes: Six Stars in the Window ★★★
53. Has anyone heard from George?

Spring, 1945: Through the winter of 1944–1945, Art, Oscar, and Johnny received regular letters from their sisters and even a few letters from their brother Reuben and their oldest brother Al.

Reuben was serving at the Great Lakes Naval Training Facility near Chicago and managed to get home several times. Eleanor reported, "I had a letter from Reuben today. He is bored with the Navy. He wants to see action. He said the only action he has seen is swabbing the deck. If he only realized how lucky he is. He will see action soon enough and wish the rest of his life that he hadn't. As for me, I dread seeing action at sea. I would rather have it on land anytime. Reuben is such a man of action, even in civilian life. He has so much energy he could win the war single handed if they would only let him."

Alfred had been promoted to the rank of warrant officer junior grade and was serving in Washington state with the 212th Anti-Aircraft Artillery Automatic Weapons Battalion.

But there was very little word from their brother George. Early in the war, the FBI had interviewed George's friends and family, ostensibly as part of a background check for a security clearance. In several letters, George hinted that he was involved with intelligence work of some sort, but nobody really knew for sure what he was doing in the service.

★ Click here for Web Info

Figure 53-1: George Koski with his youngest sister Edna Mae, outside the Koski house during George's leave in the summer of 1944.

George was home on leave in the summer of 1944, but he didn't talk about his Army assignments, not even with Oscar, who was home at the same time.

★ Click here to watch video

Figure 53-2: Operation Varsity was the last major airborne assault of the war.

After stints with the Signal Corps, Ordinance, Anti-aircraft, and Artillery units, George's military records indicate he left the U.S. on February 11, 1945, arriving in Europe on February 23.

There are two very different accounts of what happened next. In the version of events that he told his brothers, George was attached to an airborne unit and climbed aboard a glider to participate in an airborne attack, possibly Operation Varsity.

It is a matter of record that Operation Varsity began early on the morning of March 24. A massive air armada, consisting of some 3,500 transport planes, gliders, and fighters, crossed the Rhine River near Wessel, Germany. There were so many planes, they literally darkened the sky for two-and-a-half hours as they passed overhead. Their mission was simple, to establish positions on the German side of the Rhine River so engineers could build bridges to funnel Allied troops and equipment into the German heartland.

But the Germans knew that the Rhine was their last line of defense. No invading army had successfully crossed the Rhine since Napoleon, 140 years earlier. The Germans were not about to let the Allies cross it unopposed.

As Allied paratroopers and gliders neared the ground, they came under heavy fire. Casualties mounted. Plywood gliders broke apart on landing. Paratroopers were shot while floating to earth under their parachutes or as they struggled to disentangle themselves from their harnesses.

The glider carrying George Koski approached its designated landing area. One wing caught a tree. The plywood glider ripped apart on impact, spilling men and equipment over the ground. George was thrown clear of the wreckage.

George regained consciousness several hours later. He could see, he could hear, but he could not move anything below his jaw. He couldn't even turn his head. He didn't feel any pain, so he assumed his neck was broken when he was thrown from the glider.

He called out, but the only reply was a low moaning somewhere out of his line of sight. After a while the moaning stopped and he was left very much alone.

George was desperately thirsty. He had a canteen attached to his belt, but it might as well have been on the moon, since he couldn't move his hand to get it. He faded in and out of consciousness. Time passed.

Two days later, a squad from Graves Registration arrived at the crash site to collect bodies. One of the men called out in surprise, "Hey! Over here! This one's still alive!"

They carefully examined George, placed him on a stretcher, and drove him back to a field hospital for treatment. George spent the next several months recuperating from a broken neck in a hospital in France.

As he lay immobilized in the hospital bed, George dictated a short letter to his fiancée Rochelle. In the letter to Rochelle, George downplayed his injury, telling her a completely different version of the story: "I injured my neck in a stupid accident. I feel so useless, taking up space in this hospital, alongside men who were wounded in combat. Don't worry, I'm going to be fine. I cracked a vertebrae, but the doctors say I'm going to recover completely."

Aside from his discharge papers, some training certificates, and a few letters, there is little documentation regarding George's military experience. George survived the war, but rarely spoke about his wartime experiences. When pressed, he would say he "couldn't talk about it," implying security restrictions.

It is possible that the story of the glider crash was the boasting of a young man trying to impress his brothers with an interesting story after the war.

It is also possible that his explanation to Rochelle was an attempt to tone down the facts to keep her from worrying about him.

Perhaps the truth lies somewhere in between. As is the case with so many veterans, the true story may never be known.

★ Click here to watch video

Figure 53-3: George Koski (left) and an unidentified buddy at the 587th Signal Depot Company.

★★★ Ordinary Heroes: Six Stars in the Window ★★★
54. Lie in the dark

April, 1945: During the first week of April, Oscar and his crew traveled to the Isle of Capri for rest and recuperation. It was a fantastic, yet disorienting experience. Capri is a small island just a few miles off the coast of Italy. Its white beaches, craggy cliffs, olive groves, and spectacular blue-water views have made it a popular tourist destination since Roman times. Oscar stayed in a luxurious hotel with maid service and slept in a real bed with a feather pillow. For ten days, he could do as little or as much as he wanted. He had no duties and no cares. As he relaxed in the beautiful surroundings, he started to feel that maybe, just maybe, there might be something good in the future that lay ahead.

Oscar did his best to forget the war. Like tourists on holiday, he and the crew toured the famed Blue Grotto, a beautiful cave bathed in blue sunlight shining through the water. Later, they explored the ruins of a castle built by the Roman emperor Tiberius. The beautiful surroundings were like a tonic, reinvigorating Oscar's youthful exuberance and his wry sense of humor.

But they weren't tourists and they weren't on holiday. As they left the castle of Tiberius, a B-24 buzzed the ruins, flying low to the ground. Suddenly an engine cut out. The B-24 didn't pull up and it crashed into the mountains. There wasn't anything they could do, so the airmen just stood there and watched the burning wreckage, a grim reminder of the war that still had to be won.

Even irrepressible Oscar found it difficult to get back in the holiday spirit after the crash. His mood was reflective as he sipped a quiet cup of coffee and watched the sun sparkle on the water. He was on leave, but all over the world men were fighting and dying. In just a few days, the wake-up guy would shake him on the shoulder once again and tell him it was time to suit up for another mission. He realized these could be the last pleasant days of his life.

That evening Oscar looked through the few English language books in the lobby of the hotel. He picked up a book of poetry, and found the poem *Lie in the Dark and Listen* by Noël Coward. Oscar was so impressed with the poem that he read it to Skillings. The poem described the RAF bomber crews, flying high over England towards enemy territory while the English civilians lay safe in their beds below.

After he finished reading the poem, Oscar and Skillings sat and looked out the window towards the beautiful Mediterranean Sea.

After a while, Skillings took a deep breath and remarked, "When this is all over, I wonder if anyone will care about what we did. If we lose, they'll blame us. The Nazis will write the history books and we'll come out as the bad guys. If we win, they'll think it was inevitable. If we die, they'll forget us, and if we live through it, they'll roll their eyes and yawn when we try to tell them what it was like. The fella that wrote that poem got it right 'Theirs is a world you'll never know.' Hell, my own kids probably won't even care what we went through."

★★★ Ordinary Heroes: Six Stars in the Window ★★★
55. Where I'm going

April, 1945: Looking back, most of the men of F Company would remember the first weeks of April as a blur of foxholes, inadequate sleep, K-rations, cold nights, and incoming artillery shells. They spent the daylight hours crouched in their foxholes. At night, one man would crawl out to collect rations and water.

German shells continued to fall unpredictably, sometimes just a shell or two, other times a whole series of shells that pummeled the entire hillside. After a few weeks, many of the men found it difficult to remember a time when they weren't living in a foxhole under near-constant shelling.

Life in the foxholes of Mount della Spe was an isolated existence. Except for Bobby Kraft, Johnny didn't see many other people. He couldn't see the Germans and he didn't see any other Americans except when he crawled back for rations and water. Sometimes, during the long nights, it seemed like everybody else had gone home and it was just him and Kraft sitting in their foxhole, while the Germans lobbed shells at them.

As F Company sniper, Leif Syversen had been issued a bolt action Springfield with a scope. During the first week of April, he expanded his foxhole with a small notch in the front that he could crawl into for protection from tree bursts—artillery shells that hit trees and exploded, raining shrapnel and splinters on the men below. At night he put his sniper rifle and helmet in the bottom of his foxhole, then curled up on the covered shelf to sleep.

One night an 88 mm shell landed on the edge of Syversen's fox hole. The GIs in nearby foxholes called for him, but he didn't answer. They were sure he had been killed. After a few minutes, Syversen's head appeared over the edge of his foxhole. "I'm all right!" he said. "It just stunned me for a bit. My helmet, rifle, and scope are ruined, but I'm okay. I sure am glad I dug that little shelf in my foxhole."

One more soldier was wounded when a shell exploded in a tree and sent splinters flying through the air. Another GI got too far from his foxhole and was wounded in the arm by shrapnel, but overall, casualties were light.

The loneliest nights were spent on sentry duty in an outpost. The first night on outpost duty, Johnny and Kraft waited until it was fully dark, then crawled to a foxhole a few hundred yards in front of the rest of the men. As they got close to the outpost, the sentries heard them in the dark. "Who's there?" they challenged.

"It's us, Koski and Kraft!" whispered Johnny.

"What's the password?" demanded the sentry.

Johnny and Kraft looked at each other, trying to remember the current password. Johnny knew the password was typically a word or phrase that would be difficult for German-speakers to correctly pronounce. Then he remembered: "Wild rabbit!"

That was the correct password and the sentry whispered for them to "Come on in!"

Johnny and Kraft tumbled into the foxhole and the two soldiers who had been on outpost duty slithered back towards the main line. Then the waiting began. For the rest of the night and all the next day, Johnny and Kraft sat in the foxhole and took turns watching and listening for Germans. They couldn't leave the foxhole for their entire time on watch. It was boring, but in this case boring was good and they hoped it would stay that way.

The outposts were an early warning system, designed to alert the rest of the men if the Germans attacked. Two sentries couldn't stop an attack, but they could warn the rest of the Company. The sentries would probably sacrifice their lives to give the rest of the men a few minute's warning.

The next night, as Johnny and Bobby Kraft crouched in the outpost foxhole, they were very glad when they heard their replacements crawling up from behind. As soon as the new men settled in, they scrambled out of the foxhole and crawled back to their own foxhole.

Johnny smiled as he settled into his foxhole. Two days ago, he'd figured it was about the worst place in the world. After a night and a day at the outpost, his old foxhole looked pretty good. Johnny was trying to decide if it was safe enough to crawl back for a cup of hot coffee when he heard the distinctive whistle of incoming shells. Johnny crouched in his foxhole next to Kraft as the shells exploded, showering dirt and shrapnel all around. For the hundredth time, he was thankful for the heavy logs and sandbags that covered their foxhole.

The shelling ended and Johnny cautiously peered over the edge of his foxhole. Other men emerged from their foxholes and started checking for casualties. They found a soldier crouched in the bottom of his foxhole. Thinking he was dead, one of the other soldiers dropped into the hole with him. The man was alive: he wasn't even wounded. He was just sitting on the bottom of his foxhole, his arms wrapped tightly around his legs, and his face pressed between his knees. He didn't respond to anything. He remained curled up tight, withdrawn from the world and the war. The men finally hoisted him out of the foxhole by his elbows and carried him over the hill, still curled up in a ball.

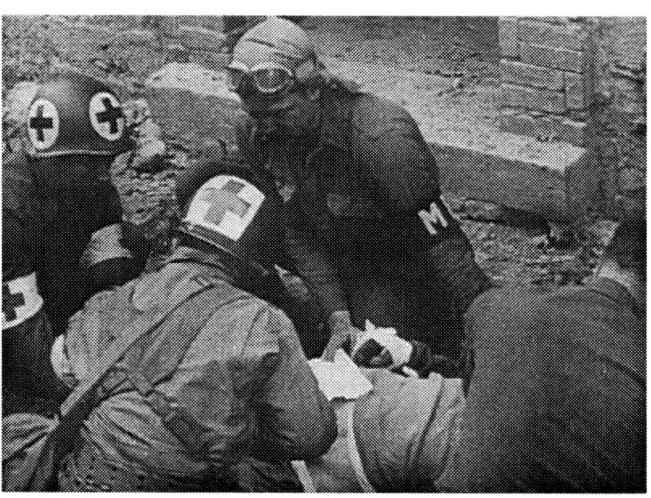

★ Click here to watch video

Figure 55-1: Medics, ambulance drivers, nurses, and doctors worked tirelessly to try to save the lives of wounded GIs.

As the medics drove the man away in a Jeep, one of the men who had carried him said, "You know, back in Camp Hale, I would have called that man a coward. But after what we've been through, I can't criticize him. He didn't run. He stayed here on the line. He just finally reached a point where couldn't take it any more. I can't blame him for that. It could happen to any of us." In a quieter voice, he added, "It could happen to me."

On the night of April 6, Johnny crawled back and ran into Wally Krusell, the big guy whose front teeth had been knocked loose. Wally had been sent back to attend a memorial service at the military cemetery near Florence. The endless rows of crosses in the cemetery made a strong impression on Wally. "You see men lying on the ground, and you see new replacements come in, but you don't realize how many have died. Seeing all those crosses sure gives a guy something to think about."

Figure 55-2: Memorial service for fallen comrades held in the military cemetery in Florence Italy on April 6, 1945.

The men of F Company kept hearing rumors about the "Big Push." According to the latest rumors, the Army strategists were waiting for the snow to melt so they could move vehicles and armor through the mountain passes. The rumors were basically correct, the "Big Push," code-named Operation Craftsman, was scheduled for early April.

Everyone knew the next attack was going to be tough. The Germans occupied heavily fortified positions all along the next ridge and had been improving their defenses for months.

If the Germans held the hills, the war would drag on. If the Allies took those hills, the last German defenses would be broken open and U.S. Armored units could move up Highway 64, getting behind the German lines. At that point, the war in Italy would be all but over.

But taking those hills would not be easy. In order to reach them, the men of the 10th would have to go down the slopes of Mount della Spe and cross the open valley, where they would be exposed to withering fire from machine guns, artillery, and mortars. They would then have to fight their way uphill while the Germans fired down from their entrenched positions.

On April 10, James Winterbottom was promoted to sergeant and was put in charge of a five-man squad consisting of himself, Armstrong, Smieska, Kraft, and Johnny. Sergeant Winterbottom carried his knee mortar. The rest of the squad loaded up with ammo shells.

That night, Johnny and Bobby Kraft were awakened by the sound of American artillery firing on German positions. Johnny muttered, "This is different, and different isn't good."

The next morning, Sergeant Winterbottom crawled by and dropped into their foxhole. Winterbottom was all business. "This is it, the push for the Po River valley! The 92nd and the 442nd Nisei attacked this morning. We move out tomorrow morning. It will start with an air attack followed by a heavy artillery barrage."

He pointed toward the valley. "We'll advance across the valley and up Hill 860. Companies E and G will consolidate their positions on Hill 860 while we veer left, up Hill 909. We're going to advance with the rifle platoons. When they get held up by a bunker or machine-gun nest, we'll take it out. We're going to need all the ammo we can carry. Each of the riflemen will carry one mortar shell tied around his neck. We'll collect them as we go. You guys should take a full load of ammo, but carry your rifles and a few grenades as well. Stay spread out as we cross the valley—there are a lot of mines out there."

He stopped for a moment, looking each of them in the eye in turn. "This won't be easy. They know we're coming and they know they have to stop us."

Throughout that long day, Johnny and Bobby checked and rechecked their weapons and gear. Through the long, dark night, they tried to mentally prepare themselves for the coming attack.

Like so many of the men around him, Johnny prayed. "Lord, I don't want to die in this place. But if that's your will, give me the courage to do what must be done. That's all I ask. Just give me enough courage to do what I have to do."

He turned to his foxhole buddy, Bobby Kraft, and asked, "Bobby, if I don't make it, would you get word to my family that I died as a Christian? It would mean a lot to them."

Kraft agreed to do so and both men tried to get some rest.

As dawn grudgingly brightened the sky on the morning of April 12, Johnny saw heavy clouds looming overhead. A few minutes later they received word that the attack would be postponed for one day because the planes couldn't provide ground support through the heavy overcast.

Figure 55-3: Soldiers of the 10th Mountain Infantry Division at the entrance to their foxhole on Mount della Spe.

They had been ready that morning, as ready as men could be. Now that readiness seeped away as they huddled in their foxhole for yet another day. Neither Johnny nor Bobby felt like talking. They rechecked their weapons and waited as the minutes and the hours ticked by.

When Johnny woke up early the next morning, the sky was still heavily overcast.

Bobby looked up at the sky and said, "Damn! They're going to postpone again! If we've got to do this thing, I'd just as soon get it over with. How many times do we have to go through this?"

Johnny just grunted. There wasn't anything to say. It was one of those times that occurs in every life, one of those times when something momentous is about to happen. You can't avoid it, you can't slow it down, and you can't make it happen any sooner. You just have to wait and ride it out.

As expected, a short time later they received word that the attack would be postponed for yet another twenty-four hours. Some of the men believed the attack had been postponed because the Army didn't want to jinx it by attacking on Friday the 13th. Others blamed the cloudy weather.

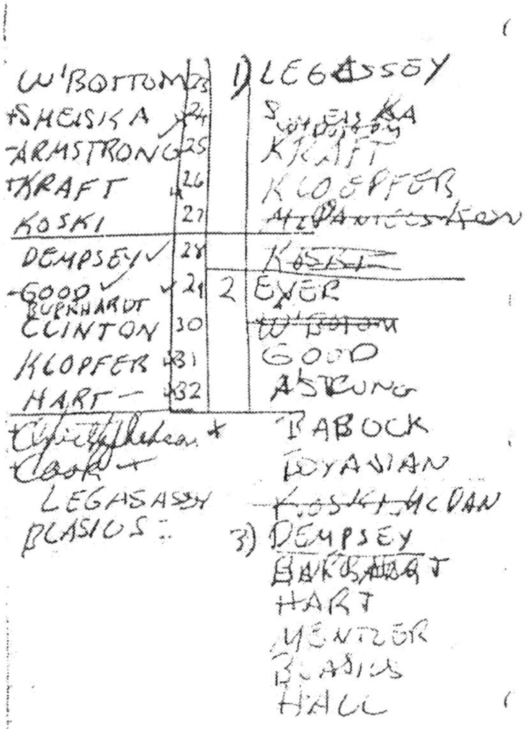

Figure 55-4: A page from Platoon Sergeant James Orwig's notebook showing 4th platoon squad members in April, 1945. At this point, Johnny was a member of James Winterbottom's five-man mortar squad.

None of the men were happy with the postponement. For two nights they had waited anxiously in their foxholes for the coming attack. For two mornings they had tried to put themselves in the mental state needed to advance across the open valley. And two times they were told to stand down and wait for another day. They just wanted to get it over with.

★ Click here to watch video

Figure 55-5: The Big Push was delayed several times.

Later that day, someone passed the word that President Roosevelt had died. The disheartening news rippled over the foxholes like a black wave. Most of the soldiers understood that it was Roosevelt who had prepared the country for the inevitable war with the Axis powers. It was Roosevelt who had turned America into the arsenal of democracy. It was Roosevelt who looked deep into the soul of America and said, "This is the toughest war of all time. We need not leave it to historians of the future to answer the question whether we are tough enough to meet this unprecedented challenge. We can give that answer now. The answer is 'Yes'."

Roosevelt had been a stalwart leader. But that leader had fallen. Like knights on a battlefield of old, the soldiers instinctively understood that if their leader could fall so near the end, any one of them could fall as well. With a renewed sense of their own mortality, the soldiers of the 10th Mountain Infantry Division prepared themselves for battle.

Platoon Sergeant James Orwig made one more entry in his diary:

```
The big drive is on. We will push them into the Alps.
This will be the last big operation of the Italian
front. When I again will be able to write in this
book depends on the course of the battle and my own
fortunes for which I am hoping the best...
```

Like many soldiers who have been in combat too long and have suffered too much, Johnny began to think that he was not going to survive the war. He wrote pessimistic letters to his sisters, letters that drove them frantic with worry.

His sister Eleanor wrote:

```
I had a letter from Johnny. He has seen a lot of
action, but not a scratch yet. However, he knows his
luck will run out. The rest of his letter is about
Dad. "Please comfort him after I am gone. Why do I
know I am going to die? I know because I feel
Christ's presence so strongly. I can almost see Him
and I know he is here with me.

I am not afraid. Tell Dad my sins are forgiven me
because Christ died to save me. Through His grace I
shall enter the Kingdom of Heaven. Dad is the most
important person to me in the world. My only regret
is leaving him sorry because of my death."

I had sent him a clipping where congress had passed
the G.I. Bill of Rights. I thought it would cheer
Johnny up to know he could go to college with expens-
es paid. He answered, "Where I am going I won't need
a college education. Had I survived this war, I would
have gone to Flat Rock and stayed there forever. I
really love that place in the wilderness."

Then he said "Thanks for all the support you have
given me all these years. God's peace. Johnny"

I hope none of his predictions come true, and that it
is only combat fatigue he is suffering from. I am
praying hard. Oh, when is this nightmare going to end?
I have forgotten what normal living is like.
```

★ Click here to watch video

Figure 55-6: The "Soldier's Bill" was to have a profound impact on the lives of many GIs after the war.

★★★ Ordinary Heroes: Six Stars in the Window ★★★
56. Give 'em heck boys

April 8, 1945: Oscar and his crew returned to Lucera 8 after their leave in Capri. The 301st had flown six missions while they were gone. Most of the missions sought to stop the Germans from moving men and materials to the front lines by destroying railroad bridges and marshaling yards.

The Germans weren't giving up. On April 5, during a raid over northern Italy, almost every plane from the 301st was hit by flak. Two sustained heavy flak damage and twenty-six sustained minor damage. If the war was almost over, it seemed someone had forgotten to tell the Germans.

The British Eighth Army was scheduled to attack the eastern flank of the German line on April 9. That morning, Oscar flew in a formation of 866 bombers that pounded the German lines with 1,692 tons of fragmentation, softening them up for the infantry advance. German antiaircraft and fighter resistance was relatively light, but a B-24 was lost when it moved out of position and was hit by bombs dropped from the planes above.

On April 11, Oscar flew again, this time as part of a 112-plane formation attacking the Vipiteno Railroad Bridge. One plane from the 301st was lost. Its crew was on its seventh mission. The pilot, Lieutenant Walter Haaser, reported an oil leak on the #3 engine before reaching the target. He feathered the prop, but managed to stay with the formation and dropped his bombs on the target. Flak over the target was very heavy and two more engines quit. Haaser's plane fell out of formation. Airmen in other planes reported seeing black smoke pouring from one engine as the crew jettisoned loose equipment in an attempt to lighten the load so they might make it back to base.

The desperate measures that had helped Oscar's crew just a few months before, didn't work for Lieutenant Haaser's crew. They were unable to gain enough altitude and bailed out near the Swiss border. Most of the crewmen were picked up by neutral Swiss forces and interned until the end of the war. One man drifted into German territory and spent the rest of the war in a German prisoner-of-war camp.

On April 12, Oscar watched from the runway as the planes of the 301st returned from a mission to the Padua Railroad Bridge in northern Italy. As a damaged B-17 touched down, the #4 engine accelerated uncontrollably and the plane veered off the runway. The plane ran into five C-47 transport planes that were parked on the runway, shearing off their noses. The B-17 and several of the damaged C-47s burst into flames. All but one of the crew members of the B-17 managed to escape the burning plane. Three British crewmen were killed in the parked planes.

On April 14, the Fifth Army launched a major ground offensive. On April 15, the 15th AAF launched its biggest single day of operations. Every plane capable of flying was hurled at the German supply lines to prevent them from reinforcing the troops at the front. One group attacked ground targets around Bologna, while a second group attacked a railroad bridge to prevent supplies from being brought in for the German troops. The 858 bombers in the first group dropped 1,577 tons of bombs on gun positions, troops, supply dumps, and German headquarters.

Oscar didn't fly that day, but as he watched the bombers take off, he thought, "Give 'em heck boys! My little brother is out there somewhere."

★★★ Ordinary Heroes: Six Stars in the Window ★★★
57. Valley of the shadow

April 14, 1945: Johnny crouched in his foxhole and watched as the clouds cleared, revealing the stars and the sliver of a new moon in an inky sky. With a clear sky, it seemed certain the attack would proceed the next morning. Johnny knew many men would die and he wondered if he was looking up at the stars for the last time. He felt very small, huddled in the bottom in his foxhole with the vast night sky stretched overhead. He hoped God was looking down on him.

He couldn't sleep. Instead he thought about the good times at Flat Rock, Dead River, and Cooper Lake. He wondered if he'd ever see those places again. He hoped it wouldn't all end for him today. He tried to encourage himself with the old saying, "Not everybody dies in a war!"

As the stars of night gave way to dawn, the deep shadows of night lifted, unveiling the valley between the American and the German positions—the valley they would cross that day. Bobby Kraft looked up at the sky and casually remarked, "No clouds—we're gonna go today for sure."

The bombardment was scheduled to begin at 8:30 a.m. German positions would be pummeled by planes and artillery. Then the order would be given and the GIs would climb out of their foxholes and advance into that valley under the German guns.

The minutes dragged on. Johnny kept checking his watch: 8:28, 8:29, 8:30, 8:31, 8:32, 8:33.

No artillery, no planes, nothing. The men crouched in their foxholes, waiting.

It began just after 9:00 a.m. First came the planes, raining bombs and napalm on the facing hills. Plane after plane passed low over the German positions. Clouds of smoke and debris rose high into the air.

As the last plane disappeared in the distance, the artillery bombardment started. All up and down the line, American artillery shells whistled overhead then smashed into German positions on the facing hills. Johnny had never seen such a concentrated bombardment. Shells pounded every foot of the German lines. Soon, the hills were hidden behind smoke from the explosions. When it seemed the hills themselves must have been blown away, the artillery stopped.

★ Click here to watch video

Figure 57-1: On the morning of April 14, the men of F-85 watched as the mountains across from them went up in flames.

Peering from the edge of his foxhole, Bobby Kraft said, "Would ya look at that! There can't be any Germans left up there! This might not be so bad after all!"

After almost half an hour, the bombardment stopped and the valley grew quiet once more.

Like all the GIs on the hill, Johnny knew they'd soon receive the order to advance across that valley. He waited and he prayed.

At 9:45 a.m., Sergeant Winterbottom yelled, "Get moving!" Up and down the hill, olive-clad GIs struggled out of their foxholes. Johnny and Bobby Kraft grabbed their gear and followed Sergeant Winterbottom into the valley.

The 2nd Battalion was to move down Mount della Spe, across the Pra del Bianco and up Hill 860. E and G Companies were in the lead, with F Company following behind. The rifle platoons moved in a skirmish line, the men spread out to minimize casualties from mines and artillery. The 4th Platoon moved along with the rifle platoons, ready to set up their mortars and machine guns as needed. Sergeant Winterbottom was in the lead, his knee mortar dangling from a strap over his shoulder. Johnny, Kraft, Smieska, and Armstrong followed, each carrying extra mortar shells and a pistol, carbine, or rifle.

As the platoon advanced down the flanks of Mount della Spe and into the valley below Hill 860, it encountered only scattered small arms fire. Johnny thought, "Maybe most of the Germans were killed by the artillery barrage." He hardly dared hope, "Maybe this is going to be easy after all."

But on the hills above him, the Germans crawled out of their bunkers, back to their firing positions. The smoke from the bombardment began to clear. Johnny could see the German positions in the hills above and he knew with a sinking heart that the Germans could see him.

★ Click here to watch video

Figure 57-2: The men of the 10th took heavy casualties as they advanced down into the valley below Mount della Spe.

The organized German defense started with a single shot. A GI fell backwards and lay still. More shots rang out. German machine guns, mortars, and artillery poured fire into the valley. Now many men were falling. Artillery shells punched into the ground, sending plumes of smoke and sometimes men high into the air. The GIs surged forward, desperate to get across the valley and close with the enemy.

Johnny saw 2nd Lieutenant William F. Callahan leading a rifle platoon through the field ahead. A mortar shell hit and the platoon was shrouded by shrapnel and smoke. Moments later, the rest of the platoon emerged from the smoke, but Lieutenant Callahan was no longer running with them. This was Lieutenant Callahan's first significant combat action. He had joined the company just two weeks earlier.

Johnny dove for cover behind a boulder. Near him, lay another soldier. He was saying something to himself. Through a lull in the fire, Johnny heard the man praying, "Yea, though I walk through the valley of the shadow of death, I will fear no evil, for thou art with me." Then Sergeant Winterbottom jumped to his feet and Johnny and the rest of the squad chased after him.

Johnny was beyond the point of being afraid. It was like the civilized part of his brain shut down, leaving just primal functions. His only thoughts were for the task at hand and immediate threats to his own survival. Maybe that was courage. Maybe that was just animal instinct. Maybe it didn't matter.

Johnny and Kraft ran with the squad along a rough track. He heard an explosion and two men running ahead of them were blown into the air. Someone yelled, "Land mines!" and the squad veered into a shallow ditch along the side of the road.

A squad of soldiers pushed their way into a hedge. The hedge exploded. Two more men went down, one staggered back, bleeding in many places.

"Booby traps!" someone yelled.

Sergeant Winterbottom ran to the spot where the booby traps had gone off, muttering "Better here than anywhere!" The squad pushed through the hedge and broke into the field beyond.

The 2nd Battalion made it across the valley and by 10:00 a.m. was fighting its way up Hill 860. By the time F Company reached the hill, the ground had been churned into near-frozen mud. Sometimes on their hands and knees, the men worked their way up the muddy slope, struggling to keep their rifles out of the mud.

Johnny saw Phil Lane sitting in the mud, looking into his rifle barrel and cursing. Johnny yelled, "Phil! Are you hit?"

Lane replied disgustedly, "No, damn it! I tripped and stuck the barrel of my gun in the mud. Now it's frozen in there and I can't clear it. I can't attack the Germans with a club!"

While E and G Companies consolidated their hold on Hill 860, F Company veered off to attack Hill 909. Fighting was fierce, and often at close range. Many Germans stubbornly refused to surrender and had to be killed or forced out of their foxholes and bunkers with grenades and bayonets.

About 10:00 a.m., the men of F Company were pinned down on a ridge by machine-gun and mortar fire. Don Montgomery, the runner for the 2nd Platoon, and Bill Kehres, the runner from the 3rd Platoon, were with Captain King, waiting to take his orders back to their respective platoons. Montgomery looked down into the valley, saw a platoon taking heavy fire from the Germans and whistled, "Look at those poor bastards getting hammered down there!"

Captain King replied, "That's Dole's platoon from I Company."

Back on Hill 909, the squad followed Sergeant Winterbottom up as he raced up the hill. George Armstrong got hit in the leg. He cursed and fell heavily onto his side. Winterbottom and Smieska grabbed his arms and dragged him behind a grassy knoll. Smieska checked his wound. Johnny and Bobby Kraft pulled off Armstrong's mortar vest and distributed the mortar shells he had been carrying. They patted him on the shoulder, then left him for the medics. The squad was now down to four men–Winterbottom, Smieska, Kraft, and Johnny.

★ Click here to watch video

Figure 57-3: For many soldiers of the 10th, the war ended on April 14, 1945.

The Germans pummeled the men on Hill 909. As he lay panting on the side of the hill, Johnny saw a GI tossed up into the air as a German mortar shell landed at his feet. Captain King and another soldier ran to his side to try to help.

Sergeant Winterbottom's knee mortar proved itself many times that day. Each time the advance was slowed by a stubborn group of entrenched Germans, Winterbottom dropped to the ground, wedged the base of the mortar against the ground, then lobbed shells at the Germans as fast as he could drop shells in the barrel. When Winterbottom stopped firing, riflemen advanced to finish off the Germans with rifles or grenades.

As Carl Cossin later recalled, "On occasion, a machine gun would chatter away for a time. If one of our mortar men got a fix on its location, he would put it out of action before the squad could work in close to it. His name was Winterbottom, but they called him Summertop. He fired his mortar without a base plate. He could look at a target, adjust the tube, and fire quick. He was a natural for firing any type of missile and found it hard to understand why everybody could not fire with the same accuracy. His fast firing with extreme accuracy balanced the difference in our favor."

By late afternoon Johnny's squad reached the top of Hill 909. The men tumbled into German foxholes and trenches along the crest of the hill.

Johnny watched as a Lieutenant ordered a couple of GIs to take up positions in a small gap in the line. One of the GIs replied, "Sir, you've got too many men too close together up there. Any minute now, the Germans are going to hit that line with artillery and we're going to lose a lot of men."

The lieutenant loosened the flap of his .45 pistol and said, "Soldier, you know I could shoot you for that."

The lieutenant glanced over and saw the other GI pointing his M1 rifle at his gut. Without a word, the lieutenant snapped his holster shut and stalked off. Minutes later, two GIs climbed up the hill and took positions in the gap the lieutenant had pointed out. Shortly afterwards, an artillery shell landed on their position and both men were killed.

At dusk, the Germans tried to retake the hill, but were beaten back as the Americans fired their rifles and rolled grenades down on the advancing Germans. When the Germans retreated, Johnny and Kraft crawled around to the riflemen, gathering the mortar shells that each man carried.

As night fell, the 2nd Battalion held most of Hill 909. Pockets of Germans still defended scattered positions around the hill, but most of it was occupied by Americans. The GIs dug in deep, determined to hold the hill. E Company took positions on the east side, F Company was in the center, and G Company was on the west side.

Johnny and Bobby Kraft took cover for the night in an abandoned German foxhole. The rest of the squad, Sergeant Winterbottom and Ed Smieska, shared a foxhole a few yards to their right. Johnny started to shake. He couldn't tell if it was from the cold, from fear, or from leftover adrenaline.

As they settled in for the night, a lieutenant crawled by and whispered, "There are Germans all around us. Stay in your foxholes. If you hear anything moving, toss a grenade at it. Don't shoot or you'll give away your position."

The lieutenant slithered on to the next foxhole. When they could no longer hear the lieutenant crawling away, Johnny whispered, "Why would he think we'd be stupid enough to crawl around out there?"

Sometime later, Johnny heard a noise over to the right. Someone tossed a grenade. Someone yelled, "Damn it! It's me!" then the hill fell silent.

Johnny turned to Bobby Kraft, "Do you think that was the Lieutenant?"

Kraft just shook his head.

As they huddled in their foxhole, Kraft asked Johnny, "Did you see that fellow charge the machine-gun nests as we came up that hill today?"

"No, I don't think I did."

"If you saw him, you'd remember. His squad was pinned down by a machine-gun nest near a farmhouse at the base of the hill. When that machine gun opened up, everybody else in the squad hit the dirt, but this guy charged around the house. He came around the back and shot the German gunners with his M1. Then he grabbed the German machine gun and chased a squad of Germans up the hill, machine gun blazing all the while. I lost sight of him after that. I don't know who that crazy son of a bitch was, but I sure hope someone gives him a medal."

As Bobby tried to get some sleep, Johnny peered over the edge of their foxhole, watching and listening for the telltale sound of a dislodged pebble or a cracked stick that would indicate someone trying to creep up on him. Crouched there, Johnny felt vaguely surprised to have made it that far.

The determined GIs of the 10th Mountain Infantry Division had successfully crossed the valley. They had forced the Germans from their positions on Hills 860 and 909, also known as Serre D'Aino. Tomorrow, they would drive the Germans from Hill 915, breaking the back of their last defensive line. "Maybe, just maybe," thought Johnny, "we are going to live through this."

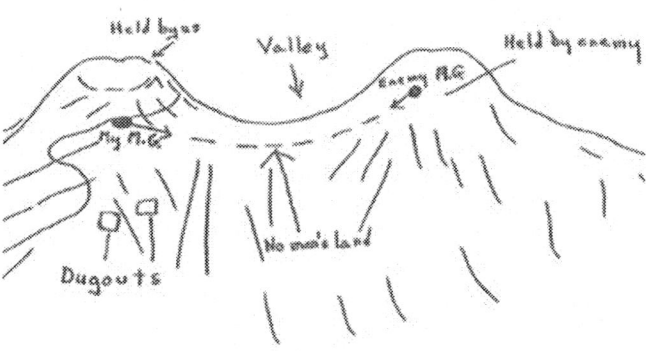

★ Click here to watch video

Figure 57-4: Sergeant Robert Ellis drew this sketch of positions on Hills 915 and 909, the morning of April 15, 1945. Hills 909 and 915 are just little marks on a map, but it took the heroic efforts of many men to drive the Germans from those hills. James "Ed" Welch of F-85 was one of the men awarded the Silver Star for his actions on those hills.

In a foxhole not far from Johnny, Sergeant Robert Ellis of the 4th Platoon scribbled a more somber assessment in his notebook.

```
We now faced the heartstopping task of getting out of
our protective foxholes in the face of machine gun
fire and bursting artillery shells and advancing
across the saddle and up the slopes of Hill 915 which
lay before us. The best solution was to advance as
fast as possible to minimize the time we would be
exposed to incoming fire, and we knew that it was
solely a matter of chance whether we'd be hit. Combat
experience, or what the press liked to call
"battle-seasoning" offered no advantage in an action
of this kind. It was luck, pure and simple, which
would determine our fate.
```

★ Click here to watch video

Figure 57-5: Johnny's Platoon Sergeant, James Orwig, did not make it across the valley on the morning of April 14.

★★★ Ordinary Heroes: Six Stars in the Window ★★★
58. One bridge too far

Figure 58-1: Carl "Art" Koski on the banks of the Elbe River near Magdeburg.

April, 1945: Art bounced along in the back of the survey crew's half-track as it clanked towards a damaged bridge over the Elbe River near Magdeburg. Art had heard rumors the Russians were approaching the Elbe from the east, but so far he hadn't seen any Russian troops. Captain Towne warned the survey crew to be extremely careful about approaching Russian troops. "If you guys start shooting at each other, we don't know where it will end."

An armored unit had moved into Magdeburg a few days earlier. Organized German resistance dissolved into swarms of disheartened veterans, anxious to surrender to the Americans.

They knew the Russians were coming and were desperate to stay out of the clutches of their hated enemy. But not all Germans were ready to quit. Small groups of Nazi fanatics fought to the death. Many of them were just boys, the last believers in the myth of Nazi invincibility.

Art held his rifle at the ready as the half-track came to a halt near the ruins of the Magdeburg bridge. The rest of the crew took up defensive positions while Art and Private First Class Alfred Spicer cautiously approached the damaged bridge.

★ Click here to watch video

Figure 58-2: Near the end of the war, many captured German soldiers were old men or young boys.

They were supposed to cross the bridge and hold the survey rods so the men on the west side of the river could survey the bridge for reconstruction. The two GIs carefully made their way across the heavily damaged bridge, trying to keep their M1 rifles ready as best they could.

As they neared the far end of the bridge, they heard voices. A group of soldiers wearing unfamiliar uniforms came around the corner, weapons ready. One soldier saw Art crouched in the wreckage of the bridge. He pointed and yelled something that Art couldn't understand. Spicer tried to pull Art out of sight, but it was too late. The entire group of soldiers ran toward them.

Art didn't know what he should do. If he shot, the soldiers would shoot back and he and Spicer would surely die. In a hoarse whisper, he warned Spicer, "Don't shoot! Don't shoot!"

Captain Towne and Sergeant Jones looked on in horror from the west side of the bridge as the unidentified soldiers ran toward Art and Spicer. Several engineers took aim, but Captain Towne ordered them to hold their fire.

Jones and Towne could see the soldiers yelling and gesturing for Art and Spicer to climb down from the bridge. Art and Spicer were crouched on the bridge, shaking their heads, refusing to climb down. From the far side of the river Jones and Towne couldn't tell if the soldiers were telling Art and Spicer to surrender or if they were German troops, trying to surrender to the first Americans they'd seen.

As the situation settled into a standoff, Towne and Jones crawled across the bridge to see if they could help. As he got closer, Jones realized the soldiers were not wearing German uniforms. Suddenly he understood. He yelled, "They're Russians! Don't shoot, they're Russians!"

Unfortunately none of the Engineers spoke Russian. Captain Towne tossed some cigarettes down to the Russian soldiers, yelling "Americans! Americans!"

From the corner of his eye, Art saw a Russian officer running towards them, holding a bundle in his arms. "What the heck is this?" he muttered to himself.

The Russian officer stopped and tossed the bundle up to the GIs on the bridge. Spicer neatly caught it. Art exhaled with relief when it didn't explode. The Russian officer had tossed them a bundle of flowers, tied with signal wire. It was clearly a gesture of goodwill.

The Russian officer saluted the American GIs. Captain Towne stood up and gravely returned the salute, then ordered his men to "Salute and get back across that bridge before he changes his mind!"

Art and Spicer saluted the Russian officer, then turned and crawled across the bridge. Spicer didn't dare drop the flowers for fear of insulting the Russians, so he carried them with him across the bridge. Back on their own side of the bridge, the survey crew laughed and slapped each other on the back. The flowers were a good omen. Maybe the war was really coming to an end.

★ Click here to watch video

Figure 58-3: In this photo, an unidentified soldier of the 332nd Engineers picks his way across a damaged bridge. It was on a bridge much like this that the men of the 332nd met the Russians near the end of the war.

Several hours later Captain Towne received official word that the Russians had reached the Elbe at Magdeburg. The 332nd was ordered to hold its position on the west side of the Elbe. Everything on the east side was to be left for the Russians.

For over three years, the men of the 332nd Engineer Regiment had built and fought their way across the continent. From Utah Beach, across France, through Belgium, and into Germany, they had worked tirelessly to push the Germans to the east. Now they'd met the Russians who were advancing from the east. At least in this part of Germany, the German Army no longer existed.

★★★ Ordinary Heroes: Six Stars in the Window ★★★
59. For him, the war was over

April 16, 1945: Allied air operations entered a new phase as General Spaatz announced that the strategic air war had been won. The Germans had no significant remaining infrastructure worth attacking. All future missions would be flown in support of the ground troops. The strategic air war was over, but the men of the 301st still had important work to do in support of the ground troops.

Figure 59-1: U.S. Army Air Forces photo from 301st Bomb Group raid on Bologna, Italy on April 17, 1945.

After almost a week on the ground, Oscar flew again on April 17 as 785 bombers attacked targets in Bologna, Italy in support of the ground troops who had smashed through the Gothic line and were racing toward the Po River Valley. Many of the targets were German positions just ahead of the U.S. lines, so all possible precautions were taken to prevent bombs from falling on Allied troops. The ground troops put up ground markers, colored smoke, and fired antiaircraft bursts to mark the approach and the position of the front lines.

Up to this point in the war, the bomber crews cranked open the bomb bay doors some distance before reaching the target. When the crew cranked open the bomb bay doors, any bombs that had worked loose from the racks fell out of the plane, creating an unpleasant surprise for any Germans below.

It was one thing if an errant bomb occasionally fell on a German village or town. It was enemy territory anyway. But loose bombs became a significant problem when the B-17s flew in close support of ground troops. American soldiers understandably did not appreciate being bombed by their own planes.

On this mission, to prevent any loose bombs from falling on Allied soldiers, all bomb bay doors were opened over water before approaching the lines. This turned out to be a wise move as a number of 120-pound fragmentation bombs fell into the water when the bombers opened their bomb bay doors. The stringent precautions were successful and no U.S. casualties were reported from the bomb runs.

As he flew back over the Allied lines, Oscar said to himself, "Johnny, wherever you are, I hope God is with you."

Oscar flew again on April 23, 24, and 25 as the 301st pounded railroad bridges and marshaling yards to prevent reinforcements and supplies from reaching the German troops being overrun by the Fifth Army.

The Germans were down, but they were not out. During the mission of the 25th, fifteen bombers—three percent of the planes on the mission—were shot down by flak. Three B-17s from the 301st suffered major damage and four suffered minor damage.

Oscar left the ground thirteen times in April, but many missions were recalled due to bad weather, so Oscar received credit for six additional combat missions in April. He had now flown a total of thirty-five combat missions. For him, the war was over.

★ Click here for Web Info

Figure 59-2: Oscar Koski's missions in April, 1945.

★★★ Ordinary Heroes: Six Stars in the Window ★★★
60. The last hill

April 15, 1945: As the darkness slowly brightened into morning, Johnny was able make out the shapes of the hills around him. The Americans had taken and held Hill 909, but the battle wasn't over. The Germans had fallen back to defensive positions on the next hill, Hill 915. Once again, the American GIs were going to have to leave their foxholes, advance through an unprotected valley, and attack uphill.

Bobby Kraft could hear Johnny whispering to himself, "It's not that far. It's not that far."

Kraft peered over the edge of the foxhole next to him. "You're right Johnny, it isn't that far. We could run up there in twenty minutes."

Johnny replied dryly, "Yeah, if no one was shooting at us. One way or another, I believe we'll take that hill by the end of the day. I just wonder how many of us will live to walk on it."

Kraft was quiet as they ate a breakfast of K-rations. Johnny finally asked him, "What are you thinking about Bobby?"

Bobby replied, "Do you remember that magician back at Montecatini? He said the war would end on April 15. Well that's today. If the Germans are going to surrender, this would be a damned good time to do it."

Johnny peered over the edge of his foxhole at the war-torn valley below them, let out a long sigh, and agreed, "Yeah. This would be a good day for the war to end."

As the first rays of dawn groped for the valley floor, the battle started once again. German mortar and artillery shells pounded the American positions, searching for any man foolish enough to be caught in the open.

Bullets from machine guns and sniper rifles peppered the ground. Most of the fire seemed to come from German positions on Hill 915 across the shallow valley. Aside from the occasional flash of a machine gun, Johnny couldn't see any Germans. But he knew they were there, crouched in their trenches and foxholes. The Germans were waiting. The Americans were waiting. Both sides knew it had to start soon.

The valley between the hills was pitted with shell holes. The ragged trunks of a few trees extended splintered branches to the sky. Nothing green remained.

Johnny turned his head slightly. Yes, he could hear gunfire, screams, and grenades from the direction of Hill 860 behind them. "The Germans must be trying to retake Hill 860," he said to Kraft. "I almost wish they'd attack us here. Then they'd have to cross that valley under fire, instead of us."

Their orders were passed down the line, whispered from foxhole to foxhole. The Company was to move out at 7:00 a.m. in a frontal attack on Hill 915.

From his foxhole, a few yards to their left, Sergeant Winterbottom told the men of his squad what he wanted them to do. "We have to cross the valley lickety-split. If we get stuck down there, we're dead. See that machine-gun nest on the left, about two-thirds of the way up? That's our first target. We'll work our way up toward it, then take it out with the mortar. We'll continue up the hill, taking out targets as they appear. Stay close."

At 6:40 a.m., American artillery started pounding the German positions. Just before 7:00 a.m., the guns went silent. Sweaty palms gripped rifles as the men of F Company readied themselves for the order to advance.

At 7:00 a.m., someone blew a whistle. All along the hill, tired men in dirty green uniforms emerged from their foxholes. Soldiers crouched and ran, then dove to the ground. After a short pause, they would jump up and sprint to the next piece of cover.

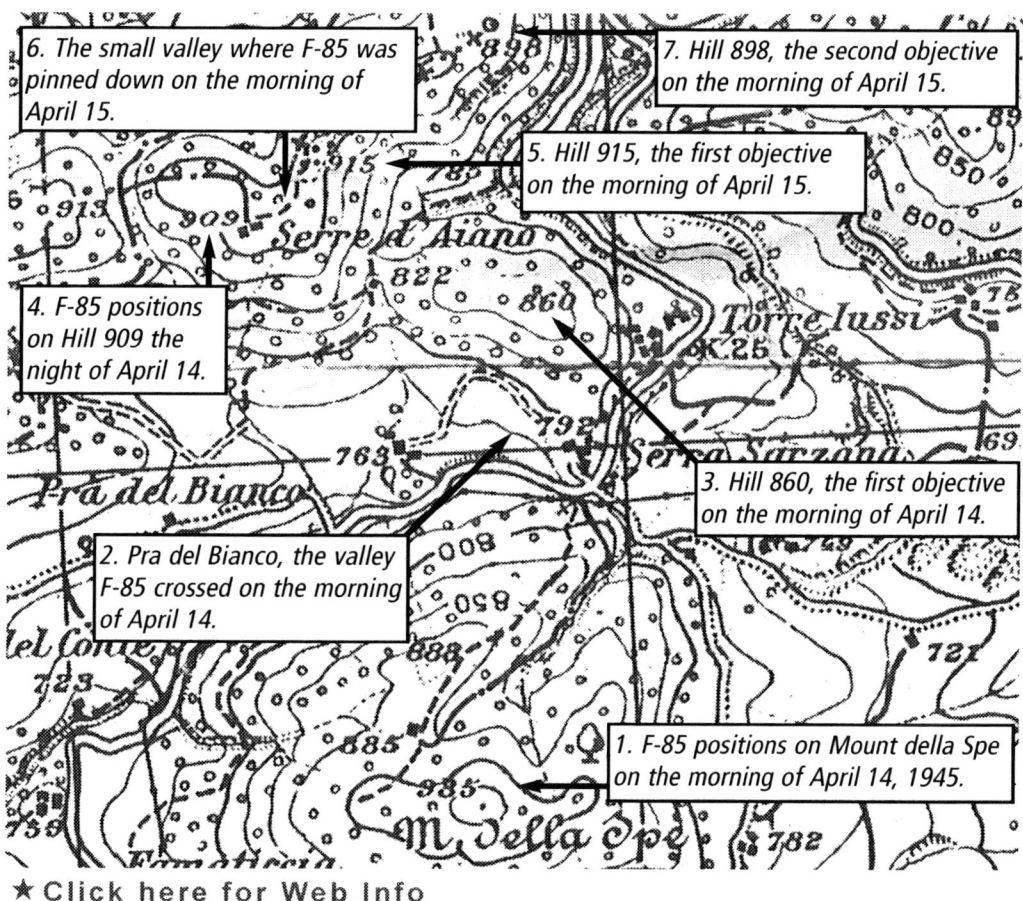

Figure 60-1: Detailed map of the movements of F-85 on April 14 and April 15, 1945.

As the GIs advanced down the hill, the German fire seemed to ease off. For a moment, Johnny thought the enemy might have decided to retreat. Then he understood why the Germans weren't firing. They weren't giving up. They were just waiting for the Americans to reach the kill zone.

When the GIs reached the floor of the valley, the Germans hit them with everything they had. Artillery, mortars, sniper rifles, machine guns—the entire German Army seemed to be firing at once. Men fell to the ground. Some huddled behind the nearest rock or mound. Others sprawled lifeless in the dirt.

Johnny saw a soldier curled behind a rock just a few yards to his right. The man turned his head and Johnny realized it was Nesbur Brandt, one of the replacements who had ridden up with him from the replacement depot so very long ago.

A wounded soldier lay on the open hillside, moaning.

Suddenly, Brandt jumped to his feet. He sprinted through the exploding shells and flying bullets, threw the wounded man on his back, and carried him to safety.

Nesbur Brandt looked back and saw that his squad sergeant had been hit and was lying wounded in the open. Once again, Brandt got up and ran to the rescue.

This time he was not so lucky. As he ran, Private Nesbur Brandt was hit by an artillery shell and killed.

Johnny didn't have time to think about Brandt's actions, or what might motivate a man to risk his life to save another man. It was just another thing that happened, another scene in a war movie that was all too real. Perhaps he'd think about it later, if there was a later.

The heavy fire continued. Those brave men who tried to advance were killed almost as soon as they left cover. The attack ground to a halt and the men of F Company began to take heavy casualties, trapped in the shallow valley between Hills 909 and 915.

By 10:00 a.m., the situation was extremely serious. F Company was pinned down. Units on the left and the right had already moved forward. If F Company did not advance, the Germans would be able to attack the unprotected flanks of those units. The entire attack could fail. Somehow, F Company had to find a way to move forward through the hail of bullets and artillery shells.

Johnny caught a glimpse of Sergeant Winterbottom in a shell hole a few yards away, with Smieska and Kraft. They were burrowed into the dirt, trying to avoid the bullets and shrapnel that buzzed through the air.

Lieutenant Mackin crawled towards them and yelled, "Captain King's been hit! I'm in command. Get your squad up that hill and take out that machine gun."

Johnny saw Sergeant Winterbottom checking his knee mortar. He was about to make his move. The rest of the squad would have to back him up as best they could.

Sergeant Winterbottom leapt to his feet and sprinted up the hill, his knee mortar gripped in both hands, his long legs pumping. Smieska and Kraft glanced at each other, then sprinted after Winterbottom. Johnny left the shelter of the boulder and ran after them, the heavy mortar shells jiggling in his mortar vest.

Partway up the hill, Johnny saw a young soldier propped against a stump. Johnny figured he must know him, but he didn't recognize him. His face wasn't the right color and he looked old somehow. Then Johnny saw that the man's insides had been blown out and were draped over the bushes next to him. He wasn't dead and strangely he didn't seem to be in too much pain. His lips were moving and he was looking back over the valley. A medic knelt beside him and injected him with morphine. Johnny took a step towards them, thinking the medic might need help to evacuate the man. The medic looked at Johnny and shook his head slightly as if to indicate there wasn't anything that could be done.

Johnny felt a chill run through him as he realized what the medic meant. With his insides gone, there was no surgery that could save the wounded man. There wasn't any point in moving him. It would only take other soldiers out of the battle and hasten the man's death. The medic could only fill him with morphine and leave him there, alone, to wait for death. Johnny said a silent prayer for the man, then continued running up the endless hill.

Johnny dropped into a shell hole where the rest of the squad had taken cover, about halfway up the hill. Some twenty yards further, they could see the machine-gun nest pouring heavy fire onto the men trapped in the valley below.

★ Click here to watch video

Figure 60-2: German artillery, machine guns, mortars, and small arms poured concentrated fire on the advancing GIs.

Sergeant Winterbottom yelled, "Stay put!" He crawled with his knee mortar towards the machine gun nest, taking advantage of every rock and depression along the way. The Germans were firing at the men in the valley and didn't see him crawling towards them.

Winterbottom crawled around to the left side of the machine-gun nest. He braced the mortar against a mound of dirt and fired into the machine-gun nest at point-blank range. The explosion was followed by a short scream that quickly died away. The machine gun stopped firing.

One German staggered from the back of the machine-gun position, then fell backwards and lay still. Sergeant Winterbottom slumped to the ground and closed his eyes for a moment, then pulled himself to his feet and continued up the hill.

Johnny saw a group of riflemen crawling towards another machine-gun nest on the right side of the hill. They tossed grenades and that machine gun fell silent as well.

With the machine guns eliminated, the men of F Company scrambled towards the top of the hill. Using grenades, rifles, and bayonets, they relentlessly drove the Germans back from the crest of the hill.

Johnny and the rest of the squad ran up Hill 915, jumping over shell holes and bodies, trying to catch up with Sergeant Winterbottom. Smieska was in the lead, followed by Kraft, then Johnny. Bullets peppered the ground as they ran and mortar and artillery shells dropped all around them.

Suddenly Ed Smieska went down, hit in the left leg. Johnny saw him roll behind a rock, but there was no time to stop. The squad was now down to three men. Johnny and Bobby Kraft struggled to catch up to Sergeant Winterbottom. Their boots dug deep into the muddy hillside and their breath came in labored gasps.

Three artillery shells arced down towards them. One shell hit ahead of them, then one to the right.

Johnny never heard the shell that hit him.

His first thought was that something very strange had happened. One moment he was running up the hill, with artillery shells landing all around. The next moment he was lying on his back looking up at the clear blue sky.

The sound of gunfire seemed muted and things that seemed crucial just moments ago—like getting up that hill—seemed somehow less urgent.

As Johnny looked up, the sky seemed to darken and he saw a figure, dressed in white, approaching in the distance. At first he thought it was an angel, but as it came closer it seemed somehow familiar.

Then he recognized the figure. It was his mother, Elizabeth. He hadn't seen her since she had died almost fifteen years before, but as she came closer, he knew that it was her.

He wondered, "Why is she here, on a battlefield in Italy?"

He noticed she was barefoot and the mud of Italy had worked its way between her toes. He tried to ask her why she wasn't wearing any shoes, but he could not speak. She seemed to be saying something to him. As she got closer, the sounds of combat faded away. Then she leaned down, reached out her arms, said, "Come with me dear Johnny, your work here is done."

For Johnny, the war was over.

★ Click here to watch video

Figure 60-3: Photo taken in the vicinity of Mount della Spe, not far from where Johnny was killed.

★★★ Ordinary Heroes: Six Stars in the Window ★★★
61. I'm not gonna lose my whole damn squad

April 15, 1945: Bobby Kraft was knocked down by the concussion of the shell that killed Johnny. He staggered to his feet and saw Johnny lying dead on the hillside. With a quick breath, he turned and continued running up the hill.

Kraft flopped to the ground next to Sergeant Winterbottom, breathing heavily from the run. "Koski and Smieska are down! You and me, we're the only ones left."

Sergeant Winterbottom didn't answer, he just stared at Kraft for a moment, like he didn't understand, then continued crawling doggedly toward the top of the hill.

German resistance fell off as the soldiers of F Company neared the top of the hill. Lieutenant William Douglas and the men of the 2nd Platoon were the first to reach the top of Hill 915 as the Germans fled down the far side of the hill, many taking cover in a stone farmhouse partway down the hill.

The GIs dropped into positions along the crest of the hill and started shooting at the fleeing Germans. A German machine gun defiantly spat shells from the farmhouse and German artillery pounded the exposed side of the hill. The GIs pulled back from the crest of the hill, out of the line of fire.

Lieutenant Twomey was in charge at the top of the hill. He positioned his squads to hold the hill against a counterattack, then tried to find a way to advance.

The machine-gun nest in that stone farmhouse had to be eliminated. Lieutenant Twomey directed one squad to the right to try to outflank the farmhouse. They were spotted and hit hard with fire from machine guns, mortars, and German 88s. He directed another squad to sneak around on the left. They also came under heavy fire and were forced to withdraw.

Sergeant Winterbottom crawled up next to Lieutenant Twomey. The two men grimly surveyed the scene below. Winterbottom's face was hard, but his voice was calm as he said, "Don't send any more squads down there. I'll take care of those sons of bitches."

He crawled back to Kraft and ordered, "Stay here! I'm not gonna lose my whole damn squad!"

Sergeant Winterbottom tucked two mortar shells under his belt, slung his knee mortar over his shoulder, and crawled to the crest of the hill to observe. The German 88s and machine guns couldn't fire continuously, so they alternated fire. The 88s fired a barrage of shells. A few seconds after the last 88 shell hit, the machine guns opened up. When the next round of 88 shells hit, the machine guns stopped to reload and let the barrels cool.

Sergeant Winterbottom watched this cycle a few times. He saw his opportunity in the machine-like efficiency of the highly trained German soldiers. "1, 2, 3, 4, 5, 6." Six 88's fired during each salvo. "1, 2, 3, 4" He counted about four seconds before the machine guns started to fire. He waited for the next cycle. As soon as the sixth shell hit, he took off like a rabbit counting out loud, "1, 2, 3, 4!"

On four, he dove for cover just as the machine guns opened up. He repeated this maneuver, once, twice, then a third time, sprinting down the hill in the brief interval between the 88 shells and the machine-gun fire.

He worked his way down to a small depression about thirty yards from the door of the farmhouse. It was a typical Italian stone farmhouse with rough openings for a door and windows. He couldn't see the machine gun or the crew. He could only see the muzzle flashes in the darkened doorway. Even a mortar shell would bounce off the thick stone walls of the ancient farmhouse. He'd have to lob a shell right in the doorway.

He placed the tube of the knee mortar on the ground and dropped in a shell. The first shell hit the farmhouse wall, just to the right of the door. He nudged the barrel slightly to the left, then quickly dropped in another shell.

"Whuff, whuff!" coughed the mortar. One shell, then another, went right through the front door. He heard two explosions in quick succession. Smoke poured from the windows of the house and Germans started streaming out the back door.

The machine gun nest was gone, but German 88s continued to pound the hill. Sergeant Winterbottom sprinted back up the hill, diving for cover as the first shell hit. He stayed down until the sixth shell exploded. He reached the top, rolled over the crest of the hill, then lay exhausted in the relative safety of the far side of the hill.

With the machine gun nest in the farmhouse destroyed, F Company resumed its relentless advance. The men swarmed over the hill, past the farmhouse, down into the shallow valley, and over the trenches and foxholes on Hill 898. Foxhole by foxhole, they drove the Germans from the hill. The Germans launched a counterattack, but the soldiers of F Company refused to yield.

Hills 909, 913, and 898 were in American hands. The Allies now controlled the entire Ruffeno Ridge. That same day the 86th and 87th Mountain Infantry Regiments also broke through the German lines, pushing to Monte Pigna, Rocco Ruffeno, and beyond. The battles of April 14 and 15 broke the back of the last German defenses in Italy. The Allies exploited the break in the lines, and pushed rapidly towards the Po River valley cutting off the Germans before they could retreat into the Alps.

★ Click here to watch video

Figure 61-1: James Winterbottom was a charming young man who reached deep into his soul and there found the strength to do the things that needed to be done.

In the attack of April 14 and 15, the 85th Mountain Regiment of the 10th Mountain Infantry Division suffered 462 casualties with ninety-eight men killed in action. April 15 had been a particularly tough day for F Company with twenty men wounded and six killed. Private John L. Koski was one of the men who gave his life to take those hills.

On April 16, Sergeant Robert Ellis of the 4th Platoon wrote the following in his diary:

```
April 16-We attacked and before we reached the L.D., one
lieutenant was killed 50 yards behind me. Dug in in a draw.
Shells very close. Crossed the road and dug in again. Orwig,
Eyer, Olsen, Oldham hit. G Company taking a terrific beat-
ing. Dead GI's all around.

Held down by MG fire. Dug in on reverse slope just around
corner from Burp fire. Perry shot himself. I walked over
thinking a hidden Heine had shot him and found one in a
dugout. As he turned toward me I shot him with my .45
through the head.

This morning Capt. King got MG slugs through his stomach
about two feet from my foxhole. Under cover of our four 30's
we assaulted the hill and took 60 prisoners. Lost contact
with the Company, wondering what to do. Found out where the
company was and rejoined them in a very dangerous position.
Many dead-Taylor, Moses, Koski and others. Our casualties so
heavy we were relieved and went to a rearward rest area.

Luth, one of my oldest friends, and Goodal killed. 74 men
left.
```

Every member of F Company lost friends and comrades on April 14 and April 15, friends and comrades who would never be forgotten. On the night of April 15, Carl Cossin sat in his foxhole staring at the hill above him. He wasn't thinking about anything in particular. He was just staring at the hill for which they had paid such a high price.

A captain from E Company walked up to his foxhole and asked, "You lost a good friend up there, didn't you, soldier?"

"Yes sir, I lost a very good friend," replied Cossin.

The captain walked a few steps, then stopped, looked back at him and asked, "Soldier, do you believe in God?"

Cossin thought for a moment, then gave the answer he thought the Captain wanted, "Yes sir, everybody in the world does."

The captain replied, "No soldier, not everybody does, but you keep on believing in God."

The captain then walked away. Carl Cossin sat in his foxhole, wondering what that captain meant, wondering if he would ever make sense of the events of those days.

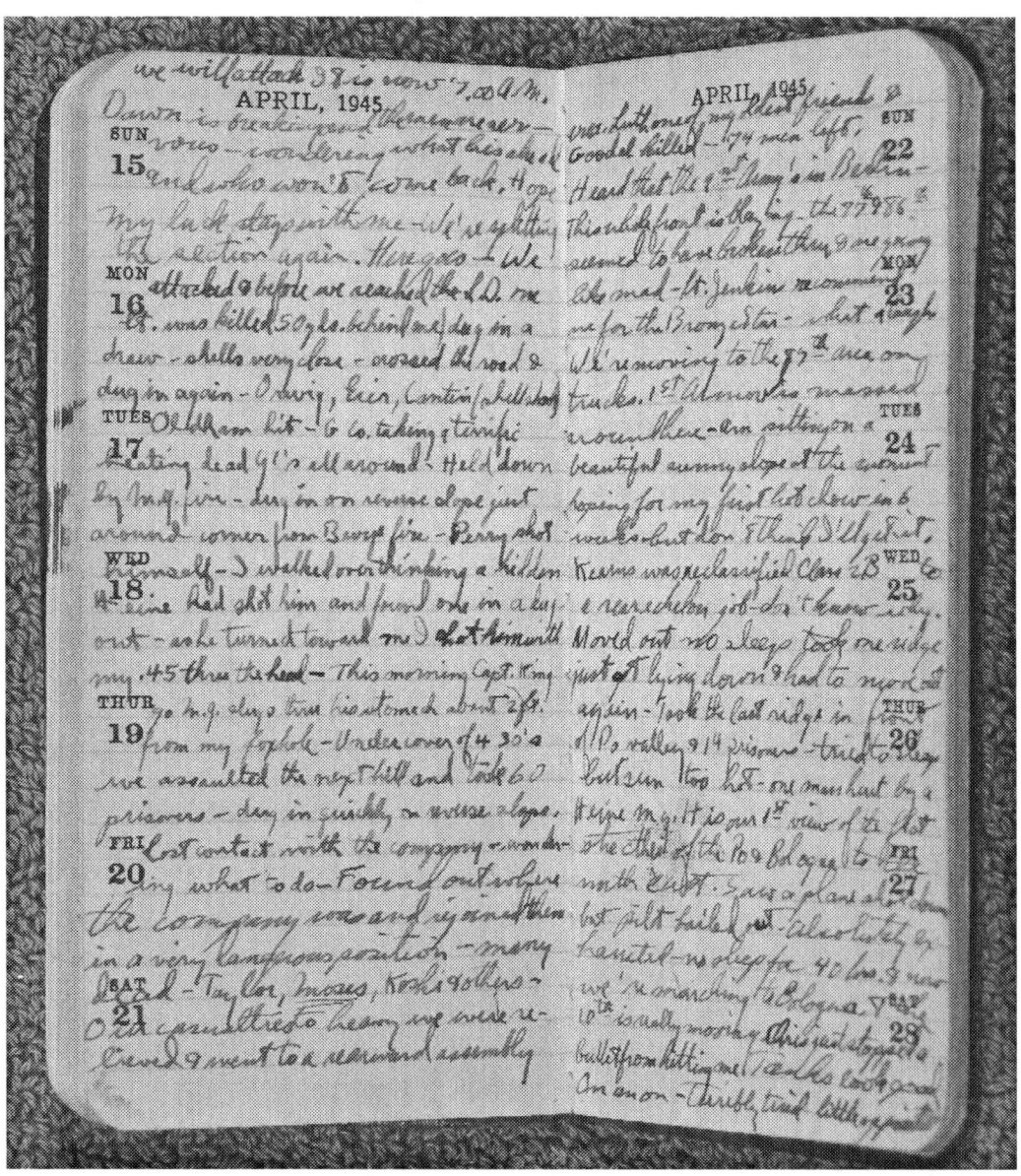

★ Click here for Web Info

Figure 61-2: Photo of the April 16, 1945 entry from Sergeant Ellis' diary. Johnny is mentioned on the left page, third line up from the bottom.

★★★ Ordinary Heroes: Six Stars in the Window ★★★
62. SUD to KIA

April 16, 1945: General Hayes decided that the 85th and other 10th Mountain Regiments had taken too many casualties and needed time to regroup so they were moved back from the front.

On April 21, a graves registration unit located Johnny's body, lying where he had fallen, partway up Hill 915. He was placed in a white body bag and loaded on a truck which brought him to the American Cemetery in Florence, Italy where he was buried with his comrades.

The F Company morning reports for April 22 include the following entry:

> Burrows Lawrence   PFC
>
> Koski, John L   Pvt
>
>   Above 2 EM abs SUD to KIA 15 Apr 45
>
>   Vic Mt Della Spe Italy EM entitled to CIP

The last two lines translate to "the above two enlisted men, previously listed as absent, status undetermined, are now listed as killed in action on April 15, 1945 in the vicinity of Mount della Spe, Italy. Both of the enlisted men are entitled to Combat Infantry Pay."

★ Click here to watch video

Figure 62-1: For John Leslie Koski, the war ended on April 15, 1945, in the hills just north of Mount della Spe.

Larry "Jaggers" Burrows and John Leslie Koski would fight no more.

John Leslie Koski ended his military career as a private, the lowest rank in the U.S. Army. He was awarded two medals during his military career—the Expert badge for the M1 Rifle, earned during basic training, and a posthumous award of the Purple Heart.

The story of F Company and the soldiers of the 10th Mountain Infantry Division did not end on April 15. By April 20, F Company was back in action, charging across the Po River and on to Lake Garda. More GIs were killed and wounded, but the German Army was in retreat and the worst of the fighting was over.

On May 2, barely two weeks after Johnny was killed, the German armies in Italy surrendered. Less than a week later, the German armies in Germany surrendered. By May 8, 1945, the war in Europe was over.

Sergeant Winterbottom's courageous attack helped break open the German defenses and allowed F Company to move out of the valley and take Hill 915 and Hill 898. For his actions, Sergeant Winterbottom was later awarded the Silver Star. On July 16, 1945, the Johnstown, NY newspaper carried the following account of the attack:

> Observing that the forward elements of his company were being prevented by enemy machine-gun and rifle fire from continuing their onslaught, Sergeant Winterbottom personally took his knee-mortar forward. Fired one round, with the second round Sgt Winterbottom scored a direct hit on a hostile machine-gun nest killing three of its personnel, and with subse-

quent fire forced the withdrawal of the opposing enemy riflemen. Rather then risk his squad in this action, Sgt Winterbottom went over the crest of the mountain and down the open forward slope, deliberately exposing himself to intense machine-gun, mortar, artillery and rifle fire from all adjacent enemy troops. As a direct result of his courageous and efficient actions, Sgt Winterbottom's company resumed its advance with no further immediate casualties.

Sergeant Winterbottom was not the only man from F Company to earn the Silver Star. Three men earned the Silver Star for actions on Mount Belvedere and della Torraccia, one each on February 21, 22, and 23. One man earned the Silver Star for his actions on April 14.

On April 15, the day that Johnny was killed, ten men from F Company earned the Silver Star. Another earned the Silver Star on April 22 as the Company moved into the Po River Valley. Seventy-eight men from F Company were awarded the Bronze Star.

Four men from F Company were awarded both the Bronze Star and the Silver Star, although only one of them—Sergeant James Winterbottom—was awarded the Silver Star and the Bronze Star for actions while serving with F Company:

★ Sergeant James Winterbottom

★ S/Sergeant Albert Wiedorn (for actions while serving with H Company)

★ 1st Lieutenant Robert Beck (for actions while serving with G Company)

★ Captain William Shepard (for actions while serving with HQ-2)

The Combat History of the 10th Mountain Infantry Division prepared by the Infantry School at Fort Benning, GA indicates that the "the success of the attack had hinged on the taking of Hills 913, 909, and 898. With these strategic hills in Allied hands, the 87th Mountain Regiment was able to move rapidly to the northeast, taking Mt. Pigna and Rocca di Roffeno."

In just over three months of combat, 3,124 soldiers of the 10th Mountain Infantry Division were wounded and 996 were killed. John Leslie Koski, youngest of the six Koski brothers, beloved son and brother, was one of the 996, one of the 405,399 ordinary American soldiers—ordinary heroes—who gave their lives during World War II so the rest of us could live in freedom.

Another of those soldiers was 2nd Lieutenant William F. Callahan, who was killed on the slopes of Mount della Spe on the morning of April 14. He was the son of the chairman of the Massachusetts Turnpike Authority. After the war, the tunnel leading to Logan International Airport in Boston was named after him.

The platoon that Bill Kehres and Don Montgomery saw taking fire in the valley on the morning of April 14 was led by 2nd Lieutenant Robert Dole. Dole was seriously wounded that morning, but he eventually recovered. After a long career in politics, Robert Dole was nominated as the 1996 Republican candidate for President of the United States.

The soldier who took out multiple machine-gun nests on Hill 909 was Private First Class John D. Magrath. Later that day, Private Magrath volunteered to run through heavy shelling to gather a casualty report. Two mortar shells hit him almost simultaneously and he was killed instantly. John D. Magrath was posthumously awarded the Congressional Medal of Honor.

Major General George Hays, commander of the 10th Mountain Infantry Division, wrote a letter to the men of the 85th Mountain Regiment dated November 23, 1945:

> Members of the 85th Mountain Infantry, you should all retain a just pride and lasting satisfaction in your magnificent combat achievements and heroic sacrifices. You played a vital role in the success of the 10th Mountain Infantry Division. You spearheaded our first Division operation in the capture of Mount Gorgelesco and your advance to the base of Mount Torraccia. You captured Monte della Spe and Mount Castellano and held these vital terrain features against determined counterattacks. You again spearheaded the Divisions' final attack on April 14th against the bulk of the German 334th Infantry Division, broke through their heavily mined and defended lines, and captured heights which enabled the remainder of the Division to advance to the northeast. You played an important role in our advance to the Alps. Your courage and determination are an inspiration to me and all members of the Division. I am proud of you and extend to each of you my best wishes for your future success and happiness.

The legacy of the 10th Mountain Infantry Division continues to this day. Soldiers of the 10th Mountain Infantry Division, Fort Drum, NY, have served in countries around the world, including Somalia, Afghanistan and Iraq.

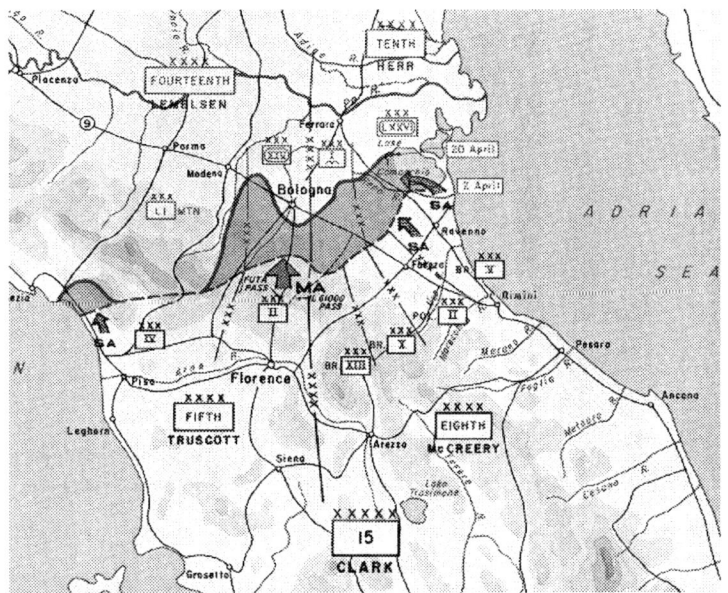

★ Click here for Web Info

Figure 62-2: Allied gains from April 1 to April 20, 1945. The 10th Mountain Infantry Division advanced along the line of the large center arrow, heading toward Bologna. It doesn't look like a great distance on the map, but many young men died to force the Germans from that narrow strip of Italy.

★ Click here for Web Info

Figure 62-3: Statue at Fort Drum, New York, depicts a WWII 10th Mountain Infantry Division soldier assisting a present-day soldier.

★★★ Ordinary Heroes: Six Stars in the Window ★★★
63. Forget it, forget all of it

May 2, 1945: Oscar was in the 301st Bomb Group Headquarters when the teletype started chattering. First came the usual message, "Stand by... Stand by..."

"That's strange," Oscar thought curiously, "I didn't think we were flying any more missions."

Shortly afterwards, the teletype started to chatter again. With mounting excitement, Oscar read the message. SS Major General Wolf had surrendered his armies in Italy. The war in Italy was over!

Oscar rushed out of the tent to tell the rest of the crew. He found them in the briefing hut. They'd been watching a movie when an Italian shepherd had burst into the darkened hut, yelling "War is over! War is over!"

The airmen didn't believe the shepherd. They chased him out and sat down to watch the rest of the show. Oscar was still trying to convince them that the Germans had surrendered when an announcement came over the loudspeaker: "Attention all personnel. We need about twenty enlisted volunteers for a special detail on the double."

★ Click here to watch video

Figure 63-1: The German armies in Italy surrendered on May 2. The remaining German armies surrendered on May 9, 1945, ending the war in Europe.

No one responded. They'd been in the Air Force long enough to know not to volunteer for anything. The loud speaker came to life again, "Okay, you sons of bitches! The war's over and we've got about twelve cases of whiskey that have to be moved to the enlisted mens' club."

That got the mens' attention and a three-day party followed.

After a few days of wild celebration, the airmen began to wonder what the Air Force planned for them next. The war wasn't really over. The Japanese were still fighting. None of the airmen knew if they had flown their last combat mission or if they had an appointment over Japan.

Many of the men had a difficult time with the sudden peace. One week they were flying missions over enemy territory. The Germans were shooting at them. They were dropping bombs on the Germans. Men were dying on both sides. Then someone signed a paper and said the war was over. But the emotions of war are not put to rest that easily.

As an editorial in one military newsletter sarcastically put it:

> The Jerries aren't really bad guys, once you get to know them. They couldn't possibly have had anything to do with shooting our medics. Or with driving Italian women out of strong points dressed in German uniforms to draw our fire. A few minutes of conversation with any of the 3/4 million German soldiers in Italy, and you can see for yourself that it must have been some other guys.

Dachau, the unspeakable? Forget it. Forget the freight cars stacked with whip scarred dead, the smooth efficiency of the crematory, reception room for stripping living and dead, shower room for washing and gassing victims, furnace room. Forget the ingenious system of pulleys and hooks on which victims hung by thumbs or necks or any other way that amused the SS men, to be tortured as they watched their comrades slip into the furnace.

Forget it, all of it. It doesn't mean anything. It's just a coincidence that such places flourished all over Germany. It's just a coincidence that such bestiality existed on a national scale. The German nation had nothing to do with it. It was some other guys.

So let's not be mean to the Krauts. They meant well... you must not hold it against them because they didn't really like the regime. You can forget about the kid we used to drink beer with, the one who got it through the red cross on his helmet.

After they've told us how much they like us, it isn't polite to mention that they killed a lot of our friends. Killed them in the name of a government that slaughtered Poles—men, women, and children—by millions. Let's not remind them that they shot to kill while the going was good and then they surrendered to save their skins. Oh no. Don't embarrass these fine people, who are very sentimental about flowers and adore little children. Give them a sportsmanlike pat on the back and wish them better luck next time. Otherwise you might discourage them. The sons of bitches are terribly sensitive.

Gradually, the anger cooled. The soldiers who had fought the war would never forget what they had been through. They could never forget their friends and comrades who had been killed. But they resolutely locked those memories away in special compartments in their minds.

The war had taken many of their friends, it had taken their innocence and their youth. It had left them scarred, but most of them resolved not to let it ruin the rest of their lives. Like so many other soldiers, Oscar decided he would put the war behind him. He would go home and he would make something of his life.

Not all of the men who had served with the 301st would be going home. The 301st Bomb Group Heavy lost a total of 137 B-17s in combat or accidents. All together, 516 airmen had been killed, 579 captured, and 208 were rescued or evaded capture. Those losses were reflected throughout the Army Air Forces, which lost 6,700 bombers and listed 62,000 airmen as killed, captured, or missing.

★ Click here to watch video

Figure 63-2: Some veterans were deeply scarred by their combat experience. Others were not so deeply affected. Most did not complain as they knew that others had it worse.

The question "What next?" was soon answered for them. Men who had flown less than twenty-five combat missions were given thirty days leave, after which they were to report for assignment in the Pacific. Men who had flown more than twenty-five combat missions would be discharged. For First Lieutenant Oscar Henry Koski, it was time to go home.

★ Click here to watch video

Figure 63-3: As the war ended, thousands of Allied prisoners of war were freed from German POW camps, including 1,100 airmen returned to Foggia in April, 1945.

Oscar had spent eight months with the 301st, flying a total of thirty-five combat missions over enemy territory. He was awarded the Air Medal with two oak leaf clusters and the European Theater Ribbon with four battle stars.

Oscar was discharged from the U.S. Army Air Forces at Ellington Field, Texas on October 23, 1945. He promptly boarded a train and headed home to West Ishpeming.

Among the papers he carried with him was a certificate for meritorious service, extending the gratitude of the United States Army Air Forces to Oscar Henry Koski, 1st Lieutenant, "whose whole-hearted and sincere services contributed to the successful prosecution of World War II against those who sought to subjugate the civilized world."

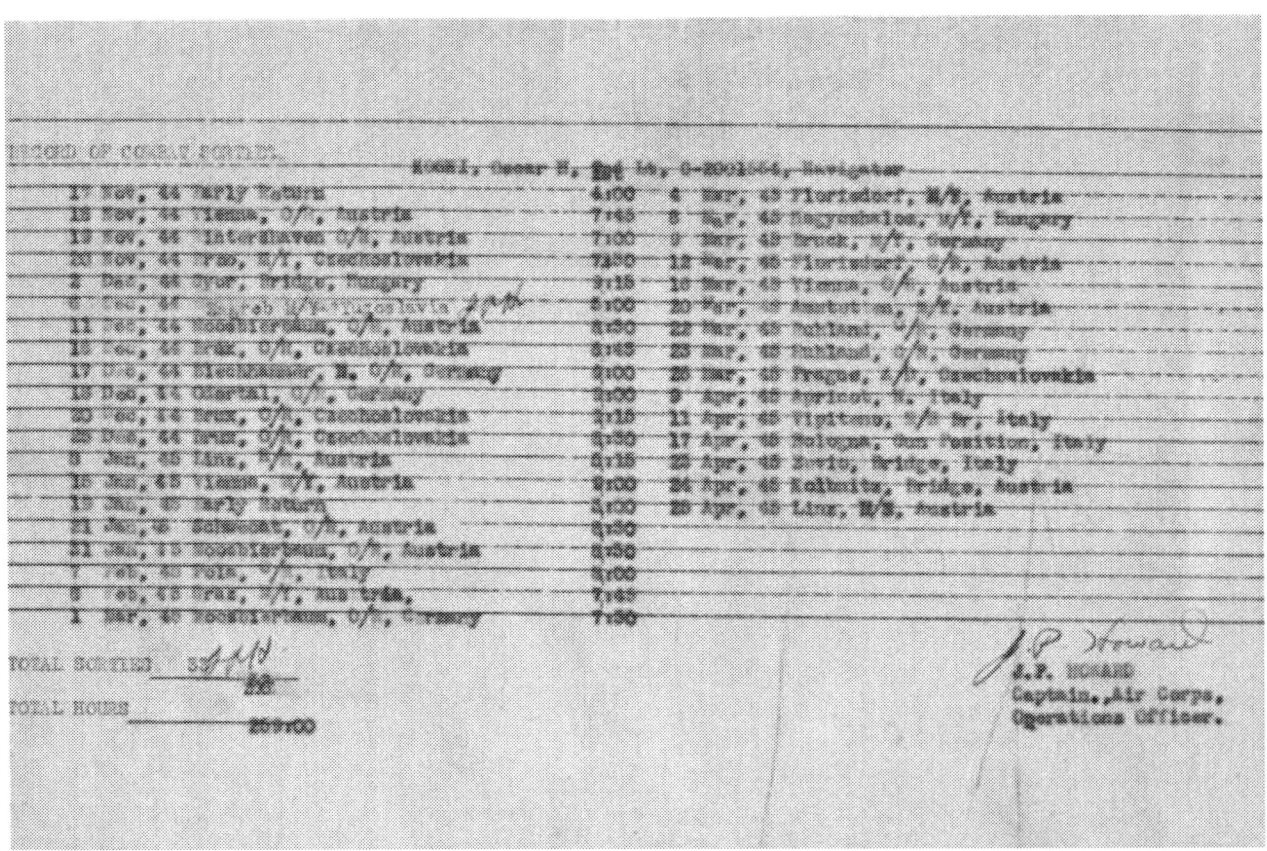

★ Click here for Web Info

Figure 63-4: Oscar Koski's final record of combat sorties, which includes only those missions flown into enemy airspace.

★★★ Ordinary Heroes: Six Stars in the Window ★★★
64. We have to let it go

Late April, 1945: Art sat in a railway car as the H&S Company train clacked its way towards Gohfeld, Germany. He was reading a letter he just had received from Johnny. In the letter, Johnny wrote about one of his buddies who had been killed on Easter Sunday. Art refolded the letter and prayed Johnny would be all right. "We're moving into Germany from all sides," he tried to reassure himself. "The war will be over soon and everybody will be okay."

On April 25, the H&S Company train left Gohfeld and moved to the Krupp Steel Works in Rheinhausen, Germany. When they got off the train, some of the men spotted a large concrete water tank, used to store water for fighting fires after bombing raids. The dirty GIs stripped off their clothes and jumped in for a refreshing swim. Art didn't swim, but he removed his boot and sock and rested his injured leg in the warm sunshine. His leg hadn't really healed, but it hadn't gotten much worse. The skin had healed and some circulation had slowly returned.

On May 1, Art and the men of the 332nd Engineers heard on the radio that the German armies in Italy had surrendered. "Thank God!" thought Art. "Oscar and Johnny should be safe now." Art didn't yet know that for Johnny, the war was already over.

On May 2, the 332nd and related units started work on the "Victory Bridge" over the Rhine River. The 2,815-foot railroad bridge, consisting of 38 spans, was built in a record time of six days, fifteen hours, and twenty minutes.

Later that week, the 332nd Engineers received the following commendation from W. H. Simpson, Command General, 9th Army:

> Upon your departure from the 9th Army area, I wish to express my appreciation for the work you have accomplished in support of the Army. Your expeditious rehabilitation of the rail lines has contributed materially to the recent rapid advance of the army. The wholehearted cooperation exhibited by the officers and men of your unit in assisting with Army Engineers in numerous instances and their ability to meet or better target dates for opening rail lines at all times is worthy of the highest commendations.

A few days later, the 332nd established a command post at Kassel, Germany. That's where they received the news that the German Army had surrendered. The war in Europe was over!

The 332nd held a victory review near one of their reconstruction projects to celebrate the end of the war in Europe.

A few days later, the mood changed as the 332nd Regiment received word it would be transferred to the Pacific for the invasion of Japan. Some of the men hoped they'd get a furlough in the States before the transfer. Others figured they'd be put on a ship and sent directly through the Panama Canal.

In mid-May, the 332nd moved further into Germany. Art and a friend hitched a ride into Berlin. They located the Reichstag and gave a guard a carton of cigarettes to let them in. The once grand

Figure 64-1: The 332nd Engineers Regiment held a review to celebrate completion of the Victory Bridge and the end of the war.

building had been severely damaged and ransacked. In one room, they saw Iron Crosses and other medals strewn over the floor. As they walked through the imposing building, they saw a number of U.S. officers busily removing souvenirs. One officer was up on a ladder, removing light fixtures. Too late, they noticed that almost everyone in the building was an officer. They worked their way to the door, fell in step behind a group of officers, and followed them outside.

As the two war-weary GIs wandered through the ruins of Berlin, Art thought about that German prisoner of war, who so long ago had taunted the Engineers: "Hey GIs! We're going to New York! Where are you going!?" Art thought, "It's been a long, hard road and a lot of men have died, but we made it, we made it all the way to Berlin."

★ Click here to watch video

Figure 64-2: Berlin was in ruins, as was much of Germany.

After the Germans surrendered, Art was reassigned to courier duty. He shuttled messages between various units of the 332nd Engineers, sometimes driving through Russian-occupied areas. Many GIs had been robbed by Russian soldiers. To help prevent incidents, U.S. troops were ordered to carry only three rounds for their M1 Garand rifles. Art didn't feel safe driving through Russian-held territory with only three rounds, so he kept a captured Luger pistol under his shirt in case the Russians tried to rob him.

Near the end of May, Art received a letter from his sister Eleanor indicating that Johnny had been killed in action in Italy. Art read the letter, then carefully folded it and tucked it in his shirt pocket. He took a long, long walk alone through the woods outside of town. As he walked, he thought about his little brother Johnny, Johnny who would never again hunt the plains of Flat Rock. Yes, the war was won, but the cost, the cost had been so very high. Americans, Canadians, British, Australians, Russians, Germans, Japanese, Finns, Jews—so many people had died.

★ Click here to watch video

Figure 64-3: The full horror of the Nazi death camps only became known near the end of the war.

That spring and summer, rumors began to circulate about horrible Nazi death camps—places of unspeakable evil where millions of people had been systematically starved and slaughtered. Art refused to believe those stories. He could not believe—he would not believe—that human beings could do such things to other human beings.

On June 29, the 332nd Engineers received a surprise visit from a U.S. intelligence officer and a German scientist named Werner Von Braun. Nine men from the 332nd, headed by Sergeant Joe Schwartz, accompanied the intelligence officer on a secret mission to five sites near Bad Sachs, in Russian-controlled territory. They recovered five boxes of documents that had been buried in various locations. They did not know it at the time, but those documents contained plans for advanced rocket systems that later proved instrumental in development of the U.S. rocket program.

Although the 332nd was a service regiment, it had routinely operated in the combat zone. Members of the 332nd Engineers Regiment were awarded Battle Participation Credit for five North European campaigns: Normandy, Ardennes, Central Europe, Northern France, and Rhineland. The men didn't care so much about the award, but they were very happy to hear it would increase their points and speed their transfer home. After three years in the service, the men of the 332nd were desperate to return home and build their lives as civilians.

Later that summer, the 332nd was sent to a rest camp near Kassel, Germany. They received word that men with 85 or more points would be transferred home. Art was ecstatic, he was going home! Men with less than 85 points were less happy. They would be shipped to the Pacific to participate in the invasion of Japan.

★ Click here to watch video

Figure 64-4: The atomic bombs at Hiroshima and Nagasaki killed hundreds of thousands of Japanese, but they saved the lives of millions of soldiers and civilians who would have died in an invasion of the Japanese mainland.

On the morning of August 6, Art wrote another letter to Jenny, "I hear by way of the grapevine that I am next in line for the start back home and I hope they hurry up about it, I've been over here long enough. Only catch to it is we will be transferred to another outfit, which is slated to go back this month, so if you don't hear from me for a few weeks, just keep smiling 'cuzz I'll be on my way home."

The next day, rumors spread that the Allies had exploded a new kind of super bomb over Japan, a bomb that could vaporize an entire city. These rumors proved to be true. But the Japanese refused to surrender. Plans continued for Operation Downfall, the invasion of Japan. Casualties were expected to be heavy: perhaps a million Americans and two million Japanese. Some experts predicted that more American soldiers could die in the invasion of Japan than had died in the entire war up to that point.

On August 9, the U.S. dropped a second atomic bomb on Japan. The next day, the Japanese proposed a conditional surrender. The Allies did not accept the offer. The U.S. prepared to drop a third atomic bomb on Japan.

On August 10, Art wrote to Jenny, "I'm still sitting over here when as to my way of thinking I should have left for home long ago. I can't understand why the heck we haven't got men going home like other units when we have two or more years of service over seas than they have. Well honey, I shouldn't be wailing to you about that, I hope you excuse my frame of mind. If I were home we could be going out this afternoon like we used to. I wonder if all those trails are grown over with trees and brush. In three or more years, they change a bit."

Finally, on August 14, six days after the second bomb was dropped, the Japanese surrendered. Victory over Japan was declared on August 15. Everyone was going home!

Every soldier was desperate to get home as soon as possible, but the Army couldn't possibly ship sixteen million men home all at once. So, the troops waited impatiently and did what they could to pass the time. Warren Babcock from H&S Company, found an old top hat and clowned around in an attempt to cheer the men up.

On August 19, Art wrote to Jenny again: "Three nights in succession I've dreamed about being home and Gee!, it sure is wonderful to see you again, but I hate to wake up and find myself back here instead. Well, someday that dream will come true. I only hope it isn't too far off."

In September, the men of the 332nd who had at least 85 points were packed railroad cars and sent to Camp Lucky Strike near St. Valery on the French coast to await transfer back to the states. The straw in the railway car was infested with bugs and all the men got scabies.

At Camp Lucky Strike, the men were assigned to units for the trip home and eventual discharge. Art and Warren Babcock of H&S Company were assigned to Company A of the 424th Regiment of the 106th Infantry Division—the division that had borne the brunt of the German attack in the Battle of the Bulge.

There were thousands of men in the large camp, including German prisoners of war, liberated Allied prisoners of war, and veterans who had accumulated at least 85 points during their service in the war. The meals at Camp Lucky Strike were served by German prisoners of war and emotions often ran high, particularly among GIs who had spent time in German prisoner-of-war camps.

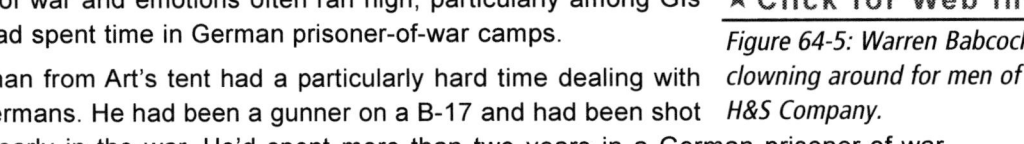

★ Click for Web Info

Figure 64-5: Warren Babcock clowning around for men of H&S Company.

One man from Art's tent had a particularly hard time dealing with the Germans. He had been a gunner on a B-17 and had been shot down early in the war. He'd spent more than two years in a German prisoner-of-war camp, a camp that had one section for American prisoners and a separate section for Russian prisoners of war.

One day, the gunner tried to jump over the counter to attack a German sergeant who was dishing out food in the chow line. The other GIs struggled to hold him back. He yelled, "That Nazi son of a bitch! He looks just like one of the prison guards! You should'a seen what they did to us! You should'a seen what they did to those Russians! They lost the war and now he's serving up our food and smiling at me like that! Look at him! He's still smiling!"

The GIs dragged the struggling gunner outside, sat him down on the grass, and gave him a cigarette. After he smoked for a few minutes, he seemed to calm down. Art sat down next to the gunner and started talking to him. "I know it's hard, but you gotta let that hate go. It'll burn you up inside. We all got reason to hate 'em—they killed our buddies, they gave me this gimpy leg, and they killed my little brother."

The gunner seemed to be listening, so Art continued, "I'm not going to let them have anything else. I'm not going to live the rest of my life filled with bitterness and hate. The war is over. We have to let it go. For us, the war is over. We have to let it be over."

★ Click here for Web Info

Figure 64-6: Camp Lucky Strike in the summer of 1945.

The small group of soldiers sat quietly in the grass, thinking about what they'd been through, thinking about the buddies who'd been killed. They knew Art was right, they had to find some way to let it go, so they could get on with their lives.

Aside from roll call and waiting in lines, the men had little to do. It rained steadily, so they sat in their tents and talked, mostly about home, but also about their experiences in the war. Art and Warren learned that many of the men in Company A had been transferred from other units, but some of the men had been with the company since the Battle of the Bulge. The survivors of the 424th had been on the line for just over a week before the attack. Many of their weapons were still packed in cosmoline when they were attacked. They did their best, but they were greatly outnumbered by the attacking Germans.

One day, a Sergeant from the 106th, told them about trying to stop a German tank with a bazooka during the initial attack. He'd only gotten off one shot before the German infantry surrounded his squad, killed several men and took the rest prisoner. He spent the rest of the war in a German prison camp.

Another day, Art found himself sitting next to a man who introduced himself as Rudy Landolt. Rudy asked Art, "Have you been with the 106th long?"

Art replied, "No, not really. I was with the 332nd Engineers from the spring of '42 through most of this summer. I had 85 points, so I was transferred to the 106th for the trip home."

Rudy Landolt replied:

> I wasn't with the 106th too long myself. I was drafted in the fall of '42 and served with the Quartermaster Corps as we moved across Africa and up into Italy. By the fall of '44, it looked to me like the war was almost over. My family was from Germany and I still had relatives there. I wanted to get to Germany after the war, to look up some of my relatives, so I requested a transfer to the infantry. I went through some infantry retraining and by November I was on my way. I joined Company A of the 424th Infantry on December 11th, 1944.
>
> I didn't have any experience in the infantry, but when I got to the 424th I found it was a brand new outfit, just off the boats the week before. They didn't have any more combat experience than I did. I was happy to hear that we were stationed in a quiet part of the front, 'just there to get a little experience on the line' before being moved to a more active area.
>
> Well, my timing wasn't too good. Five days later, those Panzers rolled right over us. The 422nd and 423rd Regiments were surrounded and forced to surrender. The 424th was hit hard, but we managed to pull back. After the first few days, Company A was down to nineteen men—nineteen out of two hundred. I don't know what happened to the rest of them. I keep hoping more of them will turn up here, but I haven't seen any so far.
>
> Then we regrouped and counterattacked. We fought our way back to St. Vith, then continued to push the Germans through the Ardennes and finally back into Germany.
>
> That winter and spring, so many replacements came, and died. I can still see their faces. It doesn't seem right. I remember their faces. I remember how they died. But I never knew their names.
>
> We fought our way into Germany. I saw the devastation and couldn't help wondering what had happened to my relatives. After the fighting ended, I made it to our village and tracked down my aunt and uncle. Their house was demolished, but they were alive. I asked them about my other two uncles and my cousin.
>
> One of my uncles, an interpreter with the German army in France, was killed during the invasion of Normandy. Another uncle was wounded on the Russian front. He spent time in a Russian POW camp, but did get home. My cousin

★ Click here to watch video

Figure 64-7: Memories of combat and lost comrades often created tension between GIs and German prisoners.

had been a motorcycle dispatch rider on the Russian front. He won the Iron Cross, but was later captured by the Russians. We were told he died while working as a forced laborer in a prisoner-of-war camp in Russia. My father's family line was pretty well wiped out.

This war cost so many families so much. Hitler and the Nazis have a lot to answer for.

Figure 64-8: Ships carrying 332nd Engineers and other soldiers as they near New York Harbor.

Art just looked at the ground, lost in thought. "Yeah. They caused so much pain and so much suffering for so many millions of people. It doesn't hardly seem that hell will be punishment enough for the likes of them."

After three weeks at Camp Lucky Strike, the men boarded the USS Frederick, a Kaiser boat. On September 27, Art left Europe. The ship ran into a major storm with fifty-foot waves, but the boat survived the storm and made it safely back to New York City.

After disembarking, Art was sent to Camp Shank, NY, pending release from the Army. To Art, each day was an eternity. He watched as groups of discharged men boarded trains and headed for home. It had been over three years since he left home and he was desperately anxious to get back to West Ishpeming to see Jenny and to get on with his life.

On October 16, 1945, Carl Arthur "Art" Koski was discharged as a "T5" or Technician 5th Class from Company A of the 424th Infantry Regiment. His discharge papers list Normandy, Rhineland, Ardennes, Central Europe, and Northern France under Battles and Campaigns. He was awarded the Good Conduct Medal and the European African Middle Eastern Service Medal with 5 Bronze Service Stars.

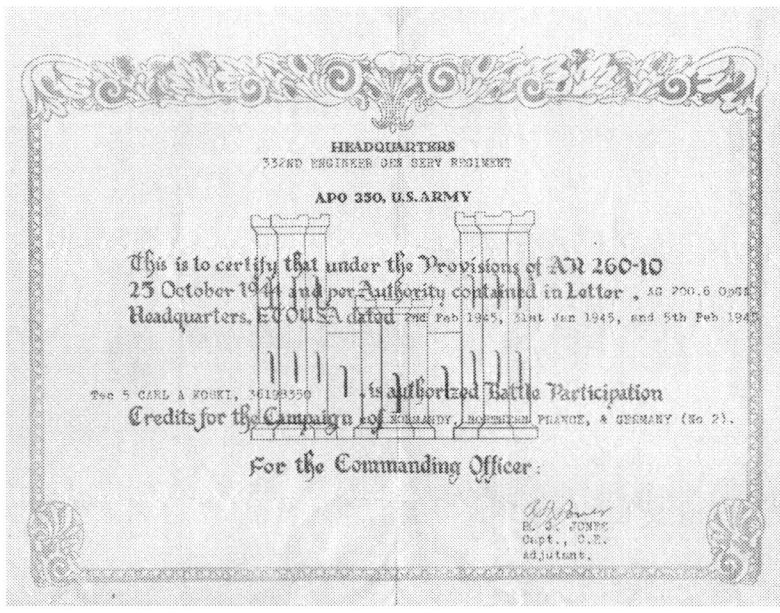

★ Click here for Web Info

Figure 64-9: Carl "Art" Koski's battle participation certificate.

★★★ Ordinary Heroes: Six Stars in the Window ★★★
65. To our graves

April 15, 1945: Al, the oldest Koski brother, sat in his barracks in the state of Washington, and wrote the following letter to his little brother:

```
15 April 45

Dear Johnny,

Read your letter yesterday and sure glad to hear from
you and it is comforting to know you are physically
still intact though we all suffer wounds that will stay
with us to our graves. Sometimes, and often lately, I
wonder if one is capable of enjoying and receiving
pleasure from the same things we used to during our
normal course of life, for instance if one still can
breathe deeply of pine scented air and feel the exhila-
ration we used to.

Rec'd a letter from Art several days ago and he seemed
to be in high spirits, he seemed anxious to get home
to see the rocky soil of U.P. once again. Well Art
sure deserves it having been gone 3 years without see-
ing home. Oscar doesn't write much and can't blame him
fully realizing what his life is like, though he, the
same as Art, remarked receiving letters from you and
they seemed much concerned over you and feel the same
as I that we could change places with you because we
feel you deserve a better break.

It is likely that by the time you receive this letter
extensive action will have terminated and being a wish-
ful thinker and sticking my neck out making predictions
am very much for an early ending of hostilities in the
Pacific Theater. Well concerning Bill Lucas, he hasn't
written to me since last year, don't know why.

Maybe it is the eternal woman danger. Shall close and
good luck Johnny and may God Bless You,

Your Bro. Al

P.S. Rube or George don't correspond with me so I don't
know a thing about them except what Lillie writes, have
had one letter from Anna and only one from El this
year so far, often wonder if the home folks are getting
tired of writing to me, of course, I can not blame
them, as for myself it is hard to write, things which
would be of interest are forbidden, So long.

                                             Al
```

Al placed the letter in a mailbox later that day. It was postmarked April 18 and slowly made its way to Italy.

In the last week of May, that letter was returned to Al. Tears formed in his eyes when he saw the word "Deceased" and "Verified" stamped across the front of the envelope.

Over the next few weeks, more letters addressed to Johnny were returned to Al. Each letter was stamped "Deceased" and "Verified" across the front. Al opened the letters, reread them carefully, then placed them in his footlocker.

Al never talked about those letters. They were found, years later, by his son, John W. Koski, carefully saved with Al's other important papers.

★ Click here for Web Info

Figure 65-1: Al wrote a letter to Johnny on April 15, the day Johnny was killed. The letter was postmarked on April 18, then later returned to Al stamped "Deceased."

★★★ Ordinary Heroes: Six Stars in the Window ★★★
66. Aftermath

May 4, 1945: Lilly numbly held the telegram in her hand, unwilling to read it.

Lilly blinked the tears from her eyes. The telegram was addressed to Alfred Koski. It was from the War Department. This didn't look like a mistake. Lilly slowly read the telegram.

```
TA07 1945 MAY 4 AM 2 11

T.WA12 30 GOVT=WASHINGTON DC 4 231A

MR. ALFRED KOSKI:

RT #1 BOX 231, ISHPEMING MI,

=THE SECRETARY OF WAR DESIRES ME TO EXPRESS HIS DEEP REGRET
THAT YOUR SON PVT KOSKI JOHN L WAS KILLED IN ACTION IN ITALY
15 APR 45 CONFIRMING LETTER FOLLOWS=

J A ULIO THE ADJUTANT GENERAL.

1945
```

Tears streamed down Lilly's face. She didn't want to believe it. This couldn't be happening. Little Johnny couldn't be dead.

Lilly's mind filled with memories of Johnny. She saw him as a young boy, running around the house with a bag of bismarcks over his head. She remembered his gentleness as he cared for the little bear cub with an injured foot. She remembered how grown-up he looked in his Army uniform when they brought him to the train station the last time he was home—the last time he was ever coming home...

She thought of all the things that would not be: Johnny getting married, Johnny with his own little girl, Johnny as a middle-aged man. She thought of Johnny, dying, alone on a battlefield in Italy.

Lilly didn't resist as the sisters helped her into the car. Tears streamed down her face. Lost in her own thoughts, she rocked gently back and forth in the front seat of the car.

Jack drove the sisters to the mine where their father was working. He talked briefly to a man at the gate and a short time later, Alfred Koski walked out of the mine.

Alfred approached the car and saw his daughters sobbing inside. Jack got out and handed him the telegram. Alfred slowly read the telegram, handed it back, and then, without saying a word, turned and slowly walked back into the mine. Jack stood outside the car for a while, waiting, but Alfred didn't return, so he finally drove the Koski sisters home.

By six o'clock, Alfred hadn't come home from work and the family started to get worried. He was always home by four o'clock to milk the cows. Jack drove back to the mine. The road was empty. Jack drove to the family farm at Cooper Lake. There he found Alfred Koski walking alone through the fields. He pulled alongside him and stopped the car. Alfred climbed into the car and pulled the door shut. Silently, the two men drove back to the Koski house.

When they arrived back at the Koski house, Alfred went in and found his daughters still weeping. He watched them for a moment, then said, "Death is only an end to things made of clay. Johnny's gone home to Heaven's Glory and he has seen God." His daughters looked up at him through their tears.

Alfred continued with conviction, "Your Mother rejoices to see Johnny coming home. Keep your faith in good conscience that no man taketh away your crown, and you will see Johnny again, one day." With that, he turned and went to bed, leaving his daughters in the darkening room.

On May 6, a memorial service for Johnny was held in the Apostolic Lutheran Church in Ishpeming. The next day, page six of the *Mining Journal* carried the article, "John L. Koski With Army in Italy, Killed."

On May 8 news of the German surrender reached Ishpeming. Martha and her family were at Dead River, but they heard horns, sirens, and bells, so they knew something important had happened. They jumped into their car and raced to town. The streets were filled with jubilant people celebrating the end of the war.

In an attempt to take her mind off of Johnny, Martha read the special Victory Edition of the *Mining Journal*. The headline proclaimed, "VICTORY! GERMANY QUITS!" She leafed through the paper and she saw many ads congratulating the soldiers on their victory over Germany, while cautioning that the job wouldn't be over until Japan had been defeated. Her breath caught when she spied a full page ad placed by the Schneider Brother Lumber Company.

The ad showed soldiers and a large headline, "When Johnny Comes Marching Home." Smaller text underneath read, "Johnny has licked the Hun again. We are celebrating here. He is cheering over there. Axis might has been crushed in Europe! Japan is next! Let's do the job quickly. Speed the day when the bands will play, the men will cheer, the boys will shout, and the ladies will all turn out—when Johnny comes marching home to stay!"

Martha let the paper fall into her lap. The long awaited victory had arrived, yet there was little joy, not for the Koski family, not for the families of the hundreds of thousands of young men who had paid the ultimate price during the war.

Figure 66-1: Mining Journal article about the memorial service for John Leslie Koski held on May 7, 1945.

★ Click here to watch video

Figure 66-2: As others celebrated the end of the war, the Koski family grieved for Johnny.

The days and weeks passed and the grief began to slowly ease. Al, Art, George and Oscar still hadn't come home from the war. To little Edna Mae, it seemed like Johnny was still out there somewhere, and might yet return.

Jackie Bennett sometimes lay in her bed and dreamed that Johnny wasn't really dead, that he had been injured or captured and would be coming home again. After all, he had promised to come and take her away. He couldn't really be gone for good.

The next week, the Koski family received two letters confirming Johnny's death, one from the War Department and another from the chaplain of the 10th Mountain Infantry Division.

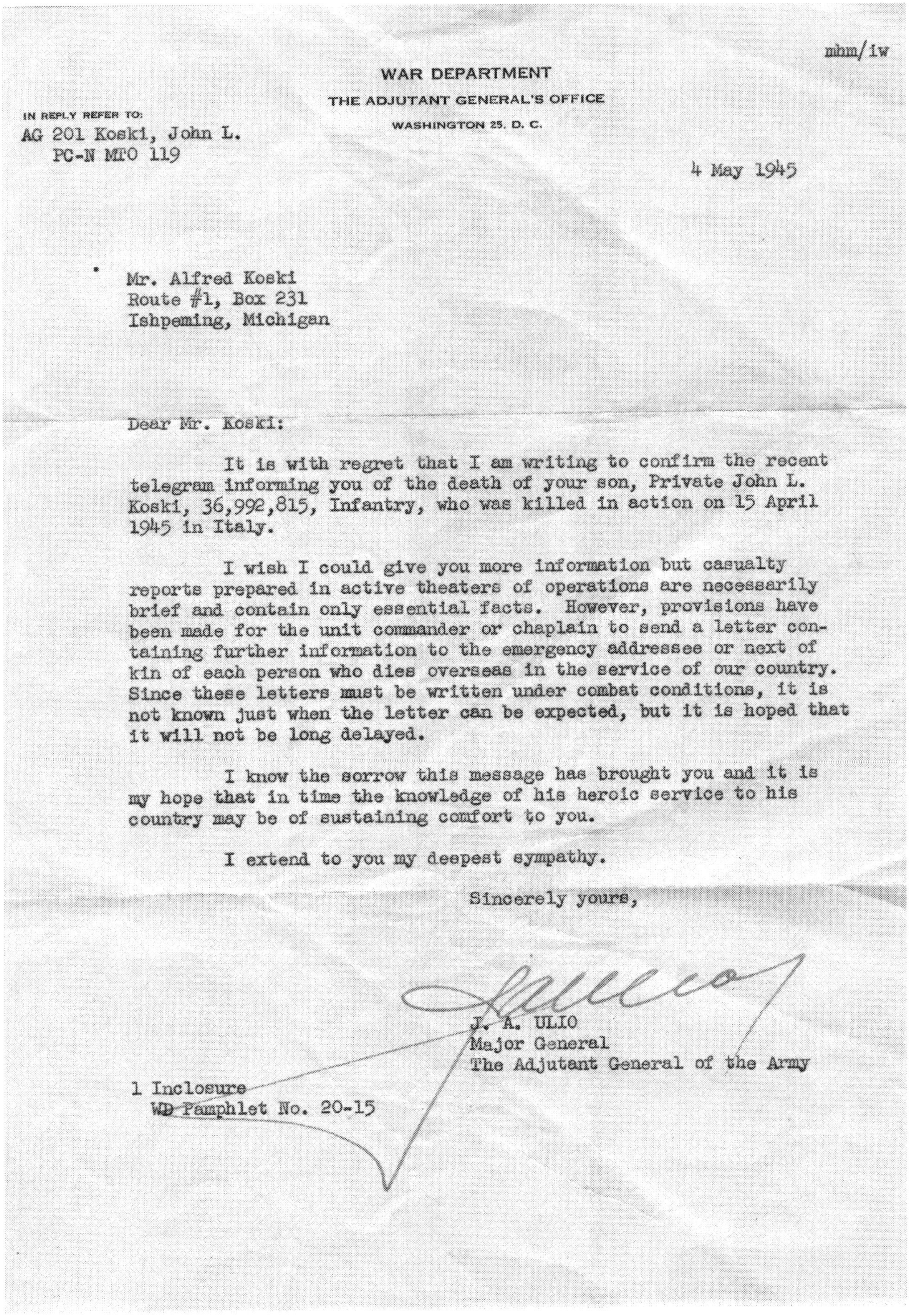

```
                            WAR DEPARTMENT                                    mhm/lw
                        THE ADJUTANT GENERAL'S OFFICE
                            WASHINGTON 25, D. C.
IN REPLY REFER TO:
AG 201 Koski, John L.
PC-N MTO 119
                                                          4 May 1945


        Mr. Alfred Koski
        Route #1, Box 231
        Ishpeming, Michigan




Dear Mr. Koski:

        It is with regret that I am writing to confirm the recent
telegram informing you of the death of your son, Private John L.
Koski, 36,992,815, Infantry, who was killed in action on 15 April
1945 in Italy.

        I wish I could give you more information but casualty
reports prepared in active theaters of operations are necessarily
brief and contain only essential facts. However, provisions have
been made for the unit commander or chaplain to send a letter con-
taining further information to the emergency addressee or next of
kin of each person who dies overseas in the service of our country.
Since these letters must be written under combat conditions, it is
not known just when the letter can be expected, but it is hoped that
it will not be long delayed.

        I know the sorrow this message has brought you and it is
my hope that in time the knowledge of his heroic service to his
country may be of sustaining comfort to you.

        I extend to you my deepest sympathy.

                                            Sincerely yours,


                                            J. A. ULIO
                                            Major General
                                            The Adjutant General of the Army

1 Inclosure
    WD Pamphlet No. 20-15
```

Figure 66-3: The official letter from the War Department, sent to Johnny's father, Alfred Koski.

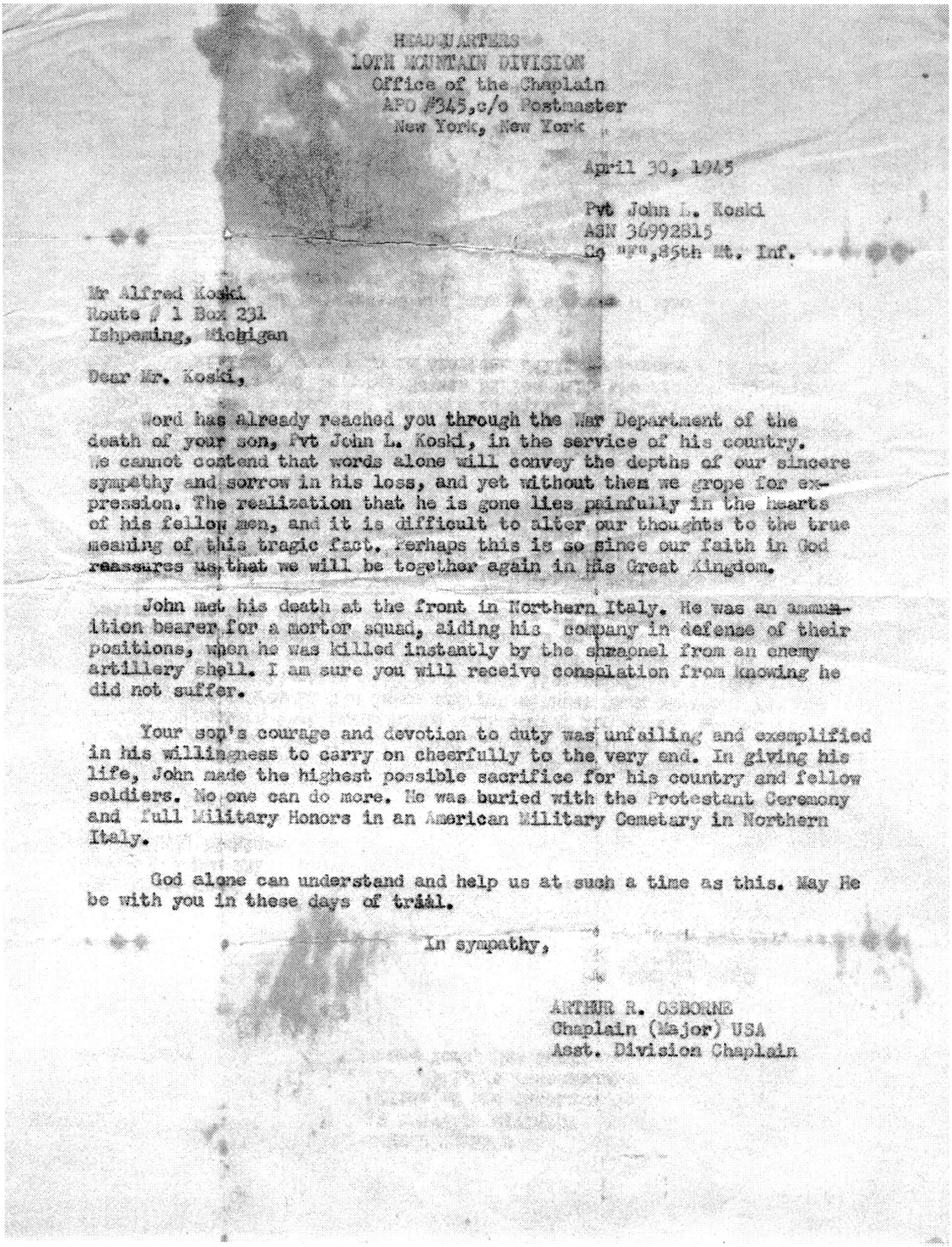

```
                HEADQUARTERS
              10TH MOUNTAIN DIVISION
               Office of the Chaplain
               APO #345, c/o Postmaster
                New York, New York
```

April 30, 1945

Pvt John L. Koski
ASN 36992815
Co "F", 85th Mt. Inf.

Mr Alfred Koski
Route # 1 Box 231
Ishpeming, Michigan

Dear Mr. Koski,

Word has already reached you through the War Department of the death of your son, Pvt John L. Koski, in the service of his country. We cannot contend that words alone will convey the depths of our sincere sympathy and sorrow in his loss, and yet without them we grope for expression. The realization that he is gone lies painfully in the hearts of his fellow men, and it is difficult to alter our thoughts to the true meaning of this tragic fact. Perhaps this is so since our faith in God reassures us that we will be together again in His Great Kingdom.

John met his death at the front in Northern Italy. He was an ammunition bearer for a mortor squad, aiding his company in defense of their positions, when he was killed instantly by the shrapnel from an enemy artillery shell. I am sure you will receive consolation from knowing he did not suffer.

Your son's courage and devotion to duty was unfailing and exemplified in his willingness to carry on cheerfully to the very end. In giving his life, John made the highest possible sacrifice for his country and fellow soldiers. No one can do more. He was buried with the Protestant Ceremony and full Military Honors in an American Military Cemetary in Northern Italy.

God alone can understand and help us at such a time as this. May He be with you in these days of trial.

In sympathy,

ARTHUR R. OSBORNE
Chaplain (Major) USA
Asst. Division Chaplain

Figure 66-4: The letter from the chaplain.

On May 14, sister Eleanor sent copies of those letters to her oldest brother Al, along with a letter in which she talked about the grief felt by the entire family:

Ishpeming, Michigan

May 14, 1945

Dearest Al,

I am forwarding copies of letters sent by Johnny's chaplain and another officer as I know you would like an official explanation on it. I believe the chaplain's letter will make you feel a bit better, at least it did us.

I am praying to God that He may console you in your great sorrow and give us all more faith to see us through these dark days. It is such a terrible price we pay for loving someone, isn't it? Fear throughout the lifetime and sorrow and anguish at the final parting. No greater love could have existed between brothers than did exist between you and Johnny and now the hurt is greater too. I have noted a thread of fear for his safety in all your letters no matter how cheerful the content may have been.

Johnny loved life but had no qualms about dying in his youth and repeatedly warned us not to grieve in event he should not return. When I think of it, he had a nice life and I give you credit for making it beautiful. You gave him more love and guidance than an average parent would have and built him up mentally and physically too. You allowed him to go to camp long before the others. He owned a gun and enjoyed privileges at an earlier age than the others and was the toast of the hunting gang. No one could have done more than you did for the boys so at least you have no regrets.

He did the hardest job on earth with strength and courage that we should be proud of and when he took his place among the stars he left us with a memory that will never fade. God picks His most beautiful flowers first and I suppose it is because He would not find his Kingdom as enticing were it composed of all withered ones and gray beards.

I am glad to report that Lil and the others are taking things very well. I suppose it is because their faith in God surpasses their grief. I feel as though mine were tottering in its weakness. The very sight of my friends or thoughts of recreation nauseates me and if I had my way I would hide away forever and wait for the day that I could see my brother again. It is so easy to forget ones debt to the living in times like this.

Love, El

★ Click here for Web Info

Figure 66-5: A transcript of the letter sent from Eleanor to her brother Al, shortly after the telegram arrived.

In August of 1945, Alfred Koski received two additional documents about his son from the U.S. Army. One was a posthumous award of the Purple Heart, which reads as follows:

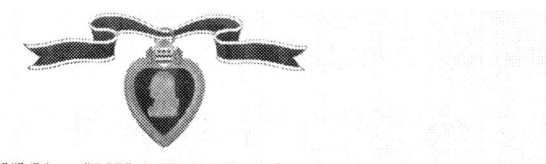

Figure 66-6: John Leslie Koski's Purple Heart documentation.

The other document was signed by President Harry S. Truman.

Figure 66-7: Document signed by President Harry S. Truman.

★★★ Ordinary Heroes: Six Stars in the Window ★★★
67. Don't you recognize me?

October 20, 1945: It was the middle of the night when the "Old 400" pulled into the Ishpeming train station. Art threw his duffel bag over his shoulder and set out on foot for West Ishpeming. He trudged up the hill towards the house and saw a light in the kitchen window.

"Who would be up at this hour?" he wondered. "My letters couldn't have arrived yet. No one knows I'm coming home."

He opened the door and stepped across the old familiar threshold. As Art stepped into the kitchen he saw his father drinking coffee at the kitchen table. His father looked up. When he saw it was Art, a broad smile lit his face. The normally reserved Alfred Koski strode across the room, hugged his son and cried, "My son! My son! Thank God! Thank God!"

Minutes later, Reuben and the sisters stumbled down the stairs to see what the fuss was about. Everyone talked excitedly, asking questions so fast that Art couldn't hope to answer them. Art yawned deeply and they decided they should let him get some sleep.

Art went upstairs to the boy's room and stretched out on his old bed. It was strange to see so many empty bed in this room that used to be so full of Koski brothers. Al and George used to sleep here. Oscar, Reuben, and Johnny slept over there.

Art lay in the dark and tried unsuccessfully to fall sleep. He was finally home, after almost three and a half years, but the war was not yet through with him. Each time he closed his eyes, memories flooded back: airplanes strafing the H&S train, the German scout car coming down the snowy road, and the blond baby floating down the river. Each time he almost fell asleep, he'd jerk awake, thinking he was back in the war. It didn't feel right to lie down unprotected. After a few hours, Art went downstairs and got his hunting rifle. He lay down in his bed with his rifle at his side, closed his eyes, and finally fell asleep.

The next morning, Reuben found Art asleep in his bed, his rifle cradled in his arms. Reuben touched Art's arm. Art sat up with a start, his rifle at the ready, a wild look in his eyes.

"Easy, easy Art!" said Reuben. "You're home. You're safe now."

As he realized where he was, Art slowly put the rifle down and climbed out of bed.

Art dressed and went downstairs. He drank a quick cup of coffee and asked if his old Ford was still running. Lilly said she thought it was. The keys were on a nail by the door. Art took the keys and said he had to go to catch Jenny as she walked to work.

Art drove through the streets of Ishpeming, marveling at how quiet and peaceful the town seemed. "I'm never going to leave the U.P. again!" he promised himself.

Art pulled to the side of the street outside the Gossard Manufacturing Building, where Jenny worked. A steady stream of women walked toward the entrance of the building to start their shifts for the day. Then he saw Jenny, walking down the sidewalk.

She was even prettier than he remembered, her red hair glistening in the morning sun. Art drove slowly down the street. He pulled even with her and whistled out the window. She put her nose in the air and walked even faster.

Chuckling, Art called out, "Don't you recognize me? Don't you know your old friend Art?"

Jenny turned and stared at him. Art turned off the car, then jumped out. They hugged and laughed and cried. The car was still in the street blocking traffic, but no one honked his horn or yelled. The other motorists just smiled at the happy reunion between the young GI and his girl, then steered carefully around the empty car.

Art and Jenny got into the car and drove away, talking excitedly about all of the things they were going to do, now that the war was finally over. For the first time in her life, Jenny completely forgot about going to work.

Art proposed to Jenny soon after his return. Jenny wanted to get married right away, but Art thought they should wait until after deer season. He felt it just wouldn't be right to get married and then head off to deer camp. He loved Jenny, but he had no intention of missing another deer season. After rather heated discussions, they set the date for December 10, 1945, so Art could go to deer camp.

Three of the Koski brothers—Art, Oscar, and Reuben—went to deer camp at Flat Rock for the hunting season of 1945. Art and Oscar had been discharged in mid-October and had been home for only a few weeks. Reuben had been discharged from the Navy earlier that summer.

Al and George were not yet home. Al was scheduled to be discharged in December, 1945. George had recovered from his neck injury and been shipped to the Philippines in July of 1945. He was waiting for a ship home and expected to be discharged in January of 1946.

Art had dreamed of that hunting camp so many times during the war. Now he was finally there, but somehow the old camp didn't seem the same. He missed Al, he missed George—and he missed Johnny.

There were many deer that year, perhaps because there had been so few hunters in previous deer seasons. Art, Oscar, and Reuben all got their bucks. But their time at the camp wasn't just about hunting, it was also a healing time—a time for the brothers to adjust to the idea of civilian life, a chance to somehow learn to cope with the after-effects of the war.

★ Click here to watch video

Figure 67-1: The veterans of WWII knew that everything they had been through, everything they had done, was necessary. They knew they had done their duty, they had fought "the good war."

As so many veterans have discovered, Art and Oscar found that war was not easily left behind.

Art still slept with his rifle in his bunk. At any unusual noise, he sat up, rifle at the ready.

Oscar often found himself awake in the early morning hours, expecting the wake-up guy to burst in and tell him it was time to get dressed for yet another mission.

The brothers didn't talk too much about Johnny, but they felt his presence in the camp and on the woodland trails. They remembered his gullibility when they teased him about whistling bears. They remembered him as a boy, reciting the Gettysburg Address and *I have a Rendezvous with Death*. They remembered his quiet pride after he shot the charging bear at the age of thirteen. And, as they lay on their bunks in the quiet of the night, they tried not to think too much about their little brother Johnny, fighting, and dying, on some hill so very far from home.

★★★ Ordinary Heroes: Six Stars in the Window ★★★
68. Not forgotten

Spring, 1948: The Army announced that the families of servicemen killed in the war could have the bodies shipped home. It was a one-time offer.

Some of the brothers thought it might be best to leave Johnny buried with his comrades. Alfred Koski was ambivalent about his son's remains, "His soul is with God and the clay is not important."

Lilly said, "But we can't just leave him over there. We have to bring him home! If nothing else, I need a chance to say goodbye to him."

Art finally spoke his mind: "Lil, I think you're right on this. If I had died in the Ardennes, I would want you to bring me home so I could be buried here with mother. I wouldn't want you to leave me there."

"That's settled then!" said Lil, "We'll tell the Army to send Johnny home so he'll be close to his friends and family. That way we can visit him often."

On November 7, 1948, the U.S. Army Transport *Lawrence Victory*, one of the victory ships that helped to win the war, returned to the U.S. with the bodies of 253 American soldiers. Traveling on that ship were the bodies of twenty-one soldiers from the Upper Peninsula of Michigan, including two from the Ishpeming area: Private Arne A. Saari of Palmer and Private John L. Koski of West Ishpeming. The bodies were removed from the ship, placed on trains, and shipped back to their hometowns.

On November 16, John Leslie Koski returned to Ishpeming on the "Old 400," the same train on which he had left almost four years earlier. His flag-draped casket arrived on the 7:00 a.m. train, where it was met by the entire Koski family. Light snow fell as four soldiers carried the casket from the train to the waiting hearse.

The soldiers saluted the family, then one of them stepped forward and said, "I served with Johnny in the 10th Mountain Infantry Division. I have a message to the family from Johnny. He wanted you to know that he died a Christian."

The family followed as the hearse took Johnny's body to the Apostolic Lutheran Church for a memorial service. During the service, delivered by Reverend Tulkki, the congregation sang the familiar hymns "Safe in the Arms of Jesus" and "Abide with Me." After the memorial service, the hearse brought Johnny's body to the Ishpeming cemetery, stopping next to the grave of his mother, Elizabeth. After a short sermon, each member of the Koski family stepped to the casket and said goodbye to their youngest brother Johnny.

After Johnny's body was lowered into his grave, the honor guard fired, once, twice, then three times. In the silence that followed, the Koski brothers snapped to attention, and as one, they sharply saluted their fallen brother. Then, tears glittering in their eyes, they turned and walked away.

For the Koski family, the war was finally over.

The war was over, but it has not been forgotten.

★ Click here to watch video

Figure 68-1: John Leslie Koski's remains were returned to Ishpeming on November 16, 1948.

Christine, the young girl mentioned so fondly in Johnny's letters, is now a grown woman with children and grandchildren of her own. While discussing this book with the author, Christine's husband said, "Yes, I know about Johnny. Christine still cries for him."

For the rest of their lives, the Koski brothers and sisters found it difficult to talk about Johnny. They would start to talk about him, but would choke up and would have to walk away. This depth of feeling has not faded.

Like so many veterans, the Koski brothers rarely talked about the war. They probably had many reasons for their reticence. Perhaps they didn't think their experience was special, since so many men from their generation had similar stories to tell. They probably did not realize they were part of a unique generation that lived in exceptional times and faced exceptional challenges. Perhaps they didn't want to burden their families with stories of death and destruction. However, in declining to talk about their experiences, they made it more difficult for future generations to understand how close the world had come to domination by madmen and the extent of the sacrifice that had been required to save it.

What the Allied soldiers of WWII did is too important to be forgotten. We—the people of the United States, the people of Europe, the people of Asia, indeed all people living anywhere in the world today—owe a unpayable debt to the Allied veterans of World War II. Without their sacrifice, our world would be a much darker place.

As civilians, most of us will never really understand what it means to be a soldier. We live our lives in relative comfort and safety, far from the dangers and the stresses of the battlefield. But we should never forget that our way of life does not come cheap. It was won—and is preserved—through the sacrifice of soldiers.

★ Click here to watch video

Figure 68-2: In 2005, the surviving Koski siblings—Oscar Koski, Reuben Koski, and Edna Mae Koski Oja—joined members of the extended Koski family and F-85 veterans as they celebrated their shared heritage and the life of John Leslie Koski.

★ Click here to watch video

★ Click here for Web Info

Figure 68-3: John Leslie Koski is buried next to his mother and his father. His dear sister Lilly, who raised him from the age of four, is buried just one hundred steps away.

John Leslie Koski.
Loved and honored always.

★★★ Ordinary Heroes: Six Stars in the Window ★★★
Afterword

The author presents James Orwig with a special reunion copy of Ordinary Heroes signed by veterans and members of the Koski family. James Orwig was the platoon sergeant for the 4th Platoon of F Company of the 85th Regiment of the 10th Mountain Infantry Division. John Leslie Koski served as an ammunition carrier in the 1st mortar squad of that platoon.

"I never knew him—I never *really* knew him." This phrase was on my mind as we drove north to Michigan's Upper Peninsula for the final reunion of F Company of the 85th Mountain Infantry. The main feature of this event was to be the honoring of Pvt. John Koski who was killed in action in our North Apennines campaign. John had joined the 4th Platoon as one of a dozen replacements to fill in for those we lost in the battle of Mount Belvedere. His name is listed several times in my combat notes which as platoon sergeant I had used to keep track of our men.

During that reunion I came to know about as completely as one could the real John Koski behind the name on my list in what amounted to a kind of revelation. I came to know a remarkable family of 11 children the six sons of which were all in service in WWII. I came to know a strong ethnic group of Finnish people. I learned about work in the iron mines and how essential it was in the support of this and most families in the region. I came to know a community of hard working people with strong fundamental values, true to each other, which surrounded the Koski family. I came to know of a rigorous region with hard winters and a challenging environment in which hunting, fishing and outdoor living were essential elements of the full life.

Dan Oja in this volume has presented in rich and faithful detail all of these elements in John's background in telling the story of the Koski family. And he has gone to great lengths to cover John's time in service and his untimely end carrying his mortar rounds in the thick of action. But this story becomes part of a larger account of the experiences of two older brothers who also faced the awful stresses of live combat—Oscar as a navigator on a B-l7 bomber and Art as an army engineer fighting across France from D-Day to the end of the war.

Oja skillfully interweaves these three combat narratives in a manner that fully engages our interest. The dialogue throughout rings true although some of it is fictionalized out of necessity. Yet the realism of it speaks well for his careful and extensive research and interviewing efforts. I feel assured that this book is an important contribution to the literature of WWII.

One might be tempted to say, "Oh, just another book about someone's war experiences." But what a story this one is! From beginning to end, the significance of this unique Koski family shines forth as its six sons go off to war and six blue stars are in the window of the family home. Then in the final weeks of the war one star becomes golden, marking the supreme sacrifice of the youngest brother, John Koski, who became to me infinitely more than just a name in my notebook.

James K. Orwig

★★★ Ordinary Heroes: Six Stars in the Window ★★★
Credits

Technology:
The technology used in the interactive digital versions of *Ordinary Heroes: Six Stars in the Window* was created by MediaTechnics Corporation. For more information on the MediaTechnics BookOn™ digital publishing system visit www.mediatechnicscorp.com.

Photographs and drawings:
1. Most of the photos of Koski family members are from the Koski family collection, with contributions from the extended Koski family and friends of the family.
2. Most of the generic WWII photos are from Signal Corps photos in the Dan Oja collection.
3. Most photos pertaining to the 332nd Engineer Regiment are used courtesy of the Carl "Art" Koski family, Tom Jones, Warren Babcock, or other members of the 332nd Engineers or their families.
4. Most photos pertaining to the 10th Mountain Infantry Division are courtesy of veterans of the 10th Mountain Infantry Division, particularly members of F-85, including Bill Kehres, James Orwig, Al Wiedorn, and James Winterbottom.
5. The photo of Robert Ellis' notebook in Figure 61-2, the sketch in Figure 57-4, and the quote on page 229 are used with permission of Ted Ellis, son of Robert Ellis.
6. The following photos are used with permission of the Denver Public Library:
    a. Figure 43-4: The chapel on the rock in Gaggio Montano, 1945. Denver Public Library, Western History Collection, Call Number TMD-253.
    b. Figure 47-4: Apple blossoms bloom near Mount della Spe in the spring of 1945. Denver Public Library, Western History Collection, Call Number TMD-281.
    c. Figure 55-2: Memorial service for fallen comrades held in the military cemetery in Florence Italy, April 6th, 1945. Denver Public Library, Western History Collection, Call Number TMD-76.
    d. Figure 57-1: Photo of the bombardment of the German positions as seen from Mount della Spe. Denver Public Library, Western History Collection, Call Number TMD-130.
7. The following maps are used with permission of the Denver Public Library:
    a. Figure 44-3: Close-up of map of Mount della Castellana area.
    b. Figure 60-1: Close-up of map showing Hill 909, Hill 915, and Hill 898.

Videos:
1. The documentary video *Ordinary Heroes* and the trailer from that documentary are copyrighted by Dan Oja. The script was written by June Parsons and video production and editing was by Stephen Stanley.
2. The World War II video clips are from public domain video obtained from the National Archives or from the Dan Oja collection.
3. The video interviews with veterans are copyrighted by Dan Oja.
4. The news footage in Figure 68-2 is used with permission from WLUC-TV/Barrington Broadcasting LLC.

For detailed information on the photographs and videos used in this project, visit:
www.sixstarsinthewindow.com/media/photocredits.htm.

★★★ Ordinary Heroes: Six Stars in the Window ★★★
Bibliography

Most recommended sources:
For detailed information on the 301st Bomb Group see *Who Fears? The 301st in War and Peace 1942–1979* by Kenneth P. Werrell, ISBN: 0-87833-025-9
For detailed information on the 332nd Engineers see *Bridging for Victory, 332nd Engineers Regiment* by Chester W. Nichols
For detailed information on the 85th Regiment, with a particular focus on F Company and the 4th Platoon see:
The 85th Mountain Infantry Regimental History, 4 January 1945 to 31 May 1945 by John B. Woodruff, adapted by John Imbrie from the original document in the National Archives, Suitland, Maryland (Record Group 407)
I Soldiered with America's Elite 10th Mountain Division of W.W. II by Carl V. Cossin, 1st books, ISBN 0-75963-791-1
Lieutenant Mackin's 10th Mountain Men, by C.K. Moore, 1989
See Naples and Die by Robert B. Ellis, McFarland and Company, Inc., ISBN: 0-7864-0190-7

Upper Peninsula Events
Microfilm copies of The *Mining Journal* located at the Peter White Public Library, Marquette MI
POW Camps in the UP, The *Mining Journal* and WNMU-TV
52 Steps Underground, An Autobiography of a Miner, by Ernie Ronn, 2000 by Northern Michigan University, ISBN: 0-9666248-1-5 paper

Camp Croft
Camp Croft, South Carolina and Spartanburg, by the Camp Croft Post Exchange
Trainees Handbook, Infantry Replacement Training Center, Camp Croft, S.C.U.S. Army Publication
When the Soldiers Came to Town, edited by Susan Turpin, Carolyn Creal, Ron Crowley and James Crocker of the Spartanburg County Historical Association, 2004, Hub City Writers Project ISBN: 1891885375

10th Mountain Infantry Division
The 85th Mountain Infantry Regimental History, 4 January 1945 to 31 May 1945 by John B. Woodruff, adapted by John Imbrie from the original document in the National Archives, Suitland, Maryland (Record Group 407)
The Boys of Winter by Charles J. Sanders, University Press of Colorado, Boulder, CO ISBN: 0-87081-783-3
Combat History of the 10th Mountain Infantry Division 1944–1945, Infantry School Library, Fort Benning, Georgia
Good Times and Bad, A History of C Company of the 85th Mountain Regiment 10th Mountain Infantry Division, edited by John Imbrie and Hugh W. Evans, Vermont Heritage Press, ISBN: 0-911853-10-3 (pb), 0-911853-14-6 (h)
Green Cognac, The Education of a Mountain Fighter by William Lowell Putnam, printed by AAC Press ISBN: 0-930410-50-5
History of the 87th Mountain Infantry, Italy 1945, Captain George F. Earle
I Soldiered with America's Elite 10th Mountain Division of W.W. II by Carl V. Cossin, 1st books, ISBN 0-75963-791-1
Lieutenant Mackin's 10th Mountain Men, by C.K. Moore, 1989
Mountain Troops and Medics, Wartime Stories of a Frontline Surgeon in the U.S. Ski Troops by Albert H. Meinke Jr., M.D., Rucksack Publishing Company, ISBN: 0-9633742-0-6
Mountaineers, a booklet about the 10th Mountain Infantry Division by the U.S. Army
Rifleman's Diary, A an unpublished manuscript by Donald H. Montgomery
See Naples and Die by Robert B. Ellis, McFarland and Company, Inc., ISBN: 0-7864-0190-7
The North Apennines and Beyond with the 10th Mountain Division by Harris Dusenbery, Blinford and Mort Publishing, ISBN: 0-8323-0522-7
Short History of the 85th Mountain Infantry Regiment, A, 10th Mountain Infantry Division Association
Ski Troops, The by Hal Burton, Simon and Shuster, ISBN 671-20986-8
This was Italy, National Association of the 10th Mountain Infantry Division
Unpublished notes on the 4th Platoon, Company F, 85th Regiment of the 10th Mountain Infantry Division, compiled by James Orwig, Platoon Sergeant, F Company, 85th Regiment, 10th Mountain Infantry Division
Unpublished notes on the morning reports of Company F, 85th Regiment of the 10th Mountain Infantry Division, compiled by William Ballek, 1st Sergeant, F Company, 85th Regiment, 10th Mountain Infantry Division
Unpublished memoires of James Winterbottom of the 4th Platoon of Company F of the 85th Mountain Infantry Division by James Winterbottom

301st Bomb Group, 5th Wing, 15th AA Force and Related References
376th Bomb Group Mission History by Edward Frank Clendenin, Jr., published by the author
A Brief History of the Fifteenth Air Force (1 November 1943–1 January 1966) by Dr. Cornelius C. Smith, Jr., Chief, Historical Division, Directorate of Information, Headquarters, Fifteenth Air Force, March Air Base, California
A Measure of Life by Herman L. Cranman, ISBN: 0-615-12007-5

Combat Legend B-17 Flying Fortress, Martin Bowman, 2002 Airlife Publishing Ltd., Shresbury England, ISBN 1-84037-3654-2

Combat records of Oscar Koski

Flying Forts by Martin Caidin, Ballantine Books, NY ISBN: 0-345-28308-2

Forever Remembered, by Irv Broughton, Copyright 2001, Eastern Washington University Press, Spokane WA, ISBN 0-910055-71-8

Forgotten Fields of America, Volume 3, by Lou Thole, Pictorial Histories Publishing Company, Inc., Missoula, MT ISBN: 1-57510-102-5

Luck of the Draw, Reflections on the Air War in Europe, Frank D. Murphy, FPN Military Division, ISBN 0-917678-51-6

Navigator's Information File, a U.S.A.A.F. restricted publication

Serenade to the Big Bird, Bert Stiles, Schiffer Publishing Ltd., Atglen Pa, ISBN: 0-7643-1396-7

The Army Air Forces in World War II, 1948 by the University of Chicago, ISBM: 0-912799-03-X

The Bomber War by Robin Neillands, ISBN: 1-58567-457-5

The Wild Blue by Stephen Ambrose, ISBN: 0-7432-0339-9

The Mighty Eighth, by Gerald Astor, Dell Publishing, a Division of Random House, Inc.ISBN: 0-440-22648-1

Those Who Fall, by John Muirhead, Pocket Books, ISBN: 0-671-64944-2

Together We Fly, a U.S. Army Air Forces publication published during the war

Two Years, an unpublished history of the 5th Wing, 15th AAF, January, 1945, by Brigadier General, C.W. Lawrence USAAF

Who Fears? The 301st in War and Peace 1942–1979 by Kenneth P. Werrell, ISBN: 0-87833-025-9

332nd Engineers and Related References

320th Engineer Battalion, 1942–1945, an unpublished unit history

332nd Engineer Regiment 23rd Reunion Booklet by Gordon Schopfer, H&S Company, 332nd Engineers

Bridging for Victory, 332nd Engineers Regiment by Chester W. Nichols

Bridging the way to Victory with the 355 Engineers, an unpublished manuscript

Camp Claiborne by Cecil Atkinson and Kathy Tilley, Ack Hill Publishing Company, Forrest Hill, LA ISBN: 0-9626853-0-5

Engineering the Victory, The Battle of the Bulge by Col. David Pergrin, Schiffer Publishing, LTD., Atglen, PA ISBN: 0-7643-0163-2

The History of the 341st Engineer Regiment, July 29, 1943–March 22, 1946, an unpublished manuscript

History of the Fourth Major Port, Cherbourg France, June 1944–Oct 1945, an unpublished manuscript, author unknown

Hitler's Fortress Cherbourg, The Conquest of a Bastion, by William B. Bauer, published by Stein and Day, Briarcliff Manor, NY 10510, ISBN 0-8128-2952-2

Unpublished War Scrapbook of Carl Arthur Koski, H&S Company, 332nd Engineers

General WWII References

The American Axis, Henry Ford, Charles Lindbergh, and the Rise of the Third Reich by Max Wallace, copyright 2003,St. Martin's Press, New York, ISBN: 0-312-29022-5

Countdown to Victory, the Final European Campaigns of World War II, Barry Turner, HarperCollins Publishers, New York, ISBN 0-06-074067-1

Franklin and Winston, An intimate portrait of an epic friendship, by John Meacham, Random House Publishing, ISBN 0-8129-7282-1

The German Army,1933–1945 by Matthew Cooper, 1978 by Cooper and Lucas Ltd., ISBN 0-8128-8519-8

The Gothic Line The Italian Campaign, Autumn 1944, by Dougliss Orgill, 1967, W.W. Norton & Company Inc. New York, Library of Congress Catalog Card No. 67-15816

Hitler's War, Germany's Key Strategic Decisions 1940–1945, Heinz Mageneimer, Barnes & Noble Books, Copyright 1997, ISBN: 0-7607-3531-X

Lie in the Dark and Listen from Noël Coward Collected Verse edited by Graham Payne and Martin Tickner , 1987 Methuen Publishing Ltd., ISBN: 0413551504j, The Estate of Noël Coward

The Longest Day 1959 by Cornelius Ryan, Touchstone Books, NY ISBN: 0671-89091-3

On Killing, The Psychological Cost of Learning to Kill in War and Society by Lieutenant Col. Dave Grossman, 1995/1996, Little, Brown, and Co., ISBN 0-316-33000-0 (hc), 0-316-33011-6 (pb)

Once in a Lifetime, A World War II Memoir, Robert A. Nusbaum, Merriam Press, ISBN: 1-57638-170-6

Photographic History of the Peninsular Base Section, Volume II, United States Army, published 1945

Why the Allies Won, Richard Overy, W. W. Norton & Company Inc. New York, ISBN: 0-393-03925-03

The Winter War by Eloise Engle and Lauri Paananen, StackPole books, ISBN 0-8117-2433-6

World War II, The Axis Assault, 1939–1942, The New York Times Living History, Times Books, Henry Holt and Company, LLC, Edited by Douglas Brinkley, 2003, ISBN: 0-8050-7246-2 (vol. 1)

World War II, The Allied Counteroffensive, 1942–1945, The New York Times Living History, Times Books, Henry Holt and Company, LLC, Edited by Douglas Brinkley, 2003, ISBN: 0-8050-7246-2 (vol. 1)

★★★ Ordinary Heroes: Six Stars in the Window ★★★
Index

106th Infantry Division, Battle of the Bulge 125, Camp Lucky Strike 250-251
10th Mountain Infantry Division, Kiska 44, Riva Ridge and Belvedere 155-156, John Koski assigned to 159, Montecatini 196, Mount della Spe 204-205, April 1, 195 212, April 1945 221, The Big Push April 14 1945 229, April 15, 1945 239, April 16, 1945 241-243, Letters from 256-258, Honor Guard 263
15th Army Air Force, Oscar Koski assigned to 100, Oscar first mission with 122, Loss of Ralph Steuve 172, Berlin mission 201
213th Anti-aircraft Battalion, 44
223rd Combat Crew Training School, 77
301st Bomb Group Heavy, Oscar Koski assigned to 100, Oscar Koski first combat mission 112, November 1944 121, December 1944 129, Psychological effects and jokes 133, Oxygen hose 139, Knittelfeld mission 148, Luck 163, Loss of Ralph Steuve 172, March 1945 199, April 1945 224, End of war 232, Return home 244
30th Infantry Training Battalion, 70, 91
332nd Engineer Regiment, Carl "Art" Koski assigned to 37, Going overseas 45, Arrive in England 48, D-day prep and invasion 64, Utah Beach and Cherbourg 79, Breakout 92, Strafing 120, Battle of the Bulge 125, Ditch defense 142, Resume advance 144, Into Germany 186, March 1945 211, Meet Russians 231, End of war 247
333rd Engineer Regiment, 82
342nd Engineer Regiment, 82
34th Infantry Division, 156
352nd Squadron, 100, 115, 199
442nd Nisei Regimental Combat Team, 153, 221
5th Wing of the 15th Army Air Force, 100
60 mm mortar, 109, 175
63rd Coast Artillery, 44
81 mm mortar 109, 175
85th Mountain Regiment, John Koski assigned to 159-160, Big Push 239
87th Mountain Combat Team, 43-44
8th Replacement Depot, Empoli, Italy, John Koski assigned to 151, John Koski leaves 159

A
Aachen, Germany, 96, 145, 147
Adriatic, 114, 129, 140, 199
Alaska, 40, 41, 42, 44, 45
Albert Canal, Belgium, 144
Aleutian islands, Alaska, 41, 42
Allegheny College, 59, 62
Antwerp, 126, 127
Apostolic Lutheran Church, 5, 213, 256, 263
Ardennes, 26, 125, 127, 151, 207, 248, 251, 252, 263
Argentina, USS, 46-48
Armstrong, PFC George, John Koski meets 161, 168, 180-181, 221, Wounded 226-227
Army Specialized Training Program (ASTP), 54
Atomic bomb, 249
Attu, Alaska, 41-43
Aubel, Belgium, 96
Axis Sally, 127

B
B-17 bomber, 60, 61, 78, 101, 104, 107-108, 114, 121-122, 130-133, 140, 148, 157-158, 160, 164, 172, 224
B-24 bomber, 130, 199, 201
Baal, Germany, 186
Babcock, Sergeant Warren, Party 50, Ice cream maker 51, Waterproof vehicles 66, 80, Requisition parts 94, Buzz bombs 98-99, Strafing 119-120, 142, 210-211, Clowning 249, 250
Bailey bridge, 50
Bastogne, Belgium, 126, 142
Battle of Britain, 28, 29
Battle of San Pietro, 155
Battle of the Bulge, 126, 127, 138, 143, 144, 146, 250
Bayless, Lieutenant, 96, 97
Beck, Lieutenant Robert, 242
Belpedio, Nataline, 32
Benham Valence Castle, England, 49-50
Bennet, Jack, 2, 3, 13, 88, 255
Bennet, Jacqueline (Jackie), 2, 117, 270
Bennet, Martha, 2, 3, 88, 117, 256
Bennett, Martha (Nonny), 117
BerMar, 169
Birchette, 1st Lieutenant James, 186
Blechhammer, Germany, 121, 131
Blizzard, 194
Blue Grotto, Isle of Capri, 218
Bogrow, Morris, 148-149
Bohm, Richard, 85
Bologona, Italy, 232
Bonetti, Guido, 32
Boyajian, PFC Lawrence, 167-168
Brandt, PVT Nesbur, 168, 235
Brazilian Expeditionary Force (BEF), 153, 212
Bridges, William, 167
British Auxiliary Territorial Army, 50
Brno, Czechoslovakia, 121, 131
Brown, PFC William, 167
Browning Automatic Rifle (BAR), 56, 86, 96, 104, 136-138, 153, 230
Brux, Czechoslovakia, 101, 103, 124, 130, 133, 135
Burrows, PFC Lawrence, 178, 208, 241

C
Caerleon, England, 49
Callahan, Lieutenant William, 226, 242
Camp Callan, California, 32
Camp Claiborne, Louisiana, 37-38, 40, 45
Camp Croft, Spartanburg, South Carolina, 69, 70-71, 86-87, 89, 91, 109, 177
Camp Hale, Colorado, 162, 166-167, 183, 220
Camp Kilmer, New Jersey, 45-46, 49
Camp Lucky Strike, France, 250, 252
Camp Shank, New York, 252
Camp Swift, Texas, 166
Campo Tizzoro, Italy, 159, 160, 166, 171
Canham, PFC Ray, 193-194
Capri, Isle of, Italy, 218, 224, 233
Carney Matheny, Private, 97
Carney, Sergeant Bernard, 97, 161-162, 168, 180, 192
Carson, Sergeant Lorin, 167
Castel D'Aiano, Italy, 179, 189, 208
Chamberlain, Neville, 17, 20-21, 22, 26
Cherbourg, France, 67, 81-85, 92, 95-96
Churchill, Winston, 26-30, 68
Civilian Public Service Camp, 135 75
Clancy, Lieutenant Thomas, 199
Clark, Nina, 8-9
Coast Artillery, 3, 36, 41, 44, 54, 60, 122
Concentration camps, 248
Condon, PFC Thomas, 167-168
Conscientious objectors, 75-76
Cotentin peninsula, France, 81
Cooper Lake, Michigan, 6, 58, 86, 89
Cossin, Sergeant Carl, 166, 228, 240
Coughlin, Father Charles, 19
Coward, Noël 169, 218
Cowesfield House, England, 64-65
Creel, PFC Tommie, 168

D
Daladier, Edourd, 20, 22
Dam busters 65
D-day, 67-68, 72, 79-81
Dead River, Michigan, 6, 37, 77, 86, 214, 225, 256
Dearborn Independent, 18-19
Dempsey, John 161
Dole, Lieutenant Robert, 207
Douglas, Lieutenant William, 207, 238
Drava River, Europe, 199
Dresden, Germany, 172
Dreux River, France, 94
Dreux, France, 93
Dunbridge House, England, 52
Dunkirk, France, 27, 40
Dutch Harbor, Alaska, 42
Dyersburg, Tennessee, 77

E
E-6B Aerial Dead Reckoning Computer, 62, 157
Edison, Thomas, 18-19
Eisenhower, General Dwight D., 65, 67, 212
Elbe River, Europe, 230
Ellington Field, Houston, Texas, 62, 246
Ellis, Sergeant Robert, 161, 194, 229, 239, 240
Ellison, Sergeant Tustin, 161, 167-168, 175
Elmer, PFC Richard 167
Emmanuelson, Robert (Bobby), 24-25, 56, 58, 90
Eschweiler, Germany, 145
Essential civilian workers, 73
Eyer, Sergeant Oliver, 161, 239

F
F Company, 85th Regiment, 10th Mountain Infantry Division, John Koski assigned to 159, 161, Camp Tizzoro 166-168, 171, Mount della Castellana 176-180, 182, 184, 188-191, 193, Montecatini 195-196, Mount della spe 203, 206, April 1, 1945 213-214, 219-220, The Big Push April 14, 1945 226-228, April 15, 1945 234-242
Firth of Clyde, Scotland, 48

Flat Rock, Michigan, 6, 13, 15, 58, 77, 116, 117, 169, 178, 194, 215, 223, 225, 248, 262
Florence, Italy, 151-152, 220, 241
Florisdorf Oil Refinery, Vienna, Austria, 112, 124, 199
Foggia, Italy, 100, 107, 151, 246
Ford, Henry, 18-19, 32
Fort Sheridan, Illinois 54
Frechette, Arthur, 165
Frederick, USS ,252
Fritz, Clyde, 38
Fritz, Lieutenant, 82, 94
Ft. Patrick Henry, Virginia, 150

G
Geilenkirchen, Germany, 186
Gemmenich, Belgium, 98
Germfask, Michigan, 75-76
Gettysburg Address, 262
Golden Lions (106th Infantry Division), 125
Göring, Hermann, 21
Gossard, 1, 3, 261
Gothic line, Italy, 212, 232
Gott mit uns, 184-185
Greenock, Scotland, 48
Grims Ditch, Dorset, England 64
Gulley, 2nd Lieutenant Atlee, 199
Gyor, Hungary, 129, 135

H
H&S Company, 332nd Engineers, Carl "Art" Koski assigned to 37-38,, 40, England 49, 51-52, D-day preparations 64-67, To Utah Beach 79, 93, Battle of the Bulge 98-99, 119-120, 127-128, 142-143, 145, 186, 247, 249, 250
Haaser, Lieutenant Walter, 224
Haines, Shapley, At 8th Replacement Depot 152, 154, Assigned to F-85 159-160, Montecatini 195-198, 203-205, 208-209, Killed in action 212-214
Hall, Sergeant Harold (Midge), 194
Hampton Roads, Virginia, 100
Hardaway, Brigadier General F.P., 32
Harlingen Field, Laguna Madre, Texas, 62
Hart, Robert, 72
Hartnet, Private, 71
Hassinger, Ben, 57
Hayhä, Corporal, 23
Hays, General George, 207, 242
Hegyeshalom, Hungary, 199
Heibel, Arthur, 56
Herzogenrath, Germany, 145
Hester, Major General, 87
Hill 860, Italy, 221, 226-227, 229, 234, 235
Hill 898, italy, 235, 239, 241-242
Hill 909, Italy, 221, 227-229, 234-235, 239, 242
Hill 913, Italy, 239, 242
Hill 915, Italy, 229, 234, 235, 237-238, 241
Hillman, Albert, 32
Hitler, Adolph, 1, 17, 19, 20-21, 22, 26, 28-31, 33, 35, 80, 100, 123, 143, 215, 251
Honkala, Roy, 58, 154
Honkala, Ted, 71, 94
Hotel Chalfonte, Atlantic city, New Jersey, 54, 59
Hughes, PVT Thomas, 186

I
I Have a Rendezvous with Death, 24, 197, 262
Ilse de Monsin bridge, Belgium, 144
In Flanders Fields, 2
Interventionists, 31
Iron mines, 73
Ishpeming High School, Michigan, 3, John Koski graduation 56-57
Ishpeming, MI, 1-3, 5- 6, 9, 13-14, 18, 32-33, 45, 49, 56-57, 68-69, 72-74, 77, 116-118, 246, 252, 255, 256, 259, 261, 263, 264
Isigny, France, 92
Isolationists, 31, 55

J
Jones, Sergeant Tom, 45, 51, 52, Painting 65, 79, 84, 93, 128, 136, 187, 231
Julich, Germany, 145, 147

K
Kallatsa's store, West Ishpeming, 10, 117
Karchner, Private, 71
Kassel, Germany, 247, 249
Kearns, 2nd Lieutenant Michael, 132
Kehres, PFC William, 192, 213-214, 227, 242
Keiser, 1st Lieutenant Ted, 133
Kemper, Squadron Operations Officer, Othmer 158
Kerekes, Lieutenant Carl, 207
King, Captain Charles, 179, 192-193, 196, 227, Wounded 236, 239
Kintner, PVT Mancle, 159
Kiska, Alaska, 41-44
Kitts, PVT 71, 109-110
Kleby Airfield, Czechoslovakia 202
Klopfer, Adolph, 159, 161, 166-169, 180
Knee mortar, James Winterbottom gets 175-176, 181-183, 203, 221, 226-227, 236, Use on farmhouse 238-239
Knittelfeld, Austria, 148-149
Koch, (first name unknown) 148

Koski Lake, Michigan, 117
Koski, Alfred, 5-6, 8-11, 14, 16, 24, 26, 32, 36, 42, 69, 91, 154, 216, 255, 260-261
Koski, Ann, 1-3, 38, 57, 64, 71, 77, 87- 91, 110
Koski, Carl Arthur (Art), 3, 6, Come down from the roof 8, 17-18, 30, 33-34, Inducted 37-41, Leave U.S. 45-52, 54, D-day preparations 64, 66-68, Letter from 72, To Utah Beach 79-80, Cherbourg 82-84, 87, Breakout into France 91-97, Strafing 119-120, Battle of the Bulge 125, Christmas eve 1945 128, Ditch defense 136-138, 141-147, 154, Sniper 186-187, 210-211, 215-216, Meet Russians 230-231, End of war 247-253, Return home 261-262
Koski, Edna Mae, Telegram 2-4, 8-10, 12, 36, 50, Watch 118, 216, 256
Koski, Eleanor, Telegram 2-4, 7, 50, Letter from 57, Letter from 68-69, Letter from 72, Letter from 88-89, Letter from 155, Letter from 216, Letter from 223, 248, 253, Letter from 259
Koski, Elizabeth, 5, 7- 8, 149, 237, 263
Koski, Evelyn, 3, 9, 12
Koski, Frank Alfred (Al), 3, 10, 13-14, Deer hunting 16-18, 30, Inducted 32-34, Recalled to service 36, Sent to Alaska 41-42, 44, 54, 69, 72, 91, 116, Letter to 122, 146, 154-155, 192, 216, Letters to John Koski 253-254, 256, Letter to 259, 261-262
Koski, George Harold (Jiggs), 3, 6, 14-15, 18, 26, 29, 33-34, Inducted 36, 54, 64, 68, 71, Furlough 77, 87, 91, 154, Injury 216-217, 253, 262
Koski, John Leslie (Johnny), 3, Poetry 6, Bad things 7, Dreams 9, Deer hunting 13-16, 24-25, Bear 30, 34, 54, Graduation 56-58, 64, Inducted 69-71, To Camp Croft 86, Letter from 88-91, Letter from 109-111, Furlough 116-118, Overseas 150-156, Assigned to 10th Mountain Infantry Division 159-162, 166-169, Mount della Castellana 176-185, 188-189, 191, Montecatini 194-198, Mount della Spe 203-209, 212-216, 219-223, The Big Push April 14, 1945 225-229, Killed in action 233-242, 248, Letter to 253, 255-256, 259, 262-264
Koski, John W., 254
Koski, Karen 122
Koski, Lillian, 1, Receives telegram 3-4, 7, Postponed relationship with George Sarberg 9-13, 15, 18, 36, 57, 90, Chicken dinner 116-117, Letter to 154, 200-201, Letter to 214, 253, Reads telegram 255, 261, 263, 264
Koski, Oscar Henry, 4, 6, Jam incident 10, 34, 36, Join service 54-55, Allegheny College 59, Navigator training 61-63, 68, Furlough 77-78, 88, 91, To Italy 100-109, Second mission 112-115, Third mission 121-124, December 1944 129-134, Oxygen line incident 139-140, Knittelfeld mission 148-149, Knittelfeld return 157-158, Promotion to 2nd Lieutenant 163, Loss of friend Ralph Steuve 172-174, March 1945 199-202, 216, Leave on Isle of Capri 218, April 1945 224, Last combat missions 233, End of war 244-246, 262
Koski, Reuben (Rube), 3, 10, 18, 30, 34, Deferment 36, 54, 64, Iron mining 73-74, Enters Navy 89-91, 116, 216, 253, 261, 262
Kovach, George, 159
Kraft, PFC Robert, 159, Assigned to mortar squad 161, 166-169, 177, Mount della Castellana 180-182, 184-185, 189, 193, 205-207, 212, 214, Mount della Spe 219-222, The Big Push April 14, 1945 225- 229, 234, 236-238
Krusell, PFC Wallace (Wally), 166, 220

L
La Hutte, Coulumbiers, France 93
Laitinen, Toivo, 90
Lake Lesina, Italy, 158
Landing Craft Tank, (LCT) 79-81
Lane, PVT Phillip, 205, 207, 227
Langley Woods, England 66
LeGassy, Sergeant George, 194
Legion of Merit, 84
Leinonen, Leonard, 32
Leversen, Richard L., 84
Levy, PFC Henry, 97
Lie in the Dark and Listen, 218
Liege, Belgium, 98-99, 126-128, 136, 144
Lindbergh, Anne Morrow, 19
Lindbergh, Charles, 19, 31
Lindholm, Mrs., 2-3
Linz, Austrailia, 139-140, 163, 173, 233
Liverno (Leghorn), Italy, 151
Lobau Oil Refinery, Vienna, Austria, 172
Longfellow, Henry Wadsworth, 25
Lowecke brothers, 72
Lucera 8, Italy, 100, 103, 114, 124, 135, 140, 148, 158, 174, 202, 224, 233
Ludwig, Captain William, 115
Luftwaffe, 28-29, 78, 95, 120, 149, 160, 201
Lukkarinen, Arthur, 116
Lukkarinen, Fred, 116

M
M1 Garand rifle, 45, 86, 89, 93, 96-97, 111, 136, 160, 230, 248
Maastricht, Belgium, 98
Magdeburg, Germany, 230-231
Magrath, PFC John, Actions in Italy 228-229, Medal of Honor 242
Malpus Court, South Wales, 48
Manse, Leroy, 159
Maribor Marshaling Yard, Germany, 199
Marquette, Michigan, 37, 56
Mayenne, France, 92
Mein Kampf, 30
Memphis Belle ,78
Messier, Sergeant James, 161, 167-168, Newspaper 194

Meuse River, Europe, 127, 144
Michigan College of Mines, Michigan, 32
Michigan Technological University, Michigan, 32
Miller, Ona, 120
Mills, David, 148-149, 157-158
Mining Journal The, 32, 34, 116, 256
Molotov, Vyacheslav, 23
Monte Pigna, Italy, 239
Montecatini, Italy, 195-197, 203-204, 214, 234
Moore, Danny, 134, 148, 173-174
Moore, Norbert F., 148
Moosbierbaum, Austria, 130, 135, 163, 199, 202
Morris, Lieutenant Cliff, 130
Moses, Sergeant Lawrence, 239
Mount Belvedere, Italy, 155-156, 160, 162, Veterans recall 166-170, 176, 193-194, 203, 242
Mount della Castellana, Italy, 179-180, 182-184
Mount della Spe, Italy, 179, 183-184, 193, 198, 204-206, 212-213, 219, 221, 226, 235, 237, 241-243
Mount della Torraccia, Italy, 170, 176, 242-243
Mount Gorgolesco, Italy, 155, 167, 170, 176, 193
Muchen-Gladbach, Germany, 210
Mulberry, 81
Munster, Germany, 210
Murphy, Sergeant Maurice (Speed), 176-177
Murray, PFC George, 203
Murrow, Edward, 26, 29
N
Namur, Belgium, 127-128
Naples, Italy, 64, 100, 150-151, 190
Negaunee, Michigan, 18, 57, 74, 116
Neutrality, 26, 31
Newport News, Virginia, 150
Newport, Wales, 48
Nissen Hut, 48
Norden bombsight, 60
Northway Camp, England, 51
Novi Pazar, Yugoslavia, 102
O
O'Callaghan, Lieutenant, 199
Obersalzberg Speech, 20
Odertal, Germany, 131, 133, 135
Omaha Beach, France, 67-68
Operation Clarion, 172
Operation Downfall, 249
Operation Overlord, 65, 67
Operation Varsity 216
Orwig, Sergeant James, John assigned to his Platoon 161-162, Remembers mules on Mount Belvedere 169, Boot size list from diary 175-176, 184, Diary entry Mount della Castellana 190-191, 195, 203, 205, Diary entry on Mount della Spe 207, Diary entry before the Big Push 222-223, Wounded 229, 239, Talks about John Koski 241
Over There 195
P
Paddock, PVT Leonard, 167
Padua Railroad Bridge, Italy, 224
Passatore, Italy, 195, 204
Patton, General George, 92-93
Pearl Harbor, Hawaii Attack on 33-34, 41, 60, 153
Pearson, Lieutenant, 165
Pepinster Bridge, Belgium, 97
Perho, Finland, 5
Petain, Philippe, 28
Pierce, Sergeant Leonard, 167
Pliscek, Sergeant Michael, 167
Plombiers, Belgium, 119, 125-126, 144
Po River Valley, Italy, 212, 221, 232, 239, 242
POW camps in Upper Michigan, 76
Pra del Bianco, Italy, 206, 226, 235
Propaganda, 26, 42, 113, 127, 190
Protocols of the Learned Elders of Zion, 19
Putnam, Lieutenant William, 207
Q
Quonset Hut, 42, 48, 103
R
Raley, James, 164
Recycling drives, 75
Regensburg Oil Refinery, 133
Rhine River, Europe, 216-217, 247
Richards, Bill, 72
Riva Ridge, Italy, 155-156, 160, 169
Rocco Ruffeno, Italy, 239
Roer River, Europe, 145, 186
Ronk, Clifford, 77, 139
Roosevelt, Franklin D., 35-36, 46, 222-223
Royal Air Force (RAF), 29, 61, 218
Ruhland, Germany, 201-202
Russo, Strom, 32
S
Saari, PVT Arne, 263
Salisbury Congregational Church, 64
Sarberg, George, 11-12, 18, 36, 200-201
Sarvanto, Lieutenant, 23
Schu mine, 145, 186

Seeger, Alan, 24
Selman Field, Monroe, Louisiana, 62
Serra Sarzana, Italy, 207
Sevareid, Eric, 33
Shepard, Captain William, 242
Sisu 26
Sitzkreig, 26
Skillings, William (Bill), 77, 101-102, 104, 107, 112, 114, 139, 140, 164, 218
Smieska, PFC Edward, 161, 168, 176, 179-181, 183, 221, 226-228, Wounded 236-238
Solka, Christine, 57, 64, 88-90, 110, 153, 264
Solka, John (Buster), 38, 57
Sommers, 1st Lieutenant Ralph, 199
Spaatz, General, 232
Spice, Robert, 77, 112, 132, 140
Spicer, PVT Alfred, 128, 230, 231
Stalin, Joseph, 20, 30
Stark, Donald Sergeant, 119-120
Steiner, PFC Warren, 167
Stepnowski, Sergeant Edward, 167
Stockbridge Hospital, 52
Stone, George, 98
Stueve, Ralph, 130, 132, 173
Summertop (James Winterbottom), 161, 175, 228
Syversen, Sergeant Leif, 219
T
Taylor, Sergeant Arthur, 239
Tillotson, Eugene 1st. Lieutenant, 129
Tippett, Lieutenant James, 207
Tokle, Torger, 183
Tora, Italy, 179, 180
Towne, Captain, 66, 128, 136, 230-231
Traise, Jeannette (Jenny), 12, 34, Letter to 37-38, 40, 45-47, Telegram and V-mail to 49-51, 64, 80, Letter to 84, Letter to 94-95, 137, 144, Letter to 146-147, Letter to 211, Letter to 249-250, 252, Reunion with 261-262
Trench foot, 43-44, 142
Tuskegee airmen, 133
Twomey, Lieutenant Albert, 238
U
Unalaska, Alaska, 41
Utah Beach, France, 67, 79, 85, 231
V
V1 rocket, 98, 127
V2 rocket, 98, 123, 127
Verviers, 97
Vesuvius, Mount, 150
Vichy France, 28
Vienna, Austria, 19, 112, 121, 123-124, 130-131, 133, 148, 163, 172, 199, 202
Viney, Col. Albert, 81
Vipiteno Railroad Bridge, Ital,y 224
V-mail, 50
Von Schirach, Baldur, 19
Vreeland, Wilbur, PFC, 119-120
W
Wacht am Rhein, 125
Watson, PFC William, 167
Wesser River, Europe, 210
West Ishpeming, Michigan, 1, 2, 5, 9, 32-33, 49, 57, 116-117, 246, 252, 261, 263
Wheeler, Sam, 165
Wickwrath, Germany, 210
Wiedorn, Sergeant Albert, 167, 242
Winterbottom, Sergeant James, At Camp Croft 70, John Koski assigned to squad 161, Talks about Mount Belvedere experience 168-171, Knee mortar 175-176, Mount della Castellana 180-183, Incident with General 191-193, 203, Bury pilot 205, Promoted to sergeant 221-222, The Big Push April 14, 1945 226-228, April 15, 1945 234, 236-239, Silver Star 241-242
Wolf, Major General, 244
Woodward, John, 120
Y
Yellowham Camp, Dorchester, England, 79
Yougken, PVT Milton, 186
Z
Zagreb, Yugoslavia, 130, 135, 199